THE RINGERS
IN THE TOWER

Harold Bloom

THE RINGERS

IN THE TOWER

Studies in Romantic Tradition

The
University of Chicago Press
Chicago & London

International Standard Book Number: 0–226–06048–9
Library of Congress Catalog Card Number: 73–149595
The University of Chicago Press, Chicago 60637
The University of Chicago Press, Ltd., London
© 1971 by The University of Chicago
All rights reserved. Published 1971
Printed in the United States of America

For Geoffrey Hartman

Have you not heard, have you not seen that corps
Of shadows in the tower, whose shoulders sway
Antiphonal carillons launched before
The stars are caught and hived in the sun's ray?

—Hart Crane

I shall find the dark grow luminous, the void
fruitful when I understand I have nothing, that
the ringers in the tower have appointed for the
hymen of the soul a passing bell.

—W. B. Yeats

Contents

Preface

Though most of these essays first appeared in other places, almost all were intended to find their context in this gathering. Their major subject is poetic influence (perhaps rather poetic misprision), conceived as an anxiety principle or variety of melancholy, particularly in regard to the relation between poets in the Romantic tradition. The three essays concerning prose works—on *Frankenstein*, Ruskin's criticism, *Marius The Epicurean*—are closely connected to prevalent themes in the poetry: Promethean quest and its failure; the estrangement of landscape from the imaginative quester; the sensibility of skepticism when intimately allied with the "privileged moment" or secularized epiphany. One purpose of this book is to suggest that our poets, if they are to survive the anxieties of influence, must learn to master and unify these themes, which remain inescapable.

Acknowledgments are made to the editors and publishers of the following essays, in their first appearance and original form: 1. *Studies in Romanticism*. 2. W. W. Norton and Company, for the introduction to the anthology, *Romanticism and Consciousness*. 3. *Partisan Review*. 4. *Proceedings of the Modern Language Association*. 5. *Eighteenth Century Studies*. 6. *Yale French Studies*. 7. The New American Library, for the Introduction to *Selected Poetry and Prose of Shelley*. 8. *Partisan Review*. 9. Oxford University Press, essay in *From Sensibility to Romanticism: Essays Presented to Frederick A. Pottle*, ed. F. W. Hilles and H. Bloom. 11. Mr. Coburn Britton and *Prose*. 12. Doubleday-Anchor Books, for the introduction to *The Literary Criticism of John Ruskin*. 13. The New American Library, for the introduction to *Marius The Epicurean*. 14. Southern Illinois University Press, from *A D. H.*

Lawrence Miscellany, ed. H. T. Moore. 15. *The New Republic, The Yale Review.* 16. *The Massachusetts Review.* 17. Prentice-Hall, from *Wallace Stevens,* ed. Marie Borroff. 19. *Southern Review.* 20. *Midway.*

THE RINGERS
IN THE TOWER

1
Introduction:
First and Last Romantics

The Odyssey is the fundamental quest romance, and the first Romantic poem. Romance is a journey toward home, the hero's home though not the reader's, nor even a home where the hero might bear to abide. Or, romance is a journey toward a supreme trial, after which home is possible, or else homelessness will suffice. At the least, we are given a quester and his quest, antagonists and temptations, a presiding goal. Demonic romance, as Borges shows, the art of Browning or Kafka or Yeats, unwillingly exposes the goal as delusive, but even such gnostic romance values the journey more than the destination, and leaves us something other than a sense of loss. Hart Crane's *The Bridge,* if we arranged the poem in its most effective order, that of its composition, with *Atlantis* as ecstatic starting-point and the desperate but heroic hysteria of *Cape Hatteras* as conclusion, would be seen more clearly as demonic romance, quest fulfilled to no consequence, or fulfillment revealed as a parody of the goal, a darkness known to Crane already at the commencement of his vision.

Romanticism stems from the enchantment of the marvelous, the roots of romance, Calypso's cave and the Siren's song, the Perilous Chapel and the Whore Duessa, but from contrary sources also. The quester bound for home or shrine, tempted by all that opposes, begins with a literal vision of what he seeks, but has no word of his own to deliver, is not himself the vehicle of a message, the trumpet of a prophecy. Romanticism fused romance and prophecy, and Saint John the Apocalyptic may be called, as well as any, the first Romantic, rather than the poet of *The Odyssey*, or the public orator who composed the book of Ezekiel. What the late eighteenth and early nineteenth-century Romantics named as vision might better be termed a making and a hearing, or a making heard, and came to them from the *nabi* and his calling.

First Romantics are as plentiful as last, and both can be nominated freely wherever the theorist chooses his date, from Viconian postulates of Hermetic men divining their own immortality to Yeatsian enlargements of family and friends finding and making their masks in disappointments and defeats. Choose your first Romantic, or your first Romanticism, and you tell us what kind of a last Romantic you yourself are, or what kind of last anti-Romantic you ache to be. If you want a late start, far on in the eighteenth century, insisting on High Romanticism as the Romantic proper, then you may be discomfited by voices rising out of the Renaissance:

> I know more than Apollo,
>   For oft when he lies sleeping
> I see the stars at bloody wars
>   And the wounded welkin weeping
> The moon embrace her shepherd
>   And the Queen of Love her warrior,
> While the first doth horn the Star of Morn
>   And the next, the Heavenly Farrier.

This is an anonymous voice and, by tradition, a mad one. But there are other voices:

> Decay nor age there nothing knows,
> There is continual youth,
> As time on plant or creature grows
> So still their strength reneweth.
>
> The poets' paradise this is,
> To which but few can come;
> The Muses' only bower of bliss
> Their dear Elizium.

That English Romanticism, as opposed to Continental, was a renaissance of the Renaissance, is happily now a critical commonplace. When Collins or Cowper or Blake or Keats looked back, he saw Spenser and Shakespeare and Milton, not Donne and Jonson and Pope, as the splendors of his language. The return to older modes was a selective one, like all returns, and disrespectful therefore of much that was most valuable and disciplined in the imaginative past. To this disrespect, Dr. Samuel Johnson, the greatest anti-Romantic critic in the language, addressed his intellect:

> To select a singular event, and swell it to a giant's bulk by fabulous appendages of spectres and predictions, has little difficulty, for he that forsakes the probable may always find the marvelous. And it has little use; we are affected only as we believe; we are improved only as we find something to be imitated or declined.

This massive dismissal of a return to Romantic invention is directed at Gray's *The Bard*, which with its sister ode, *The Progress of Poesy*, always excited the Johnsonian critical glee. These were to him "the *Wonderful Wonder of Wonders*," and even "but cucumbers after all." Traditional invention, to Johnson, was an oxymoron and an evasion of the poet's true burden.

"The highest praise of genius is original invention." We do well to remember that, of all English critics, Johnson was most impatient of poetic influence. Homer had come first, and all other poets were impoverished by their great original's wealth. Only God's influence, in Johnson's vision, worked so as not to famish the receiver. Johnson, whose own exuberance could scarcely be reduced by the horror of dying, revered invention because he associated originality with vitalism, and found in any fresh fiction what naturalism discovers anew with every Spring. We learn always, in reading Johnson or reading about him, that he fears only annihilation and sloth, two antipodes of invention. Because Milton stands so firmly against these evils, Johnson set aside his own fierce prejudices and celebrated the maker of *Paradise Lost* as "the least indebted" of Homer's borrowers: "he did not refuse admission to the thought or images of his predecessors, but he did not seek them." Johnson, who wrote only a few strong poems, had felt deeply the anxiety of influence, as yet another variety of melancholy to add to his afflictions.

A parable of Borges tells of a dream in which the Gods returned, to occupy a platform in a lecture hall before an audience of the School of Philosophy and Letters. The professors first applauded, tearfully, but then began to suspect that the Gods were dumb and degenerate, "cunning, ignorant and cruel like old beasts of prey." Lest the Gods destroy them, the scholars "took out our heavy revolvers . . . and joyfully killed the Gods." The tears were authentic, yet so was the joy; we applaud enchantment, but celebrate the success of our resistance to it. "We are improved only as we find something to be imitated or declined," and we long to be improved. The Gods are a fiction never obsolete enough to cease from menacing the probable world, yet there is no Romanticism without a return, in

5

some form, of the Gods. For the Gods are poets whose auguries all have been fulfilled, men who somehow learned never to die, men who mastered divination, according to Vico. Hermes Thoth, God of commerce and so of all property, invented all names, establishing the certainties of ownership, and so goes on writing all books whatsoever. Emerson is Viconian when he associates the poet with "the common wealth" and observes that "the young man reveres men of genius, because, to speak truly, they are more himself than he is." "The poets are thus liberating gods," free themselves from the ultimate poverty of death, saved by their power of divining what can kill and when, and their consequent power of vital evasion:

> Olympian bards who sung
> Divine ideas below,
> Which always find us young,
> And always keep us so.

This kind of evasion is an extravagance, a yielding to the vagrant impulse that is Romanticism. "And there I found myself more truly and more strange." When the greatest precursor of High Romanticism found himself, he accepted the darkness of his fate, in the hope that renown accompanied the darkness:

> . . . but chief
> Thee *Sion* and the flowrie Brooks beneath
> That wash thy hallowd feet, and warbling flow,
> Nightly I visit: nor somtimes forget
> Those other two equal'd with me in Fate,
> So were I equal'd with them in renown,
> Blind *Thamyris* and blind *Maeonides*,
> And *Tiresias* and *Phineus* Prophets old.

What is this renown but a divination, not so much of one's glory to come but of the glory one already is? Byron, the most anti-Romantic of authentic High Romantics, is accurate in assigning such divination to its proper element:

> And so great names are nothing more than nominal,
> And love of glory's but an airy lust,
> Too often in its fury overcoming all
> Who would as 'twere identify their dust
> From out the wide destruction . . .

Just so: "an airy lust" followed by the universally wide entombing, but Byron knowingly gives us only half the poet's life-cycle *qua* poet. The Idiot Questioner divining by air, and the Real Man, the

Imagination, destroying self into earth come after the movement from a heavier to a lighter element, water to fire, the Ephebe to the Promethean Quester, even as the latter movement is from lighter to heavier, air to earth. When the poet is freshly incarnated, it is by the side of ocean. If the "beau linguist" or "crystal hypothesis" rightly

> himself lay lounging by the sea,

> Drowned in its washes, reading in the sound,
> About the thinker of the first idea,
> He might take habit, whether from wave or phrase,

> Or power of the wave, or deepened speech,
> Or a leaner being, moving in on him,
> Of greater aptitude and apprehension,

> As if the waves at last were never broken,
> As if the language suddenly, with ease,
> Said things it had laboriously spoken.

And, after this self-divination, must come the upward movement to the quester's own element, the generous fire of a fearful renown, not a burning fountain but an ocean aflame:

> Yet—yet—one brief relapse, like the last beam
>   Of dying flames, the stainless air around
> Hung silent and serene—a blood-red gleam
>   Burst upwards, hurling fiercely from the ground
>   The globéd smoke,—I heard the mighty sound
> Of its uprise, like a tempestuous ocean.

Self-recognition, or the apprehension of the Poetic Character in oneself, is a kind of divination because this self is in the future rushing toward us, and never in the present moment. That Romanticism, or the internalization of quest, should have returned poetry to the dangerous shamanism of its origins, is a rebuke to the humanism also prevalent in the line of vision. Yeats's occultries, like the table-rappings by which Hugo indulged his credulous spirit, play at one kind of Romantic divination, yet border always on the same concern that is Wordsworth's hidden theme, the poetic spirit's obsessive need for a literal immortality. Not to know separation, not to experience even the altogether necessary freedom of some discontinuity, not to have a consciousness of dying: this is the implicit prayer of *Tintern Abbey*, and the sorrow of the great lyrics of 1802.

The return of the Gods means then, for Romanticism, the divination of immortality for and by poets, and such divination is literally intended by the consciousness that has been raised to apocalyptic pitch. More than our humanism is baffled by this literalness; what of the reality principle, which teaches us, finally, an acceptance not ignoble? Does Romanticism found itself upon a visionary lie? Don Quixote, Kierkegaard says, is the prototype for that subjective madness in which the infinite passion of inwardness embraces a particular fixed idea, necessarily finite. Never to die, not to know death, is a particular idea, but turns upon infinity, and he who has this passion is no Quixote, but a Magus, reminding us of that Simon Magus who was the ancestor of Faust.

When we seek the ancestors of the Romantics among the greatest poets of the English Renaissance we tend to slight the poet of *Faustus*, whose hero's faith holds that "A sound Magician is a mighty god" and who tries his brains to gain a deity. His influence, even in Byron, came through Shakespeare's, who subsumed his precursor more fully than even Milton could subsume Spenser. The Marlovian Prometheanism of Shakespeare's unnatural invokers of nature has lost its innocence; Tamburlaine and Faustus are more grotesquely attractive than Richard III and Edmund, for desiring an immortality seems less of an element in the power drives of Shakespeare's more complex creations. As the dream of divination wanes, an obsession with transformations takes its place. The poet, if he cannot dodge his death through prolepsis, may delude death by offering it many substitute forms for himself. Spenser retains something of the spirit of the shamans; his principal knights and ladies may touch disaster, but a proleptic sense in their creator so devises the shape of disaster that always they do draw back from each final abyss. Milton, whose immense disasters preceded his major poems, seems to have feared from the start that a demon of transformations would mock his career. *Lycidas* laments the loss of the poetic power of divination, and no monitory promptings in *Paradise Lost* can avail, for no death (or fall that is a little death) can be evaded. Is this why Milton, throughout his life, was obsessed with the myth of Circe? From the *First Elegy* through Comus, son of Circe, and on to Dalila-Circe, Milton's poetry engages *The Odyssey*'s demoness-lover in many guises, as though she must lurk wherever divination has lost its power of sidestepping.

E. R. Dodds traced the origin of Puritanism to the Greek shamans, and our current irrationalism, in many of the young and their occasional middle-aged cultural converts, shows a similar engendering of

Puritanism out of a version of shamanism. Though there are shamanistic elements in Yeats and Lawrence, and yet more artificially
in Robert Graves and some of his disciples (like Ted Hughes), the
major phase of High Romanticism is largely free of it. The spirit
in man that needs cleansing, to the High Romantics, from Blake
through Browning, is rational, and not magical, and calls for a catharsis that is imaginative or more-than-rational but that first includes the rational. Stevens, when he chants of reasoning with a
"later reason" or calls the imaginative the "more than rational distortion," is wholly within central Romantic tradition, as Emerson
was before him. The shamanism of Empedocles, so strangely reborn
in Yeats's *A Vision*, Lawrence's *Fantasia of the Unconscious*, and
Graves's *The White Goddess*, proposes a preternatural catharsis to
heal a magical spirit in us. Dodds, surveying Greek irrationalisms,
pointed to ritual and musical incantation as supplementary shamanistic therapies, but placed the emphasis on *askesis*, a conscious training of psychic powers, the living of life in a particular way.

The primal sin, in shamanistic tradition as I understand it, was
the slaying, cooking, and devouring of the infant god Dionysos by
our wretched, direct ancestors, the Titans. Dodds points out that this
is late Orphic tradition, but something like it appears to be at the
root of all shamanisms, including our current rabblement. We then
are to be regarded as murderous cannibals with just a saving pinch
of the baby Dionysos in us, and we need (on this view) to enlarge
and liberate that pinch of divine roasted baby-fat, which alone makes
us gods as well as sinful mortals. This would connect divination with
Dionysiac release, a formula that has failed late or Decadent Romanticism before, and evidently will now fail it again.

We can observe, in this melancholy glance at some fresh Last
Romantics, their revealing placements of First Romantics. For Lawrence, they were the Etruscans; for Yeats, the Byzantines under
Justinian; for Graves, more persuasively, they are the Sufis, and
the Provencal and Celtic romancers whom Graves regards as the
Sufi's immediate disciples. Graves, responding recently to our current *schwärmerei*, has speculated happily that a religious revolution
may be upon us. Rahab, the Queen of Heaven, so fiercely denounced
by Jeremiah and by Blake, may be worshipped again at least by the
young and their university fellow-travelers. Divination has come
back into fashion already, though in vulgarized form, and much else
may follow, at least for a time.

Dodds, lecturing upon *The Greeks and the Irrational* at that fated university, Berkeley, in 1949, prophesied the troubles to come some fifteen years later when he quoted T. H. Huxley as epigraph to his last lecture: "A man's worst difficulties begin when he is able to do as he likes." Romantic poetry, in its long history, has been saved from those worst difficulties by its sense of its own tradition, by the liberating burden of poetic influence. Yeats, Lawrence, Graves—despite their varied and real poetic successes—willfully placed their First Romantics too freely and too far away, and were saved from too crippling a freedom by the relative proximity of their true Romantic ancestors: Blake and Shelley for Yeats, Whitman and Hardy for Lawrence, Keats and Hardy for Graves. The High Romantics were more fortunate in finding their First Romantics in Spenser, Shakespeare, Milton, however high the shadow of such greatness hovered before them. Spenser, Shakespeare, and Milton together formed a colossal Covering Cherub, who prevented the Romantics from certain achievements, but they compelled Blake and Wordsworth, Shelley and Keats, to invent continuously where otherwise they might have yielded to phantasmagoria, as Yeats, Lawrence, Graves, and younger poets so often have done.

For invention is a positive mode of divination (as Johnson wonderfully realized when he called invention the essence of poetry) even as the shamanistic, magical divination is a negative mode, since it seeks not the heterocosm, but actual power over nature, over things as they are. The strong Romantic poet, when he is most himself, makes a world in which his Real Man, the Imagination, can never die. His spectral self, which must die in nature, never enters the world of his invention. Though Wordsworth's spectre could not know this, the early vision in *Tintern Abbey* is comprehensive enough as invention to make the poem's later anxieties unnecessary. Every Romantic has a tendency to drink unnecessarily from the Circean cup of illusion, thus confirming Milton's deepest fears by his descendants' dallyings with the demoness of transformations. The greatest such encounter, in Romantic poetry, destroys Rousseau, archetype of the natural man, in Shelley's *The Triumph of Life*. When we turn to the major descendants of Romanticism in modern poetry, we behold a competition to drink of Circe's cup, with only a few notable exceptions. The *daimon* is our destiny, Yeats says, and our destiny is even a kind of justice, but then we discover that this justice means only the exhaustion of every possible illusion, the completion of every possible emotional relationship. Or, to descend to a lower comedy, Graves tells us that Freud projected a private

10

fantasy upon the world and then Graves offers us the assurance that true poetry worships a barbaric lunar Muse. Both Yeats and Graves show us the nightmare cyclic world of Blake's *The Mental Traveller*, but what Blake tells us is mere unnecessary masochism Yeats and Graves affirm as imaginative truth, though only Graves insists also on the mutual rendings of poet and Muse as being true love.

All rationalisms, from Greek to Late Victorian, fail in turn, as do all Romanticisms, for less than all cannot satisfy man. The Freudian rationalism, wisely refusing heroic failure, insists that less than all had better content man, for there can be no satisfaction in satisfaction anyway. Though this is wisdom, it can be found in only a few modern poets who do not darken it with extrapoetic persuasions, in the manner of Eliot and his followers. I can think only of Hardy and of Stevens as modern poets who divine by invention, without phantasmagoria or doctrine, without the cup of Circe or the cup of communion. If our current poets are to help us in an increasingly bad time, if they are to make the dark grow luminous, the void fruitful, they had best be found by the right precursors among the ringers in the tower of Romantic tradition.

1969

2
The Internalization of
Quest Romance

Freud, in an essay written sixty years ago on the relation of the poet to daydreaming, made the surmise that all aesthetic pleasure is forepleasure, an "incitement premium" or narcissistic fantasy. The deepest satisfactions of literature, on this view, come from a release of tensions in the psyche. That Freud had found, as almost always, either part of the truth or at least a way to it, is clear enough, even if a student of Blake or Wordsworth finds, as probably he must, this Freudian view to be partial, reductive, and a kind of mirror-image of the imagination's truth. The deepest satisfactions of reading Blake or Wordsworth come from the realization of new ranges of tensions in the mind, but Blake and Wordsworth both believed, in different ways, that the pleasures of poetry were only forepleasures, in the sense that poems, finally, were scaffoldings for a more imaginative vision, and not ends in themselves. I think that what Blake and Wordsworth do for their readers, or can do, is closely related to what Freud does or can do for his, which is to provide both a map of the mind and a profound faith that the map can be put to a saving use. Not that the uses agree, or that the maps quite agree either, but the enterprise is a humanizing one in all three of these discoverers. The humanisms do not agree either; Blake's is apocalyptic, Freud's is naturalistic, and Wordsworth's is—sometimes sublimely, sometimes uneasily—blended of elements that dominate in the other two.

Freud thought that even romance, with its element of play, probably commenced in some actual experience whose "strong impression on the writer had stirred up a memory of an earlier experience, generally belonging to childhood, which then arouses a wish that finds a fulfillment in the work in question, and in which elements of the recent event and the old memory should be discernible." Though this is a brilliant and comprehensive thought, it seems inadequate to the complexity of romance, particularly in the period during which romance as a genre, however displaced, became again the dominant form, which is to say the age of Romanticism. For English-speaking readers, this age may be defined as extending from the childhood of Blake and Wordsworth to the present moment. Convenience dictates that we distinguish the High Romantic period proper, during which a half-dozen major English poets did their work, from the generations that have come after them, but the distinction is difficult to justify critically.

Freud's embryonic theory of romance contains within it the potential for an adequate account of Romanticism, particularly if we interpret his "memory of an earlier experience" to mean also the recall of an earlier insight, or yearning, that may not have been experiential. The immortal longings of the child, rather variously interpreted by Freud, Blake, and Wordsworth, may not be at the roots of romance, historically speaking, since those roots go back to a psychology very different from ours, but they do seem to be at the sources of the mid-eighteenth-century revival of a romance consciousness, out of which nineteenth-century Romanticism largely came.

J. H. Van den Berg, whose introduction to a historical psychology I find crucial to an understanding of Romanticism, thinks that Rousseau "was the first to view the child as a child, and to stop treating the child as an adult." Van den Berg, as a doctor, does not think this was necessarily an advance: "Ever since Rousseau the child has been keeping its distance. This process of the child and adult growing away from each other began in the eighteenth century. It was then that the period of adolescence came into existence." Granting that Van den Berg is broadly correct (he at least attempts to explain an apparent historical modulation in consciousness that few historians of culture care to confront), then we are presented with another in a series of phenomena, clustering around Rousseau and his age, in which the major change from the Enlightenment to Romanticism manifested itself. Changes in consciousness are of course very rare, and no major synthesizer has come forth as yet, from any discipline, to demonstrate to us whether Romanticism marks a genuine change in consciousness or not. From the Freudian viewpoint, Romanticism is an "illusory therapy" (I take the phrase from Philip Rieff), or what Freud himself specifically termed an "erotic illusion." The dialectics of Romanticism, to the Freudians, are mistaken or inadequate, because the dialectics are sought in Schiller or Heine or in German Romantic philosophy down to Nietzsche, rather than in Blake or the English Romantics after him. Blake and Coleridge do not set intellect and passion against one another, any more than they arrive at the Freudian simplicity of the endless conflict between Eros and Thanatos. Possibly because of the clear associations between Jung and German Romanticism, it has been too easy for Freudian intellectuals to confound Romanticism with various modes of irrationalism. Though much contemporary scholarship attempts to study English and Continental Romanticism as a unified phenomenon, it can be argued that the English Romantics tend to lose more than they gain by such study.

Behind Continental Romanticism there lay very little in the way of a congenial native tradition of major poets writing in an ancestral mode, particularly when compared to the English Romantic heritage of Spenser, Shakespeare, and Milton. What allies Blake and Wordsworth, Shelley and Keats, is their strong mutual conviction that they are reviving the true English tradition of poetry, which they thought had vanished after the death of Milton, and had reappeared in diminished form, mostly after the death of Pope, in admirable but doomed poets like Chatterton, Cowper, and Collins, victims of circumstance and of their own false dawn of Sensibility. It is in this highly individual sense that English Romanticism legitimately can be called, as traditionally it has been, a revival of romance. More than a revival, it is an internalization of romance, particularly of the quest variety, an internalization made for more than therapeutic purposes, because made in the name of a humanizing hope that approaches apocalyptic intensity. The poet takes the patterns of quest-romance and transposes them into his own imaginative life, so that the entire rhythm of the quest is heard again in the movement of the poet himself from poem to poem. M. H. Abrams brilliantly traces these patterns of what he calls "the apocalypse of imagination." As he shows, historically they all directly stem from English reactions to the French Revolution, or to the intellectual currents that had flowed into the Revolution. Psychologically, they stem from the child's vision of a more titanic universe that the English Romantics were so reluctant to abandon. If adolescence was a Romantic or Rousseauistic phenomenon of consciousness, its concomitant was the very secular sense of being twice-born that is first discussed in the fourth chapter of *Émile*, and then beautifully developed by Shelley in his visionary account of Rousseau's second birth, in the concluding movement of *The Triumph of Life*. The pains of psychic maturation become, for Shelley, the potentially saving though usually destructive crisis when the imagination confronts its choice of either sustaining its own integrity or yielding to the illusive beauty of nature.

The movement of quest-romance, before its internalization by the High Romantics, was from nature to redeemed nature, the sanction of redemption being the gift of some external spiritual authority, sometimes magical. The Romantic movement is from nature to the imagination's freedom (sometimes a reluctant freedom), and the imagination's freedom is frequently purgatorial, redemptive in direction but destructive of the social self. The high cost of Romantic internalization, that is, of finding paradises within a renovated man, tends to manifest itself in the arena of self-consciousness. The quest is to widen consciousness as well as intensify it, but the quest is shadowed by a spirit that tends to narrow consciousness to an acute preoccupation with self. This shadow of imagination is solipsism, what Shelley calls the Spirit of Solitude or *Alastor*, the avenging daimon who is a baffled residue of the self, determined to be compensated for its loss of natural assurance, for having been awakened from the merely given condition that to Shelley, as to Blake, was but the sleep of death-in-life. Blake calls this spirit of solitude a Spectre, or the genuine Satan, the Thanatos or death-impulse in every natural man. Modernist poetry in English organized itself, to an excessive extent, as a supposed revolt against Romanticism, in the mistaken hope of escaping this inwardness (though it was unconscious that this was its prime motive). Modernist poetry learned better, as its best work, the last phases of W. B. Yeats and Wallace Stevens, abundantly shows, but criticism until recently was tardy in catching up, and lingering misapprehensions about the Romantics still abide. Thus, Irving Howe, in an otherwise acute essay on literary Modernism, says of the Romantic poets that "they do not surrender the wish to discover in the universe a network of spiritual meaning which, however precariously, can enclose their selves." This is simply not true of Blake or Wordsworth or Shelley or Keats, nor is the statement of Marius Bewley's that Howe quotes approvingly, that the Romantics' central desire is "to merge oneself with what is greater than oneself." Indeed, both statements are excellent guides to what the major Romantics regarded as human defeat or a living death, as the despairing surrender of the imagination's autonomy. Since neither Howe nor Bewley is writing as an enemy of the Romantics, it is evident that we still need to clear our mind of Eliotic cant on this subject.

Paul De Man terms this phenomenon the post-Romantic dilemma, observing that every fresh attempt of Modernism to go beyond Romanticism ends in the gradual realization of the Romantics' continued priority. Modern poetry, in English, is the invention of Blake and of Wordsworth, and I do not know of a long poem written in English since then that is either as legitimately difficult or as rewardingly profound as *Jerusalem* or *The Prelude*. Nor can I find a modern lyric, however happily ignorant its writer, that develops beyond or surmounts its debt to Wordsworth's great trinity of *Tintern Abbey*, *Resolution and Independence*, and the *Intimations of Immortality* Ode. The dreadful paradox of Wordsworth's greatness is that his uncanny originality, still the most astonishing break with tradition in the language, has been so influential that we have lost sight of its audacity and its arbitrariness. In this, Wordsworth strongly resembles Freud, who rightly compared his own intellectual revolution to those of Copernicus and Darwin. Van den Berg quietly sees "Freud, in the desperation of the moment, turning away from the present, where the cause of his patients' illnesses was located, to the past; and thus making them suffer from the past and making our existence akin to their suffering. It was not necessary." Is Van den Berg right? The question is as crucial for Wordsworth and Romanticism as it is for Freud and psychoanalysis. The most searching critique of Romanticism that I know is Van den Berg's critique of Freud, particularly the description of "The Subject and his Landscape":

> Ultimately the enigma of grief is the libido's inclination toward exterior things. What prompts the libido to leave the inner self? In 1914 Freud asked himself this question—the essential question of his psychology, and the essential question of the psychology of the twentieth century. His answer ended the process of interiorization. It is: the libido leaves the inner self when the inner self has become too full. In order to prevent it from being torn, the I has to aim itself on objects outside the self; ". . . ultimately man must begin to love in order not to get ill." So that is what it is. Objects are of importance only in an extreme urgency. Human beings, too. The grief over their death is the sighing of a too-far-distended covering, the groaning of an overfilled inner self.

Wordsworth is a crisis-poet, Freud a crisis-analyst; the saving movement in each is backward into lost time. But what is the movement of loss, in poet and in analyst? Van den Berg's suggestion is that Freud unnecessarily sacrificed the present moment, because he came at the end of a tradition of intellectual error that began with the extreme Cartesian dualism, and that progressively learned to devalue contact between the self and others, the self and the outer world, the self and the body. Wordsworth's prophecy, and Blake's, was overtly against dualism; they came, each said, to heal the division within man, and between man and the world, if never quite between man and man. But Wordsworth, the more influential because more apparently accessible of the two (I myself would argue that he is the more difficult because the more problematic poet), no more overcame a fundamental dualism than Freud did. Essentially this was Blake's complaint against him; it is certainly no basis for us to complain. Wordsworth made his kind of poetry out of an extreme urgency, and out of an overfilled inner self, a Blakean Prolific that nearly choked in an excess of its own delights. This is the Egotistical Sublime of which Keats complained, but Keats knew his debt to Wordsworth, as most poets since do not.

Wordsworth's Copernican revolution in poetry is marked by the evanescence of any subject but subjectivity, the loss of what a poem is "about." If, like the late Yvor Winters, one rejects a poetry that is not "about" something, one has little use for (or understanding of) Wordsworth. But, like Van den Berg on Freud, one can understand and love Wordsworth, and still ask of his radical subjectivity: was it necessary? Without hoping to find an answer, one can explore the question so as to come again on the central problem of Romantic (and post-Romantic) poetry: what, for men without belief and even without credulity, is the spiritual form of romance? How can a poet's (or any man's) life be one of continuous allegory (as Keats thought Shakespeare's must have been) in a reductive universe of death, a separated realm of atomized meanings, each discrete from the next? Though all men are questers, even the least, what is the relevance of quest in a gray world of continuities and homogenized enterprises? Or, in Wordsworth's own terms, which are valid for every major Romantic, what knowledge might yet be purchased except by the loss of power?

Frye, in his theory of myths, explores the analogue between quest-romance and the dream: "Translated into dream terms, the quest-romance is the search of the libido or desiring self for a fulfillment that will deliver it from the anxieties of reality but will still contain that reality." Internalized romance, and *The Prelude* and *Jerusalem* can be taken as the greatest examples of this kind, traces a Promethean and revolutionary quest, and cannot be translated into dream terms, for in it the libido turns inward into the self. Shelley's *Prometheus Unbound* is the most drastic High Romantic version of internalized quest, but there are more drastic versions still in our own age, though they present themselves as parodistic, as in the series of marvelous interior quests by Stevens, that go from *The Comedian As the Letter C* to the climactic *Notes Toward a Supreme Fiction*. The hero of internalized quest is the poet himself, the antagonists of quest are everything in the self that blocks imaginative work, and the fulfillment is never the poem itself but the poem beyond that is made possible by the apocalypse of imagination. "A timely utterance gave that thought relief" is the Wordsworthian formula for the momentary redemption of the poet's sanity by the poem already written, and might stand as a motto for the history of the modern lyric from Wordsworth to Hart Crane.

The Romantics tended to take Milton's Satan as the archetype of the heroically defeated Promethean quester, a choice in which modern criticism has not followed them. But they had a genuine insight into the affinity between an element in their selves and an element in Milton that he would externalize only in a demonic form. What *is* heroic about Milton's Satan is a real Prometheanism and a thoroughly internalized one; he can steal only his own fire in the poem, since God can appear as fire, again in the poem, only when he directs it against Satan. In Romantic quest the Promethean hero stands finally, quite alone, upon a tower that is only himself, and his stance is all the fire there is. This realization leads neither to nihilism nor to solipsism, though Byron plays with the former and all fear the latter.

The dangers of idealizing the libido are of course constant in the life of the individual, and such idealizations are dreadful for whole societies, but the internalization of quest-romance had to accept these dangers. The creative process is the hero of Romantic poetry, and imaginative inhibitions, of every kind, necessarily must be the antagonists of the poetic quest. The special puzzle of Romanticism is the dialectical role that nature had to take in the revival of the mode of romance. Most simply, Romantic nature poetry, despite a long critical history of misrepresentation, was an antinature poetry, even in Wordsworth who sought a reciprocity or even a dialogue with nature, but found it only in flashes. Wordsworthian nature, thanks to Arnold and the critical tradition he fostered, has been misunderstood, though the insights of recent critics have begun to develop a better interpretative tradition, founded on A. C. Bradley's opposition to Arnold's view. Bradley stressed the strong side of Wordsworth's imagination, its Miltonic sublimity, which Arnold evidently never noticed, but which accounts for everything that is major in *The Prelude* and in the central crisis lyrics associated with it. Though Wordsworth came as a healer, and Shelley attacked him, in *Mont Blanc*, for attempting to reconcile man with nature, there is no such reconciliation in Wordsworth's poetry, and the healing function is performed only when the poetry shows the power of the mind over outward sense. The strength of renovation in Wordsworth resides only in the spirit's splendor, in what he beautifully calls "possible sublimity" or "something evermore about to be," the potential of an imagination too fierce to be contained by nature. This is the force that Coleridge sensed and feared in Wordsworth, and is remarkably akin to that strength in Milton that Marvell urbanely says he feared, in his introductory verses to *Paradise Lost*. As Milton curbed his own Prometheanism, partly by showing its dangers through Satan's version of the heroic quest, so Wordsworth learned to restrain his, partly through making his own quest-romance, in *The Prelude*, an account of learning both the enormous strength of nature and nature's wise and benevolent reining-in of its own force. In the covenant between Wordsworth and nature, two powers that are totally separate from each other, and potentially destructive of the other, try to meet in a dialectic of love. "Meet" is too hopeful, and "blend" would express Wordsworth's ideal and not his achievement, but the try itself is definitive of Wordsworth's strangeness and continued relevance as a poet.

If Wordsworth, so frequently and absurdly called a pantheist, was not questing for unity with nature, still less were Blake, Shelley, and Keats, or their darker followers in later generations, from Beddoes, Darley, and Wade down to Yeats and Lawrence in our time. Coleridge and Byron, in their very different ways, were oddly closer both to orthodox Christian myth and to pantheism or some form of nature-worship, but even their major poems hardly approximate nature poetry. Romantic or internalized romance, especially in its purest version of the quest form, the poems of symbolic voyaging that move in a continuous tradition from Shelley's *Alastor* to Yeats's *The Wanderings of Oisin*, tends to see the context of nature as a trap for the mature imagination. This point requires much laboring, as the influence of older views of Romanticism is very hard to slough off. Even

Northrop Frye, the leading romance theorist we have had at least since Ruskin, Pater, and Yeats, says that "in Romanticism the main direction of the quest of identity tends increasingly to be downward and inward, toward a hidden basis or ground of identity between man and nature." The directional part of this statement is true, but the stated goal I think is not. Frye still speaks of the Romantics as seeking a final unity between man and his nature, but Blake and Shelley do not accept such a unity as a goal, unless a total transformation of man and nature can precede unity, while Wordsworth's visions of "first and last and midst and without end" preserve the unyielding forms both of nature and of man. Keats's closest approach to an apocalyptic vision comes when he studies Moneta's face, at the climax of *The Fall of Hyperion*, but even that vision is essentially Wordsworthian, seeing as it does a perpetual change that cannot be ended by change, a human countenance made only more solitary in its growing alienation from nature, and a kind of naturalistic entropy that has gone beyond natural contraries, past "the lily and the snow." Probably only Joyce and Stevens, in later Romantic tradition, can be termed unreconstructed naturalists, or naturalistic humanists. Late Romantics as various as Eliot, Proust, and Shaw all break through uneasy natural contexts, as though sexuality was antithetical to the imagination, while Yeats, the very last of the High Romantics, worked out an elaborate sub-myth of the poet as antithetical quester, very much in the mode of Shelley's poetry. If the goal of Romantic internalization of the quest was a wider consciousness that would be free of the excesses of self-consciousness, a consideration of the rigors of experiential psychology will show, quite rapidly, why nature could not provide adequate context. The program of Romanticism, and not just in Blake, demands something more than a natural man to carry it through. Enlarged and more numerous senses are necessary, an enormous virtue of Romantic poetry clearly being that it not only demands such expansion but begins to make it possible, or at least attempts to do so.

The internalization of romance brought the concept of nature, and poetic consciousness itself, into a relationship they had never had before the advent of Romanticism in the later eighteenth century. Implicit in all the Romantics, and very explicit in Blake, is a difficult distinction between two modes of energy, organic and creative (Orc and Los in Blake, Prometheus bound and unbound in Shelley, Hyperion and Apollo in Keats, the Child and the Man, though with subtle misgivings, in Wordsworth). For convenience, the first mode can be

21

called Prometheus and the second "the Real Man, the Imagination" (Blake's phrase, in a triumphant letter written when he expected death). Generally, Prometheus is the poet-as-hero in the first stage of his quest, marked by a deep involvement in political, social, and literary revolution, and a direct, even satirical attack on the institutional orthodoxies of European and English society, including historically oriented Christianity, and the neoclassic literary and intellectual tradition, particularly in its Enlightenment phase. The Real Man, the Imagination, emerges after terrible crises in the major stage of the Romantic quest, which is typified by a relative disengagement from revolutionary activism, and a standing-aside from polemic and satire, so as to re-center the arena of search within the self and its ambiguities. In the Prometheus stage, the quest is allied to the libido's struggle against repressiveness, and nature is an ally, though always a wounded and sometimes a withdrawn one. In the Real Man, the Imagination, stage, nature is the immediate though not the ultimate antagonist. The final enemy to be overcome is a recalcitrance in the self, what Blake calls the Spectre of Urthona, Shelley the unwilling dross that checks the spirit's flight, Wordsworth the sad perplexity or fear that kills or, best of all, the hope that is unwilling to be fed, and Keats, most simply and perhaps most powerfully, the Identity. Coleridge calls the antagonist by a bewildering variety of names since, of all these poets, he is the most hagridden by anxieties, and the most humanly vulnerable. Byron and Beddoes do not so much name the antagonist as they mock it, so as to cast it out by continuous satire and demonic farce. The best single name for the antagonist is Keats's Identity, but the most traditional is the Selfhood, and so I shall use it here.

Only the Selfhood, for the Romantics as for such Christian visionaries as Eckhart before them, burns in Hell. The Selfhood is not the erotic principle, but precisely that part of the erotic that cannot be released in the dialectic of love, whether between man and man, or man and nature. Here the Romantics, all of them, I think, even Keats, part company with Freud's dialectics of human nature. Freud's beautiful sentence on marriage is a formula against which the Romantic Eros can be tested: "A man shall leave father and mother—according to the Biblical precept—and cleave to his wife; then are tenderness and sensuality united." By the canons of internalized romance, that translates: a poet shall leave his Great Original (Milton, for the Romantics) and nature—according to the precept of Poetic Genius—and cleave to his Muse or Imagination; then are the generous and solitary halves united. But, so translated, the formula has ceased to be Freudian and has become High Romantic. In Freud, part of the ego's own self-love is projected onto an outward object, but part always remains in the ego, and even the projected portion can find its way back again. Somewhere Freud has a splendid sentence that anyone unhappy in love can take to heart: "Object-libido was at first ego-libido and can be again transformed into ego-libido," which is to say that a certain degree of narcissistic mobility is rather a good thing. Somewhere else Freud remarks that all romance is really a form of what he calls "Family-romance"; one could as justly say, in his terms, that all romance is necessarily a mode of ego-romance. This may be true, and in its humane gloom it echoes a great line of realists who culminate in Freud, but the popular notion that High Romanticism takes a very different view of love is a sounder insight into the Romantics than most scholarly critics ever achieve (or at least state). All romance, literary and human, is founded upon en-chantment; Freud and the Romantics differ principally in their judg-ment as to what it is in us that resists enchantment, and what the value of that resistance is. For Freud it is the reality-principle, work-ing through the great disenchanter, reason, the scientific attitude, and without it no civilized values are possible. For the Romantics, this is again a dialectical matter, as two principles intertwine in the resist-ance to enchantment, one "organic," an anxiety-principle masquer-ading as a reality-principle and identical to the ego's self-love that never ventures out to others, and the other "creative," which resists enchantment in the name of a higher mode than the sympathetic imagination. This doubling is clearest in Blake's mythology, where there are two egos, the Spectre of Urthona and Los, who suffer the enchantments, real *and* deceptive, of nature and the female, and who resist, when and where they can, on these very different grounds. But, though less schematically, the same doubling of the ego, into passive and active components, is present in the other poets wher-ever they attempt their highest flights and so spurn the earth. The most intense effort of the Romantic quest is made when the Prome-thean stage of quest is renounced and the purgatorial crisis that fol-lows moves near to resolution. Romantic purgatory, by an extraor-dinary displacement of earlier mythology, is found just beyond the earthly paradise, rather than just before it, so that the imagination is tried by nature's best aspect. Instances of the interweaving of pur-gatory and paradise include nearly everything Blake says about the state of being he calls Beulah, and the whole development of Keats, from *Endymion* with its den or cave of Quietude on to the structure of *The Fall of Hyperion* where the poet enjoys the fruit and drink of paradise just before he has his confrontation with Moneta, whose shrine must be reached by mounting purgatorial stairs.

Nothing in Romantic poetry is more difficult to comprehend, for me anyway, than the process that begins after each poet's renunciation of Prometheus; for the incarnation of the Real Man, the Imagination, is not like psychic maturation in poets before the Romantics. The love that transcends the Selfhood has its analogues in the renunciatory love of many traditions, including some within Christianity, but the creative Eros of the Romantics is not renunciatory though it is self-transcendent. It is, to use Shelley's phrasing, a total going-out from our own natures, total because the force moving out is not only the Promethean libido but rather a fusion between the libido and the active or imaginative element in the ego; or simply, desire wholly taken up into the imagination. "Shelley's love poetry," as a phrase, is almost a redundancy, Shelley having written little else, but his specifically erotic poems, a series of great lyrics and the dazzling *Epipsychidion*, have been undervalued because they are so very difficult, the difficulty being the Shelleyan and Romantic vision of love.

Blake distinguished between Beulah and Eden as states of being, the first being the realm of family-romance and the second of apocalyptic romance, in which the objects of love altogether lose their object-dimension. In family-romance or Beulah, loved ones are not confined to their objective aspect (that would make them denizens of Blake's state of Generation or mere Experience), but they retain it nevertheless. The movement to the reality of Eden is one of re-creation or better, of knowledge not purchased by the loss of power, and so of power and freedom gained *through* a going-out of our nature, in which that last phrase takes on its full range of meanings. Though Romantic love, particularly in Wordsworth and Shelley, has been compared to what Charles Williams calls the Romantic theology of Dante, the figure of Beatrice is not an accurate analogue to the various Romantic visions of the beloved, for sublimation is not an element in the movement from Prometheus to Man. There is no useful analogue to Romantic or imaginative love, but there is a useful contrary, in the melancholy wisdom of Freud on natural love, and the contrary has the helpful clarity one always finds in Freud. If Romantic love is the sublime, then Freudian love is the pathetic, and truer of course to the phenomenon insofar as it is merely natural. To Freud, love begins as ego-libido, and necessarily is ever after a history of sorrow, a picaresque chronicle in which the ever-vulnerable ego stumbles from delusion to frustration, to expire at last (if lucky) in the compromising arms of the ugliest of Muses, the reality-principle. But the saving dialectic of this picaresque is that it is better thus, as there is no satisfaction in satisfaction anyway, since in the Freudian view all erotic partners are somewhat inadequate replacements for the initial sexual objects, parents. Romantic love, to Freud, is a particularly intense version of the longing for the mother, a love in which the imago is loved, rather than the replacement. And Romantic love, on this account, is anything but a dialectic of transformation, since it is as doomed to overvalue the surrogate as it compulsively overvalues the mother. Our age begins to abound in late Romantic "completions" of Freud, but the Romantic critiques of him, by Jung and Lawrence in particular, have not touched the strength of his erotic pessimism. There is a subtly defiant attempt to make the imago do the work of the imagination by Stevens, particularly in the very Wordsworthian *The Auroras of Autumn*, and it is beautifully subversive of Freud, but of course it is highly indirect. Yet a direct Romantic counter-critique of Freud's critique of Romantic love emerges from any prolonged, central study of Romantic poetry. For Freud, there is an ironic loss of energy, perhaps even of spirit, with every outward movement of love away from the ego. Only pure self-love has a perfection to it, a stasis without loss, and one remembers again Van den Berg's mordant observation on Freud: "Ultimately the enigma of grief is the libido's inclination toward exterior things." All outward movement, in the Freudian psychodynamics, is a fall that results from "an overfilled inner self," which would sicken within if it did not fall outward, and downward, into the world of objects and of other selves. One longs for Blake to come again and rewrite *The Book of Urizen* as a satire on this cosmogony of love. The poem would not require that much rewriting, for it now can be read as a prophetic satire on Freud, Urizen being a superego certainly overfilled with itself, and sickening into a false creation or creation-fall. If Romantic love can be castigated as "erotic illusion," Freudian love can be judged as "erotic reduction," and the prophets of the reality-principle are in danger always of the Urizenic boast:

> I have sought for a joy without pain,
> For a solid without fluctuation
> Why will you die O Eternals?
> Why live in unquenchable burnings?

The answer is the Romantic dialectic of Eros and Imagination, unfair as it is to attribute to the Freudians a censorious repressiveness.

But, to Blake and the Romantics, all available accounts of right reason, even those that had risen to liberate men, had the disconcerting tendency to turn into censorious moralities. Freud painfully walked a middle way, not unfriendly to the poetic imagination, and moderately friendly to Eros. If his myth of love is so sparse, rather less than a creative Word, it is still open both to analytic modification and to a full acceptance of everything that can come out of the psyche. Yet it is not quite what Philip Rieff claims for it, as it does not erase "the gap between therapeutic rationalism and self-assertive romanticism." That last is only the first stage of the Romantic quest, the one this discussion calls Prometheus. There remains a considerable gap between the subtle perfection to which Freud brought therapeutic rationalism and the mature Romanticism that is self-transcendent in its major poets.

There is no better way to explore the Real Man, the Imagination, than to study his monuments: *The Four Zoas, Milton,* and *Jerusalem; The Prelude* and the *Recluse* fragment; *The Ancient Mariner* and *Christabel; Prometheus Unbound, Adonais,* and *The Triumph of Life;* the two *Hyperions; Don Juan; Death's Jest-Book;* these are the definitive Romantic achievement, the words that were and will be, day and night. What follows is only an epitome, a rapid sketch of the major phase of this erotic quest. The sketch, like any that attempts to trace the visionary company of love, is likely to end in listening to the wind, hoping to hear an instant of a fleeting voice.

The internalization of quest-romance made of the poet-hero not a seeker after nature but after his own mature powers, and so the Romantic poet turned away, not from society to nature, but from nature to what was more integral than nature, within himself. The widened consciousness of the poet did not give him intimations of a former union with nature or the Divine, but rather of his former self-less self. One thinks of Yeats's Blakean declaration: "I'm looking for the face I had/Before the world was made." Different as the major Romantics were in their attitudes toward religion, they were united (except for Coleridge) in *not* striving for unity with anything but what might be called their Tharmas or id component, Tharmas being the Zoa or Giant Form in Blake's mythology who was the unfallen human potential for realizing instinctual desires, and so was the regent of Innocence. Tharmas is a shepherd-figure, his equivalent in Wordsworth being a number of visions of man against the sky, of actual shepherds Wordsworth had seen in his boyhood. This Romantic pastoral vision (its pictorial aspect can be studied in the woodcuts of Blake's Virgil series, and in the work done by Palmer, Calvert, and Richmond while under Blake's influence) is biblical pastoralism, but not at all of a traditional kind. Blake's Tharmas is inchoate when fallen, as the id or appetite is inchoate, desperately starved and uneasily allied to the Spectre of Urthona, the passive ego he has projected outward to meet an object-world from which he has been severed so unwillingly. Wordsworth's Tharmas, besides being the shepherd image of human divinity, is present in the poet himself as a desperate desire for continuity in the self, a desperation that at its worst sacrifices the living moment, but at its best produces a saving urgency that protects the imagination from the strong enchantments of nature.

In Freud the ego mediates between id and superego, and Freud had no particular interest in further dividing the ego itself. In Romantic psychic mythology, Prometheus rises from the id, and can best be thought of as the force of libido, doomed to undergo a merely cyclic movement from appetite to repression, and then back again; any quest within nature is thus at last irrelevant to the mediating ego, though the quest goes back and forth through it. It is within the ego itself that the quest must turn, to engage the antagonist proper, and to clarify the imaginative component in the ego by its strife of contraries with its dark brother. Frye, writing on Keats, calls the imaginative ego *identity-with* and the selfhood ego *identity-as*, which clarifies Keats's ambiguous use of "identity" in this context. Geoffrey Hartman, writing on Wordsworth, points to the radical Protestant analogue to the Romantic quest: "The terror of discontinuity or separation enters, in fact, as soon as the imagination truly enters. In its restraint of vision, as well as its peculiar nakedness before the moment, this resembles an extreme Protestantism, and Wordsworth seems to quest for 'evidences' in the form of intimations of continuity." Wordsworth's greatness was in his feeling the terror of discontinuity as acutely as any poet could, yet overcoming this terror nevertheless, by opening himself to vision. With Shelley, the analogue of the search for evidences drops out, and an Orphic strain takes its place, as no other English poet gives so continuous an impression of relying on almost literal inspiration. Where Keats knew the Selfhood as an attractive strength of distinct identity that had to be set aside, and Wordsworth as a continuity he longed for yet learned to resist, and Blake as a temptation to prophetic wrath and withdrawal that had to be withstood, Shelley frequently gives the impression of encountering no enchantment he does not embrace, since every enchantment is an authentic inspiration. Yet this is a false impression, though Yeats sometimes received it, as in his insistence that Shelley, great poet as he certainly was, lacked a Vision of Evil. The contrary view to Yeats is that of C. S. Lewis, who held that Shelley, more than any other "heathen" poet (the word is from Lewis), drove home the truth of Original Sin. Both views are mistaken. For Shelley, the Selfhood's strong enchantment, stronger even than it is for the other Romantics, is one that would keep him from ever concluding the Prometheus phase of the quest. The Selfhood allies itself with Prometheus against the repressive force Shelley calls Jupiter, his version of Blake's Urizen or Freud's superego. This temptation calls the poet to perpetual revolution, and Shelley, though longing desperately to see the tyrannies of his time overturned, renounces it at the opening of *Prometheus Unbound*, in the Imagination's name. Through his renunciation, he moves to overturn the tyranny of time itself.

There are thus two main elements in the major phase of Romantic quest, the first being the inward overcoming of the Selfhood's temptation, and the second the outward turning of the triumphant Imagination, free of further internalizations, though "outward" and "inward" become cloven fictions or false conceptual distinctions in this triumph, which must complete a dialectic of love by uniting the Imagination with its bride, a transformed, ongoing creation of the Imagination rather than a redeemed nature. Blake and Wordsworth had long lives, and each completed his version of this dialectic. Coleridge gave up the quest, and became only an occasional poet, while Byron's quest, even had he lived into middle age, would have become increasingly ironic. Keats died at twenty-five, and Shelley at twenty-nine; despite their fecundity, they did not complete their development, but their death-fragments, *The Fall of Hyperion* and *The Triumph of Life*, prophesy the final phase of the quest in them. Each work breaks off with the Selfhood subdued, and there is profound despair in each, particularly in Shelley's, but there are still hints of what the Imagination's triumph would have been in Keats. In Shelley, the final despair may be total, but a man who had believed so fervently that the good time would come, had already given a vision of imaginative completion in the closing act of *Prometheus Unbound*, and we can go back to it and see what is deliberately lacking in *The Triumph of Life*. What follows is a rapid attempt to trace the major phase of quest in the four poets, taking as texts *Jerusalem* and *The Prelude*, and the *Fall* and *Triumph*, these two last with supplementary reference to crucial earlier erotic poems of Keats and Shelley.

28

Of Blake's long poems the first, *The Four Zoas*, is essentially a poem of Prometheus, devoting itself to the cyclic strife between the Promethean Orc and the moral censor, Urizen, in which the endless cycle between the two is fully exposed. The poem ends in an apocalypse, the explosive and Promethean *Night the Ninth, Being The Last Judgment*, which in itself is one of Blake's greatest works, yet from which he turned when he renounced the entire poem (by declining to engrave it). But not before he attempted to move the entire poem from the Prometheus stage to the Imagination, for Blake's own process of creative maturation came to its climax while he worked on *The Four Zoas*. The entrance into the mature stage of the quest is clearly shown by the different versions of *Night the Seventh*, for the later one introduces the doubling of the ego into Spectre of Urthona and Los, Selfhood or *Identity-As*, and Imagination or *Identity-With*. Though skillfully handled, it was not fully clarified by Blake, even to himself, and so he refused to regard the poem as definitive vision. Its place in his canon was filled, more or less, by the double-romance *Milton* and *Jerusalem*. The first is more palpably in a displaced romance mode, involving as it does symbolic journeys downward to our world by Milton and his emanation or bride of creation, Ololon, who descend from an orthodox Eternity in a mutual search for one another, the characteristic irony being that they could never find one another in a traditional heaven. There is very little in the poem of the Prometheus phase, Blake having already devoted to that a series of prophetic poems, from *America* and *Europe* through *The Book of Urizen* and on to the magnificent if unsatisfactory (to him, not to us) *The Four Zoas*. The two major stages of the mature phase of quest dominate the structure of *Milton*. The struggle with the Selfhood moves from the quarrel between Palamabron (Blake) and Satan (Hayley) in the introductory Bard's Song on to Milton's heroic wrestling match with Urizen, and climaxes in the direct confrontation between Milton and Satan on the Felpham shore, in which Milton recognizes Satan as his own Selfhood. The recognition compels Satan to a full epiphany, and a subsequent defeat. Milton then confronts Ololon, the poem ending in an epiphany contrary to Satan's, in what Blake specifically terms a preparation for a going-forth to the great harvest and vintage of the nations. But even this could not be Blake's final Word; the quest in *Milton* is primarily Milton's and not Blake's, and the quest's antagonist is still somewhat externalized. In *Jerusalem, The Prelude's* only rival as the finest long poem of the nineteenth century, Blake gives us the most comprehensive single version of Romantic quest. Here there is an alternation between vision sweeping outward into the nightmare world of the reality-principle, and a wholly inward vision of conflict in Blake's ego, between the Spectre and Los. The poet's antagonist is himself, the poem's first part being the most harrowing and tormented account of genius tempted to the madness of self-righteousness, frustrate anger, and solipsistic withdrawal, in the Romantic period. Blake-Los struggles on, against this enchantment of despair, until the poem quietly, almost without warning, begins to move into the light of a Last Judgment, of a kind passed by every man upon himself. In the poem's final plates (Blake's canonical poems being a series of engraved plates), the reconciliation of Los and his emanative portion, Enitharmon, begins, and we approach the completion of quest.

Though Blake, particularly in *Jerusalem*, attempts a continuity based on thematic juxtaposition and simultaneity, rather than on consecutiveness, he is in such sure control of his own procedure that his work is less difficult to summarize than *The Prelude*, a contrast that tends to startle inexperienced readers of Blake and of Wordsworth. *The Prelude* follows a rough, naturalistic chronology through Wordsworth's life down to the middle of the journey, where it, like any modern reader, leaves him, in his state of preparation for a further greatness that never came. What is there already, besides the invention of the modern lyric, is a long poem so rich and strange it has defied almost all description.

The Prelude is an autobiographical romance that frequently seeks expression in the sublime mode, which is really an invitation to aesthetic disaster. *The Excursion* is an aesthetic disaster, as Hazlitt, Byron, and many since happily have noted, yet there Wordsworth works within rational limits. *The Prelude* ought to be an outrageous poem, but its peculiar mixture of displaced genre and inappropriate style *works*, because its internalization of quest is the inevitable story for its age. Wordsworth did not have the Promethean temperament, yet he had absolute insight into it, as *The Borderers* already showed. In *The Prelude*, the initial quest phase of the poet-as-Prometheus is diffuse but omnipresent. It determines every movement in the growth of the child's consciousness, always seen as a violation of the established natural order, and it achieves great power in Book VI, when the onset of the French Revolution is associated with the poet's own hidden desires to surmount nature, desires that emerge in the great passages clustered around the Simplon Pass. The Promethean quest fails, in one way in the Alps when chastened by nature, and in another with the series of shocks to the poet's moral being when England wars against the Revolution, and the Revolution betrays itself. The more direct Promethean failure, the poet's actual abandonment of Annette Vallon, is presented only indirectly in the 1805 *Prelude*, and drops out completely from the revised, posthumously published *Prelude* of 1850, the version most readers encounter. In his crisis, Wordsworth learns the supernatural and superhuman strength of his own imagination, and is able to begin a passage to the mature phase of his quest. But his anxiety for continuity is too strong for him, and he yields to its dark enchantment. The Imagination phase of his quest does not witness the surrender of his Selfhood and the subsequent inauguration of a new dialectic of love, purged of the natural heart, as it is in Blake. Yet he wins a provisional triumph over himself, in Book XII of *The Prelude*, and in the closing stanzas of *Resolution and Independence* and the Great Ode. And the final vision of *The Prelude* is not of a redeemed nature, but of a liberated creativity transforming its creation into the beloved:

> Prophets of Nature, we to them will speak
> A lasting inspiration, sanctified
> By reason, blest by faith: what we have loved
> Others will love, and we will teach them how;
> Instruct them how the mind of man becomes
> A thousand times more beautiful than the earth
> On which he dwells, above this frame of things . . .

Coleridge, addressed here as the other Prophet of Nature, renounced his own demonic version of the Romantic quest (clearest in the famous triad of *Kubla Khan, Christabel,* and *The Ancient Mariner*), his wavering Prometheanism early defeated not so much by his Selfhood as by his Urizenic fear of his own imaginative energy. It was a high price for the release he had achieved in his brief phase of exploring the romance of the marvelous, but the loss itself produced a few poems of unique value, the *Dejection* Ode in particular. These poems show how Coleridge preceded Wordsworth in the invention of a new kind of poetry that shows the mind in a dialogue with itself. The motto of this poetry might well be its descendant Stevens's "The mind is the terriblest force in the world, father,/ Because, in chief, it, only, can defend/Against itself. At its mercy, we depend/Upon it." Coleridge emphasizes the mercy, Wordsworth the saving terror of the force. Keats and Shelley began with a passion closer to the Prometheus phase of Blake than of Wordsworth or Coleridge. The fullest development of Romantic quest, after Blake's mythology and Wordsworth's exemplary refusal of mythology, is in Keats's *Endymion* and Shelley's *Prometheus Unbound*. In this second generation of Romantic questers the same first phase of Prometheanism appears, as does the second phase of crisis, renounced quest, overcoming of the Selfhood, and final movement toward imaginative love, but the relation of the quest to the world of the reality-principle has changed. In Blake, dream with its ambiguities centers in Beulah, the purgatorial lower paradise of sexuality and benevolent nature. In Wordsworth, dream is rare, and betokens either a prolepsis of the imagination abolishing nature or a state the poet calls "visionary dreariness," in which the immediate power of the mind over outward sense is so great that the ordinary forms of nature seem to have withdrawn. But in Keats and Shelley, a polemical Romanticism matures, and the argument of the dream with reality becomes an equivocal one. Romanticism guessed at a truth our doctors begin to measure; as infants we dream for half the time we are asleep, and as we age we dream less and less, while we sleep. The doctors have not yet told us that utterly dreamless sleep directly prophesies or equals death, but it is a familiar Romantic conceit, and may prove to be true. We are our imaginations, and die with them.

Dreams, to Shelley and Keats, are not wish-fulfillments. It is not Keats but Moneta, the passionate and wrong-headed Muse in *The Fall of Hyperion*, who first confounds poets and dreamers as one tribe, and then overreacts by insisting they are totally distinct, and even sheer opposites, antipodes. Freud is again a clear-headed guide; the manifest and latent content of the dream can be distinct, even opposite, but in the poem they come together. The younger Romantics do not seek to render life a dream, but to recover the dream for the health of life. What is called real is too often an exhausted phantasmagoria, and the reality-principle can too easily be debased into a principle of surrender, an accommodation with death-in-life. We return to the observation of Van den Berg, cited earlier; Rousseau and the Romantics discovered not only the alienation between child and adult, but the second birth of psychic maturation or adolescence. Eliot thought that the poet of *Adonais* and *The Triumph of Life* had never "progressed" beyond the ideas and ideals of adolescence, or at least of what Eliot had believed in his *own* adolescence. Every reader can be left to his own judgment of the relative maturity of *Ash Wednesday* and *The Witch of Atlas*, or *The Cocktail Party* and *The Cenci*, and is free to formulate his own dialectics of progression.

The Promethean quest, in Shelley and in Keats, is from the start uneasy about its equivocal ally, nature, and places a deeper trust in dream, for at least the dream itself is not reductive, however we reduce it in our dissections. Perhaps the most remarkable element in the preternatural rapidity of maturation in Keats and Shelley is their early renunciation of the Prometheus phase of the quest, or rather, their dialectical complexity in simultaneously presenting the necessity and the inherent limitation of this phase. In *Alastor*, the poem's entire thrust is at one with the poet-hero's self-destruction; this is the cause of the poem's radical unity, which C. S. Lewis rightly observed as giving a marvelous sense of the poet's being at one with his subject. Yet the poem is also a daimonic shadow in motion; it shows us nature's revenge upon the imagination, and the excessive price of the quest in the poet's alienation from other selves. On a cosmic scale, this is part of the burden of *Prometheus Unbound*, where the hero, who massively represents the bound prophetic power of all men, rises from his icy crucifixion by refusing to continue the cycles of revolution and repression that form an ironic continuity between himself and Jupiter. Demogorgon, the dialectic of history, rises from the abyss and stops history, thus completing in the macrocosmic shadow what Prometheus, by his renunciation, inaugurates in the microcosm of the individual imagination, or the liberating dream taken up into the self. Shelley's poetry after this does not maintain the celebratory strain of Act IV of his lyrical drama. The way again is down and out, to a purgatorial encounter with the Selfhood, but the Selfhood's temptations, for Shelley, are subtle and wavering, and mask themselves in the forms of the ideal. So fused become the ideal and these masks that Shelley, in the last lines he wrote, is in despair of any victory, though it is Shelley's Rousseau and not Shelley himself who actually chants:

> . . . thus on the way
> Mask after mask fell from the countenance
> And form of all; and long before the day
>
> Was old, the joy which waked like heaven's glance
> The sleepers in the oblivious valley, died;
> And some grew weary of the ghastly dance,
>
> And fell, as I have fallen, by the wayside—

For Shelley, Rousseau was not a failed poet, but rather the poet whose influence had resulted in an imaginative revolution, and nearly ended time's bondage. So, Rousseau speaks here not for himself alone, but for his tradition, and necessarily for Coleridge, Words-worth, and the Promethean Shelley as well, indeed for poetry itself. Yet, rightly or wrongly, the image Shelley leaves with us, at his end, is not this falling-away from quest but the image of the poet forever wakeful amidst the cone of night, illuminating it as the star Lucifer does, fading as the star, becoming more intense as it narrows into the light.

The mazes of romance, in *Endymion*, are so winding that they suggest the contrary to vision, a labyrinthine nature in which all quest must be forlorn. In this realm, nothing narrows to an intensity, and every passionate impulse widens out to a diffuseness, the fate of Endymion's own search for his goddess. In reaction, Keats chastens his own Prometheanism, and attempts the objective epic in *Hyperion*. Hyperion's self-identity is strong but waning fast, and the fragment of the poem's Book III introduces an Apollo whose self-identity is in the act of being born. The temptation to go on with the poem must have been very great, after its magnificent beginnings, but Keats's letters are firm in renouncing it. Keats turns from the enchantments of Identity to the romance-fragment, *The Fall of Hyperion*, and engages instead the demon of subjectivity, his own poetic ambitions, as Wordsworth had done before him. Confronted by Moneta, he meets the danger of her challenge not by asserting his own Identity, but by finding his true form in the merged identity of the poethood, in the high function and responsibilities of a Words-worthian humanism. Though the poem breaks off before it attempts the dialectic of love, it has achieved the quest, for the Muse herself has been transformed by the poet's persistence and integrity. We wish for more, necessarily, but only now begin to understand how much we had received, even in this broken monument.

I have scanted the dialectic of love, in all of these poets. Romantic love, past its own Promethean adolescence, is not the possessive love of the natural heart, which is the quest of Freudian Eros, moving always in a tragic rhythm out from and back to the isolate ego. That is the love Blake explicitly rejected:

> Let us agree to give up Love
> And root up the Infernal Grove
> Then shall we return and see
> The worlds of happy Eternity
>
> Throughout all Eternity
> I forgive you you forgive me . . .

The Infernal Grove grows thick with virtues, but these are the selfish virtues of the natural heart. Desire for what one lacks becomes a habit of possession, and the Selfhood's jealousy murders the Real Man, the Imagination. All such love is an entropy, and as such Freud understood and accepted it. We become aware of others only as we learn our separation from them, and our ecstasy is a reduction. Is this the human condition, and love only its mitigation?

> To cast off the idiot Questioner who is always questioning,
> But never capable of answering . . .

Whatever else the love that the full Romantic quest aims at may be, it cannot be a therapy. It must make all things new, and then marry what it has made. Less urgently, it seeks to define itself through the analogue of each man's creative potential. But it learns, through its poets, that it cannot define what it is, but only what it will be. The man prophesied by the Romantics is a central man who is always in the process of becoming his own begetter, and though his major poems perhaps have been written, he as yet has not fleshed out his prophecy, nor proved the final form of his love.

1968

3
Visionary Cinema of Romantic Poetry

The inventor of my subject in this essay is, unsurprisingly, Eisenstein, who wrote insightfully on the cinematic elements in Milton and Shelley. I want to deviate from Eisenstein's concern a little, and I choose my motto from a poem of Wallace Stevens, *The Creations of Sound*. Speaking of one X, a poet I take to have been Eliot, Stevens says of his poems, in courteous but firm disapproval: "They do not make the visible a little hard to see." Blake, Wordsworth, and Shelley meant somewhat different things by vision, and their intentions in this matter were certainly not identical, but they all of them, in their poems, do tend to make the visible at least a little hard to see.

Critics have noted, during these last decades, the apparent conflict between theory and performance in this regard in these poets, particularly in Wordsworth. Blake seems just as odd when one starts to know him well. "General Knowledge," he insisted, "is Remote Knowledge. It is in Particulars that Wisdom consists & Happiness too. Both in Art & Life General Masses are as Much Art as a Pasteboard Man is Human."

An experienced reader of Blake's major poems, his epics, learns to set aside the very early impression that there is anything cloudy or indefinite about the figures or actions in those poems. Yet there is a subtler problem in visualization that presents itself everywhere in Blake's poetry at its most characteristic; Blake invites the reader's ocular powers to the enjoyment of a dangerous freedom, dangerous I think not to Blake as a poet, but certainly to Blake as a visual artist and critically somewhat dangerous to the reader. I read one of the most eloquent descriptive passages in the language, I stare, disbelievingly, at an inadequate engraved illumination and then try, too strenuously, to isolate an image that

37

Blake, as a poet, knew better than to isolate. Blake, I think, like his master Milton (as Eisenstein hinted), wants us to be more of a film-script reader or even a director than a film-viewer. He wants us to hear the fierce arguments between his Giant Forms, and he wants how we hear those disputes to waver depending upon our own state of being. And he wants us to see the transformations in his ruined worlds, but how we see and even at times what we see will depend upon the self-purging of our own eyes. Blake suggests a principle that I have seen applied only at scattered moments in a handful of films, one that might be called both auditory and visual counterpoint. The Urizen in us is meant to see one thing, the suffering Tharmas another, and so on down that sorrowing cast of internalized Titans.

There is an equivalent or parallel counterpoint in Wordsworth, a cinematic dialectic in which natural sight and sound reach their horizon and blend into a seeing and hearing of processes that cannot, in mere nature, be seen and heard. To Blake, Wordsworth's visionary cinema seemed not a counterpoint but a movingly fragmented single voice, the voice of Tharmas, a splintered but still visual, still instinctual unity, quaveringly seeking his harmony again in a context that could never afford him such harmony. But Wordsworth makes his blendings work, and invents the modern crisis poem by doing so. That a strictly controlled synesthesia should have been the mark, not of disaster, but of salvation in the Coleridgean-Wordsworthian crisis poem is of importance in understanding how the Romantics suggest a more imaginative cinema than we can see in our theaters.

Shelley is the crucial case, and no originality is possible here, because of the brilliant commentary by Eisenstein on visual detail in Shelley's lyricism. Shelley, as always, is an imaginative extremist, and does not deal in visual or auditory counterpoint as do Blake and Wordsworth. His desire is to make the visible almost impossible to see, and his cinema is too visionary for any techniques devised in our time to encompass. The sight or sound too keen for more than a flash of apprehension is the staple of his imagination, and seems to suggest the art of the lighting expert or of the sound-effects specialist more than that of the film creator. But, at his greatest moments, Shelley earns his assignment to Phase 17 of Yeats's *A Vision*, one of the *daimonic* men whose Body of Fate is "Loss." Where Blake struggles to *see* an imaginative gain, and Wordsworth to *hear* the conversion of experiential loss into such gain, Shelley sees, hears, and describes imaginative loss. The dissolving of sight is given us, by him, as a presage of a greater fading of integrity, a yielding of every natural particular to what he ironically terms the Triumph of Life.

Keats is not primarily the creator of a visionary cinema, though *Endymion* acts itself out before us as a dissolving series of visions, and *The Fall of Hyperion* stations its scene and figures with a monumental sense of visual possibility that transcends what is ordinarily visible. A feeling for the weight of things, and a deliberate pacing, too slow for the impatience of the eye, combine to render Keats a maker poised before things-in-their-greeting, even as Blake, Wordsworth, and Shelley, in different ways, deal with things-in-their-farewell. Keats is nevertheless more than a naturalistic artist, however heroically we conceive his naturalism; like the other major Romantics, though to a lesser extent, he was, despite his yearnings, a Miltonic poet, and the central principle that organizes his art is not a particularly dramatic one. If *To Autumn* is rightly accounted his masterpiece, it presents us with a scenario of, first, an enacted process too slow for the eye to see; second, a sight so ambiguously blended that we cannot know for sure whether we love landscape or woman; third, a series of sounds, of autumnal music, that inevitably betoken death by their gentle tentativeness. Blake would have had no quarrel with the ode *To Autumn*; it gives firm outline, but spiritual as opposed to corporeal form.

I propose in what follows to sketch the rough outlines of a visionary cinema in Blake, Wordsworth, and Shelley, not in order to cast any illumination upon the nature of any mere pragmatic cinema we already know, and not much in the hope that a study of poetry will ever make any particular cinematic artist any more gifted in his work. The burden of Romantic poetry is absolute freedom, including freedom from the tyranny of the bodily eye, and this freedom appears to have resulted in part from the specifically Protestant influencing that made modern poetry possible. When Wordsworth seeks the middle passage between the sensual, sleeping the sleep of death in their vacancy and vanity, and the ascetics, studying their nostalgias and insisting that all earthly paradises have been lost, he is presumably not immediately conscious that he seeks what radical Protestantism so frequently sought, a renewal of the biblical program of hallowing the commonplace. It takes a while to realize that this Wordsworthian hallowing is not enacted through the eye. Wordsworth would rouse us from sleep by words, he says, that speak of nothing more than what we *are*, rather than of nothing more than what we *see*. Who could have thought, Stevens asks, in one of his more explicitly humanist declarations—who could have thought to make, out of what one sees and what one hears, so many separate selves. Wordsworth was too aware that his freedom was precarious to make so trusting a statement. In him the Christian Liberty of Milton had become what it nearly became in Coleridge, the power of the mind over a universe of death.

Christian Liberty, as a doctrine, led to Milton's conception of a sect of one (Abdiel), a church of one (himself). He appealed to the holy light to shine inward, and created English Romanticism by doing so. The implicit distrust of the visible in Blake and Wordsworth, in particular, has some relation to Milton's blindness, for Milton is the greatest visionary poet in the English language, as Isabel McCaffrey remarks. He yearns, most movingly, for the visible, but he does not need it, and its absence became one of the greatest of his astonishing panoply of strengths.

There is, I think, a profound sense in which poetry *is* antithetical to cinema, an opinion expressed rather strongly by Valéry. My concern here is not to say anything about the nature of cinema, but to apply the principle of Borges, that artists create their own precursors and force us to read the precursors differently. Art forms do the same, and the consciousness of films compels us to read past poetry differently. That this difference is sometimes loss is beyond dispute; *Paradise Lost* has yielded some of its *primary* excitement to our cinematic experiences. But, if controlled, the difference becomes gain, becomes indeed another working of Wordsworth's compensatory imagination. I want, in this investigation, to bring a critical eye conditioned by cinema freshly to bear upon Blake's visionary procedure and Wordsworth's and Shelley's after that. Somewhere along the roads that led from the major Romantics to our poets who matter most—to Stevens and Hart Crane particularly—the distrust of the merely visible dissipated. One wants so badly for Tennyson to have freed his inner eye, to have yielded himself to the phantasmagoria that was his truest mode; and Browning, particularly in the greatest of his lyrics, *"Childe Roland to the Dark Tower Came,"* does yield momentously to vision, and renews something of the Romantic freedom. Stevens hesitates, endlessly, at the verge of that freedom. But, to this day, for a full-scale emancipation from a mere appearance of objects, we need to go back to the founders of modern poetry, to Blake and to Wordsworth.

If I ask myself what I remember most vividly, at all times, about

Blake's three long poems—*The Four Zoas, Milton,* and *Jerusalem*—
the answer is always argument—passionate, beautiful argument between mutually tormented consciousnesses—and never actions or
sights as such. But Blake does more than make us hear these arguments; he stations the disputants in a context informed by conceptual images, images that either poise themselves just within the visible or compel a new kind of visibility to appear. From their starts,
his long poems refuse to seek the visually remembered world. Even
Wordsworth, of course, is found not by the visually remembered
world, but by that world taken up into the mind and seen again by
the eye of the mind, as Geoffrey Hartman suggests. Blake shatters
this blending with a single insistence; as he does not behold the outward creation, so he can affirm for himself that his Giant Forms are
stationed in no remembered landscape but only in the visionary finding of his own pulsation of an artery, that moment in each day that
Satan's Watch-Fiends cannot find.

At the end of Night the Fourth of *The Four Zoas,* the Giant Form
named Los, who will at last compel an imaginative salvation, wearies
of the terrible task of hammering the falling Urizen into some kind
of definite shape. Himself a malformed Imagination, Los, the affrighted Titan, at this point, cannot bear the consequences of his own
necessary labor. Instead of the heroic stance of the artificer before
his own free creation, we are given the wavering of an enforced illu-
sionist who "became what he beheld / He became what he was doing
he was himself transformed." The final lines of Night IV read:

> The bones of Urizen hurtle on the wind the bones of Los
> Twinge & his iron sinews bend like lead & fold
> Into unusual forms dancing & howling stamping the Abyss

This vehement grotesquerie seems, at first, only an instance of
what Blake's friend Fuseli charmingly called "Meester Blake's emancipated anatomy," prompting those Blakean manuscript sketches
that impress our skepticism as being only so many flying geeks. But
the rhetoric this vision emancipates in Blake at the very start of the
next book, Night the Fifth, is monumentally impressive by any standards. This is the *totentanz* of Los:

> Infected Mad he dancd on his mountains high & dark as heaven
> Now fixd into one stedfast bulk his features stonify
> From his mouth curses & from his eyes sparks of blighting
> Beside the anvil cold he dancd with the hammer of Urthona
> Terrific pale. Enitharmon stretchd on the dreary Earth

Felt her immortal limbs freeze stiffning pale inflexible
His feet shrunk withring from the deep shrinking & withering
And Enitharmon shrunk up all their fibres withring beneath
As plants witherd by winter leaves & stems & roots decaying
Melt into thin air while the seed drivn by the furious wind
Rests on the distant Mountains top. So Los & Enitharmon
Shrunk into fixed space stood trembling on a Rocky cliff
Yet mighty bulk & majesty & beauty remaind but unexpansive
As far as highest Zenith from the lowest Nadir. So far shrunk
Los from the furnaces a Space immense & left the cold
Prince of Light bound in chains of intellect among the furnaces
But all the furnaces were out & the bellows had ceast to blow

He stood trembling & Enitharmon clung around his knees
Their senses unexpansive in one stedfast bulk remain
The night blew cold & Enitharmon shriekd on the dismal wind

Her pale hands cling around her husband & over her weak head
Shadows of Eternal Death sit in the leaden air

But the soft pipe the flute the viol organ harp & cymbal
And the sweet sound of silver voices calm the weary couch
Of Enitharmon but her groans drown the immortal harps
Loud & more loud the living music floats upon the air
Faint & more faint the daylight wanes. The wheels of turning darkness
Began in solemn revolutions. Earth convulsd with rending pangs
Rockd to & fro & cried sore at the groans of Enitharmon
Still the faint harps & silver voices calm the weary couch
But from the caves of deepest night ascending in clouds of mist
The winter spread his wide black wings across from pole to pole
Grim frost beneath & terrible snow linkd in a marriage chain
Began a dismal dance. The winds around on pointed rocks
Settled like bats innumerable ready to fly abroad

If Wordsworth's method, as Pottle remarked, was one of transfiguration, then Blake's, in this terrific passage, seems to be poised
between the phantasmagoria of the surrealists and the massive and
detailed visionary realism of Milton. The matter of common perception is wholly absent here; no descriptive detail awaits transfiguration. Yet the greatness of the passage does not dwell only in its carry-
ing-over of the Miltonic sublime into a conceptualized night-world.
Like every major passage in Blake, it is polemical, and it fights not
only the technologists and materialists of Blake's own time, but also
the servants of Urizen who abound in our own technological dreari-

ness. To explore the dens of Urizen is to come to terms with a fallen world, but to see the irrelevance of that world to the imagination, as Blake does in the passage that I've quoted, is to see what an intellectual fighter must see, if he believes, as Blake did, that the Eternal Great Humanity Divine can tear Himself free from any local, time-bound accidents of context, whether the context be provided by nature or by the technological extensions of nature. For Blake, as for Wordsworth and Shelley, there are no extensions of man; there are only more Humanized or less Humanized men. Explorations that are not apocalyptic are, to Blake, exploitations; they lead to religions of concealment. The passage I have quoted from Blake is about the completion of the Fall of man, which is made final when the imagination accepts unnecessary limitations. The terror felt by Los is founded on his stupidity; he cannot see that the hammering of error into definite shape, however repugnant, will lead to salvation. The great description of the dance of Los founds its irony on visionary counterpoint; the imagination is accepting a naturalization that is wholly unnecessary; it is yielding itself to the context of space. But it is recalcitrant to that context, and the landscape cannot hold it. With an eye made active by an awareness of cinema, we see what Blake gives us in his passage, a series of shifting views that are not in continuity with one another, and whose juxtapositions suggest an intolerable confusion between an inward world rolling outward and an outward world that stands apart and is objectified as a mockery of our visual powers. Los is "Infected" because he is becoming what he beheld in the changes of Urizen; he is "Mad" because he cannot bear such transformations in himself. He dances "on his mountains," which are truly his, for they are forsaken elements of his own self. In the earth of Eden, before the Fall, the Imagination dwelt in underground caves, which were the auricular nerves of man, and identical with the apocalyptic sense of hearing. In Blake, the Fall turns everything inside out; the stonified ears have become the mountains on which the deafened Los dances. We see, in succession, but again without continuity, the following images: a mad Titan dancing on mountains as high and dark as an inhuman heaven; then a steadfast bulk, a horror of natural sculpture, with stony features, a cursing mouth, and eyes from which sparks of blighting come at us. Next we see the dancer again, but he is pale, and dances beside a cold anvil, ironically brandishing the now useless hammer of Urthona, his name in Eternity. The next shot shows us his female, emanative portion, Enitharmon, stretched on a denuded earth, and freezing and stiffening into that ground of unbeing. In the eye of vision we suddenly see both figures shrinking and withering from the feet up, and immediately the next frame shows us two plants withered by winter, uprooted, decaying, and then dissolving in a furious wind that carries the unseen seeds to a distant mountaintop. We see the two more-than-human figures again, still mighty in bulk and majesty and beauty, but curiously confined-looking, and then a shot of the cold furnaces and unused bellows is given us. The two figures tremble on a cliff at the edge of an abyss, the female clinging round Los's knees. The wind blows, and we hear her shriek; there is a chorus of soft instruments and silvery voices, but she shrieks louder to drown it out as the daylight wanes. The darkness comes in the shapes of the turning wheels of giant mills, as though industrial spectres were planted in the skies, and the earth responds to the dread revolutions of those dark wheels by rocking to and fro, convulsed in the rending pangs of some enormous childbirth. As Enitharmon groans again, the music of comfort attempts to return:

> But from the caves of deepest night ascending in clouds of mist
> The winter spread his wide black wings across from pole to pole
> Grim frost beneath & terrible snow linkd in a marriage chain
> Began a dismal dance. The winds around on pointed rocks
> Settled like bats innumerable ready to fly abroad

I have re-quoted these last five lines because their visionary power is so intense. Here, the Winter wind is an enormous bat flying over the frozen chain of Jealousy that symbolizes all fallen marriage for Blake, and the dance of the weather completes Los's dance of death. Beneath the black bat and the white chain there now comes rending forth, out of the earth, the crimson form of natural man in revolt, the hellish figure of Orc, Rousseau's dream of man become a nightmare of revolt and unrestrained violence. A ghastly decomposition in layers of black, white, and red ends a scene that began with a maddened but still titanically heroic figure dancing itself on, through a frenzy of incomprehension, into its own destruction. The ear has heard a blowing wind, a silvery music too soft to endure, and a female howling in pangs of childbirth. The eye has seen human forms vacillating between stony masses and ruined vegetation, and eye and ear together end with a vision of a howling red child, menacing all of the senses it seeks to release; a vision of natural existence so violent that it can give vision no field in which to continue the labors of salvation.

44

What Blake has compelled us to see and to hear is not the redemption of physical reality, which Kracauer states as the central thesis of his theory of film, but rather the ocular and aural demonstration that physical reality cannot be redeemed by the art of the eye and the ear. Uneasily but inevitably, the passage, like every major passage in Blake's mature poetry, makes us confront the abyss of the five senses, makes us realize, in Stevensian terms, the necessity for a violence from within to overcome this violence from without. In the war between the sky and the mind, Blake fights on the mind's side always, and he will resort to no external image for its own sake, but only as yet another index to our Fall. We cannot be saved by images, in Blake, and yet the emblem of salvation for Blake remains a central image, the Human Form Divine, a perfect human body stationed in no context but itself, seen against no background but the artifacts it itself has made, but artifacts poised against the created world. What Blake finally wants us to see breaks the confines of a possible cinema—a greater human form, male and female together, containing the world *within* it, from the caves of middle-earth to the starry wheels above. To visualize a poem, and a visionary poem at that, is to see what cannot be seen. In the closing lines of *Jerusalem* Blake speaks of what Stevens terms a seeing and unseeing in the eye, as an *identifying* of all human forms. He asks for too much, and perhaps at last we will be condemned to judge him as he judged Milton, a true poet when he wrote of visual torment, but a fettered bard of the absolute when he asked us to go beyond the abyss of the eye. Yet his eternal appeal is in his demand that we must and can do so.

With Wordsworth, we move to a more overt defeat of the eye, though the consequences of the defeat are deliberately mitigated *by* the poet, in contrast to Blake's grim delight in our apprehension of the defeat of sight by vision. Though Blake might have seen our movie theaters as so many more temples of Urizen, he would have found them demonically relevant, mills of the mind in retreat from the work of creation that might burn up *the* creation. But to Wordsworth, they would have been merely irrelevant to the inward eye of solitude, which is the eye of his song. As I have chosen what Blake himself termed one of his more "terrific" passages, I take, for contrast, Wordsworth in his eerie, his preternatural *quietness*, showing a strength of being perhaps more primordial in its effect than that of any other poet whatsoever. *The Ruined Cottage*, the tragic tale of Margaret, supplies the passages. Where, with Blake, we are rhetorically compelled to know that we are in the presence of a poet's prophetic *power*, here in Wordsworth the rhetoric makes us know the strength of a prophetic *endurance* that only an extraordinarily exalted poet possesses. Blake moves us by a counterpoint that turns on the irony of unnecessary limitations; Wordsworth moves us, possibly more deeply, by a counterpoint that turns on the anti-ironic, on the necessity of a suffering so permanent, obscure, and dark that it overcomes its own status as limitation, and shares the nature of infinitude. Blake shows us vision collapsing into space and time; Wordsworth shows a spot of time or moment of space that holds vision precariously open to further experience. For Blake the mind is always lord and master, even if the mastery belongs, at times, to Urizen, the writer of the great poem of winter. For Wordsworth, there is always a precise extent and a *howness*, to the mind's mastery, and always therefore an abiding recalcitrance in which outward sense is not only the servant of the mind's will, but has an unsuspended and dangerous will of its own. The tyranny of the eye, that most despotic of our senses, is only the most celebrated aspect of this recalcitrance. The tyranny of the ear, which Wordsworth would never acknowledge, subtly imposes itself by the compulsive repetition of the sound of universal waters far inland. Deep in his journey to the interior, Wordsworth is obsessed by the oceanic sense, the waters of judgment rushing all about his ears. It takes a while for the constant reader of Wordsworth to be disheartened by the excessive recurrence of this auricular image, but disheartened one can become. Yet compulsion in Wordsworth *is* strength, whatever it may be in the rest of us, and perhaps it is even, finally, an aesthetic strength.

That ruin should come out of the more than natural, the apocalyptic strength of hope and love, is the awful meaning of the tale of Margaret, as harrowing a poem as any of us have read, a warning against the destructive power of the imagination. All through the old man's discourse that *is* the poem, the eye of the narrative pauses, with a racking slowness, on the outward signs of Margaret's inner self-destruction, and in a way that avoids the tyranny of the camera-eye. I quote, in progression, three such passages, torn from their context but forming a unit between them:

> The sun was sinking in the west and now
> I sate with sad impatience. From within
> Her solitary infant cried aloud;
> The spot though fair seemed very desolate
> The longer I remained more desolate.
> And looking round I saw the corner stones

> Till then unmarked, on either side the door
> With dull red stains discoloured, and stuck o'er
> With tufts and hairs of wool as if the sheep
> That feed upon the commons thither came
> As to a couching-place and rubbed their sides
> Even at her threshold. The church-clock struck eight,
> I turned and saw her distant a few steps.
> Her face was pale and thin, her figure too
> Was changed. As she unlocked the door she said
> "It grieves me you have waited here so long
> But in good truth I've wandered much of late";

A step further on, and we are given this:

> I turned towards the garden gate, and saw
> More plainly still the poverty and grief
> Were now come nearer to her; the earth was hard
> With weeds defaced and knots of withered grass;
> No ridges there appeared of clear black mould,
> No winter greenness. Of her herbs and flowers
> It seemed the better part were gnawed away
> Or trampled on the earth; a chain of straw
> Which had been twisted round the tender stem
> Of a young apple-tree lay at its root,
> The bark was nibbled round by truant sheep.
> Margaret stood near, her infant in her arms
> And seeing that my eye was on the tree
> She said, "I fear it will be dead and gone
> Ere Robert come again."

And finally, the end, abrupt, and arousing in us that brother's love
in which we bless her in the impotence of grief:

> Meanwhile her poor hut
> Sank to decay, for he was gone, whose hand
> At the first nippings of October frost
> Closed up each chink, and with fresh bands of straw
> Chequered the green-grown thatch. And so she lived
> Through the long winter, reckless and alone;
> Till this reft house, by frost, and thaw, and rain
> Was sapped, and, when she slept, the nightly damps
> Did chill her breast, and in the stormy day
> Her tattered clothes were ruffled by the wind
> Even at the side of her own fire. Yet still
> She loved this wretched spot, nor would for worlds
> Have parted hence, and still that length of road

And this rude bench one torturing hope endeared,
Fast rooted at her heart; and here, my friend,
In sickness she remained, and here she died,
Last human tenant of these ruined walls.

Three visions of a spot made progressively more wretched by the
yearning strength of a hope too willing to be fed, and yet three visions in which the visible is either very hard to see indeed, or else
does not yield up to the eye the full purchase it has made upon reality. In the first, the aged narrator sits against a sunset, hears the cry
of a solitary infant, and stares at the corner stones on either side the
door. He sees a pastoral emblem, but one that shows a falling-away;
the discolored stones, with their dull red stains, their tufts and hairs
of wool, subtly tell of a collapse from cultivation back to the wild.
The red-stained stone is itself a sunset, and the infant's cry of loneliness is another sunset, the three together betokening the twilight
figure of Margaret, that lingering sunset whose slow self-destruction
is the process that the poem enacts. In the second passage, the old
man scrutinizes Margaret's ruined garden, and sees again a series of
tokens that only the eye of the mind can link together. Where fixities
and definites in the first passage dissolve into the sad unity of the
pastoral sunset, here they dissolve into the image of a pastoral hunger shared both by the earth and by the wintry sheep. Again the
hand of the human is missing, and the wild claims its own—the earth
is hard, the withered grass is knotted, the herbs and flowers gnawed
away and trampled, and the young apple-tree gradually dies into its
longest winter, its bark nibbled round by the hungry sheep. What
the scene speaks of is at the borders of the visible, for the abandonment does not indicate despair, but grimly once again tells of the
destructive strength of outrageously sustained hope. It is an instance
where Valéry is proved correct, for here the poem is antithetical to
its own cinema; what camera eye could gaze upon this scene, and
tell us, mutely, that the voice that will rise from this solitude and
wilderness will be the voice of a woman transfigured by an infinite
hope, and not by a despair?

In the third passage, ending the poem, the torturing hope attains
its visionary climax. Nature has been abandoned to apocalyptic
yearnings, and it replies as it must, in the killing image of winter.
The cottage and the woman fuse together, and both reach the borders of the visible, for the artifact and the human alike slide over into
a blending where they are merely vegetal and animal, exposed rem-
nants of nature yielding to natural entropy. The cottage is reft and

sapped by frost and thaw and rain, and Margaret is chilled, asleep, by nightly damps and, awake, by a wind that blows by her own fireside. The last *more-than-visual* image is one of dreadful naturalization, even of a Blakean sort; the endearing but torturing hope holds her to the wretched and now deathly spot, "fast rooted at her heart." The final image is purely *visual*—the ruined walls of the cottage, but visual presentation has little to do with the Wordsworthian power of this final image. It is a complex of emotions that falls apart in this abandoned spot, and the falling-apart is truly one of the credences of winter.

We need not puzzle as to why Blake distrusted the merely visual, and insisted on the visionary in its place. But, despite the great line of Wordsworthian critics, from Bradley and Abercrombie through Wilson Knight and Hartman—that alternative convention that has insisted against Arnold that Wordsworth was *not* the poet of nature —despite that splendid array the Wordsworthian distrust of the eye remains a partial mystery. Wordsworth, at his very greatest, feared both the outward eye of nature and the inward eye of vision, though the fears never kept him from his courageous assaults upon both modes of seeing. Hartman suggests the influence of Burke on Wordsworth, quoting Burke's notion that the business of poetry "is, to affect rather by sympathy than imitation; to display rather the effect of things on the mind of the speaker, or of others, than to present a clear idea of the things themselves." Pottle cites Wordsworth's letter to Landor, where what moves Wordsworth most in poetry is spoken of as that point of vision "where things are lost in each other, and limits vanish, and aspirations are raised." The strength of hope, in Wordsworth as in Margaret, is more-than-natural, and perhaps the clue to his distrust of the bodily eye is to be found in the apocalyptic power of his hope. His sense of possible sublimity is always with him, and his poetry holds us, ultimately, by our own sense that it will reveal "something evermore about to be." The visible has been, and is, and even its actual sublimity is always a betrayal of its possible grandeur. The spirit of the unvisited haunts Wordsworth, and the unvisited resists even the counterpoint of the visual and the visionary.

Blake lived in apocalyptic hope also, but his response to that hope was unequivocal; the expanding eyes of Man would *see*, and in that revelation the deeps would shrink to their foundations. The blending or dual element in Wordsworth refuses a clarified sight as the gift of revelation; either common sight must suffice or, since it does not, a synaesthetic blend of seeing-hearing must return, as once it existed for the young child. And, when this return is doubted or modified, the synaesthetic phenomenon, the sober coloring that is also a still, sad music, must yield to hearing alone, as nothing in nature will satisfy the eye that quests for evidences of the mind's excursive powers. The things not seen provide the substance of hope, and Wordsworth at last approximates Milton in practicing an art of the eye's abyss, in taking us down to that inward depth where no modern prophet of the eye has followed. An art so deep is a lasting reproof to our cinema, and to ourselves.

My epilogue is in Shelley, who went on until he had stopped eye and ear together. As I have used such melancholy passages of Blake and Wordsworth, I am happy to quote Shelley at his most loving. Here is one of the dazzling passages of his *Epipsychidion*, where he describes, or rather does not describe, the beauty of Emilia Viviani, that soul out of his soul:

> The glory of her being, issuing thence,
> Stains the dead, blank, cold air with a warm shade
> Of unentangled intermixture, made
> By Love, of light and motion; one intense
> Diffusion, one serene Omnipresence,
> Whose flowing outlines mingle in the flowing,
> Around her cheeks and utmost fingers glowing
> With the unintermitted blood, which there
> Quivers, (as in a fleece of snow-like air
> The crimson pulse of living morn may quiver,)
> Continuously prolonged, and ending never
> Till they are lost, and in that Beauty furled
> Which penetrates and clasps and fills the world;
> Scarce visible from extreme loveliness.
> Warm fragrance seems to fall from her light dress
> And her loose hair; and where some heavy tress
> The air of her own speed has disentwined,
> The sweetness seems to satiate the faint wind;
> And in the soul a wild odour is felt,
> Beyond the sense

I don't recall that any actual cinema I've seen does much to make the beauty of a woman a little hard to see. Shelley, unlike Milton, Blake, and Wordsworth, both liked and desired women; the three older prophet-poets desired women, but evaded the full portrayal of the total or spiritual form of that desire. Shelley was, intellectually, a ruthless skeptic, as tough-minded as you are, whoever you are.

Rhetorically, he was, all critical misrepresentation to the contrary, an urbane ironist, but emotionally he was, to his eternal credit but personal sorrow, a passionate idealist. As an intellectual skeptic, he knows, too well, the narrow limits of both poetry and love; as an ironist he is too cultivated to indulge in the vulgarity of constantly showing us that he knows those limits. As an idealist, he merely keeps falling in love. Put together the skepticism, the urbanity, and the idealism, and you leave little reason for any visible appearance to move this poet. Intellectually he doubts that he can know its reality; rhetorically he doubts that it can be expressed with any decorum, and emotionally he doubts that it can satisfy a desire that will not settle for any outermost form whatsoever. Set him the task of describing the beauty of his beloved, and you get this extravagant and magnificent passage, not so much a description of a human female as a fireworks display of what Stevens called "lights astral and Shelleyan."

Yet a close inspection of the passage makes us dissatisfied, not with it, but with the ways we ordinarily describe a woman's beauty, and even more, with the grossness of the motion picture camera, or its manipulator, when an attempt is made to show us such beauty. "See where she stands!" Shelley cries in exultation, and we try to see. But the glory of her being is not visible in any ordinary sense. We cannot *see* a warmth compounded of light and motion, nor can we see the aura of love surrounding this beauty. And yet, as Shelley's poem knows and shows us, phenomenologically just *this* is given to us in the privileged moments of our lives. The problem is to describe a secularized epiphany that cannot be described, but Shelley was a specialist in the indescribable. I don't know the critical technique that would permit *us* to describe accurately just *what* happens in this passage that confronts the idealized Emilia. Confrontation takes place in the second person; all analysis or description takes place in the third. The Intellectual Beauty, a gleam just beyond the range of our senses to apprehend it, gets into this passage, but phenomenologically what counts most is what Shelley beautifully calls "the air of her own speed." The miracle of Shelley's art is in its continual impression of speed. Like the Psalmist, when his soul is uplifted, Shelley in moments of glory moves with a speed that reproves the slow dullness of the ordinarily visible. His nuances are subtler than Blake's or Wordsworth's; too subtle for the outward eye to apprehend, but not too subtle for the awakened spirit seeking, as Yeats said of Shelley, more in this world than any can understand.

51

The final use of Romantic poetry, or of poetry written in that tradition down to Yeats, Lawrence, Stevens, and Crane, is to teach us that we do not know either what our senses, just as they are, can reveal to us, or what can be revealed to us, perfectly naturalistically, and yet seemingly just beyond the range of our senses. All actual cinema that I know, including the rubbish that currently passes for experimental or "new" cinema but seems designed merely to bring on a saving myopia—all cinema yet made has failed in imagination, has absurdly fallen short of the whole aesthetic needs of the awakened consciousness of man. One does not ask a film to be a poem; films-as-literature bore, and will go on boring. But one waits for an artist, and an art, to go beyond the relative crudity of what one has been offered. The burden of Romantic poetry, and the true though frequently evaded burden of post-Romantic poetry, is either to offer an apocalypse of the order of physical reality, as in Blake or Shelley or Yeats, or to move us toward that adventure in humanity in which, at last, we would be a race completely physical in a physical world, the dream of Keats and of the colder Stevens after him. Between these fierce alternatives there is the blending vision of Wordsworth, seeking the difficult rightness of a nature "first and last and midst and without end," in which the Characters of the Great Apocalypse could be read in every countenance and on every blossom. No medium has inherent limitations so great that the Imagination cannot overcome them, and no medium is its own message. Films will either become more imaginative, will either achieve their own apocalyptic form, whatever that may be, or they will die, leaving us again with those astral and Shelleyan lights that our poetic tradition throws upon us, adding nothing to our reality but themselves, and yet reimagining our lives in that addition. Wallace Stevens, commenting in a letter on one of his own poems, concludes the matter as I would have it concluded. He writes:

> The astral and Shelleyan lights are not going to alter the structure of nature. Apples will always be apples, and whoever is a ploughman hereafter will be what the ploughman has always been. For all that, the astral and the Shelleyan will have transformed the world.

1967

4
Dialectic of
The Marriage of Heaven and Hell

The Marriage of Heaven and Hell assaults what Blake termed a "cloven fiction" between empirical and a priori procedure in argument. In content, the *Marriage* compounds ethical and theological "contraries"; in form it mocks the categorical techniques that seek to make the contraries appear as "negations." The unity of the *Marriage* is in itself dialectical, and cannot be grasped except by the mind in motion, moving between the Blakean contraries of discursive irony and mythical visualization.

Apocalypse is dialectical in the *Marriage,* as much so as in Shelley's *Prometheus* or the poems by Yeats written out of *A Vision,* or in Blake's own Night the Ninth of *The Four Zoas.* The great difficulty of dialectical apocalypse is that it has got to present itself as prophetic irony, in which the abyss between aspiration and institution is *both* anticipated and denounced. The specific difficulty in reading *The Marriage of Heaven and Hell* is to mark the limits of its irony: where does Blake speak straight? In Blake, rhetoric subsumes dialectic, and usurps its place of privilege. But the process of usurpation is not clear, though this is no flaw in Blake as poet and polemicist. *The Marriage of Heaven and Hell* is a miniature "anatomy," in Northrop Frye's recently formulated sense of the term, and reserves to itself the anatomy's peculiar right to mingle satire with vision, furious laughter with the tonal complexity involved in any projection of the four or more last things.

I suggest that we need to distinguish between the *Marriage* as in itself dialectical and the dialectic it attempts to present. The same distinction, rigorously set forth, would clear away much of Yeats's deliberate perverseness in *A Vision,* and might help in the comprehension of the epics of Blake. The *schemata* of those epics, though dialectical, are yet systematic; the local life in them maddeningly (but gratefully) defies the system. The *schemata*, as Frye in particular has extracted them, present *the* dialectics, early and late, of Blake; the texture, of *Jerusalem* especially, is so dialectical as to put *the* dialectics in doubt. Not that Blake mocks himself; only that he mocks the Corporeal Understanding (including his own) and refuses unto death to cease setting traps for it. There is, in consequence, a true way of reading Blake, put forward by Blake himself, a first-class critic of his own works. But this is a true way which, as Kafka once remarked of true ways in general, is like a rope stretched several inches above the ground, put there not to be walked upon but to be tripped over.

I shall attempt to reduce the *Marriage* to Blake's own overt dialectic in what follows, but because it is not primarily a discursive work I make this attempt in a spirit of tentativeness, respecting its innate trickery.

The poem that opens the *Marriage* as "argument" has not been much admired, nor much understood. Rintrah, the angry man in Blake's pantheon, rears and shakes his fires in the burdened air; clouds, hungry with menace, swag on the deep. The poem is a prelude, establishing the tone of prophetic fury that is to run beneath the *Marriage;* the indignation of Rintrah presages the turning over of a cycle.

The poem itself has the cyclic irony of *The Mental Traveller.* The "just man" or "Devil" now rages in the wilds as outcast, having been driven out of "perilous paths" by the "villain" or "Angel." This reversal is simple enough, if it is true reversal, which it is not. The initial complication is provided by the sixth to ninth lines of the poem:

> Roses are planted where thorns grow,
> And on the barren heath
> Sing the honey bees.

Grow, not *grew; sing*, not *sang.* We are already involved in the contraries. Cliff is opposed to river, tomb to spring, bleached bones to the red clay of Adam (literal Hebrew meaning). The turning of this cycle converts the meek just man into the prophetic rager, the easeful villain into the serpent sneaking along in mild humility. The triple repetition of "perilous path" compounds the complication. First the just man keeps the perilous path as he moves toward death. But "*then* the perilous path was planted . . ./ *Till* the villain left the path of ease,/ To walk in perilous paths."

We grasp the point by embracing both contraries, not by reconciling them. There is progression here, but only in the ironic sense of cycle. The path, the way of generation that can only lead to death, is always being planted, the just man is always being driven out; the villain is always usurping the path of life-in-death. When the just man returns from being a voice in the wilderness, he drives the villain back into the nonexistence of "paths of ease." But "just man" and "villain" are very nearly broken down as categories here; the equivocal "Devil" and "Angel" begin to loom as the *Marriage*'s contraries. The advent of the villain upon the perilous path marks the beginning of a new "heaven," a "mild humility" of angelic restraint. So Blake leaves his argument and plunges into his satiric nuptial song:

> As a new heaven is begun and it is now thirty-three years
> since its advent, the Eternal Hell revives.

Swedenborg, writing in his *True Christian Religion*, had placed the Last Judgment in the spiritual world in 1757, the year of Blake's birth. In 1758 Swedenborg published *his* vision of judgment, *Heaven and Hell*. Now, writing in 1790, at the Christological age of thirty-three, Blake celebrates in himself the reviving of the Eternal Hell, the voice of desire and rebellion crying aloud in desert places against the institution of a new divine restraint, albeit that of the visionary Swedenborg, himself a Devil rolled round by cycle into Angelic category.

Before the *Marriage* moves into diabolical gear, Blake states the law of his dialectic:

> Without Contraries is no progression. Attraction and Re-
> pulsion, Reason and Energy, Love and Hate, are necessary to
> Human existence.

The key here is *Human*, which is both descriptive and honorific. This is a dialectic without transcendence, in which heaven and hell are to be married but without becoming altogether one flesh or one family. By the "marriage" of contraries Blake means only that we are to cease valuing one contrary above the other in any way. Echoes of Isaiah xxxiv and xxxv crowd through the *Marriage*, and a specific reference to those chapters is given here by Blake. Reading Isaiah in its infernal sense, as he read *Paradise Lost*, Blake can acknowledge its apocalypse as his own. As the imaginative hell revives, the heaven of restraint comes down.

> And all the host of heaven shall be dissolved, and the heav-

ens shall be rolled together as a scroll: and all their host shall
fall down.

(Isaiah xxxiv. 4)

The Promethean release that has come to Blake with his full maturity is related to the titanic fury of French revolution and English
unrest that is directly contemporary with the *Marriage*. The Revolution is the active springing from Energy, called Evil by the "religious," who assign it to Hell. Frye has stated the central idea of the
Marriage as being the analogy of this unrest to the biblical time of
troubles that precedes the end of the world. The *Marriage* thus enters the category not of "How long O Lord?" prophecy but of the
"turn now" injunction based on Hillel's famous question, "If not
now, when?" So that its dialectic must cease to be purely descriptive
and cyclic, which is to say, must cease to be merely dialectic. Apocalypse does not argue, and hardly needs to convince. The verse of the
Negro spiritual carries in a kernel the authoritative message of apocalypse, taking place between the sardonic warning and the dreaded
effect: "You will shout when it hits you, yes indeed."

Therefore, the contraries, when next stated in the famous "Voice
of the Devil" passage, have ceased strictly to be contraries. Blake's
lower or earthly paradise, Beulah Land, is a state of being or place
where contraries are equally true, but the *Marriage* is written out of
the state of Generation, our world in its everyday aspect, where progression is necessary. Christian dualism is therefore a negation, hindrance, not action, and is cast out beyond the balance of contraries.
Blake does not build truth by dialectic, being neither a rational mystic like Plato nor a mystic rationalist like Hegel. Nothing eternal
abides behind forms for Blake; he seeks reality in appearances,
though he rejects appearance as it is perceived by the lowest-com-
mon-denominator kind of observer. Between the cloven fiction of St.
Paul's mind-body split and the emotionalism of the celebrator of a
state of nature exists the complex apocalyptic humanism of the *Marriage*, denying metaphysics, accepting the hard given of this world,
but only insofar as this appearance is altogether human.

Here it has been too easy to mistake Blake—for Nietzsche, for
D. H. Lawrence, for Yeats, for whatever heroic vitalist you happen
most to admire. The *Marriage* preaches the risen body breaking
bounds, exploding upward into psychic abundance. But here Blake
is as earnest as Lawrence, and will not tolerate the vision of recurrence, as Nietzsche and Yeats do. The altogether human escapes

cycle, evades irony, cannot be categorized discursively. But Blake is unlike Lawrence, even where they touch. The Angel teaches light without heat, the vitalist—or Devil—heat without light; Blake wants both, hence the marriage of contraries. The paradise of Milton needs the heat of hell; the earth of Lawrence needs the light of Eden, the rational fire of intellect and creation. Rhetoric now carries the *Marriage* through its implicit irony; Blake speaks straight for once before subjecting *Paradise Lost* to the play of dialectic:

> Energy is the only life, and is from the Body; and Reason is
> the bound or outward circumference of Energy.
> Energy is Eternal Delight.

This does not mean that Reason, the bound, is Eternal Torment; it does mean that Reason's story would hold that unbounded Energy *is* such torment. Hence the *Marriage*'s curious double account of fall and negative creation, whether of hell or heaven:

> For this history has been adopted by both parties.
> It indeed appear'd to Reason as if Desire was cast out; but
> the Devil's account is, that the Messiah fell, and formed a
> heaven of what he stole from the Abyss.

In crude terms, the problem is where the stuff of life comes from; where does Reason, divinity of the "Angels," obtain the substance that it binds and orders, the energy that it restrains? By stealing it from the *Urgrund* of the abyss, is Blake's diabolic answer. We are almost in the scheme of *The Four Zoas:* the Messiah *fell,* stole the stuff of creativity, and formed "heaven." One contrary is here as true as another: this history has been adopted by both parties. One party, come again to dominance among us, now condemns Blake as a persuasive misreader of *Paradise Lost.* When, in another turn of the critical wheel, we go back to reading *Paradise Lost* in its infernal or poetic sense, as Blake, Shelley, and a host of nineteenth-century poets and scholars did, we will have to condemn a generation of critical dogmatists for not having understood the place of dialectic in literary analysis.

The "Memorable Fancies," brilliant exercises in satire and humanism, form the bulk of the *Marriage,* and tend to evade Blake's own dialectic, being, as they are, assaults, furious and funny, on Angelic culpability. The dialectic of the *Marriage* receives its definitive statement once more in the work, in the opposition of the Prolific and the Devouring. If one grasps that complex passage, one is fortified to move frontally against the most formidable and properly most famous section of the *Marriage*, the "Proverbs of Hell," where dialectic and rhetoric come together combatively in what could be judged the most brilliant aphorisms written in English, seventy gnomic reflections and admonitions on the theme of diabolic wisdom.

The Titanic myth, the story of "the Antediluvians who are our Energies," is always present in Blake, though frequently concealed in some contrapuntal fiction. In the *Marriage* the myth is overt and "Messiah *or* Satan" is identified with these Giant Forms. The *or* establishes again the marriage of contraries. The Giant Forms, huge ids, or Orcs, to use Blake's vocabulary, are bound down by the cunning of weak and tame minds:

> Thus one portion of being is the Prolific, the other the Devouring: to the Devourer it seems as if the producer was in his chains; but it is not so, he only takes portions of existence and fancies that the whole.
>
> But the Prolific would cease to be Prolific unless the Devourer, as a sea, received the excess of his delights.

This terrifying vision of the economy of existence is mitigated by its irony, and yet moves into mystery in its final statement. Reason and the senses do not bound our energies; Eternal Delight, the primal Exuberance that is Beauty, exists beyond the bounds. Blake is not predicating an unconscious mind, for that would be only a widening of the circumference of the bound. The Freudian hypothesis of the unconscious would have represented for Blake what it does to the phenomenologists—a premature cessation of mental activity, a refusal to analyze all of the given. But Blake more than anticipates Husserl here; he gives a definitive statement of the phenomenology of existence, the ceaseless dialectic of daily appearance. Yeats, in *A Vision*, proudly asserted his refusal to be logical, lest he be trapped by his own dialectic. He had never believed with Hegel, he wrote, that the spring vegetables were refuted because they were over. In this he was caught up in Blake's spirit, in the vision of existential contraries. The Angel or Devourer takes all the negative force of Blake's rhetoric, but dialectically he is a necessity. The Prolific will not be confined, but it needs constraint, it thirsts for battle. The Devourer is a sea, a moat imprisoning the creator, who would otherwise be choked in the excess of his own delight. Without the hard given (a wall is as good a symbol as a moat) we do not engage in the mutable struggle. This war cry passes into the most defiant sentences in the *Marriage*:

Some will say: "Is not God alone the Prolific?" I answer: "God only Acts and Is, in existing beings or Men."

These two classes of men are always upon earth, and they should be enemies: whoever tries to reconcile them seeks to destroy existence.

Religion is an endeavour to reconcile the two.

The nontheism of Blake is never more clearly stated than here, and yet is still being misread by many. If God only acts *and is* in Men, then *God* has become an unnecessary hypothesis, having no abstract being beyond our powers of visualization and confrontation. To destroy enmity between Prolific and Devourer would destroy existence, such destruction being religion's attempt to inflict upon us the greatest poverty of not living in a physical world. Blake's dialectical stance, with its apotheosis of the physical and its rejection of the merely natural, is most frequently misunderstood at just this point. Against the supernaturalist, Blake asserts the reality of the body as being all of the soul that the five senses can perceive. Against the naturalist, he asserts the unreality of the merely given body as against the imaginative body, rising through an increase in sensual fulfillment into a realization of its unfallen potential.

Religion seeks to end the warfare of contraries because it claims to know a reality *beyond* existence; Blake wants the warfare to continue because he seeks a reality *within* existence. Milton's heaven knows no strife, and therefore no progression, and is to Blake—hell.

We can see Blake's interplay between dialectic and espousing one pole of the dialectic most vividly in the "Proverbs of Hell," where the revelation of the laws of process and a fierce antinomianism are frequently interleaved:

> The road of excess leads to the palace of wisdom. (3)
>
> Prudence is a rich, ugly old maid courted by Incapacity. (4)
>
> He who desires but acts not, breeds pestilence. (5)
>
> If the fool were to persist in his folly he would become wise. (18)
>
> The Tygers of wrath are wiser than the horses of instruction. (44)
>
> You never know what is enough unless you know what is more than enough. (46)
>
> Exuberance is Beauty. (64)
>
> Sooner murder an infant in its cradle than nurse unacted desires. (67)
>
> Where man is not, nature is barren. (68)

61

Each of these proverbs depends for its true meaning on a dialectic definition of desire and act, though rhetorically the meaning is overtly antinomian. Desire is positive; it leads to an action which is not the hindrance of another. Act is positive and is virtue; Blake, commenting on Lavater, defines its contrary as "accident":

> Accident is the omission of act in self & the hindering of act in another; This is Vice, but all Act is Virtue. To hinder another is not an act; it is the contrary; it is a restraint on action both in ourselves & in the person hinder'd, for he who hinders another omits his own duty at the same time.

The road of excess has therefore nothing to do with sadism or self-destruction, but is the way to that all, less than which cannot satisfy us. Incapacity, which courts Prudence, is a mode of hindrance. Desire which does not lead to action is also "accident," vice, and is self-destructive. The fool persisting in his folly at least acts; ceasing, he is merely foolish, and falls into self-negation. Instruction may draw you on, but wrath will take you sooner into wisdom, for wrath embodies desire. The boundary of desire you learn only by moving beyond, and the furious energy of this liberation is definitive of beauty. To *nurse* an unacted desire *is* to murder an infant in its cradle; overt murder is at least more positive. Last, take man and his struggle of contraries out of nature, and you are left with the barren, with the same dull round over again, the merely cyclic movement, if such it can be termed, of negations.

The last plate of the *Marriage* has upon it the figure of King Nebuchadnezzar eating grass like an ox, in a hideous emblem of the return to a state of nature. Nebuchadnezzar haunted Blake; Blake meant him to haunt us. When you forget the contrary of vision, when waking you reject the lessons of the night, then you suffer the negation: you feed like beasts upon the grass.

1957

5
Blake's *Jerusalem:*
The Bard of Sensibility
and the Form of Prophecy

also out of the midst thereof came the
likeness of four living creatures. And this
was their appearance; they had the likeness of a man.

Ezekiel 1:5

"The midst thereof" refers to "a fire infolding itself," in the
Hebrew literally "a fire taking hold of itself," a trope for a series
of fire-bursts, one wave of flame after another. Blake's *Jerusalem*
has the form of such a series, appropriate to a poem whose
structure takes Ezekiel's book as its model. *The Four Zoas*, like
Young's *Night Thoughts*, is in the formal shadow of *Paradise Lost*,
and *Milton* less darkly in the shadow of Job and *Paradise Regained*.
In *Jerusalem*, his definitive poem, Blake goes at last for prophetic
form to a prophet, to the priestly orator, Ezekiel, whose situation
and sorrow most closely resemble his own.

Ezekiel is uniquely the prophet-in-exile, whose call and labor are
altogether outside the Holy Land. Held captive in Babylon, he
dies still in Babylon, under the tyrant Nebuchadnezzar, and so
never sees his prophecy fulfilled:

> Thus saith the Lord God; In the day that I shall have
> cleansed you from all your iniquities I will also cause you to
> dwell in the cities, and the wastes shall be builded.
> And the desolate land shall be tilled, whereas it lay deso-
> late in the sight of all that passed by.
> And they shall say, This land that was desolate is become
> like the garden of Eden; and the waste and desolate and
> ruined cities are become fenced, and are inhabited.

Everything in Ezekiel except this ultimate vision is difficult, more
difficult than it at first appears. Blake's *Jerusalem* is less difficult
than it first seems, even to the informed reader, but still is difficult.
Both books share also a harsh plain style, suitable for works
addressed to peoples in captivity. Ezekiel, like *Jerusalem*, is replete
with the prophet's symbolic actions, actions at the edge of social

65

sanity, violence poised to startle the auditor into fresh awareness of his own precarious safety, and the spiritual cost of it. As early as *The Marriage of Heaven And Hell,* Blake invokes Ezekiel as one who heightens the contradictions of merely given existence:

> I then asked Ezekiel. why he eat dung, and lay so long on his right and left side? he answered the desire of raising other men into a perception of the infinite

The central image of Blake, from whenever he first formulated his mythology, is Ezekiel's; the *Merkabah,* Divine Chariot or form of God in motion. The Living Creatures or Four Zoas are Ezekiel's and not initially Blake's, a priority of invention that Blake's critics, in their search for more esoteric sources, sometimes evade. Ezekiel, in regard to Blake's *Jerusalem,* is like Homer in regard to the *Aeneid:* the inventor, the precursor, the shaper of the later work's continuities. From Ezekiel in particular Blake learned the true meaning of prophet, visionary orator, honest man who speaks into the heart of a situation to warn: if you go on so, the result is so; or as Blake said, a seer and not an arbitrary dictator.

I have indicated elsewhere the similarities in arrangement of the two books, and the parallel emphases upon individual responsibility and self-purgation. Here I want to bring the poets closer, into the painful area of the anxiety of influence, the terrible melancholy for the later prophet of sustained comparison with the precursor, who died still in the realm of loss, but in absolute assurance of his prophetic call, an assurance Blake suffered to approximate, in an isolation that even Ezekiel might not have borne. For Ezekiel is sent to the house of Israel, stiffened in heart and rebellious against their God, yet still a house accustomed to prophecy. God made Ezekiel as hard as adamant, the *shamir* or diamond-point of the engraver, and that was scarcely hard enough; Blake knew he had to be even harder, as he wielded his engraver's tool.

Jerusalem begins with the Divine Voice waking Blake at sunrise and "dictating" to him a "mild song," which Blake addresses in turn to Albion, the English Israel, at once Everyman and an exile, a sleeper in Beulah, illusive land of shades. When the Divine Voice orders Ezekiel to begin his ministry, the prophet has already had a vision of the four cherubim and their wheels, a manifestation of glory that sustains him in the trials ensuing. But Blake has never seen the Living Creatures of the *Merkabah,* his Four Zoas as one in the unity of a restored Albion. The fourth, final book of *Jerusalem* begins with a demonic parody of the *Merkabah*, with the Wheel of Natural Religion flaming "west to east against the current of / Creation." A "Watcher & a Holy-One," perhaps Ezekiel himself, "a watchman unto the house of Israel," identifies this antagonist image for Blake, who is afflicted throughout by demonic epiphanies, as Ezekiel was not. The form of Ezekiel's prophecy depends upon the initial vision, for the glory is thus revealed to him before his task is assigned, though the emphasis is on the *departure* of the *Merkabah*, interpreted by the great commentator David Kimchi as a presage of the Lord's withdrawal from the Jerusalem Temple, thus abandoned to its destruction.

In the England of *Jerusalem*, everything that could be seen as an image of salvation has been abandoned to destruction. No poem could open and proceed in a profounder or more sustained despair, for the next level down is silence. The temptation of silence, as in the self-hatred of Browning's ruined quester, Childe Roland, type of the poet who has given up, is to turn, "quiet as despair," into the path of destruction. Blake's antagonist, in *Jerusalem*, is what destroys Browning's quester: selfhood. What menaces continued life for the imaginative man is the quality of his own despair:

> But my griefs advance also, for ever & ever without end
> O that I could cease to be! Despair! I am Despair
> Created to be the great example of horror & agony: also my
> Prayer is vain I called for compassion: compassion mocked,
> Mercy & pity threw the grave stone over me & with lead
> And iron, bound it over me for ever: Life lives on my
> Consuming: & the Almighty hath made me his Contrary
> To be all evil, all reversed & for ever dead: knowing
> And seeing life, yet living not; how can I then behold
> And not tremble; how can I be beheld & not abhorrd

The imaginative man's despair is the Spectre of Urthona, who speaks these lines, and who may be thought of as holding the same relation to Blake the poet as the Solitary of *The Excursion* has to Wordsworth the poet. For the Spectre of Urthona is every prophet's own Jonah, in full flight from vision for reasons more than adequate to our unhappy yet still not unpleasant condition as natural men. Though the Spectre of Urthona had his genesis, in Blake's work, as an initially menacing figure, he is very appealing in *Jerusalem*, and Blake's critics (myself included) have erred in slighting this appeal, and thus diminishing the force of Blake's extraordinary artistry. The Spectre of Urthona *is always right*, if the reductive truth of our condition as natural men be taken as truth. Nor is the poor Spectre unimaginative in his reductions; they are exuberant by their unqualified insistence at knowing by knowing the worst, particularly concerning the self and the sexual wars of the self and the other. What is most moving about the Spectre's reductive power is its near alliance with his continual grief. We are repelled by his "mockery & scorn" and his "sullen smile," but each time we hear him we see him also as one who "wiped his tears he washd his visage" and then told the terror of his truths:

> The Man who respects Woman shall be despised by Woman
> And deadly cunning & mean abjectness only, shall enjoy them
> For I will make their places of joy and love, excrementitious.
> Continually building, continually destroying in Family feuds
> While you are under the dominion of a jealous Female
> Unpermanent for ever because of love & jealousy.
> You shall want all the Minute Particulars of Life

The form of prophecy cannot sustain such reductive, natural truths, for in the context of prophecy they are not true. When we listen to the Spectre of Urthona we hear a bard, but not a prophet, and the bard belongs to Blake's own literary age, the time of Sensibility or the Sublime. Blake's lifelong critique of the poets to whom he felt the closest affinity—Thomson, Cowper, Collins, Gray, Chatterton—culminates in *Jerusalem*. The Spectre of Urthona descends from the Los of the Lambeth books, and the Bard of Experience of the *Songs*, but is closer even than they were to the archetype Blake satirizes, the poet of Sensibility, the man of imagination who cannot or will not travel the whole road of excess to the palace of wisdom.

Martin Price, studying "the histrionic note" of mid-eighteenth-century poetry, emphasized the poet as both actor and audience in "the theatre of mind." Precisely this insight is our best starting-point in understanding the Spectre of Urthona, who is so unnerving because he appears always to be "watching with detachment the passions he has worked up in himself." The grand precursor of this histrionic kind of bard is the Satan of the early books of *Paradise Lost*, whose farewell to splendor, upon Mount Niphates, sums up the agony that makes so strange a detachment possible:

> ... to thee I call,
> But with no friendly voice, and add thy name
> O Sun, to tell thee how I hate thy beams ...
> . . . .
> Me miserable! which way shall I flie

> Infinite wrauth, and infinite despair?
> Which way I flie is Hell, my self am Hell;
> And in the lowest deep a lower deep
> Still threatening to devour me opens wide,
> To which the Hell I suffer seems a Heav'n.

A detachment that can allow so absolute a consciousness of self-damnation has something Jacobean about it. What a Bosola or a Vendice sees at the end, by a flash of vision, Satan must see continuously and forever in the vast theater of his mind. There exists perpetually for Satan the terrible double vision of what was and what is, Eternity and the categories of mental bondage, the fallen forms of space and time. This twofold vision is the burden also of the Bard of Sensibility, but not of the prophet who has seen the *Merkabah*, or even studies in hope to see it, as does the Blake-Los of *Jerusalem*. Freedom for the prophet means freedom from the detachment of the histrionic mode; the prophet retains a sense of himself as actor, but he ceases to be his own audience. A passage from solipsism to otherness is made, the theater of mind dissolves, and the actor stands forth as orator, as a warner of *persons* (Ezekiel 3:17–21). Should he fail to make this passage, he is reduced to the extreme of the histrionic mode, and becomes the singer-actor of his own Mad Songs, one of the "horrid wanderers of the deep" or a destined wretch "washed headlong from on board." I take the first of these phrases from Cowper's powerful, too-little known poem, *On The Ice Islands* (dated 19 March 1799) and the second from the justly famous *The Castaway* (written evidently the following day). A year later and Cowper died, his death like his life a warning to Blake during his years at Hayley's Felpham (1800–1803) and a crucial hidden element in both *Milton* and *Jerusalem*, where Blake fights desperately and successfully to avoid so tragically wasted a death-in-life as Cowper's.

In *On The Ice Islands* Cowper translates his own Latin poem, *Montes Glaciales, In Oceano Germanica Natantes* (written 11 March 1799). The ice islands are "portents," with the beauty of treasure, but apocalyptic warnings nevertheless as they float in "the astonished tide." They appear almost to be volcano-births, yet are Winter's creations:

> He bade arise
> Their uncouth forms, portentous in our eyes.
> Oft as, dissolved by transient suns, the snow

> Left the tall cliff to join the flood below,
> He caught and curdled with a freezing blast
> The current, ere it reached the boundless waste.

This is, to Blake, his Urizen at work, a methodical demiurge who always blunders. In Cowper's phantasmagoria, this is the way things are, a Snow Man's vision, a violence from without that crumbles the mind's feeble defenses. To it, Cowper juxtaposes the creation of Apollo's summer vision:

> So bards of old
> How Delos swam the Ægean deep have told.
> But not of ice was Delos. Delos bore
> Herb, fruit, and flower. She, crowned with laurel, wore
> Even under wintry skies, a summer smile;
> And Delos was Apollo's favourite isle.
> But, horrid wanderers of the deep, to you,
> He deems Cimmerian darkness only due.
> Your hated birth he deigned not to survey,
> But. scornful, turned his glorious eyes away.

One remembers Blake's youthful *Mad Song*, written at least twenty years earlier:

> Like a fiend in a cloud
>   With howling woe,
> After night I do croud,
>   And with night will go;
> I turn my back to the east,
> From whence comforts have increas'd;
> For light doth seize my brain
> With frantic pain.

Late in his life, long after the Felpham crisis, Blake looked back upon Cowper's madness. We do not know when Blake annotated Spurzheim's *Observations on . . . Insanity* (London, 1817), and we perhaps cannot rely on the precise wording of the annotations as being wholly Blake's own rather than Yeats's, since the copy from which Yeats transcribed has been lost. But, to a student of Blake, the wording seems right:

> *Spurzheim:* ". . . the primitive feelings of religion may be misled and produce insanity . . ."

> *Blake:* "Cowper came to me & said. O that I were insane always I will never rest. Can you not make me truly insane. I

will never rest till I am so. O that in the bosom of God I was hid. You retain health & yet are as mad as any of us all—over us all—mad as a refuge from unbelief—from Bacon Newton & Locke

Spurzheim cites Methodism "for its supply of numerous cases" of insanity, and Blake begins his note by scrawling "Methodism &." The Spectre of Urthona has the same relation to Blake's Cowper that Los has to Blake's Ezekiel, and we will see more of the Spectre than we have seen if we keep in mind that he is both a poet of Sensibility and a kind of sin-crazed Methodist. Cowper ends *On The Ice Islands* by desperately warning the "uncouth forms" away:

> Hence! Seek your home, nor longer rashly dare
> The darts of Phoebus, and a softer air;
> Lest you regret, too late, your native coast,
> In no congenial gulf for ever lost!

The power of this, and of the entire poem, is in our implicit but overwhelming recognition of Cowper's self-recognition; he himself is such an ice island, and the uncongenial gulf in which he is lost is one with the "deeper gulfs" that end *The Castaway*:

> No voice divine the storm allayed,
>   No light propitious shone,
> When, snatched from all effectual aid,
>   We perished, each alone:
> But I beneath a rougher sea,
> And whelmed in deeper gulfs than he.

Though Cowper's terror is his own, the mode of his self-destruction is akin to that of the Bard of Sensibility proper, Gray's Giant Form:

> "Fond impious Man, think'st thou yon sanguine cloud,
> Rais'd by thy breath, has quench'd the orb of day?
> To-morrow he repairs the golden flood,
> And warms the nations with redoubled ray,
> Enough for me: with joy I see
> The different doom our fates assign.
> Be thine despair, and scept'red care,
> To triumph, and to die, are mine."
> He spoke, and headlong from the mountain's height
> Deep in the roaring tide he plung'd to endless night.

71

That is not the way the Spectre of Urthona ends:

> Los beheld undaunted furious
> His heavd Hammer; he swung it round & at one blow,
> In unpitying ruin driving down the pyramids of pride
> Smiting the Spectre on his Anvil & the integuments of his Eye
> And Ear unbinding in dire pain, with many blows,
> Of strict severity self-subduing, & with many tears labouring.

> Then he sent forth the Spectre all his pyramids were grains
> Of sand & his pillars; dust on the flys wing; & his starry
> Heavens; a moth of gold & silver mocking his anxious grasp.

Cowper and the Bard drown to end an isolation, whether terrible or heroic; the theater of mind dissolves in the endless night of an original chaos, the abyss always sensed in the histrionic mode. The Spectre of Urthona is both shattered and unbound, his anxious grasp of self mocked by his selfhood's reduction to a fine grain, to the Minute Particulars of vision. Because he cannot face the hammering voice of the prophetic orator, the Spectre is at last divided "into a separate space," beyond which he cannot be reduced. The theater of mind is necessarily a Sublime theater of the Indefinite, but the prophet compels definite form to appear.

Jerusalem's quite definite form is the form of prophecy, Blake's mythologized version of the story of Ezekiel, even as the form of Revelation is demonstrated by Austin Farrer to be Saint John's mythologized rebirth of Ezekiel's images. When the visionary orator steps forward, he shares the courage of Gray's Bard, but goes further because his words are also acts. Emerson, in one of his eloquent journal broodings upon eloquence, fixes precisely this stance of Blake's Los:

> Certainly there is no true orator who is not a hero. His attitude in the rostrum, on the platform, requires that he counterbalance his auditory. He is challenger, and must answer all comers. The orator must ever stand with forward foot, in the attitude of advancing. His speech must be just ahead of the assembly, ahead of the whole human race, or it is superfluous. His speech is not to be distinguished from action.
>
> (*Journal,* June 1846)

Speech that is act cannot be reconciled with excessive self-consciousness; the prophetic mind is necessarily a mind no longer turned in upon itself. The man of Young's *Night Thoughts* ("I tremble at myself / And in myself am lost!") is succeeded by prophetic Man, the "identified" Human Form, as Blake exaltedly wishes him phrased. This transition, from representative man as poet of Sensibility, inhabiting the theater of mind, to prophetic Man, a transition made again in Wordsworth and in Shelley, is in Blake at least founded upon biblical precedent. What drew Blake to Ezekiel is the denunciation, first made by that prophet, of the entire spiritual tradition of collective responsibility. As Buber remarks, "Ezekiel individualizes the prophetic alternative." The larger covenant has broken down, because the collectivity of Israel or Albion is no longer a suitable covenant partner.

For the theater of mind, though an Ulro-den of self-consciousness, is founded upon a collective Sublime. The man of Burke, Young, Gray, Cowper, is still the universal man of humanist tradition, still the man Pope and Johnson longed to address. Wordsworth is enough of a Burkean to retain the outline of such a figure, but Blake knows that continuity to be broken down, and forever. Blake's God, like Ezekiel's, sends a "watchman" to admonish individuals, and Los, as that watchman, delivers a message that no collectivity is capable of hearing. The Sublime terror, founded as it is upon a universal anxiety, is dismissed by Blake as the Spectre's rhetoric, his deception of others, while the Sublime transport is similarly dismissed as the Spectre's sentimentality, or self-deception. "Los reads the Stars of Albion! the Spectre reads the Voids/Between the Stars." To see the Burkean Sublime is to see: "a Disorganized/And snowy cloud: brooder of tempests & destructive War."

The bounding outline, or organized vision, Blake rightly found in Ezekiel and the other prophets, who gave him the harsh but definite form in which *Jerusalem* is organized, perhaps even over-organized. The form of prophecy, particularly fixed in Ezekiel, is the unique invention of the writing prophets who sustained the destruction of the Northern kingdom and the subsequent Babylonian exile. Since the *nabi*'s teaching emphasizes return, or salvation by renovation, the form the teaching takes emphasizes a process of return, the *Merkabah*'s fire-bursts from within itself, a declaration that is also a performance. For the *Merkabah*, to surmise largely, is a giant image for the prophetic state-of-being, for the *activity of prophecy*, though it presents itself as something larger, as the only permitted (if daring) image of the divine imagelessness. If we think back to the first of the writing prophets, the sheep-breeder Amos, we find the *situation* of the *Merkabah* without its image. Prophecy comes among us as a sudden onslaught from a stranger, a divine judgment in a storm of

73

human speech, circling in until it addresses itself against the house of Israel. The image favored by Amos is not the storm of the rushing chariot's own splendor, the wind that is the spirit, but the waters of judgment, a more Wordsworthian emblem than Blake could care to accept.

In the writing prophets between Amos and Ezekiel, the image of judgment or form of prophecy departs more and more from the natural. Hosea's emphasis is upon the land, but the land's faithlessness, the wife's whoredoms, presented as unnatural, rather than all-too-natural, as they would be by Blake. Isaiah's vision of God's radiance, his *kabod* (wealth and glory), moves toward the vision of the *Merkabah*, subtly juxtaposing as it does the Divine Throne and the dethroned leper king Uzziah. Micah, a more vehement *nabi*, emphasizes the image of the glory's departure from the sanctuary, and is thus the true precursor of Jeremiah and Ezekiel, and through them of Blake. Jeremiah's great image, the potter's wheel upon which clay is molded into vessels, and marred vessels broken into clay again, is associated unforgettably with the prophet's own afflictions, an association which introduces into the prophetic form a new emphasis upon the *nabi* as person, but only insofar as the person is a vessel of God's message. In Ezekiel, the potter's wheel is taken up into the heavens in the wheels within wheels of the *Merkabah*, whose departure is at one with the advent of the prophet's inner afflictions, his intense personal sufferings.

Blake, a close and superb reader of the prophets, knew all this, better than we can know it because he knew also his election, following Milton, to the line of prophecy. But his immediate poetic tradition was the theater of mind, and he struggled throughout his writing life first partly to reconcile Sensibility and prophecy, and at last largely to disengage the lesser mode from the greater. In *Jerusalem,* the Bard is identified with the Spectre of Urthona, and the *nabi* not with Los or Blake, but with the Los-Blake-Jesus composite who achieves unified form at the poem's close. Cowper's suffering is not redressed, but rather is cast away, for Blake is concerned to distinguish it sharply from the suffering of the prophet, the more fruitful afflictions of Jeremiah and Ezekiel. And, since *Jerusalem* is even more purgatorial than *Milton,* the poem's main concern is to outline firmly the distinction between the two kinds of suffering *in Blake himself.* It is his *own* Spectre of Urthona who must be overcome, though the self-realization necessary for such harsh triumph depends upon his recognition that precisely this psychic component won out in the spirit of Cowper, and in other Bards of Sensibility.

Hayley, who patronized Cowper as he did Blake, extended his interest in what he took to be the "madness" of Bards to the *Jubilate Agno* of Smart, as we know from his correspondence with the Reverend Thomas Carwardine. We do not find in *Jerusalem*, with its powerful control of Blake's emotions, a pathos as immense and memorable as Smart's. The pathos of the Spectre compels a shudder more of revulsion than of sympathy; we are not humiliated by Smart's fate, or Cowper's, but we are by the Spectre's anguish. For the Spectre is rightly associated by Blake with Ezekiel's denunciation of "the dross of silver," the impure to be cast into the terrible refining furnace of Jerusalem-under-siege. Blake is singularly harsh toward the Spectre in *Jerusalem*, not only because it is at last wholly his own Spectre and so most menacing to him, but also because he is turning at last against some of his own deepest literary identifications, and so attempting to free himself from a poetic attitude powerfully attractive to him, whether in Cowper, Gray, Chatterton—whom he had admired overtly—or in lesser figures of the Sublime school.

But to cross over from Bard to *nabi*, from the theater of mind to the orator's theater of action, was not wholly a liberation for Blake's psyche. A different, a subtler anxiety than is incarnated by the Spectre, begins to manifest itself in *Jerusalem*. This is Blake's version of the anxiety of influence, which he had labored heroically to overcome in *Milton*. *Jerusalem* is not less in the Shadow of Milton (which Blake identified with Ezekiel's Covering Cherub) than *Milton* was, and is also in what we could call, following Blake, the Shadow of Ezekiel. To see and state clearly the hidden problem concerning Blake's degree of originality in his definitive poem, we need first to achieve a firmer sense of the poem's psychic cartography than is now available to us.

Freud, in *The Problem of Anxiety*, distinguishes anxiety from grief and sorrow, first by its underlying "increase of excitation" (itself a reproduction of the birth trauma) and then by its function, as a response to a situation of danger. Anxiety, he adds, can be experienced only by the ego, not by the id as "it is not an organization, and cannot estimate situations of danger." As for the superego, Freud declines to ascribe anxiety to it, without however explaining why. In Blake, the id (fallen Tharmas, or the Covering Cherub) does experience anxiety, and so does the superego (fallen Urizen or the Spectre of Albion, the Spectre proper). But Blake and Freud agree on the crucial location of anxiety, for the Blakean ego is Los, fallen form of Urthona, and the Spectre of Urthona is Los's own anxiety, the anxiety of what Yeats calls the faculty of *Creative Mind*. Yet Blake does

75

distinguish the ego's anxiety from that of other psychic components. The Spectre of Urthona is neither the anxiety of influence, a peculiarly poetic anxiety that belongs to the Covering Cherub, with its sinister historical beauty of cultural and spiritual tradition, nor the anxiety of futurity, that belongs to fallen Urizen. Nor is it the sexual anxiety Blake assigns to Orc, the tormented libido burningly rising to a perpetual defeat. Los's anxiety is larger and more constant, resembling Kierkegaards's Concept of Dread, which must be why Northrop Frye ironically calls the Spectre of Urthona the first Existentialist. A desire for what one fears, a sympathetic antipathy, or walking oxymoron; so Kierkegaard speaks of Dread, and so we learn to see the Spectre of Urthona. To Kierkegaard, this was a manifestation of Original Sin; to Blake this manifests the final consequence of being one of Tirzah's children, a natural man caught on the spindle of Necessity.

If we combine the insights of Freud and Kierkegaard, then we approach the Spectre of Urthona's condition, though without wholly encompassing it. The missing element is the anxiety endemic in the theater of mind, or the ego's dread that it can never break through into action. To be fearful that one's words can never become deeds, and yet to desire only to continue in that fear, while remembering dimly the trauma of coming to one's separate existence, and sensing the danger (and excitation) of every threat to such separation: that horrible composite is the Spectre of Urthona's consciousness. Blake, who had known this internal adversary with a clarity only the prophets achieve, turns *Jerusalem* against him even as *Milton* was directed against the Covering Cherub, and as *The Four Zoas* identified its antagonist in fallen Urizen. But even the prophets must be all-too-human. Blake triumphs against his ego's Dread, and wards off again the Urizenic horror of futurity, yet becomes vulnerable instead throughout *Jerusalem* to the diffuse anxiety of influence, the *mimschach* or "wide-extending" Cherub. This baneful aspect of Poetic Influence produces the form of *Jerusalem*, which is the form of Ezekiel's prophecy twisted askew by too abrupt a swerve or *clinamen* away from Blake's model.

Ezekiel is both more methodical in arrangement and more prosaic in style than the writing prophets before him. Rabbi Fisch, in his Soncino edition of Ezekiel, notes the even balance of the prophet's divisions, between the siege and fall of Jerusalem and destruction of the kingdom, and the vision of a people's regeneration, twenty-four chapters being assigned to each. Blake might well have adopted this balance, but chose instead a darker emphasis. Ezekiel ends Chapter XXIV with God's definitive establishment of His prophet as a sign, to those who have escaped destruction. "Thou shalt be a sign unto them; and they shall know that I am the Lord." At the close of XXV this formula is repeated, but as a prophecy against the Ammonites, with a grimly significant addition: ". . . and they shall know that I am the Lord, when I shall lay my vengeance upon them." For the prophet has moved from the fiction of disaster to the hope of renovation, a hope dependent upon the downfall of his people's enemies. He moves steadily toward comfort, and the vision of a rebuilt City of God. Blake's directly parallel movement is from Plate 50, end of Chapter 2, to Plate 53, start of Chapter 3 of *Jerusalem*. Plate 50 concludes with an antiphonal lament, of Erin and the Daughters of Beulah, imploring the Lamb of God to come and take away the remembrance of Sin. But Chapter 3 begins with Los weeping vehemently over Albion, and with our being reminded again that this lamenting, still ineffectual prophet is himself "the Vehicular Form of strong Urthona," that is, the *Merkabah* or Divine Chariot still in departure, still mourning in exile.

Throughout *Jerusalem*, no prophetic hint from Ezekiel is adopted if it might lead to what Blake could regard as a premature mitigation of fallen travail. I do not mean to question Blake's harshness, the necessity for his augmented sense of the prophet's burden. But the bitterness of presentation, the burden placed upon even the attentive and disciplined reader, may surpass what was necessary. At the close of Plate 3, addressing the Public, Blake declares his freedom from the "Monotonous Cadence" of English blank verse, even in Milton and Shakespeare:

> But I soon found that in the mouth of a true Orator such monotony was not only awkward, but as much a bondage as rhyme itself. I therefore have produced a variety in every line, both of cadences & number of syllables. Every word and every letter is studied and put into its fit place: the terrific numbers are reserved for the terrific parts—the mild & gentle, for the mild & gentle parts, and the prosaic, for inferior parts: all are necessary to each other.

Parodying Milton's defense of his refusal to use rhyme, Blake indicates his passage beyond Milton to the cadence of Isaiah and Ezekiel, the form of a true Orator. The defense of Blake's cadence has been conducted definitively by a formidable prosodist, John Hollander, in his essay on "Blake and the Metrical Contract," to which

I can add nothing. In the passage above, Blake emphasizes, as against Milton, the prosody of the King James Version, which he does not distinguish from the Hebrew original. There is evidence that Blake, remarkably adept at teaching himself languages, had some Hebrew when he worked at *Jerusalem,* but his notions as to the variety of biblical poetic numbers seem to go back to Lowth, as Smart's notions did also. This gave him a distorted sense of the metrical freedom of his great originals, a distortion that was an imaginative aid to him. Whether his distortion of larger prophetic forms was hindrance or action is my concern in the remainder of this essay.

Blake shies away from certain symbolic acts in Ezekiel that earlier had influenced him quite directly. It has never, I think, been noted that Blake's *London* has a precise source in Ezekiel:

> I wander thro' each charter'd street,
> Near where the charter'd Thames does flow.
> And mark in every face I meet
> Marks of weakness, marks of woe.

> And the glory of the God of Israel was gone up from the cherub, whereupon he was, to the threshold of the house. And he called to the man clothed with linen, which had the writer's inkhorn by his side;
> And the Lord said unto him, Go through the midst of the city, through the midst of Jerusalem, and set a mark upon the foreheads of the men that sigh and that cry for all the abominations that be done in the midst thereof.
>
> Ezekiel 9:3–4

> How the Chimney-sweepers cry
> Every blackning Church appalls,
> And the hapless Soldiers sigh,
> Runs in blood down Palace walls.

Those that sigh and cry are to be marked and spared, but those in Church and Palace are to be slain, as God pours out his fury upon Jerusalem, and upon London. Between Ezekiel and himself Blake is more than content to see an absolute identity. But, a decade or more later, the identity troubles him. If we contrast even the serene closes of Ezekiel and *Jerusalem,* where Blake directly derives from his precursor the *naming* of the City, we confront an identity straining to be dissolved:

> And the name of the city from that day shall be "The Lord
> is there."
>
> Ezekiel 48:35

> And I heard the Name of their Emanations they are named
> Jerusalem.
>
> *Jerusalem* 99:5

"The Lord is there" because the promise of Ezekiel's prophecy is that the *Merkabah* will not depart again from His sanctuary. Jerusalem receives therefore a new name. Blake's promise is more restricted, and warier; the Judgment will restore London to Jerusalem, but Jerusalem will still be a smelting furnace of mind, subject to the alternation of Beulah and Eden, creative repose and the artist's activity. So the departed Chariot's Cherubim or restored Zoas are not invoked again at *Jerusalem*'s close, as they are by Ezekiel in his final epiphany. For an apocalyptic poem, *Jerusalem* is remarkably restrained. Blake follows Ezekiel throughout, but always at a distance, for he needs to protect himself not only from the natural history of mind (which crippled the poets of Sensibility) but also from the too-rigorous Hebraic theism that would make his apocalyptic humanism impossible. Jerusalem does not accept the dualism of God and man, which is the only dualism sanctioned by the prophets, but which to them was less a dualism than a challenge to confrontation. Blake, who had held back from identifying himself wholly with Milton and Cowper, though he saw the Divine Countenance in them, kept himself distinct at last even from his prophetic precursor, Ezekiel, that he might have his own scope, but also that he might not be affrighted out of Eden the garden of God, though it be by "the anointed cherub that covereth."

1970

6
Napoleon and Prometheus: The Romantic Myth of Organic Energy

> From my window I see the old mountains
> of France, like aged men, fading away.
> Blake, *The French Revolution*

When Napoleon died in 1821, Blake painted *The Spiritual Form of Napoleon*. The picture is lost, but was described in 1876 as showing the Emperor's form to be a "strong energetic figure grasping at the sun and moon with his hands, yet chained to earth by one foot, and with a pavement of dead bodies before him in the foreground." The fortunes of Napoleon and of France had been celebrated by Blake in the historical allegory that exists at one level of meaning in his epics, and it was fitting that Blake salute Napoleon's death with a last emblem of the Titan bound. Blake's Prometheus, the exuberant Orc (from Orcus, hell), had undergone the terrible cycle of becoming one with the sky-god Urizen (from the Greek verb "to bound" as in "horizon") against whom he had risen up, even as Napoleon had aged into yet another tyrant. The figure striving to bring down sun and moon has the apocalyptic impulse, but the dead bodies and the foot bound to nature indicate the passage of that impulse into the demonic.

Napoleon's death had a more intense effect upon Byron, who maintained a lifelong identification with Napoleon as his other self. The Third Canto (1816) of *Childe Harold's Pilgrimage* had lamented the fall of Napoleon and found the Emperor's bane in the boundless Prometheanism of man:

> But quiet to quick bosoms is a hell,
> And *there* hath been thy bane; there is a fire
> And motion of the soul which will not dwell
> In its own narrow being, but aspire
> Beyond the fitting medium of desire;
> And, but once kindled, quenchless evermore,
> Preys upon high adventure, nor can tire

81

Of aught but rest; a fever at the core,
Fatal to him who bears, to all who ever bore.

Clearly this is another portrait of Byron himself, as much as it is of
Napoleon. Waterloo, a fatal field to Byron, had reconciled the poet
again to his hero, whose abdication he had greeted with the savage
Ode To Napoleon Bonaparte (1814). This extraordinary poem lives
today because of its brilliant setting by Arnold Schoenberg, for its
warring impulses and sense of betrayed adulation reduce it to inadequate rhetoric:

'Tis done—but yesterday a King!
And armed with Kings to strive—
And now then art a nameless thing:
  So abject yet alive!
Is this the man of thousand thrones,
Who strew'd our earth with hostile bones,
  And can he thus survive?
Since he, miscall'd the Morning Star,
Nor man nor fiend hath fallen so far.

Even here, at very nearly his poetic worst, the Promethean theme
suddenly elevates Byron's impulse, and makes his diction firm:

Or, like the thief of fire from heaven,
  Wilt thou withstand the shock?
And share with him, the unforgiven,
  His vulture and his rock!
Foredoom'd by God—by man accurst
And that last act, though not thy worst,
  The very Fiend's arch mock;
He in his fall preserved his pride,
And, if a mortal, had as proudly died!

It is the poem's only stanza generous toward Napoleon, as if in remembering the Titanic trinity of Prometheus, the Emperor, and himself Byron had remembered also that the two later Titans crucified on
the rock were only mortal.

Elba and Waterloo called forth poems from Byron; the death at
Saint Helena could not. The news reached Byron at Ravenna, and
seemed to him another token of the ebb of his energies. He wrote to
his friend, the poet Thomas Moore, suggesting Napoleon as a theme
that he himself could no longer approach: "I have no spirits nor *estro*
to do so. His overthrow, from the beginning, was a blow on the
head to me. Since that period, we have been the slaves of fools." The

mood of this passage is the dominant one of Byron's last years. The decay of organic energy; the fall and death of Napoleon; the exhausted state of Europe, bound in by the Urizenic Metternich, became fused for Byron into the myth of an expiring Prometheus:

> The fire that on my bosom preys
> Is lone as some volcanic isle;
> No torch is kindled at its blaze—
> A funeral pile.

It remained for Shelley, the most Promethean of all poets, to compose the proper Romantic dirge for Napoleon. Himself the poet of the permanent Left, Shelley from his youth had regarded Napoleon as the great betrayer of the Revolution. The myth of Napoleon in Blake, the story of Orc in whom merely organic and genuinely creative energy can never be distinguished, is revived in Shelley's powerful *Lines Written On Hearing The News Of The Death Of Napoleon*. The poet cries out in wonder that Earth leaps forth as of old, still alive, even though the soul of its energy has departed. Earth's fierce reply is that she lives by feeding upon the organic energy of Promethean spirits:

> "Still alive and still bold," shouted Earth.
>   "I grow bolder and still more bold.
>   The dead fill me ten thousandfold.
> Fuller of speed, and splendour, and mirth.
> I was cloudy, and sullen, and cold,
> Like a frozen chaos uprolled,
> Till by the spirit of the mighty dead
> My heart grew warm. I feed on whom I fed."

The implied myth here is akin to that of Blake's *Mental Traveller*, where an old woman who represents Nature binds down the infant Orc and grows young by feeding upon his energies, even as the Titanic child grows older.

The myth of Napoleon continued to haunt Shelley in the remaining year of the poet's life. In *The Triumph of Life*, Shelley's last major poem, the Emperor appears as a captive, chained to the triumphal chariot of the Conqueror, Life. This apparition precipitates the most crucial of the poet's reflections:

> —I felt my cheek
> Alter, to see the shadow pass away,
> Whose grasp had left the giant world so weak

That every pigmy kicked it as it lay;
And much I grieved to think how power and will
In opposition rule our mortal day,

And why God made irreconcilable
Good and the means of good.

Power, for Shelley, is the energy of the organism; will, the creative
energy of the poet. The necessary opposition between the two provokes the desperate quietism that sees good and the means of good
as being irreconcilable. Reality is so constituted that the means of
good, in the Romantic age, fell into the hands of Napoleon, and those
hands could destroy but not create. The final myth of Napoleon in
English Romantic poetry is another demonstration of why poets had
to be the *unacknowledged* legislators of the world. In the language
that summarized the career of Napoleon, Shelley echoed the speech
that caused his own Prometheus to despair:

The good want power, but to weep barren tears.
The powerful goodness want: worse need for them.
The wise want love; and those who love want wisdom;
And all best things are thus confused to ill.

By seeing the shade of Napoleon as an emblematic confirmation
of this Promethean despair, Shelley had culminated the Romantic
story of Napoleon. The myth appears again in Hardy's *The Dynasts*
(1903), under Shelley's influence, but Hardy's Napoleon is only another toy of the Immanent Will, not a Titan whose energy could
ever have been intermixed with creative force, with human will and
imagination.

1960

7
The Unpastured Sea:
An Introduction to Shelley

It is the unpastured sea hungering for calm.
Prometheus Unbound, III, II

Mesdames, one might believe that Shelley lies
Less in the stars than in their earthy wake,
Since the radiant disclosures that you make
Are of an eternal vista, manqué and gold
And brown, an Italy of the mind, a place
Of fear before the disorder of the strange,
A time in which the poet's politics
Will rule in a poets' world.
Wallace Stevens

Percy Bysshe Shelley, one of the greatest lyrical poets in Western
tradition, has been dead for more than a hundred and forty years,
and critics have abounded, from his own day to ours, to insist
that his poetry died with him. Until recently, it was fashionable to
apologize for Shelley's poetry, if one liked it at all. Each reader
of poetry, however vain, can speak only for himself, and there will
be only description and praise in this introduction, for after many
years of reading Shelley's poems, I find nothing in them that needs
apology. Shelley is a unique poet, one of the most original in the
language, and he is in many ways *the* poet proper, as much so as
any in the language. His poetry is autonomous, finely wrought, in
the highest degree imaginative, and has the spiritual form of vision
stripped of all veils and ideological coverings, the vision many
readers justly seek in poetry, despite the admonitions of a multitude
of churchwardenly critics.

The essential Shelley is so fine a poet that one can feel absurd
in urging his claims upon a reader:

I am the eye with which the Universe
    Beholds itself and knows itself divine;
All harmony of instrument or verse,
    All prophecy, all medicine is mine,
All light of art or nature;—to my song
Victory and praise in its own right belong.

That is Apollo singing, in the *Hymn* that Shelley had the sublime
audacity to write for him, with the realization that, like Keats, he
was a rebirth of Apollo. When, in *The Triumph of Life*, Rousseau
serves as Virgil to Shelley's Dante, he is made to speak lines as
brilliantly and bitterly condensed as poetry in English affords:

And if the spark with which Heaven lit my spirit
Had been with purer nutriment supplied,

Corruption would not now thus much inherit
Of what was once Rousseau—nor this disguise
Stain that which ought to have disdained to wear it.

The urbane lyricism of the *Hymn of Apollo*, and the harshly self-conscious, internalized dramatic quality of *The Triumph of Life* are both central to Shelley. Most central is the prophetic intensity, as much a result of displaced Protestantism as it is in Blake or in Wordsworth, but seeming more an Orphic than Hebraic phenomenon when it appears in Shelley. Religious poet as he primarily was, what Shelley prophesied was one restored Man who transcended men, gods, the natural world, and even the poetic faculty. Shelley chants the apotheosis, not of the poet, but of desire itself:

Man, oh, not men! a chain of linkèd thought,
Of love and might to be divided not,
Compelling the elements with adamantine stress;
As the sun rules, even with a tyrant's gaze,
The unquiet republic of the maze
Of planets, struggling fierce towards heaven's free wilderness.

Man, one harmonious soul of many a soul,
Whose nature is its own divine control,
Where all things flow to all, as rivers to the sea. . . .

The rhapsodic intensity, the cumulative drive and yet firm control of those last three lines in particular, as the high song of humanistic celebration approaches its goal—that seems to me what is crucial in Shelley, and its presence throughout much of his work constitutes his special excellence as a poet.

Lyrical poetry at its most intense frequently moves toward direct address between one human consciousness and another, in which the "I" of the poet directly invokes the personal "Thou" of the reader. Shelley is an intense lyricist as Alexander Pope is an intense satirist; even as Pope assimilates every literary form he touches to satire, so Shelley converts forms as diverse as drama, prose essay, romance, satire, epyllion, into lyric. To an extent he himself scarcely realized, Shelley's genius desired a transformation of all experience, natural and literary, into the condition of lyric. More than all other poets, Shelley's compulsion is to present life as a direct confrontation of equal realities. This compulsion seeks absolute intensity, and courts straining and breaking in consequence. When expressed as love, it must manifest itself as mutual destruction:

> In one another's substance finding food,
> Like flames too pure and light and unimbued
> To nourish their bright lives with baser prey,
> Which point to Heaven and cannot pass away:
> One Heaven, one Hell, one immortality,
> And one annihilation.

Shelley is the poet of these flames, and he is equally the poet of a particular shadow, which falls perpetually between all such flames, a shadow of ruin that tracks every imaginative flight of fire:

> O, Thou, who plumed with strong desire
>   Wouldst float above the earth, beware!
> A Shadow tracks thy flight of fire—
>   Night is coming!

By the time Shelley had reached his final phase, of which the great monuments are *Adonais* and *The Triumph of Life*, he had become altogether the poet of this shadow of ruin, and had ceased to celebrate the possibilities of imaginative relationship. In giving himself, at last, over to the dark side of his own vision, he resolved (or perhaps merely evaded, judgment being so difficult here) a conflict within his self and poetry that had been present from the start. Though it has become a commonplace of recent criticism and scholarship to affirm otherwise, I do not think that Shelley changed very much, as a poet, during the last (and most important) six years of his life, from the summer of 1816 until the summer of 1822. The two poems of self-discovery, of mature poetic incarnation, written in 1816, *Mont Blanc* and the *Hymn to Intellectual Beauty*, reveal the two contrary aspects of Shelley's vision that his entire sequence of major poems reveals. The head and the heart, each totally honest in encountering reality, yield rival reports as to the name and nature of reality. The head, in *Mont Blanc*, learns, like Blake, that there is no natural religion. There is a Power, a secret strength of things, but it hides its true shape or its shapelessness behind or beneath a dread mountain, and it shows itself only as an indifference, or even pragmatically a malevolence, toward the well-being of men. But the Power speaks forth, through a poet's act of confrontation with it that is the very act of writing his poem, and the Power, rightly interpreted, can be used to repeal the large code of fraud, institutional and historical Christianity, and the equally massive code of woe, the

89

laws of the nation-states of Europe in the age of Castlereagh and Metternich. In the *Hymn to Intellectual Beauty* a very different Power is invoked, but with a deliberate and even austere tenuousness. A shadow, itself invisible, of an unseen Power, sweeps through our dull dense world, momentarily awakening both nature and man to a sense of love and beauty, a sense just beyond the normal range of apprehension. But the shadow departs, for all its benevolence and despite the poet's prayers for its more habitual sway. The heart's responses have not failed, but the shadow that is antithetically a radiance will not come to stay. The mind, searching for what would suffice, encountered an icy remoteness, but dared to affirm the triumph of its imaginings over the solitude and vacancy of an inadvertent nature. The emotions, visited by delight, felt the desolation of powerlessness, but dared to hope for a fuller visitation. Both odes suffer from the evident straining of their creator to reach a finality, but both survive in their creator's tough honesty and gathering sense of form.

. *Mont Blanc* is a poem of the age of Shelley's father-in-law, William Godwin, while the *Hymn to Intellectual Beauty* belongs to the age of Wordsworth, Shelley's lost leader in the realms of emotion. Godwin became a kind of lost leader for Shelley also, but less on the intellectual than on the personal level. The scholarly criticism of Shelley is full of sand traps, and one of the deepest is the prevalent notion that Shelley underwent an intellectual metamorphosis from being the disciple of Godwin and the French philosophical materialists to being a Platonist or Neoplatonist, an all but mystical idealist. The man Shelley may have undergone such a transformation, though the evidence for it is equivocal; the poet Shelley did not. He started as a split being, and ended as one, but his awareness of the division in his consciousness grew deeper, and produced finally the infernal vision of *The Triumph of Life*.

But even supposing that a man should raise a dead body to life before our eyes, and on this fact rest his claim to being considered the son of God;—the Humane Society restores drowned persons, and because it makes no mystery of the method it employs, its members are not mistaken for the sons of God. All that we have a right to infer from our ignorance of the cause of any event is that we do not know it. . . .
Shelley, *Notes on Queen Mab*

The deepest characteristic of Shelley's poetic mind is its skepticism. Shelley's intellectual agnosticism was more fundamental than either his troubled materialism or his desperate idealism. Had the poet turned his doubt against all entities but his own poetry, while sparing that, he would have anticipated certain later developments in the history of literature, but his own work would have lost one of its most precious qualities, a unique sensitivity to its own limitations. This sensitivity can be traced from the very beginnings of Shelley's mature style, and may indeed have made possible the achievement of that style.

Shelley was anything but a born poet, as even a brief glance at his apprentice work will demonstrate. Blake at fourteen was a great lyric poet; Shelley at twenty-two was still a bad one. He found himself, as a stylist, in the autumn of 1815, when he composed the astonishing *Alastor*, a blank verse rhapsodic narrative of a destructive and subjective quest. *Alastor*, though it has been out of fashion for a long time, is nevertheless a great and appalling work, at once a dead end, and a prophecy that Shelley finally could not evade.

Shelley's starting point as a serious poet was Wordsworth, and *Alastor* is a stepchild of *The Excursion*, a poem frigid in itself, but profoundly influential, if only antithetically, on Shelley, Byron, Keats, and many later poets. The figure of the Solitary, in *The Excursion*, is the central instance of the most fundamental of Romantic archetypes, the man alienated from others and himself by excessive self-consciousness. Whatever its poetic lapses, *The Excursion* is our most extensive statement of the Romantic mythology of the Self, and the young Shelley quarried in it for imaginatively inescapable reasons, as Byron and Keats did also. Though the poet-hero of *Alastor* is not precisely an innocent sufferer, he shares the torment of Wordsworth's Solitary and, like him,

> sees
> Too clearly; feels too vividly; and longs
> To realize the vision, with intense
> And over-constant yearning;—there—there lies
> The excess, by which the balance is destroyed.

Alastor, whatever Shelley's intentions, is primarily a poem about the destructive power of the imagination. For Shelley, every increase in imagination ought to have been an increase in hope, but generally the strength of imagination in Shelley fosters an answering strength

91

of despair. In the spring of 1815 Shelley, on mistaken medical advice, confidently expected a rapid death of consumption. By autumn this expectation was put by, but the recent imagining of his own death lingers on in *Alastor*, which on one level is the poet's elegy for himself.

Most critical accounts of *Alastor* concern themselves with the apparent problem of disparities between the poem's eloquent Preface and the poem itself, but I cannot see that such disparities exist. The poem is an extremely subtle internalization of the quest-theme of romance, and the price demanded for the internalization is first, the death-in-life of what Yeats called "enforced self-realization," and at last, death itself. The *Alastor* or avenging demon of the title is the dark double of the poet-hero, the spirit of solitude that shadows him even as he quests after his emanative portion, the soul out of his soul that Shelley later called the epipsyche. Shelley's poet longs to realize a vision, and this intense and overconstant yearning destroys natural existence, for nature cannot contain the infinite energy demanded by the vision. Wordsworthian nature, and not the poet-hero, is the equivocal element in *Alastor*, the problem the reader needs to, but cannot, resolve. For this nature is a mirror-world, like that in Blake's *The Crystal Cabinet*, or in much of Keats's *Endymion*. Its pyramids and domes are sepulchers for the imagination, and all its appearances are illusive, phantasmagoric, and serve only to thwart the poet's vision, and drive him on more fearfully upon his doomed and self-destructive quest. *Alastor* prophesies *The Triumph of Life*, and in the mocking light of the later poem the earlier work appears also to have been a dance of death.

The summer of 1816, with its wonderful products, *Mont Blanc* and the *Hymn to Intellectual Beauty*, was for Shelley, as I have indicated, a rediscovery of the poetic self, a way out of the impasse of *Alastor*. The revolutionary epic, first called *Laon and Cyntha*, and then *The Revolt of Islam*, was Shelley's first major attempt to give his newly directed energies adequate scope, but the attempt proved abortive, and the poem's main distinction is that it is Shelley's longest. Shelley's gifts were neither for narrative nor for straightforward allegory, and the *terza rima* fragment, *Prince Athanase*, written late in 1817, a few months after *The Revolt of Islam* was finished, shows the poet back upon his true way, the study of the isolated imagination. Whatever the dangers of the subjective mode of *Alastor*, it remained always Shelley's genuine center, and his finest poems were to emerge from it. *Prince Athanase* is only a fragment, or fragments, but its first part at least retains something of the power for us that it held for the young Browning and the young Yeats. Athanase, from a Peacockian perspective, is quite like the delightfully absurd Scythrop of *Nightmare Abbey*, but if we will grant him his mask's validity we do find in him one of the archetypes of the imagination, the introspective, prematurely old poet, turning his vision outward to the world from his lonely tower of meditation:

> His soul had wedded wisdom, and her dower
> Is love and justice, clothed in which he sate
> Apart from men, as in a lonely tower,
>
> Pitying the tumult of their dark estate.—

There is a touch of Byron's Manfred, and of Byron himself, in Athanase, and Byron is the dominant element in Shelley's next enduring poem, the conversational *Julian and Maddalo*, composed in Italy in the autumn of 1818, after the poets had been reunited. The middle portion of *Julian and Maddalo*, probably based upon legends of Tasso's madness, is an excrescence, but the earlier part of the poem, and its closing lines, introduce another Shelley, a master of the urbane, middle style, the poet of the *Letter to Maria Gisborne*, the *Hymn to Mercury*, of parts of *The Witch of Atlas* and *The Sensitive Plant*, and of such beautifully controlled love lyrics as *To Jane: The Invitation* and *Lines Written in the Bay of Lerici*. Donald Davie, who as a critic is essentially an anti-Shelleyan of the school of Dr. Leavis, and is himself a poet in a mode antithetical to Shelley's, has written an impressive tribute to Shelley's achievement as a master of the urbane style. What I find most remarkable in this mastery is that Shelley carried it over into his major achievement, the great lyrical drama, *Prometheus Unbound*, a work written almost entirely in the high style, on the precarious level of the sublime, where urbanity traditionally has no place. The astonishingly original tone of *Prometheus Unbound* is not always successfully maintained, but for the most part it is, and one aspect of its triumph is that critics should find it so difficult a tone to characterize. The urbane conversationalist, the relentlessly direct and emotionally uninhibited lyricist, and the elevated prophet of a great age to come join together in the poet of *Prometheus Unbound*, a climactic work that is at once celebratory and ironic, profoundly idealistic and as profoundly skeptical, passionately knowing its truths and as passionately agnostic toward all truth. More than any other of Shelley's poems, *Prometheus Un-*

bound has been viewed as self-contradictory or at least as containing unresolved mental conflicts, so that a consideration of Shelley's ideology may be appropriate prior to a discussion of the poem.

The clue to the apparent contradictions in Shelley's thought is his profound skepticism, which has been ably expounded by C. E. Pulos in his study, *The Deep Truth*. There the poet's eclecticism is seen as centering on the point "where his empiricism terminates and his idealism begins." This point is the skeptic's position, and is where Shelley judged Montaigne, Hume, and his own older contemporary, the metaphysician Sir William Drummond, to have stood. From this position, Shelley was able to reject both the French materialistic philosophy he had embraced in his youth, and the Christianity that he had never ceased to call a despotism. Yet the skeptic's position, though it powerfully organized Shelley's revolutionary polemicism, gave no personal comfort, but took the poet to what he himself called "the verge where words abandon us, and what wonder if we grow dizzy to look down the dark abyss of how little we know." That abyss is Demogorgon's, in *Prometheus Unbound*, and its secrets are not revealed by him, for "a voice is wanting, the deep truth is imageless," and Demogorgon is a shapeless darkness. Yeats, sensing the imminence of his apocalypse, sees a vast image, a beast advancing before the gathering darkness. Shelley senses the great change that the Revolution has heralded, but confronts as apocalyptic harbinger only a fabulous and formless darkness, the only honest vision available to even the most apocalyptic of skeptics. Shelley is the most Humean poet in the language, oddly as his temperament accords with Hume's, and it is Hume, not Berkeley or Plato, whose view of reality informs *Prometheus Unbound* and the poems that came after it. Even Necessity, the dread and supposedly Godwinian governing demon of Shelley's early *Queen Mab*, is more of a Humean than a Holbachian notion, for Shelley's Necessity is "conditional, tentative and philosophically ironical," as Pulos points out. It is also a Necessity highly advantageous to a poet, for a power both sightless and unseen is a power removed from dogma and from philosophy, a power that only the poet's imagination can find the means to approach. Shelley is the unacknowledged ancestor of Wallace Stevens' conception of poetry as the Supreme Fiction, and *Prometheus Unbound* is the most capable imagining, outside of Blake and Wordsworth, that the Romantic quest for a Supreme Fiction has achieved.

The fatal aesthetic error, in reading *Prometheus Unbound* or any other substantial work by Shelley, is to start with the assumption that one is about to read Platonic poetry. I mean this in either sense, that is, either poetry deeply influenced by or expressing Platonic doctrine, or in John Crowe Ransom's special sense, a poetry discoursing in things that are at any point legitimately to be translated into ideas. Shelley's skeptical and provisional idealism is *not* Plato's, and Shelley's major poems are mythopoeic, and not translatable into any terms but their own highly original ones. Shelley has been much victimized in our time by two rival and equally pernicious critical fashions, one that seeks to "rescue" visionary poetry by reading it as versified Plotinus and Porphyry, and another that condemns visionary poetry from Spenser through Hart Crane as being a will-driven allegorization of an idealistic scientism vainly seeking to rival the whole of experimental science from Bacon to the present day. The first kind of criticism, from which Blake and Yeats have suffered as much as Shelley, simply misreads the entire argument against nature that visionary poetry complexly conducts. The second kind, as pervasively American as the first is British, merely underestimates the considerable powers of mind that Shelley and the other poets of his tradition possessed.

Shelley admired Plato as a poet, a view he derived from Montaigne, as Pulos surmises, and he appears also to have followed Montaigne in considering Plato to be a kind of skeptic. Nothing is further from Shelley's mind and art than the Platonic view of knowledge, and nothing is further from Shelley's tentative myths than the dogmatic myths of Plato. It is one of the genuine oddities of critical history that a tough-minded Humean poet, though plagued also by an idealistic and pseudo-Platonic heart, should have acquired the reputation of having sought beauty or truth in any Platonic way or sense whatsoever. No Platonist would have doubted immortality as darkly as Shelley did, or indeed would have so recurrently doubted the very existence of anything transcendent.

The most obvious and absolute difference between Plato and Shelley is in their rival attitudes toward aesthetic experience. Shelley resembles Wordsworth or Ruskin in valuing so highly certain ecstatic moments of aesthetic contemplation precisely because the moments are fleeting, because they occupy, as Blake said, the pulsation of an artery. For Shelley these are not moments to be put aside when the enduring light of the Ideas is found; Shelley never encounters such a light, not even in *Adonais*, where Keats appears to have found a kindred light in death. There is no ladder to climb in Shelley's poetry, any more than there is in Blake's. There are more imaginative states of being and less imaginative ones, but no hierarchy to bridge the abyss between them.

> It is no longer sufficient to say, like all poets, that mirrors resemble the water. Neither is it sufficient to consider that hypothesis as absolute and to suppose . . . that mirrors exhale a fresh wind or that thirsty birds drink them, leaving empty frames. We must go beyond such things. That capricious desire of a mind which becomes compulsory reality must be manifested—an individual must be shown who inserts himself into the glass and remains in its illusory land (where there are figurations and colors but these are impaired by immobile silence) and feels the shame of being nothing more than an image obliterated by nights and permitted existence by glimmers of light.
> Jorge Luis Borges

It has been my experience, as a teacher of Shelley, that few recent students enjoy *Prometheus Unbound* at a first reading, and few fail to admire it greatly at a second or later reading. *Prometheus Unbound* is a remarkably subtle and difficult poem. That a work of such length needs to be read with all the care and concentration a trained reader brings to a difficult and condensed lyric is perhaps unfortunate, yet Shelley himself affirmed that his major poem had been written only for highly adept readers, and that he hoped for only a few of these. *Prometheus Unbound* is not as obviously difficult as Blake's *The Four Zoas*, but it presents problems comparable to that work. Blake has the advantage of having made a commonplace understanding of his major poems impossible, while Shelley retains familiar (and largely misleading) mythological names like Prometheus and Jupiter. The problems of interpretation in Shelley's lyrical drama are as formidable as English poetry affords, and are perhaps finally quite unresolvable.

It seems clear that Shelley intended his poem to be a millennial rather than an apocalyptic work. The vision in Act III is of a redeemed nature, but not of an ultimate reality, whereas the vision in the great afterthought of Act IV does concern an uncovered universe. In Act IV the imagination of Shelley breaks away from the poet's apparent intention, and visualizes a world in which the veil of phenomenal reality has been rent, a world like that of the Revelation of Saint John, or Night the Ninth of *The Four Zoas*. The audacity of Shelley gives us a vision of the last things without the sanction of religious or mythological tradition. Blake does the same, but Blake is systematic where Shelley risks everything on one sustained imagining.

I think that a fresh reader of *Prometheus Unbound* is best prepared if he starts with Milton in mind. This holds true also for *The Prelude*, for Blake's epics, for Keats's *Hyperion* fragments, and even for Byron's *Don Juan*, since Milton is both the Romantic starting point and the Romantic adversary. Shelley is as conscious of this as Blake or any of the others; the Preface to *Prometheus Unbound* refers to that demigod, "the sacred Milton," and commends him for having been "a bold inquirer into morals and religion." Searching out an archetype for his Prometheus, Shelley finds him in Milton's Satan, "the Hero of Paradise Lost," but a flawed, an imperfect hero, of whom Prometheus will be a more nearly perfect descendant. Shelley's poem is almost an echo chamber for *Paradise Lost*, but all the echoes are deliberate, and all of them are so stationed as to "correct" the imaginative errors of *Paradise Lost*. Almost as much as Blake's "brief epic," *Milton*, Shelley's *Prometheus Unbound* is a courageous attempt to save Milton from himself, and for the later poet. Most modern scholarly critics of Milton sneer at the Blakean or Shelleyan temerity, but no modern critic of Milton is as illuminating as Blake and Shelley are, and none knows better than they did how omnipotent an opponent they lovingly faced, or how ultimately hopeless the contest was.

Paraphrase is an ignoble mode of criticism, but it can be a surprisingly revealing one (of the critic as well as the work, of course) and it is particularly appropriate to *Prometheus Unbound*, since the pattern of action in the lyrical drama is a puzzling one. A rapid survey of character and plot is hardly possible, since the poem in a strict (and maddening) sense has neither, but a few points can be risked as introduction. Shelley's source is Aeschylus, insofar as he has a source, but his genuine analogues are in his older contemporary Blake, whom he had never read, and of whom indeed he never seems to have heard. Prometheus has a resemblance both to Blake's Orc and to his Los; Jupiter is almost a double for Urizen, Asia approximates Blake's Jerusalem, while Demogorgon has nothing in common with any of Blake's "Giant Forms." But, despite this last, the shape of Shelley's myth is very like Blake's. A unitary Man fell, and split into torturing and tortured components, and into separated male and female forms as well. The torturer is not in himself a representative of comprehensive evil, because he is quite limited; indeed, he has been invented by his victim, and falls soon after his victim ceases to hate his own invention. Shelley's Jupiter, like Urizen in one of his aspects, is pretty clearly the Jehovah of institutional and historical Christianity. George Bernard Shaw, one of the most enthusiastic of Shelleyans, had some illuminating remarks on *Prometheus Unbound* in *The Perfect Wagnerite*. Jupiter, he said, "is the almighty fiend into whom the Englishman's God had degenerated during two centuries of ignorant Bible worship and shameless commercialism." Shaw rather understated the matter, since it seems indubitable that the Jupiter of Shelley's lyrical drama is one with the cheerfully abominable Jehovah of *Queen Mab*, and so had been degenerating for rather more than two centuries.

Prometheus in Shelley is both the archetypal imagination (Blake's Los) and the primordial energies of man (Blake's Orc). Jupiter, like Urizen again, is a limiter of imagination and of energy. He may masquerade as reason, but he is nothing of the kind, being a mere circumscriber and binder, like the God of *Paradise Lost*, Book III (as opposed to the very different, creative God of Milton's Book VII). Asia is certainly not the Universal Love that Shaw and most subsequent Shelleyans have taken her to be. Though she partly transcends nature she is still subject to it, and she is essentially a passive being, even though the apparently central dramatic action of the poem is assigned to her. Like the emanations in Blake, she may be taken as the total spiritual form or achieved aesthetic form quested after by her lover, Prometheus. She is less than the absolute vainly sought by the poet-hero of *Alastor*, though she is more presumably than the mortal Emilia of *Epipsychidion* can hope to represent. Her function is to hold the suffering natural world open to the transcendent love or Intellectual Beauty that hovers beyond it, but except in the brief and magnificent moment-of-moments of her transfiguration (end of Act II) she is certainly not one with the Intellectual Beauty.

That leaves us Demogorgon, the poem's finest and most frustrating invention, who has been disliked by the poem's greatest admirers, Shaw and Yeats. Had Shaw written the poem, Demogorgon would have been Creative Evolution, and had Yeats been the author, Demogorgon would have been the Thirteenth Cone of *A Vision*. But Shelley was a subtler dialectician than Shaw or Yeats; as a skeptic, he had to be. Shaw testily observed that "flatly, there is no such person as Demogorgon, and if Prometheus does not pull down Jupiter himself, no one else will." Demogorgon, Yeats insisted, was a ruinous invention for Shelley: "Demogorgon made his plot incoherent, its interpretation impossible; it was thrust there by that something which again and again forced him to balance the object of desire conceived as miraculous and superhuman, with nightmare."

Yet Demogorgon, in all his darkness, is a vital necessity in Shelley's mythopoeic quest for a humanized or displaced theodicy. The Demogorgon of Spenser and of Milton was the evil god of chaos, dread father of all the gentile divinities. Shelley's Demogorgon, like the unknown Power of *Mont Blanc,* is morally unallied; he is the god of skepticism, and thus the preceptor of our appalling freedom to imagine well or badly. His only clear attributes are dialectical; he is the god of all those at the turning, at the reversing of the cycles. Like the dialectic of the Marxists, Demogorgon is a necessitarian and materialistic entity, part of the nature of things as they are. But he resembles also the shadowy descent of the Holy Spirit in most Christian dialectics of history, though it would be more accurate to call him a demonic parody of the Spirit, just as the whole of *Prometheus Unbound* is a dark parody of the Christian salvation myth. Back of Demogorgon is Shelley's difficult sense of divinity, an apocalyptic humanism like that of Blake's, and it is not possible therefore to characterize *Prometheus Unbound* as being humanistic or theistic in its ultimate vision. Martin Price, writing of Blake's religion, observes that "Blake can hardly be identified as theist or humanist; the distinction becomes meaningless for him. God can only exist within man, but man must be raised to a perception of the infinite. Blake rejects both transcendental deity and natural man." The statement is equally true for the Shelley of *Prometheus Unbound,* if one modifies rejection of transcendental deity to a skeptical opening toward the possibility of such a Power. Though Demogorgon knows little more than does the Asia who questions him, that little concerns his relationship to a further Power, and the relationship is part of the imagelessness of ultimates, where poetry reaches its limit.

The events of *Prometheus Unbound* take place in the realm of mind, and despite his skepticism Shelley at this point in his career clung to a faith in the capacity of the human mind to renovate first itself, and then the outward world as well. The story of the lyrical drama is therefore an unfolding of renovation after renovation, until natural cycle itself is canceled in the rhapsodies of Act IV. Of actions in the traditional sense, I find only one, the act of pity that Prometheus extends toward Jupiter at line 53 of Act I. Frederick A. Pottle, in the most advanced essay yet written on the poem, insists that there is a second and as crucial action, the descent of Asia, with her subsequent struggle to attain to a theology of love: "Asia's action is to give up her demand for an ultimate Personal Evil, to combine an unshakable faith that the universe is sound at the core with a realization that, as regards man, Time is radically and incurably evil." Behind Pottle's reading is a drastic but powerful allegorizing of the poem, in which Prometheus and Asia occupy respectively the positions of head and heart: "The head must sincerely forgive, must willingly eschew hatred on purely experimental grounds . . ." while the heart "must exorcize the demons of infancy." One can benefit from this provisional allegorizing even if one finds *Prometheus Unbound* to be less theistic in its implications than Pottle appears to do.

Further commentary on the complexities of the poem can be sought elsewhere, but the aesthetic achievement needs to be considered here. Dr. Samuel Johnson still knew that invention was the essence of poetry, but this truth is mostly neglected in our contemporary criticism. It may be justly observed that Shelley had conquered the myth of Prometheus even as he had transformed it, and the conquest is the greatest glory of Shelley's poem. One power alone, Blake asserted, made a poet, the divine vision or imagination, by which he meant primarily the inventive faculty, the gift of making a myth or of so re-making a myth as to return it to the fully human truths of our original existence as unfallen men. If Johnson and Blake were right, then *Prometheus Unbound* is one of the greatest poems in the language, a judgment that will seem eccentric only to a kind of critic whose standards are centered in areas not in themselves imaginative.

> Nature has appointed us men to be no base or ignoble animals, but when she ushers us into the vast universe . . . she implants in our souls the unconquerable love of whatever is elevated and more divine than we. Wherefore not even the entire universe suffices for the thought and contemplation within the reach of the human mind.
> Longinus, *On the Sublime*

Published with *Prometheus Unbound* in 1820 were a group of Shelley's major odes, including *Ode to the West Wind*, *To a Skylark*, and *Ode to Liberty*. These poems show Shelley as a lyricist deliberately seeking to extend the sublime mode, and are among his finest achievements.

Wallace Stevens, in one of the marvelous lyrics of his old age, hears the cry of the leaves and knows "it is the cry of leaves that do not transcend themselves," knows that the cry means no more than can be found "in the final finding of the ear, in the thing/Itself." From this it follows, with massive but terrible dignity, that "at last, the cry concerns no one at all." This is Stevens' modern reality of *decreation*, and this is the fate that Shelley's magnificent *Ode to the West Wind* seeks to avert. Shelley hears a cry of leaves that do transcend themselves, and he deliberately seeks a further transcendence that will metamorphosize "the thing itself" into human form, so that at last the cry will concern all men. But in Shelley's *Ode*, as in Stevens's, "there is a conflict, there is a resistance involved;/And being part is an exertion that declines." Shelley too feels the frightening strength of the *given*, "the life of that which gives life as it is," but here as elsewhere Shelley does not accept the merely "as it is." The function of his *Ode* is apocalyptic, and the controlled fury of his spirit is felt throughout this perfectly modulated "trumpet of a prophecy."

What is most crucial to an understanding of the *Ode* is the realization that its fourth and fifth stanzas bear a wholly antithetical relation to one another. The triple invocation to the elements of earth, air, and water occupies the first three stanzas of the poem, and the poet himself does not enter those stanzas; in them he is only a voice imploring the elements to hear. In the fourth stanza, the poet's ego enters the poem, but in the guise only of a battered Job, seeking to lose his own humanity. From this nadir, the extraordinary and poignantly "broken" music of the last stanza rises up, into the poet's own element of fire, to affirm again the human dignity of the prophet's vocation, and to suggest a mode of imaginative renovation that goes beyond the cyclic limitations of nature. Rarely in the history of poetry have seventy lines done so much so well.

Shelley's other major odes are out of critical favor in our time, but this is due as much to actual misinterpretations as to any qualities inherent in these poems. "To a Skylark" strikes readers as silly when they visualize the poet staring at the bird and hailing it as nonexistent, but these readers have begun with such gross inaccuracy that their experience of what they take to be the poem may simply be dismissed. The ode's whole point turns on the lark's being out of sight from the start; the poet *hears* an evanescent song, but can see nothing, even as Keats in the *Ode to a Nightingale* never actually sees the bird. Flying too high almost to be heard, the lark is crucially compared by Shelley to his central symbol, the morning star fading into the dawn of an unwelcome day. What can barely be heard, and not seen at all, is still discovered to be a basis upon which to rejoice, and indeed becomes an inescapable motive for metaphor, a dark justification for celebrating the light of uncommon day. In the great revolutionary *Ode to Liberty*, Shelley successfully adapts the English Pindaric to an abstract political theme, mostly by means of making the poem radically its own subject, as he does on a larger scale in *The Witch of Atlas* and *Epipsychidion*.

In the last two years of his life, Shelley subtly modified his lyrical art, making the best of his shorter poems the means by which his experimental intellectual temper and his more traditional social urbanity could be reconciled. The best of these lyrics would include *Hymn of Apollo, The Two Spirits: An Allegory, To Night, Lines . . . on . . . the Death of Napoleon*, and the final group addressed to Jane Williams, or resulting from the poet's love for her, including *When the lamp is shattered, To Jane: The Invitation, The Recollection, With a Guitar, to Jane*, and the last completed lyric, the immensely moving *Lines Written in the Bay of Lerici*. Here are nine lyrics as varied and masterful as the language affords. Take these together with Shelley's achievements in the sublime ode, with the best of his earlier lyrics, and with the double handful of magnificent interspersed lyrics contained in *Prometheus Unbound* and *Hellas*, and it will not seem as if Swinburne was excessive in claiming for Shelley a rank as one of the two or three major lyrical poets in English tradition down to Swinburne's own time.

The best admonition to address to a reader of Shelley's lyrics, as of his longer poems, is to slow down and read very closely, so as to learn what Wordsworth could have meant when he reluctantly conceded that "Shelley is one of the best *artists* of us all: I mean in workmanship of style":

> There is no dew on the dry grass tonight,
>   Nor damp within the shadow of the trees;
> The wind is intermitting, dry, and light;
>   And in the inconstant motion of the breeze
> The dust and straws are driven up and down,
> And whirled about the pavement of the town.
>   *Evening: Ponte Al Mare, Pisa*

This altogether characteristic example of Shelley's workmanship is taken from a minor and indeed unfinished lyric of 1821. I have undergone many unhappy conversations with university wits, poets, and critics, who have assured me that "Shelley had a tin ear," the

An Introduction to Shelley

assurance being given on one occasion by no less distinguished a prosodist than W. H. Auden, and I am always left wondering if my ears have heard correctly. The fashion of insisting that Shelley was a poor craftsman seems to have started with T. S. Eliot, spread from him to Dr. Leavis and the Fugitive group of Southern poets and critics, and then for a time became universal. It was a charming paradox that formalist and rhetorical critics should have become so affectively disposed against a poet as to be incapable of reading any of his verbal figures with even minimal accuracy, but the charm has worn off, and one hopes that the critical argument about Shelley can now move on into other (and more disputable) areas.

> Cruelty has a Human Heart,
> And Jealousy a Human Face;
> Terror the Human Form Divine,
> And Secrecy the Human Dress.
>
> The Human Dress is forged Iron,
> The Human Form a fiery Forge,
> The Human Face a Furnace seal'd,
> The Human Heart its hungry Gorge.
> Blake, *A Divine Image*

The Cenci occupies a curious place in Shelley's canon, one that is overtly apart from the sequence of his major works that goes from *Prometheus Unbound* to *The Triumph of Life*. Unlike the pseudo-Elizabethan tragedies of Shelley's disciple Beddoes, *The Cenci* is in no obvious way a visionary poem. Yet it is a tragedy only in a very peculiar sense, and has little in common with the stageplays it ostensibly seeks to emulate. Its true companions, and descendants, are Browning's giant progression of dramatic monologues, *The Ring and the Book*, and certain works of Hardy that share its oddly effective quality of what might be termed dramatic solipsism, to have recourse to a desperate oxymoron. Giant incongruities clash in *Prometheus Unbound* as they do in Blake's major poems, but the clashes are resolved by both poets in the realms of a self-generated mythology. When parallel incongruities meet violently in *The Cenci*, in a context that excludes myth, the reader is asked to accept as human characters beings whose states of mind are too radically and intensely pure to be altogether human. Blake courts a similar problem whenever he is only at the borderline of his own mythical world, as in *Visions of the Daughters of Albion* and *The French Revolution*. Shelley's Beatrice and Blake's Oothoon are either too human or not human enough; the reader is uncomfortable in not knowing whether he encounters a Titaness or one of his own kind.

Yet this discomfort need not wreck the experience of reading *The Cenci*, which is clearly a work that excels in character rather than in plot, and more in the potential of character than in its realization. At the heart of *The Cenci* is Shelley's very original conception of tragedy. Tragedy is not a congenial form for apocalyptic writers, who tend to have a severe grudge against it, as Blake and D. H. Lawrence did. Shelley's morality was an apocalyptic one, and the implicit standard for *The Cenci* is set in *The Mask of Anarchy*, which advocates a nonviolent resistance to evil. Beatrice is tragic because she does *not* meet this high standard, though she is clearly superior to every other person in her world. Life triumphs over Beatrice because she does take violent revenge upon an intolerable oppressor. The tragedy Shelley develops is one of a heroic character "violently thwarted from her nature" by circumstances she ought to have defied. This allies Beatrice with a large group of Romantic heroes, ranging from the Cain of Byron's drama to the pathetic daemon of Mary Shelley's *Frankenstein* and, on the cosmic level, embracing Shelley's own Prometheus and the erring Zoas or demigods of Blake's myth.

To find tragedy in any of these, you must persuasively redefine tragedy, as Shelley implicitly did. Tragedy becomes the fall of the imagination, or rather the falling away from imaginative conduct on the part of a heroically imaginative individual.

Count Cenci is, as many critics have noted, a demonic parody of Jehovah, and has a certain resemblance therefore to Shelley's Jupiter and Blake's Tiriel and Urizen. The count is obsessively given to hatred, and is vengeful, anal-erotic in his hoarding tendencies, incestuous, tyrannical, and compelled throughout by a jealous possessiveness even toward those he abhors. He is also given to bursts of Tiriel-like cursing, and like Tiriel or Jupiter he has his dying-god aspect, for his death symbolizes the necessity of revolution, the breaking up of an old and hopeless order. Like all heavenly tyrants in his tradition, Cenci's quest for dominion is marked by a passion for uniformity, and it is inevitable that he seek to reduce the angelic Beatrice to his own perverse level. His success is an ironic one, since he does harden her into the only agent sufficiently strong and remorseless to cause his own destruction.

The aesthetic power of *The Cenci* lies in the perfection with which it both sets forth Beatrice's intolerable dilemma, and presents the reader with a parallel dilemma. The natural man in the reader exults at Beatrice's metamorphosis into a relentless avenger, and approves even her untruthful denial of responsibility for her father's murder. The imaginative man in the reader is appalled at the degeneration of an all-but-angelic intelligence into a skilled intriguer and murderess. This fundamental dichotomy *in the reader* is the theater where the true anguish of *The Cenci* is enacted. The overt theme becomes the universal triumph of life over integrity, which is to say of death-in-life over life.

The Cenci is necessarily a work conceived in the Shakespearean shadow, and it is obvious that Shelley did not succeed in forming a dramatic language for himself in his play. Dr. Leavis has seized upon this failure with an inquisitor's joy, saying that "it takes no great discernment to see that *The Cenci* is very bad and that its badness is characteristic." It takes a very little discernment to see that *The Cenci* survives its palpable flaws and that it gives us what Wordsworth's *The Borderers*, Byron's *Cain*, and Coleridge's *Remorse* give us also in their very different ways, a distinguished example of Romantic, experimental tragedy, in which a crime against nature both emancipates consciousness and painfully turns consciousness in upon itself, with an attendant loss of a higher and more innocent state of being. The Beatrice of Shelley's last scene has learned her full autonomy, her absolute alienation from nature and society, but at a frightful, and to Shelley, a tragic cost.

> But were it not, that *Time* their troubler is,
> All that in this delightfull Gardin growes,
> Should happie be, and have immortall blis . . .
> Spenser

In the spring of 1820, at Pisa, Shelley wrote *The Sensitive Plant*, a remarkably original poem, and a permanently valuable one, though it is little admired in recent years. As a parable of imaginative failure, the poem is another of the many Romantic versions of the Miltonic Eden's transformation into a wasteland, but the limitations it explores are not the Miltonic ones of human irresolution and disobedience. Like all of Shelley's major poems, *The Sensitive Plant* is a skeptical work, the skepticism here manifesting itself

as a precariously poised suspension of judgment on the human capacity to perceive whether or not natural *or* imaginative values survive the cyclic necessities of change and decay.

The tone of *The Sensitive Plant* is a deliberate exquisitiveness, of
a more-than-Spenserian kind. Close analogues to this tone can be
found in major passages of Keats's *Endymion* and in Blake's *The
Book of Thel*. The ancestor poet for all these visionary poems, including Shelley's *The Witch of Atlas* and the vision of Beulah in
Blake's *Milton*, is of course Spenser, whose mythic version of the
lower or earthly paradise is presented as the Garden of Adonis in
The Faerie Queene, Book III, Canto VI, which is probably the most
influential passage of poetry in English, if by "influential" we mean
what influences other poets.

The dark melancholy of *The Sensitive Plant* is not Spenserian, but
everything else in the poem to some extent is. Like many poems in
this tradition, the lament is for mutability itself, for change seen as
loss. What is lost is innocence, natural harmony, the mutual inter-
penetrations of a merely given condition that is nevertheless whole
and beyond the need of justification. The new state, experiential life
as seen in Part III of the poem, is the world without imagination, a
tract of weeds. When Shelley, in the noblest quatrains he ever wrote,
broods on this conclusion he offers no consolation beyond the most
urbane of his skepticisms. The light that puts out our eyes is a darkness to us, yet remains light, and death may be a mockery of our
inadequate imaginations. The myth of the poem—its garden, lady,
and plant—may have prevailed, while we, the poem's readers, may
be too decayed in our perceptions to know this. Implicit in Shelley's
poem is a passionate refutation of time, but the passion is a desperation unless the mind's imaginings can cleanse perception of its ob-
scurities. Nothing in the poem proper testifies to the mind's mastery
of outward sense. The "Conclusion" hints at what Shelley beautifully calls "a modest creed," but the poet is too urbane and skeptical
to urge it upon either us or himself. The creed appears again in *The
Witch of Atlas*, but with a playful and amiable disinterestedness that
removes it almost entirely from the anguish of human desire.

The Witch of Atlas is Shelley's most inventive poem, and is by any
just standards a triumph. In kind, it goes back to the English Renaissance epyllion, the Ovidian erotic-mythological brief epic, but in
tone and procedure it is a new departure, except that for Shelley it
had been prophesied by his own rendition of the Homeric *Hymn to
Mercury*. Both poems are in *ottava rima*, both have a Byronic touch,

and both have been characterized accurately as possessing a tone of visionary cynicism. Hermes and the Witch of Atlas qualify the divine grandeurs among which they move, and remind us that imagination unconfined respects no orders of being, however traditional or natural.

G. Wilson Knight first pointed to the clear resemblance between the tone of *The Witch of Atlas* and Yeats's later style, and there is considerable evidence of the permanent effect of the poem's fantastic plot and properties upon Yeats. Shelley's *Witch* is Yeats's *Byzantium* writ large; both poems deal with Phase 15 of Yeats's *A Vision*, with the phase of poetic incarnation, and so with the state of the soul in which art is created. In a comparison of the two poems, the immediate contrast will be found in the extraordinary relaxation that Shelley allows himself. The nervous intensity that the theme demands is present in the *Witch*, but has been transmuted into an almost casual acceptance of intolerable realities that art cannot mitigate.

The Witch of Atlas, as Shelley says in the poem's highly ironic dedicatory stanzas to his wife, tells no story, false or true, but is "a visionary rhyme." If the Witch is to be translated at all into terms not her own, then she can only be the mythopoeic impulse or inventive faculty itself, one of whose manifestations is the Hermaphrodite, which we can translate as a poem, or any work of art. The Witch's boat is the emblem of her creative desire, and like the Hermaphrodite it works against nature. The Hermaphrodite is both a convenience for the Witch, helping her to go beyond natural limitations, and a companion of sorts, but a highly inadequate one, being little more than a robot. The limitations of art are involved here, for the Witch has rejected the love of every mortal being, and has chosen instead an automation of her own creation. In the poignant stanzas in which she rejects the suit of the nymphs, Shelley attains one of the immense triumphs of his art, but the implications of the triumph, and of the entire poem, are as deliberately chilling as the Byzantine vision of the aging Yeats.

Though the Witch turns her playful and antinomian spirit to the labor of upsetting church and state, in the poem's final stanzas, and subverts even the tired conventions of mortality as well as of morality, the ultimate impression she makes upon us is one of remoteness. The fierce aspirations of *Prometheus Unbound* were highly qualified by a consciously manipulated prophetic irony, yet they retained their force, and aesthetic immediacy, as the substance of what Shelley passionately desired. The ruin that shadows love in *Prometheus Un-*

bound, the *amphisbaena* or two-headed serpent that could move downward and outward to destruction again, the warning made explicit in the closing stanzas spoken by Demogorgon; it is these antithetical hints that survived in Shelley longer than the vehement hope of his lyrical drama. *The Sensitive Plant* and *The Witch of Atlas* manifest a subtle movement away from that hope. *Epipsychidion*, the most exalted of Shelley's poems, seeks desperately to renovate that hope by placing it in the context of heterosexual love, and with the deliberate and thematic self-combustion of the close of *Epipsychidion* Shelley appears to have put all hope aside, and to have prepared himself for his magnificent but despairing last phase, of which the enduring monuments are *Adonais* and *The Triumph of Life*.

> What man most passionately wants is his living wholeness and his living unison, not his own isolate salvation of his "soul." Man wants his physical fulfillment first and foremost, since now, once and once only, he is in the flesh and potent. For man, as for flower and beast and bird, the supreme triumph is to be most vividly, most perfectly alive. Whatever the unborn and the dead may know, they cannot know the beauty, the marvel of being alive in the flesh. The dead may look after the afterwards. But the magnificent here and now of life in the flesh is ours, and ours alone, and ours only for a time.
> D. H. Lawrence, *Apocalypse*

Except for Blake's *Visions of the Daughters of Albion*, which it in some respects resembles, *Epipsychidion* is the most outspoken and eloquent appeal for free love in the language. Though this appeal is at the heart of the poem, and dominates its most famous passage (lines 147–54), it is only one aspect of a bewilderingly problematical work. *Epipsychidion* was intended by Shelley to be his *Vita Nuova*, celebrating the discovery of his Beatrice in Emilia Viviani. It proved however to be a climactic and not an initiatory poem, for in it Shelley culminates the quest begun in *Alastor*, only to find after culmination that the quest remains unfulfilled and unfulfillable. The desire of Shelley remains infinite, and the only emblem adequate to that desire is the morning and evening star, Venus, at whose sphere the shadow cast by earth into the heavens reaches its limits. After *Epipsychidion*, in *Adonais* and *The Triumph of Life*, only the star of Venus abides as an image of the good. It is not Emilia Viviani but her image that proves inadequate in *Epipsychidion*, a poem whose most turbulent and valuable element is its struggle to record the process of image-making. Of all Shelley's major poems, *Epipsychidion* most directly concerns itself with the mind in creation. *Mont Blanc* has the same position among Shelley's shorter poems, and has the advantage of its relative discursiveness, as the poet meditates upon the awesome spectacle before him. *Epipsychidion* is continuous rhapsody, and sustains its lyrical intensity of a lovers' confrontation for six hundred lines. The mind in creation, here and in *A Defense of Poetry*, is as a fading coal, and much of Shelley's art in the poem is devoted to the fading phenomenon, as image after image recedes and the poet-lover feels more fearfully the double burden of his love's inexpressibility and its necessary refusal to accept even natural, let alone societal limitations.

There is, in Shelley's development as a poet, a continuous effort to subvert the poetic image, so as to arrive at a more radical kind of verbal figure, which Shelley never altogether achieved. Tenor and vehicle are imported into one another, and the choice of natural images increasingly favors those already on the point of vanishing, just within the ken of eye and ear. The world is skeptically taken up into the mind, and there are suggestions and overtones that all of reality is a phantasmagoria. Shelley becomes an idealist totally skeptical of the metaphysical foundations of idealism, while he continues to entertain a skeptical materialism, or rather he becomes a fantasist pragmatically given to some materialist hypotheses that his imagination regards as absurd. This is not necessarily a self-contradiction, but it is a kind of psychic split, and it is exposed very powerfully in *Epipsychidion*. Who wins a triumph in the poem, the gambler with the limits of poetry and of human relationship, or the inexorable limits? Space, time, loneliness, mortality, wrong—all these are put aside by vision, yet vision darkens perpetually in the poem. "The world, unfortunately, is real; I, unfortunately, am Borges," is the ironic reflection of a great contemporary seer of phantasmagorias, as he brings his refutation of time to an unrefuting close. Shelley too is swept along by what destroys him and is inescapable, the reality that will not yield to the most relentless of imaginings. In that knowledge, he turns to elegy and away from celebration.

Adonais, Shelley's formal elegy for Keats, is a great monument in the history of the English elegy, and yet hardly an elegy at all. Nearly five hundred lines long, it exceeds in scope and imaginative ambition its major English ancestors, the *Astrophel* of Spenser and the *Lycidas* of Milton, as well as such major descendants as Arnold's *Thyrsis* and Swinburne's *Ave Atque Vale*. Only Tennyson's *In Memoriam* rivals

it as an attempt to make the elegy a vehicle for not less than everything a particular poet has to say on the ultimates of human existence. Yet Tennyson, for all his ambition, stays within the bounds of
elegy. *Adonais,* in the astonishing sequence of its last eighteen stanzas, is no more an elegy proper than Yeats's *Byzantium* poems are.
Like the *Byzantium* poems (which bear a close relation to it) *Adonais*
is a high song of poetic self-recognition in the presence of foreshad-
owing death, and also a description of poetic existence, even of a
poem's state of being.

Whether Shelley holds together the elegiac and visionary aspects
of his poem is disputable; it is difficult to see the full continuity that
takes the poet from his hopeless opening to his more than triumphant
close, from:

> I weep for Adonais—he is dead!
> O, weep for Adonais! though our tears
> Thaw not the frost which binds so dear a head!

to:

> I am borne darkly, fearfully, afar;
> Whilst, burning through the inmost veil of Heaven,
> The soul of Adonais, like a star,
> Beacons from the abode where the Eternal are.

From frost to fire as a mode of renewal for the self: that is an archetypal Romantic pattern, familiar to us from *The Ancient Mariner*
and the *Intimations* Ode (see the contrast between the last line of
stanza VIII and the first of stanza IX in that poem). But *Adonais*
breaks this pattern, for the soul of Shelley's Keats burns through the
final barrier to revelation only by means of an energy that is set
against nature, and the frost that no poetic tears can thaw yields only
to "the fire for which all thirst," but which no natural man can drink,
for no living man can drink of the whole wine of the burning fountain. As much as Yeats's *All Souls' Night, Adonais* reaches out to a
reality of ghostly intensities, yet Shelley as well as Yeats is reluctant
to leave behind the living man who blindly drinks his drop, and *Adonais* is finally a *Dialogue of Self and Soul,* in which the Soul wins a
costly victory, as costly as the Self's triumph in Yeats's *Dialogue.*
The Shelley who cries out, in rapture and dismay, "The massy earth
and spherèd skies are riven!" is a poet who has given himself freely
to the tempest of creative destruction, to a reality beyond the natural,
yet who movingly looks back upon the shore and upon the throng he
has forsaken. The close of *Adonais* is a triumph of character over

110

personality, to use a Yeatsian dialectic, but the personality of the lyric poet is nevertheless the dominant aesthetic element in the poem's dark and fearful apotheosis.

"Apotheosis is not the origin of the major man," if we are to credit Stevens, but the qualified assertions of Shelley do proclaim such an imaginative humanism in the central poems that preceded *Adonais*. In *Adonais* the imagination forsakes humanism, even as it does in the *Byzantium* poems.

Though *Adonais* has been extensively Platonized and Neoplatonized by a troop of interpreters, it is in a clear sense a materialist's poem, written out of a materialist's despair at his own deepest convictions, and finally a poem soaring above those convictions into a mystery that leaves a pragmatic materialism quite undisturbed. Whatever supernal apprehension it is that Shelley attains in the final third of *Adonais*, it is not in any ordinary sense a religious faith, for the only attitude toward natural existence it fosters in the poet is one of unqualified rejection, and indeed its pragmatic postulate is simply suicide. Nothing could be more different in spirit from Demogorgon's closing lines in *Prometheus Unbound* than the final stanzas of *Adonais*, and the ruthlessly skeptical Shelley must have known this.

He knew also though that we do not judge poems by pragmatic tests, and the splendor of the resolution to *Adonais* is not impaired by its implications of human defeat. Whether Keats lives again is unknown to Shelley; poets are among "the enduring dead," and Keats "wakes *or* sleeps" with them. The endurance is not then necessarily a mode of survival, and what flows back to the burning fountain is not necessarily the *human* soul, though it is "pure spirit." Or if it is the soul of Keats as well as "the soul of Adonais," then the accidents of individual personality have abandoned it, making this cold comfort indeed. Still, Shelley is not offering us (or himself) comfort; his elegy has no parallel to Milton's consolation in *Lycidas*:

> There entertain him all the Saints above,
> In solemn troops, and sweet Societies
> That sing, and singing in their glory move,
> And wipe the tears forever from his eyes.

To Milton, as a Christian poet, death is somehow unnatural. To Shelley, for all his religious temperament, death is wholly natural, and if death is dead, then nature must be dead also. The final third of *Adonais* is desperately apocalyptic in a way that *Prometheus Unbound*, Act IV, was not. For *Prometheus Unbound* ends in a Saturnalia, though there are darker implications also, but *Adonais* soars beyond the shadow that the earth casts into the heavens. Shelley was ready for a purgatorial vision of earth, and no longer could sustain even an ironic hope.

> Mal dare, e mal tener lo mondo pulcro
> ha tolto loro, e posti a questa zuffa;
> qual ella sia, parole non ci appulcro.
> *Inferno* 7:58–60

> That ill they gave,
> And ill they kept, hath of the beauteous world
> Deprived, and set them at this strife, which needs
> No labour'd phrase of mine to set it off.
> Cary, *The Vision of Dante*

There are elements in *The Triumph of Life,* Shelley's last poem, that mark it as an advance over all the poetry he had written previously. The bitter eloquence and dramatic condensation of the style are new; so is a ruthless pruning of invention. The mythic figures are few, being confined to the "Shape all light," the charioteer, and Life itself, while the two principal figures, Shelley and Rousseau, appear in their proper persons, though in the perspective of eternity, as befits a vision of judgment. The tone of Shelley's last poem is derived from Dante's *Purgatorio,* even as much in *Epipsychidion* comes from Dante's *Vita Nuova,* but the events and atmosphere of *The Triumph of Life* have more in common with the *Inferno.* Still, the poem is a purgatorial work, for all the unrelieved horror of its vision, and perhaps Shelley might have found some gradations in his last vision, so as to climb out of the poem's impasse, if he had lived to finish it, though I incline to doubt this. As it stands, the poem is in hell, and Shelley is there, one of the apparently condemned, as all men are, he says, save for "the sacred few" of Athens and Jerusalem, martyrs to vision like Socrates, Jesus, and a chosen handful, with whom on the basis of *Adonais* we can place Keats, as he too had touched the world with his living flame, and then fled back up to his native noon.

The highest act of Shelley's imagination in the poem, perhaps in all of his poetry, is in the magnificent appropriateness of Rousseau's presence, from his first entrance to his last speech before the fragment breaks off. Rousseau is Virgil to Shelley's Dante, in the sense of being his imaginative ancestor, his guide in creation, and also in prophesying the dilemma the disciple would face at the point of crisis in his life. Shelley, sadly enough, was hardly in the middle of the journey, but at twenty-nine he had only days to live, and the imagination in him felt compelled to face the last things. Without Rousseau, Shelley would not have written the *Hymn to Intellectual Beauty* and perhaps not *Mont Blanc* either. Rousseau, more even than Wordsworth, was the prophet of natural man, and the celebrator of the state of nature. Even in 1816, writing his hymns and starting the process that would lead to the conception of *Prometheus Unbound*, Shelley fights against the natural man and natural religion, but he fights partly against his own desires, and the vision of Rousseau haunts him still in the *Ode to the West Wind* and in the greatest chant of the apocalyptic fourth act of the lyrical drama, the song of the Earth beginning "It interpenetrates my granite mass." Shelley knew that the spirit of Rousseau was what had moved him most in the spirit of the age, and temperamentally (which counts for most in a poet) it makes more sense to name Shelley the disciple and heir of Rousseau than of Godwin, or Wordsworth, or any of the later French theorists of Revolution. Rousseau and Hume make an odd formula of heart and head in Shelley, but they are the closest parallels to be found to him on the emotional and intellectual sides respectively.

Chastened and knowing, almost beyond knowledge, Rousseau enters the poem, speaking not to save his disciple, but to show him that he cannot be saved, and to teach him a style fit for his despair. The imaginative lesson of *The Triumph of Life* is wholly present in the poem's title: life always triumphs, for life our life is after all what the Preface to *Alastor* called it, a "lasting misery and loneliness." One Power only, the Imagination, is capable of redeeming life, "but that Power which strikes the luminaries of the world with sudden darkness and extinction, by awakening them to too exquisite a perception of its influences, dooms to a slow and poisonous decay those meaner spirits that dare to abjure its dominion." In *The Triumph of Life*, the world's luminaries are still the poets, stars of evening and morning, "heaven's living eyes," but they fade into a double light, the light of nature or the sun, and the harsher and more blinding light of Life, the destructive chariot of the poem's vision. The chariot of Life, like the apocalyptic chariots of Act IV, *Prometheus Unbound*, goes back to the visions of Ezekiel and Revelation for its sources, as the chariots of Dante and Milton did, but now Shelley gives a demonic parody of his sources, possibly following the example of Spenser's chariot of Lucifera. Rousseau is betrayed to the light of Life because he began by yielding his imagination's light to the lesser but seductive light of nature, represented in the poem by the "Shape all light" who offers him the waters of natural experience to drink. He drinks, he begins to forget everything in the mind's desire that had transcended nature, and so he falls victim to Life's destruction, and fails to become one of "the sacred few." There is small reason to doubt that Shelley, at the end, saw himself as having shared in Rousseau's fate. The poem, fragment as it is, survives its own despair, and stands with Keats's *The Fall of Hyperion* as a marvelously eloquent imaginative testament, fit relic of an achievement broken off too soon to rival Blake's or Wordsworth's, but superior to everything else in its own age.

> The great instrument of moral good is the imagination.
> *A Defense of Poetry*

Anti-Shelleyans have come in all intellectual shapes and sizes, and have included distinguished men of letters from Charles Lamb and De Quincey down to T. S. Eliot, Allen Tate, and their school in our day. To distinguish between the kinds of anti-Shelleyans is instructive, though the following categories are by no means mutually exclusive. One can count six major varieties of anti-Shelleyans, whether one considers them historically or in contemporary terms:

(1) The school of "common sense"
(2) The Christian orthodox
(3) The school of "wit"
(4) Moralists, of most varieties
(5) The school of "classic" form
(6) Precisionists, or concretists.

It is evident that examples of (1), (2), and (4) need not be confuted, as they are merely irrelevant. We may deal with (3), (5), and (6) in their own terms, rather than in Shelley's, and still find Shelley triumphant.

The "wit" of Shelley's poetry has little to do with that of seventeenth-century verse, but has much in common with the dialectical vivacity of Shaw, and something of the prophetic irony of Blake. If irony is an awareness of the terrible gap between aspiration and fulfillment, then the skeptical Shelley is among the most ironical of poets. If it is something else, as it frequently is in the school of Donne, one can observe that there are many wings in the house of wit, and one ought not to live in all of them simultaneously.

Form is another matter, and too complex to be argued fully here. The late C. S. Lewis justly maintained against the school of Eliot that Shelley was more classical in his sense of form, his balance of harmony and design, than Dryden. One can go further: Shelley is almost always a poet of the highest decorum, a stylist who adjusts his form and tone to his subject, whether it be the hammer-beat low style of *The Mask of Anarchy*, the urbane middle style of the *Letter to Maria Gisborne*, or the sublime inventiveness of the high style as it is renovated in *Prometheus Unbound*. Shelley was sometimes a hasty or careless artist, but he was always an artist, a poet who neither could nor would stop being a poet. Dr. Samuel Johnson would have disliked Shelley's poetry, indeed would have considered Shelley to be dangerously mad, but he would have granted that it was poetry of a high if to him outmoded order. Critics less classical than Johnson will not grant as much, because their notions of classical form are not as deeply founded.

The precisionist or concretist is probably Shelley's most effective enemy, since everything vital in Shelley's poetry deliberately strains away from the minute particulars of experience. But this is oddly true of Wordsworth as well, though Wordsworth usually insisted upon the opposite. The poetry of renovation in the United States, in our time, had its chief exemplars in William Carlos Williams and in Wallace Stevens, and it is Stevens who is in the line of both Wordsworth and of Shelley. Williams's famous adage, "no ideas but in things," is the self-justified motto of one valid kind of poetic procedure, but it will not allow for the always relevant grandeurs of the sublime tradition, with its "great moments" of ecstasy and recognition. Wordsworth on the mountainside looks out and finds only a sea of mist, an emblem of the highest imaginative vision, in which the edges of things have blurred and faded out. Stevens, opening the door of his house upon the flames of the Northern Lights, confronts an Arctic effulgence flaring upon the frame of everything he is, but does not describe the flashing auroras. Shelley, at his greatest, precisely chants an energetic becoming that cannot be described in the concrete because its entire purpose is to modify the concrete, to compel a greater reality to appear:

> . . . the one Spirit's plastic stress
> Sweeps through the dull dense world, compelling there,
> All new successions to the forms they wear;
> Torturing th' unwilling dross that checks its flight
> To its own likeness, as each mass may bear;
> And bursting in its beauty and its might
> From trees and beasts and men into the Heaven's light.

Had Shelley been able to accept any known faith, he would have given us the name and nature of that "one Spirit." Unlike Keats, he would not have agreed with Stevens that the great poems of heaven and hell had been written, and that only the great poem of earth remained to be composed. His own spirit was apocalyptic, and the still unwritten poems of heaven and hell waited mute upon the answering swiftness of his own imaginings, when he went on to his early finalities:

> As if that frail and wasted human form,
> Had been an elemental god.

1965

8
Frankenstein,
or The Modern Prometheus

> ... there is a fire
> And motion of the soul which will not dwell
> In its own narrow being, but aspire
> Beyond the fitting medium of desire. ...
> Byron, *Childe Harold's Pilgrimage*
> Canto III

> ... Ere Babylon was dust,
> The Magus Zoroaster, my dead child,
> Met his own image walking in the garden.
> That apparition, sole of men, he saw.
> For know there are two worlds of life and death:
> One that which thou beholdest; but the other
> Is underneath the grave, where do inhabit
> The shadows of all forms that think and live
> Till death unite them and they part no more ...
> Shelley, *Prometheus Unbound*
> Act I

The motion-picture viewer who carries his obscure but still authentic taste for the sublime to the neighborhood theater, there to see the latest in an unending series of *Frankensteins*, becomes a sharer in a romantic terror now nearly one hundred and fifty years old. Mary Shelley, barely nineteen years of age when she wrote the original *Frankenstein*, was the daughter of two great intellectual rebels, William Godwin and Mary Wollstonecraft, and the second wife of Percy Bysshe Shelley, another great rebel and an unmatched lyrical poet. Had she written nothing, Mary Shelley would be remembered today. She is remembered in her own right as the author of a novel valuable in itself but also prophetic of an intellectual world to come, a novel depicting a Prometheanism that is with us still.

"Frankenstein," to most of us, is the name of a monster rather than of a monster's creator, for the common reader and the common viewer have worked together, in their apparent confusion, to create a myth soundly based on a central duality in Mrs. Shelley's novel. A critical discussion of *Frankenstein* needs to begin from an insight first recorded by Richard Church and Muriel Spark: the monster and his creator are the antithetical halves of a single being. Miss Spark states the antithesis too cleanly; for her Victor Frankenstein represents the feelings, and his nameless creature the intellect. In her view the monster has no emotion, and "what passes for emotion . . . are really intellectual passions arrived at through rational channels." Miss Spark carries this argument far enough to insist that the monster is asexual and that he demands a bride from Frankenstein only for companionship, a conclusion evidently at variance with the novel's text.

The antithesis between the scientist and his creature in *Frankenstein* is a very complex one and can be described more fully in the larger context of Romantic literature and its characteristic mythology. The shadow or double of the self is a constant conceptual image in Blake and Shelley and a frequent image, more random and descriptive, in the other major Romantics, especially in Byron. In *Frankenstein* it is the dominant and recurrent image and accounts for much of the latent power the novel possesses.

Mary Shelley's husband was a divided being, as man and as poet, just as his friend Byron was, though in Shelley the split was more radical. *Frankenstein: or, The Modern Prometheus* is the full title of Mrs. Shelley's novel, and while Victor Frankenstein is *not* Shelley (Clerval is rather more like the poet), the Modern Prometheus is a very apt term for Shelley or for Byron. Prometheus is the mythic figure who best suits the uses of Romantic poetry, for no other traditional being has in him the full range of Romantic moral sensibility and the full Romantic capacity for creation and destruction.

No Romantic writer employed the Prometheus archetype without a full awareness of its equivocal potentialities. The Prometheus of the ancients had been for the most part a spiritually reprehensible figure, though frequently a sympathetic one, in terms both of his dramatic situation and in his close alliance with mankind against the gods. But this alliance had been ruinous for man in most versions of the myth, and the Titan's benevolence toward humanity was hardly sufficient recompense for the alienation of man from heaven that he had brought about. Both sides of Titanism are evident in earlier Christian references to the story. The same Prometheus who is taken as an analogue of the crucified Christ is regarded also as a type of Lucifer, a son of light justly cast out by an offended heaven.

In the Romantic readings of Milton's *Paradise Lost* (and *Frankenstein* is implicitly one such reading) this double identity of Prometheus is a vital element. Blake, whose mythic revolutionary named Orc is another version of Prometheus, saw Milton's Satan as a Prometheus gone wrong, as desire restrained until it became only the shadow of desire, a diminished double of creative energy. Shelley went further in judging Milton's Satan as an imperfect Prometheus, inadequate because his mixture of heroic and base qualities engendered in the reader's mind a "pernicious casuistry" inimical to the spirit of art.

Blake, more systematic a poet than Shelley, worked out an antithesis between symbolic figures he named Spectre and Emanation, the shadow of desire and the total form of desire, respectively. A reader of *Frankenstein*, recalling the novel's extraordinary conclusion, with its scenes of obsessional pursuit through the Arctic wastes, can recognize the same imagery applied to a similar symbolic situation in Blake's lyric on the strife of Spectre and Emanation:

> My Spectre around me night and day
> Like a Wild beast guards my way.
> My Emanation far within
> Weeps incessantly for my Sin.
>
> A Fathomless and boundless deep,
> There we wander, there we weep;
> On the hungry craving wind
> My Spectre follows thee behind.
>
> He scents thy footsteps in the snow,
> Wheresoever thou dost go
> Thro' the wintry hail and rain. . . .

Frankenstein's monster, tempting his revengeful creator on through a world of ice, is another Emanation pursued by a Spectre, with the enormous difference that he is an Emanation flawed, a nightmare of actuality, rather than dream of desire. Though abhorred rather than loved, the monster is the total form of Frankenstein's creative power and is *more imaginative* than his creator. The monster is at once more intellectual and more emotional than his maker; indeed he excels Frankenstein as much (and in the same ways) as Milton's Adam excels Milton's God in *Paradise Lost*. The greatest paradox and most astonishing achievement of Mary Shelley's novel is that the monster is *more human* than his creator. This nameless being, as much a Modern Adam as his creator is a Modern Prometheus, is more lovable than his creator and more hateful, more to be pitied and more to be feared, and above all more able to give the attentive reader that shock of added consciousness in which aesthetic recognition compels a heightened realization of the self. For like Blake's Spectre and Emanation or Shelley's Alastor and Epipsyche, Frankenstein and his monster are the solipsistic and generous halves of the one self. Frankenstein is the mind and emotions turned in upon themselves, and his creature is the mind and emotions turned imaginatively outward, seeking a greater humanization through a confrontation of other selves.

I am suggesting that what makes *Frankenstein* an important book, though it is only a strong, flawed novel with frequent clumsiness in its narrative and characterization, is that it contains one of the most vivid versions we have of the Romantic mythology of the self, one that resembles Blake's *Book of Urizen*, Shelley's *Prometheus Unbound*, and Byron's *Manfred*, among other works. Because it lacks the sophistication and imaginative complexity of such works, *Frankenstein* affords a unique introduction to the archetypal world of the Romantics.

William Godwin, though a tendentious novelist, was a powerful one, and the prehistory of his daughter's novel begins with his best work of fiction, *Caleb Williams* (1794). Godwin summarized the climactic (and harrowing) final third of his novel as a pattern of flight and pursuit, "the fugitive in perpetual apprehension of being overwhelmed with the worst calamities, and the pursuer, by his ingenuity and resources, keeping his victim in a state of the most fearful alarm." Mary Shelley brilliantly reverses this pattern in the final sequence of her novel, and she takes from *Caleb Williams* also her destructive theme of the monster's war against "the whole machinery of human society," to quote the words of Caleb Williams while in prison. Muriel Spark argues that *Frankenstein* can be read as a reaction "against the rational-humanism of Godwin and Shelley," and she points to the equivocal preface that Shelley wrote to his wife's novel, in order to support this view. Certainly Shelley was worried lest the novel be taken as a warning against the inevitable moral consequences of an unchecked experimental Prometheanism and scientific materialism. The preface insists that:

> The opinions which naturally spring from the character and situation of the hero are by no means to be conceived as existing always in my own conviction; nor is any inference justly to be drawn from the following pages as prejudicing any philosophical doctrine of whatever kind.

Shelley had, throughout his own work, a constant reaction against Godwin's rational humanism, but his reaction was systematically and consciously one of heart against head. In the same summer in the Swiss Alps that saw the conception of *Frankenstein*, Shelley composed two poems that lift the thematic conflict of the novel to the level of the true sublime. In the *Hymn to Intellectual Beauty* the poet's heart interprets an inconstant grace and loveliness, always just beyond the range of the human senses, as being the only beneficent force in life, and he prays to this force to be more constant in its attendance upon him and all mankind. In a greater sister-hymn, *Mont Blanc,* an awesome meditation upon a frightening natural scene, the poet's head issues an allied but essentially contrary report. The force, or power, is there, behind or within the mountain, but its external workings upon us are either indifferent or malevolent, and this power is not to be prayed to. It can teach us, but what it teaches us is our own dangerous freedom from nature, the necessity for our will to become a significant part of materialistic necessity. Though *Mont Blanc* works its way to an almost heroic conclusion, it is also a poem of horror and reminds us that Frankenstein first confronts his conscious monster in the brooding presence of Mont Blanc, and to the restless music of one of Shelley's lyrics of Mutability.

In *Prometheus Unbound* the split between head and heart is not healed, but the heart is allowed dominance. The hero, Prometheus, like Frankenstein, has made a monster, but this monster is Jupiter, the God of all institutional and historical religions, including organized Christianity. Salvation from this conceptual error comes through love alone; but love in this poem, as elsewhere in Shelley, is always closely shadowed by ruin. Indeed, what choice spirits in Shelley perpetually encounter is ruin masquerading as love, pain presenting itself as pleasure. The tentative way out of this situation in Shelley's poetry is through the quest for a feeling mind and an understanding heart, which is symbolized by the sexual reunion of Prometheus and his Emanation, Asia. Frederick A. Pottle sums up *Prometheus Unbound* by observing its meaning to be that "the head must sincerely forgive, must willingly eschew hatred on purely experimental grounds," while "the affections must exorcize the demons of infancy, whether personal or of the race." In the light cast by these profound and precise summations, the reader can better understand both Shelley's lyrical drama and his wife's narrative of the Modern Prometheus.

There are two paradoxes at the center of Mrs. Shelley's novel, and each illuminates a dilemma of the Promethean imagination. The first is that Frankenstein *was* successful, in that he did create Natural Man, not as he was, but as the meliorists saw such a man; indeed, Frankenstein did better than this, since his creature was, as we have seen, more imaginative than himself. Frankenstein's tragedy stems not from his Promethean excess but from his own moral error, his failure to love; he *abhorred his creature*, became terrified, and fled his responsibilities.

The second paradox is the more ironic. This either would not have happened or would not have mattered anyway, if Frankenstein had been an aesthetically successful maker; a beautiful "monster," or even a passable one, would not have been a monster. As the creature bitterly observes in Chapter 17:

> Shall I respect man when he contemns me? Let him live with me in the interchange of kindness, and instead of injury I would bestow every benefit upon him with tears of gratitude at his acceptance. But that cannot be; the human senses are insurmountable barriers to our union.

As the hideousness of his creature was no part of Victor Frankenstein's intention, it is worth noticing how this disastrous matter came to be.

It would not be unjust to characterize Victor Frankenstein, in his act of creation, as being momentarily a moral idiot, like so many who have done his work after him. There is an indeliberate humor in the contrast between the enormity of the scientist's discovery and the mundane emotions of the discoverer. Finding that "the minuteness of the parts" slows him down, he resolves to make his creature "about eight feet in height and proportionably large." As he works on, he allows himself to dream that "a new species would bless me as its creator and source; many happy and excellent natures would owe their being to me." Yet he knows his is a "workshop of filthy creation," and he fails the fundamental test of his own creativity. When the "dull yellow eye" of his creature opens, this creator falls from the autonomy of a supreme artificer to the terror of a child of earth: "breathless horror and disgust filled my heart." He flees his responsibility and sets in motion the events that will lead to his own Arctic immolation, a fit end for a being who has never achieved a full sense of another's existence.

Haunting Mary Shelley's novel is the demonic figure of the Ancient Mariner, Coleridge's major venture into Romantic mythology of the purgatorial self trapped in the isolation of a heightened self-consciousness. Walton, in Letter 2 introducing the novel, compares himself "to that production of the most imaginative of modern poets." As a seeker-out of an unknown passage, Walton is himself a

Promethean quester, like Frankenstein, toward whom he is so compellingly drawn. Coleridge's Mariner is of the line of Cain, and the irony of Frankenstein's fate is that he too is a Cain, involuntarily murdering all his loved ones through the agency of his creature. The Ancient Mariner is punished by living under the curse of his consciousness of guilt, while the excruciating torment of Frankenstein is never to be able to forget his guilt in creating a lonely consciousness driven to crime by the rage of unwilling solitude.

It is part of Mary Shelley's insight into her mythological theme that all the monster's victims are innocents. The monster not only refuses actively to slay his guilty creator, he *mourns* for him, though with the equivocal tribute of terming the scientist a "generous and self-devoted being." Frankenstein, the Modern Prometheus who has violated nature, receives his epitaph from the ruined second nature he has made, the God-abandoned, who consciously echoes the ruined Satan of *Paradise Lost* and proclaims, "Evil thenceforth became my good." It is imaginatively fitting that the greater and more interesting consciousness of the creature should survive his creator, for he alone in Mrs. Shelley's novel possesses character. Frankenstein, like Coleridge's Mariner, has no character in his own right; both figures win a claim to our attention only by their primordial crimes against original nature.

The monster is of course Mary Shelley's finest invention, and his narrative (Chapters 11 through 16) forms the highest achievement of the novel, more absorbing even than the magnificent and almost surrealistic pursuit of the climax. In an age so given to remarkable depictions of the dignity of natural man, an age including the shepherds and beggars of Wordsworth and what W. J. Bate has termed Keats's "polar ideal of disinterestedness"—even in such a literary time Frankenstein's hapless creature stands out as a sublime embodiment of heroic pathos. Though Frankenstein lacks the moral imagination to understand him, the daemon's appeal is to what is most compassionate in us:

> Oh, Frankenstein, be not equitable to every other, and trample upon me alone, to whom thy justice, and even thy clemency and affection, is most due. Remember that I am thy creature; *I ought to be thy Adam, but I am rather the fallen angel, whom thou drivest from joy for no misdeed.* Everywhere I see bliss, from which I alone am irrevocably excluded. I was benevolent and good; misery made me a fiend. Make me happy, and I shall again be virtuous."

The passage I have italicized is the imaginative kernel of the novel and is meant to remind the reader of the novel's epigraph:

> Did I request thee, Maker, from my clay
> To mold me man? Did I solicit thee
> From darkness to promote me?

That desperate plangency of the fallen Adam becomes the characteristic accent of the daemon's lamentations, with the influence of Milton cunningly built into the novel's narrative by the happy device of Frankenstein's creature receiving his education through reading *Paradise Lost* "as a true history." Already doomed because his standards are human, which makes him an outcast even to himself, his Miltonic education completes his fatal growth in self-consciousness. His story, as told to his maker, follows a familiar Romantic pattern "of the progress of my intellect," as he puts it. His first pleasure after the dawn of consciousness comes through his wonder at seeing the moon rise. Caliban-like, he responds wonderfully to music, both natural and human, and his sensitivity to the natural world has the responsiveness of an incipient poet. His awakening to a first love for other beings, the inmates of the cottage he haunts, awakens him also to the great desolation of love rejected when he attempts to reveal himself. His own duality of situation and character, caught between the states of Adam and Satan, Natural Man and his thwarted desire, is related by him directly to his reading of Milton's epic:

> It moved every feeling of wonder and awe that the picture of an omnipotent God warring with his creatures was capable of exciting. I often referred the several situations, as their similarity struck me, to my own. Like Adam, I was apparently united by no link to any other being in existence, but his state was far different from mine in every other respect. He had come forth from the hands of God a perfect creature, happy and prosperous, guarded by the especial care of his Creator; he was allowed to converse with and acquire knowledge from beings of a superior nature; but I was wretched, helpless, and alone. Many times I considered Satan as the fitter emblem of my condition, for often, like him, when I viewed the bliss of my protectors, the bitter gall of envy rose within me.

From a despair this profound, no release is possible. Driven forth into an existence upon which "the cold stars shone in mockery," the daemon declares "everlasting war against the species" and enters upon a fallen existence more terrible than the expelled Adam's. Echoing Milton, he asks the ironic question "And now, with the world before me, whither should I bend my steps?" to which the only possible answer is, toward his wretched Promethean creator.

If we stand back from Mary Shelley's novel in order better to view its archetypal shape, we see it as the quest of a solitary and ravaged consciousness first for consolation, then for revenge, and finally for a self-destruction that will be apocalyptic, that will bring down the creator with his creature. Though Mary Shelley may not have intended it, her novel's prime theme is a necessary counterpoise to Prometheanism, for Prometheanism exalts the increase in consciousness despite all cost. Frankenstein breaks through the barrier that separates man from God and gives apparent life, but in doing so he gives only death-in-life. The profound dejection endemic in Mary Shelley's novel is fundamental to the Romantic mythology of the self, for all Romantic horrors are diseases of excessive consciousness, of the self unable to bear the self. Kierkegaard remarks that Satan's despair is absolute because Satan, as pure spirit, is pure consciousness, and for Satan (and all men in his predicament) every increase in consciousness is an increase in despair. Frankenstein's desperate creature attains the state of pure spirit through his extraordinary situation and is racked by a consciousness in which every thought is a fresh disease.

A Romantic poet fought against self-consciousness through the strength of what he called imagination, a more than rational energy by which thought could seek to heal itself. But Frankenstein's daemon, though he is in the archetypal situation of the Romantic Wanderer or Solitary, who sometimes was a poet, can win no release from his own story by telling it. His desperate desire for a mate is clearly an attempt to find a Shelleyan Epipsyche or Blakean Emanation for himself, a self within the self. But as he is the nightmare actualization of Frankenstein's desire, he is himself an emanation of Promethean yearnings, and his only double is his creator and denier.

When Coleridge's Ancient Mariner progressed from the purgatory of consciousness to his very minimal control of imagination, he failed to save himself, since he remained in a cycle of remorse, but he at least became a salutary warning to others and made of the Wedding Guest a wiser and a better man. Frankenstein's creature can help neither himself nor others, for he has no natural ground to which he can return. Romantic poets liked to return to the imagery of the ocean of life and immortality, for in the eddying to and fro of the healing waters they could picture a hoped-for process of restoration, of a survival of consciousness despite all its agonies. Mary Shelley, with marvelous appropriateness, brings her Romantic novel to a demonic conclusion in a world of ice. The frozen sea is the inevitable emblem for both the wretched daemon and his obsessed creator, but the daemon is allowed a final image of reversed Prometheanism. There is a heroism fully earned in the being who cries farewell in a claim of sad triumph: "I shall ascend my funeral pile triumphantly and exult in the agony of the torturing flames." Mary Shelley could not have known how dark a prophecy this consummation of consciousness would prove to be for the two great Promethean poets who were at her side during the summer of 1816, when her novel was conceived. Byron, writing his own epitaph at Missolonghi in 1824, and perhaps thinking back to having stood at Shelley's funeral pile two years before, found an image similar to the daemon's to sum up an exhausted existence:

> The fire that on my bosom preys
> Is lone as some volcanic isle;
> No torch is kindled at its blaze—
> A funeral pile.

The fire of increased consciousness stolen from heaven ends as an isolated volcano cut off from other selves by an estranging sea. "The light of that conflagration will fade away; my ashes will be swept into the sea by the winds" is the exultant cry of Frankenstein's creature. A blaze at which no torch is kindled is Byron's self-image, but he ends his death poem on another note, the hope for a soldier's grave, which he found. There is no Promethean release, but release is perhaps not the burden of the literature of Romantic aspiration. There is something both Godwinian and Shelleyan about the final utterance of Victor Frankenstein, which is properly made to Walton, the failed Promethean whose ship has just turned back. Though chastened, the Modern Prometheus ends with a last word true, not to his accomplishment, but to his desire:

> Farewell, Walton! Seek happiness in tranquillity and avoid ambition, even if it be only the apparently innocent one of distinguishing yourself in science and discoveries. Yet why do I say this? I have myself been blasted in these hopes, yet another may succeed.

Shelley's Prometheus, crucified on his icy precipice, found his ultimate torment in a Fury's taunt: "And all best things are thus confused to ill." It seems a fitting summation for all the work done by Modern Prometheanism and might have served as an alternate epigraph for Mary Shelley's disturbing novel.

1965

9
Keats and the Embarrassments of Poetic Tradition

One of the central themes in W. J. Bate's definitive *John Keats* is the "large, often paralyzing embarrassment . . . that the rich accumulation of past poetry, as the eighteenth century had seen so realistically, can curse as well as bless." As Mr. Bate remarks, this embarrassment haunted Romantic and haunts post-Romantic poetry, and was felt by Keats with a particular intensity. Somewhere in the heart of each new poet there is hidden the dark wish that the libraries be burned in some new Alexandrian conflagration, that the imagination might be liberated from the greatness and oppressive power of its own dead champions.

Something of this must be involved in the Romantics' loving struggle with their ghostly father, Milton. The role of wrestling Jacob is taken on by Blake in his "brief epic" *Milton*, by Wordsworth in *The Recluse* fragment, and in more concealed form by Shelley in *Prometheus Unbound* and Keats in the first *Hyperion*. The strength of poetical life in Milton seems always to have appalled as much as it delighted; in the fearful vigor of his unmatched exuberance the English master of the sublime has threatened not only poets, but the values once held to transcend poetry:

> . . . the Argument
> Held me a while misdoubting his Intent,
> That he would ruin (for I saw him strong)
> The sacred Truths to Fable and old Song
> (So *Sampson* grop'd the Temple's Posts in spite)
> The World O'erwhelming to revenge his sight.

The older Romantics at least thought that the struggle with Milton had bestowed a blessing without a crippling; to the younger ones a consciousness of gain and loss came together. Blake's audacity gave him a Milton altogether fitted to his great need, a visionary prototype who could be dramatized as rising up, "unhappy tho' in heav'n," taking off the robe of the promise, and ungirding himself from the oath of God, and then descending into Blake's world to save the later poet and every man "from his Chain of Jealousy." Wordsworth's equal audacity allowed him, after praising Milton's invocatory power, to call on a greater Muse than Urania, to assist him in exploring regions more awful than Milton ever visited. The prophetic Spirit called down in *The Recluse* is itself a child of Milton's Spirit that preferred, before all temples, the upright and pure heart of the Protestant poet. But the child is greater than the father, and inspires, in a fine Shakespearean reminiscence:

> The human Soul of universal earth,
> Dreaming on things to come.

Out of that capable dreaming came the poetic aspirations of Shelley and of Keats, who inherited the embarrassment of Wordsworth's greatness to add to the burden of Milton's. Yielding to few in my admiration for Shelley's blank verse in *Prometheus*, I am still made uneasy by Milton's ghost hovering in it. At times Shelley's power of irony rescues him from Milton's presence by the argument's dissonance with the steady Miltonic music of the lyrical drama, but the ironies pass and the Miltonic sublime remains, testifying to the unyielding strength of an order Shelley hoped to overturn. In the lyrics of *Prometheus* Shelley is free, and they rather than the speeches foretold his own poetic future, the sequence of *The Witch of Atlas*, *Epipsychidion*, and *Adonais*. Perhaps the turn to Dante, hinted in *Epipsychidion* and emergent in *The Triumph of Life*, was in part caused by the necessity of finding a sublime antithesis to Milton.

With Keats, we need not surmise. The poet himself claimed to have abandoned the first *Hyperion* because it was too Miltonic, and his critics have agreed in not wanting him to have made a poem "that might have been written by John Milton, but one that was unmistakably by no other than John Keats." In the Great Odes and *The Fall of Hyperion* Keats was to write poems unmistakably his own, as *Endymion* in another way had been his own. Individuality of style, and still more of conception, no critic would now deny to the odes, Keats's supreme poems, or to *The Fall of Hyperion*, which was his testament, and is the work future poets may use as Tennyson, Arnold, and Yeats used the odes in the past.

That Keats, in his handful of great poems, surpassed the Milton-haunted poets of the second half of the eighteenth century is obvious to a critical age like our own, which tends to prefer Keats, in those poems, to even the best work of Blake, Wordsworth, and Shelley, and indeed to most if not all poetry in the language since the mid-seventeenth century. Perhaps the basis for that preference can be explored afresh through a consideration of precisely how Keats's freedom of the negative weight of poetic tradition is manifested in some of his central poems. Keats lost and gained, as each of the major Romantics did, in the struggle with the greatness of Milton. Keats was perhaps too generous and perceptive a critic, too wonderfully balanced a humanist, not to have lost some values of a cultural legacy that both stimulated and inhibited the nurture of fresh values.

Mr. Bate finely says, commenting on Keats's dedication sonnet to Leigh Hunt, that "when the imagination looks to any past, of course, including one's own individual past, it blends memories and images into a denser, more massive unit than ever existed in actuality." Keats's confrontation with this idealized past is most direct from the *Ode to Psyche* on, as Mr. Bate emphasizes. Without repeating him on that ode, or what I myself have written elsewhere, I want to examine it again in the specific context of Keats's fight against the too-satisfying enrichments with which tradition threatens the poet who seeks his own self-recognition and expressive fulfillment.

Most readers recalling the *Ode to Psyche* think of the last stanza, which is the poem's glory, and indeed its sole but sufficient claim to stand near the poet's four principal odes. The stanza expresses a wary confidence that the true poet's imagination cannot be impoverished. More wonderfully, the poet ends the stanza by opening the hard-won consciousness of his own creative powers to a visitation of love. The paradise within is barely formed, but the poet does not hesitate to make it vulnerable, though he may be condemned in consequence to the fate of the famished knight of his own faery ballad. There is triumph in the closing tone of *To Psyche,* but a consciousness also I think of the danger that is being courted. The poet has given Psyche the enclosed bower nature no longer affords her, but he does not pause to be content in that poet's paradise. It is not Byzantium that Keats has built in the heretofore untrodden regions of his mind but rather a realm that is precisely not far above all breathing human passion. He has not assumed the responsibility of an expanded consciousness for the rewards of self-communing and solitary musing, in the manner of the poet-hero of *Alastor,* and of Prince Athanase in his lonely tower. He seeks "love" rather than "wisdom," distrusting a reality that must be approached apart from men. And he has written his poem, in however light a spirit, as an act of self-dedication and of freedom from the wealth of the past. He will be Psyche's priest and rhapsode in the proud conviction that she has had no others before him, or none at least so naked of external pieties.

The wealth of tradition is great not only in its fused massiveness, but in its own subtleties of internalization. One does poor service by sandbagging this profoundly moving poem, yet even the heroic innovators but tread the shadowy ground their ancestors found before them. Wordsworth had stood on that ground, as Keats well knew, and perhaps had chosen a different opening from it, neither toward love nor toward wisdom, but toward a plain recognition of natural reality and a more sublime recognition-by-starts of a final reality that seemed to contain nature. Wordsworth never quite named that finality as imagination, though Blake had done so and the young Coleridge felt (and resisted) the demonic temptation to do so. Behind all these were the fine collapses of the Age of Sensibility, the raptures of *Jubilate Agno* and the *Ode on the Poetical Character*, and the more forced but highly impressive tumults of *The Bard* and *The Progress of Poesy*. Farther back was the ancestor of all such moments of poetic incarnation, the Milton of the great invocations, whose spirit I think haunts the *Ode to Psyche* and the *Ode to a Nightingale*, and does not vanish until *The Fall of Hyperion* and *To Autumn*.

Hazlitt, with his usual penetration, praises Milton for his power to absorb vast poetic traditions with no embarrassment whatsoever: "In reading his works, we feel ourselves under the influence of a mighty intellect, that the nearer it approaches to others, becomes more distinct from them." This observation, which comes in a lecture Keats heard, is soon joined by the excellent remark that "Milton's learning has the effect of intuition." The same lecture, in its treatment of Shakespeare, influenced Keats's conception of the Poetical Character, as Mr. Bate notes. Whether Keats speculated sadly on the inimitable power of Milton's positive capability for converting the splendor of the past into a private expressiveness we do not know. But the literary archetype of Psyche's rosy sanctuary is the poet's paradise, strikingly developed by Spenser and Drayton, and brought to a perfection by Milton. I am not suggesting Milton as a "source" for Keats's *Ode To Psyche*. Poets influence poets in ways more profound than verbal echoings. The paradise of poets is a recurrent element in English mythopoeic poetry, and it is perhaps part

134

of the critic's burden never to allow himself to yield to embarrassment when the riches of poetic tradition come crowding in upon him.
Poets need to be selective; critics need the humility of a bad con-
science when they exclude any part of the poetic past from "tradition," though humility is never much in critical fashion. Rimbaud
put these matters right in one outburst: "On n'a jamais bien jugé le
romantisme. Qui l'aurait jugé? Les Critiques!!"

Milton, "escap't the *Stygian* pool," hails the light he cannot see,
and reaffirms his ceaseless wanderings "where the Muses haunt/
clear Spring, or shady Grove," and his nightly visits to "*Sion* and
the flow'ry Brooks beneath." Like Keats's nightingale, he "sings
darkling," but invokes a light that can "shine inward, and the mind
through all her powers/Irradiate." The light shone inward, the
mind's powers were triumphant, and all the sanctities of heaven
yielded to Milton's vision. For the sanctuary of Milton's psyche is
his vast heterocosm, the worlds he makes and ruins. His shrine is
built, not to the human soul in love, but to the human soul glorious
in its solitude, sufficient, with God's aid, to seek and find its own
salvation. If Keats had closed the casement, and turned inward, seeking the principle that could sustain his own soul in the darkness,
perhaps he could have gone on with the first *Hyperion*, and become
a very different kind of poet. He would then have courted the fate
of Collins, and pursued the guiding steps of Milton only to discover
the quest was

> In vain—such bliss to one alone
> Of all the sons of soul was known,
> And Heav'n and Fancy, kindred pow'rs,
> Have now o'erturned th'inspiring bow'rs,
> Or curtain'd close such scene from ev'ry future view.

Yeats, in the eloquent simplicities of *Per Amica Silentia Lunae*,
saw Keats as having "been born with that thirst for luxury common
to many at the outsetting of the Romantic Movement," and thought
therefore that the poet of *To Autumn* "but gave us his dream of luxury." Yeats's poets were Blake and Shelley; Keats and Wordsworth
he refused to understand, for their way was not his own. His art,
from *The Wanderings of Oisin* through the *Last Poems and Plays*,
is founded on a rage against growing old, and a rejection of nature.
The poet, he thought, could find his art only by giving way to an
anti-self, which "comes but to those who are no longer deceived,
whose passion is reality." Yeats was repelled by Milton, and found

135

no place for him in *A Vision*, and certainly no poet cared so little as Milton to express himself through an anti-self. In Blake's strife of spectre and emanation, in Shelley's sense of being shadowed by the *alastor* while seeking the epipsyche, Yeats found precedent for his own quest toward Unity of Being, the poet as daimonic man taking his mask from a phase opposite to that of his own will. Like Blake and Shelley, Yeats sought certainty, but being of Shelley's phase rather than Blake's, he did not find it. The way of Negative Capability, as an answer to Milton, Yeats did not take into account; he did not conceive of a poet "certain of nothing but of the holiness of the Heart's affections and the truth of Imagination." (There is, of course, no irritable reaching after mere fact and reason in Yeats: he reached instead for everything the occult subimagination had knocked together in place of fact and reason. But his motive was his incapability "of being in uncertainties, mysteries, doubts," and the results are more mixed than most recent criticism will admit.)

Keats followed Wordsworth by internalizing the quest toward finding a world that answered the poet's desires, and he hoped to follow Shakespeare by making that world more than a sublime projection of his own ego. Shakespeare's greatness was not an embarrassment to Keats, but the hard victories of poetry had to be won against the more menacing values of poetic tradition. The advance beyond the *Ode to Psyche* was taken in the *Ode to a Nightingale*, where the high world within the bird's song is an expansion of the rosy sanctuary of Psyche. In this world our sense of actuality is heightened simultaneously with the widening of what Mr. Bate terms "the realm of possibility." The fear of losing actuality does not encourage the dull soil of mundane experience to quarrel with the proud forests it has fed, the nightingale's high requiem. But to be the breathing garden in which Fancy breeds his flowers is a delightful fate; to become a sod is to suffer what Belial dreaded in that moving speech Milton himself and the late C. S. Lewis have taught too many to despise.

Milton, invoking the light, made himself at one with the nightingale; Keats is deliberate in knowing constantly his own separation from the bird. What is fresh in this ode is not I think a sense of the poet's dialogue with himself; it is surprising how often the English lyric has provided such an undersong, from Spenser's *Prothalamion* to Wordsworth's *Resolution and Independence*. Keats wins freedom from tradition here by claiming so very little for the imagination in its intoxicating but harsh encounter with the reality of natural song.

The poet does not accept what is as good, and he does not exile desire for what is not. Yet, for him, what is possible replaces what is not. There is no earthly paradise for poets, but there is a time of all-but-final satisfaction, the fullness of lines 35 to 58 of this ode.

I do not think that there is, before Keats, so individual a setting-forth of such a time, anywhere in poetic tradition since the Bible. The elevation of Wordsworth in *Tintern Abbey* still trembles at the border of a theophany, and so derives from a universe centered upon religious experience. The vatic gift of Shelley's self to the elements, from *Alastor* on, has its remote but genuine ancestors in the sibylline frenzies of traditions as ancient as Orphism. Blake's moments of delight come as hard-won intervals of rest from an intellectual warfare that differs little if at all from the struggles towards a revelatory awareness in Ezekiel or Isaiah, and there is no contentment in them. What Keats so greatly gives to the Romantic tradition in the *Nightingale* ode is what no poet before him had the capability of giving— the sense of the human making choice of a human self, aware of its deathly nature, and yet having the will to celebrate the imaginative richness of mortality. The *Ode to a Nightingale* is the first poem to know and declare, wholeheartedly, that death is the mother of beauty. The *Ode to Psyche* still glanced, with high good humor, at the haunted rituals of the already-written poems of heaven; the *Ode to a Nightingale* turns, almost casually, to the unwritten great poem of earth. There is nothing casual about the poem's tone, but there is a wonderful lack of self-consciousness at the poem's freedom from the past, in the poem's knowing that death, our death, is absolute and without memorial.

The same freedom from the massive beliefs and poetic stances of the past is manifested in the *Ode on a Grecian Urn*, where the consolations of the spirit are afforded merely by an artifice of eternity, and not by evidences of an order of reality wholly other than our own. Part of this poem's strength is in the deliberate vulnerability of its speaker, who contemplates a world of values he cannot appropriate for his own, although nothing in that world is antithetical to his own nature as an aspiring poet. Mr. Bate states the poem's awareness of this vulnerability: "In attempting to approach the urn in its own terms, the imagination has been led at the same time to separate itself—or the situation of man generally—still further from the urn." One is not certain that the imagination is not also separating itself from the essential poverty of man's situation in the poem's closing lines. Mr. Bate thinks we underestimate Keats's humor in the Great

Odes, and he is probably right, but the humor that apparently ends the *Grecian Urn* is a grim one. The truth of art may be all of the truth our condition can apprehend, but it is not a saving truth. If this is all we need to know, it may be that no knowledge can help us. Shelley was very much a child of Miltonic tradition in affirming the moral instrumentality of the imagination; Keats is grimly free of tradition in his subtle implication of a truth that most of us learn. Poetry is not a means of good; it is, as Wallace Stevens implied, like the honey of earth that comes and goes at once, while we wait vainly for the honey of heaven.

Blake, Wordsworth, and Shelley knew in their different ways that human splendors had no sources but in the human imagination, but each of these great innovators had a religious temperament, however heterodox, and Keats had not. Keats had a clarity in his knowledge of the uniqueness and finality of human life and death that caused him a particular anguish on his own deathbed, but gave him, before that, the imagination's gift of an absolute originality. The power of Keats's imagination could never be identified by him with an apocalyptic energy that might hope to transform nature. It is not that he lacked the confidence of Blake and of Shelley, or of the momentary Wordsworth of *The Recluse*. He felt the imagination's desire for a revelation that would redeem the inadequacies of our condition, but he felt also a humorous skepticism toward such desire. He would have read the prose testament of Wallace Stevens, *Two Or Three Ideas*, with the wry approval so splendid a lecture deserves. The gods are dispelled in mid-air, and leave "no texts either of the soil or of the soul." The poet does not cry out for their return, since it remains his work to resolve life in his own terms, for in the poet is "the increasingly human self."

Part of Keats's achievement is due then to his being perhaps the only genuine forerunner of the representative post-Romantic sensibility. Another part is centered in the *Ode on Melancholy* and *The Fall of Hyperion*, for in these poems consciousness becomes its own purgatory, and the poet learns the cost of living in an excitement of which he affirms "that it is the only state for the best sort of Poetry —that is all I care for, all I live for." From this declaration it is a direct way to the generally misunderstood rigor of Pater, when he insists that "a counted number of pulses only is given to us of a variegated, dramatic life," and asks: "How may we see in them all that is to be seen in them by the finest senses?" Moneta, Keats's veiled Melancholy, counted those pulses, while the poet waited, rapt in an apprehension attainable only by the finest senses, nearly betrayed by those senses to an even more premature doom than his destined one. What links together *The Fall of Hyperion* and its modern descendants like Stevens's *Notes Toward a Supreme Fiction* is the movement of impressions set forth by Pater, when analysis of the self yields to the poet's recognition of how dangerously fine the self's existence has become. "It is with this movement, with the passage and dissolution of impressions, images, sensations, that analysis leaves off—that continual vanishing away, that strange, perpetual weaving and unweaving of ourselves."

Though there is a proud laughter implicit in the *Ode on Melancholy*, the poem courts tragedy, and again makes death the mother of beauty. Modern criticism has confounded Pater with his weaker disciples, and has failed to realize how truly Yeats and Stevens are in his tradition. The *Ode on Melancholy* is ancestor to what is strongest in Pater, and to what came after in his tradition of aesthetic humanism. Pater's "Conclusion" to *The Renaissance* lives in the world of the *Ode on Melancholy*:

> Great passions may give us this quickened sense of life, ecstasy and sorrow of love, the various forms of enthusiastic activity, disinterested or otherwise, which come naturally to many of us. Only be sure it is passion—that it does yield you this fruit of a quickened, multiplied consciousness.

The wakeful anguish of the soul comes to the courter of grief in the very shrine of pleasure, and the renovating powers of art yield the tragedy of their might only to a strenuous and joyful seeker. Keats's problem in *The Fall of Hyperion* was to find again the confidence of Milton as to the oneness of his self and theme, but with nothing of the Miltonic conviction that God had worked to fit that self and theme together. The shrines of pleasure and of melancholy become one shrine in the second *Hyperion,* and in that ruin the poet must meet the imaginative values of tradition without their attendant credences, for Moneta guards the temple of all the dead faiths.

Moneta humanizes her sayings to our ears, but not until a poet's courteous dialectic has driven her to question her own categories for mankind. When she softens, and parts the veils for Keats, she reveals his freedom from the greatness of poetic tradition, for the vision granted has the quality of a new universe, and a tragedy different in kind from the tragedy of the past:

> Then saw I a wan face,
> Not pined by human sorrows, but bright-blanch'd
> By an immortal sickness which kills not;

It works a constant change, which happy death
Can put no end to; deathwards progressing
To no death was that visage; it had pass'd
The lily and the snow; and beyond these
I must not think now, though I saw that face.
But for her eyes I should have fled away.
They held me back with a benignant light,
Soft mitigated by divinest lids
Half closed, and visionless entire they seem'd
Of all external things—

Frank Kermode finds in this passage a prime instance of his "Romantic Image," and believes Moneta's face to be "alive only in a chill and inhuman way," yet Keats is held back from such a judgment by the eyes of his Titaness, for they give forth "a benignant light," as close to the saving light Milton invokes as Keats can ever get. Moneta has little to do with the Yeatsian concept of the poetic vision, for she does not address herself to the alienation of the poet. M. H. Abrams, criticizing Mr. Kermode, points to her emphasis on the poet as humanist, made restless by the miseries of mankind. Shelley's Witch of Atlas, for all her playfulness, has more to do with Yeats's formulation of the coldness of the Muse.

Moneta is the Muse of mythopoeia, like Shelley's Witch, but she contains the poetic and religious past, as Shelley's capricious Witch does not. Taking her in a limited sense (since she incarnates so much more than this), Moneta does represent the embarrassments of poetic tradition, a greatness it is death to approach. Moneta's perspective is close to that of the Rilkean Angel, and for Keats to share that perspective he would have to cease to depend on the visible. Moneta's is a perfect consciousness; Keats is committed still to the oxymoronic intensities of experience, and cannot unperplex joy from pain. Moneta's is a world beyond tragedy; Keats needs to be a tragic poet. Rilke dedicated himself to the task of describing a world regarded no longer from a human point of view, but as it is within the angel. Moneta, like this angel, does not regard external things, and again like Rilke's angel she both comforts and terrifies. Keats, like Stevens, fears the angelic imposition of any order upon reality, and hopes to discover a possible order in the human and the natural, even if that order be only the cyclic rhythm of tragedy. Stevens's definitive discovery is in the final sections of Notes Toward a Supreme Fiction; Keats's similar fulfillment is in his perfect poem, To Autumn.

The achievement of definitive vision in To Autumn is the more remarkable for the faint presence of the shadows of the poet's hell that the poem tries to exclude. Mr. Bate calls the *Lines to Fanny* (written, like *To Autumn*, in October 1819) "somewhat jumbled as well as tired and flat," but its nightmare projection of the imagination's inferno has a singular intensity, and I think considerable importance:

> Where shall I learn to get my peace again?
> To banish thoughts of that most hateful land,
> Dungeoner of my friends, that wicked strand
> Where they were wreck'd and live a wrecked life;
> That monstrous region, whose dull rivers pour,
> Ever from their sordid urns unto the shore,
> Unown'd of any weedy-haird gods;
> Whose winds, all zephyrless, hold scourging rods,
> Iced in the great lakes, to afflict mankind;
> Whose rank-grown forests, frosted, black, and blind,
> Would fright a Dryad; whose harsh herbag'd meads
> Make lean and lank the starv'd ox while he feeds;
> There bad flowers have no scent, birds no sweet song,
> And great unerring Nature once seems wrong.

This may have begun as a fanciful depiction of an unknown America, where Keats's brother and sister-in-law were suffering, yet it develops into a vision akin to Blake's of the world of experience, with its lakes of menace and its forests of error. The moss-lain Dryads lulled to sleep in the forests of the poet's mind in his *Ode to Psyche*, can find no home in this natural world. This is Keats's version of the winter vision, the more powerful for being so unexpected, and clearly a torment to its seer, who imputes error to Nature even as he pays it his sincere and accustomed homage.

It is this wasteland that the auroras of Keats's *Autumn* transform into a landscape of perfecting process. Does another lyric in the language meditate more humanly "the full of fortune and the full of fate"? The question is the attentive reader's necessary and generous tribute; the critical answer may be allowed to rest with Mr. Bate, who is moved to make the finest of claims for the poem: "Here at last is something of a genuine paradise." The paradise of poets bequeathed to Keats by tradition is gone; a tragic paradise of naturalistic completion and mortal acceptance has taken its place.

There are other Romantic freedoms won from the embarrassments of poetic tradition, usually through the creation of new myth, as in Blake and Shelley, or in the thematic struggle not to create a myth, as in the earlier work of Wordsworth and Coleridge. Keats found his dangerous freedom by pursuing the naturalistic implications of the poet's relation to his own poem, and nothing is more refreshing in an art so haunted by aspirations to surpass or negate nature. Shelley, still joined to Keats in the popular though not the critical consciousness, remains the best poet to read in counterpoint to the Great Odes and *The Fall of Hyperion*. There is no acceptance in Shelley, no tolerance for the limits of reality, but only the outrageous desire never to cease desiring, the unflagging intensity that goes on until it is stopped, and never is stopped. Keats did what Milton might have done but was not concerned to do; he perfected an image in which stasis and process are reconciled, and made of autumn the most human of seasons in consequence. Shelley's ode to autumn is his paean to the West Wind, where a self-destroying swiftness is invoked for the sake of dissolving all stasis permanently, and for hastening process past merely natural fulfillment into apocalyptic renewal. Whether the great winter of the world can be relieved by any ode Keats tended to doubt, and we are right to doubt with him, but there is a hope wholly natural in us that no doubt dispels, and it is of this hope that Shelley is the unique and indispensable poet.

1964

10
Tennyson, Hallam,
and Romantic Tradition

When I began to write I avowed for my principles those of Arthur
Hallam in his essay upon Tennyson. Tennyson, who had written
but his early poems when Hallam wrote, was an example of the
school of Keats and Shelley, and Keats and Shelley, unlike
Wordsworth, intermixed into their poetry no elements from the
general thought, but wrote out of the impression made by
the world upon their delicate senses.
W. B. Yeats, *Art and Ideas*

So vivid was the delight attending the simple exertions of eye and ear,
that it became mingled more and more with trains of active thought,
and tended to absorb their whole being into the energy of sense.
Hallam on Shelley and Keats, in his review of
Tennyson's *Poems, Chiefly Lyrical* (1830)

The Laureate of *Despair* and *The Ancient Sage* is of course one of
the memorable disasters of poetic tradition, surpassing the
Wordsworth of the *Ecclesiastical Sonnets* and even the Arnold of
Merope. The whole being of Tennyson was at no single time
absorbed into the energy of sense, and for this failure of experience
the price was paid, alas even overpaid:

> And more—think well! Do-well will follow thought,
> And in the fatal sequence of this world
> An evil thought may soil thy children's blood;
> But curb the beast would cast thee in the mire,
> And leave the hot swamp of voluptuousness
> A cloud between the Nameless and thyself,
> And lay thine uphill shoulder to the wheel,
> And climb the Mount of Blessing, whence, if thou
> Look higher, then—perchance—thou mayest—beyond
> A hundred ever-rising mountain lines,
> And past the range of Night and Shadow—see
> The high-heaven dawn of more than mortal day
> Strike on the Mount of Vision!
> > So, farewell.

There are still Tennyson scholars who can read this, or say they
can, but the indefensible badness of it all is plain enough. Sixty
years or so before this, as a boy of fourteen, Tennyson possessed
the verbal exuberance of an absolute poetic genius, and manifested
it in the splendid speeches of the Devil in *The Devil and the Lady*,
and in the remarkable movement of an exercise like the *Ode:
O Bosky Brook*. The extremes of a poet's values, if they are
manifested merely as a chronological continuum, do not much

matter. Vision darkens, life triumphs, the poet becomes the man whose pharynx is bad. So went Wordsworth, the founder of modern poetry, and where a Moses was lost, other losses must follow. Yeats and Wallace Stevens appear today to be the first and only poets in the Romantic tradition who flowered anew both in middle and in old age, and yet it can be questioned if either will rival Tennyson and Browning after the fogs of fashion have been dispelled.

At the center of Tennyson the problem is not whether or why he hardened and kept hardening in poetic character, or just how his vision darkened perpetually into the abysses of much of the later verse, but why and how the sensibility of a major Romantic poet was subverted even in his earlier years. What the most sympathetic reader can still find wanting in the best of Tennyson is a power of imagination shown forth uncompromisingly in *The Fall of Hyperion* and *The Triumph of Life*, in *Resolution and Independence* and *The Mental Traveller*, and on the largest scale in *The Prelude* and *Jerusalem*. Romance, lyric, epic were raised to greatness again in the two generations just before Tennyson. In a lyrical monologue like *Andrea del Sarto*, a romance like *"Childe Roland to the Dark Tower Came,"* and in the curious epic of *The Ring and the Book* a poet of Tennyson's own generation comes close to approximating the Romantic achievement. Tennyson was as legitimately the heir of Keats as Browning was of Shelley, and as much a betrayal of Keats's imaginative honesty and autonomy as Browning was of Shelley's. To make such a point is to reveal in oneself an unreconstructed Romantic bias, like that of Swinburne, or Yeats, or Shaw or Hardy, to bring in four Shelleyans who were contemporaries of the older Browning and Tennyson. There are achievements in Tennyson that are not Romantic, but they are small enough. The Tennyson who counts for most, seen in the longest and clearest perspective we now can begin to recover, is certainly a Romantic poet, and not a Victorian anti-Romantic resembling the Arnold of *Merope* or the straining Hopkins of *The Wreck of the Deutschland*. He is a major Romantic poet, but not perhaps one of the greatest, though there is an antithetical storm-cloud drifting through the center of his work that sometimes shows us what his proper greatness should have been. His affinities in his own time were to no other poet but to Ruskin, a great ruin of a Romantic critic, and his value to us now is rather like Ruskin's, since he shows forth as a most crucial instance of the dilemma of post-Romantic art.

Hallam, who remains Tennyson's best critic, found "five distinctive excellencies" in his friend's poetic manner: (1) the control of a luxuriant imagination; (2) accuracy of adjustment in "moods of character," so that narration and feeling naturally corresponded with each other; (3) skill in emotionally fusing a vivid, "picturesque" portrayal of objects ("picturesque" being opposed here to Wordsworthian descriptiveness); (4) modulation of verbal harmony; (5) "mellow soberness of tone," addressed to the understanding heart rather than the mere understanding. Yeats, in his old age, spoke of "the scientific and moral discursiveness of *In Memoriam*," but I cannot recognize the poem from that description. What lives in the elegies for Hallam are precisely the excellences that Hallam picked out in his friend's earlier manner, and the various tracts of discursiveness one learns to step over quickly. Discursiveness became a Tennysonian vice, but it did not in itself inhibit the development of Tennyson's poetry. Tennyson, like Browning, but to a still worse extent, never achieved even a pragmatic faith in the autonomy of his own imagination. Such a faith was a ruling passion in Blake, Shelley, and Keats, and such a faith, though held with earnest misgivings, for a while allowed Wordsworth and Coleridge to yield themselves to their greatest achievements. Though the overt Victorian Romantics of the Pre-Raphaelite group struggled back to a version of this faith, it was not held again with similar intensity in Tennyson's age except by Pater, who fostered Yeats even as he gave the more disjunctive and ironical Stevens a fresh point of departure in America. To trace the conflict in Tennyson's earlier poetry between a Romantic imagination and an emergent societal censor is hardly to conduct a fresh investigation, and I will not attempt it here. Such conflicts, whether found in a Spenser or even in a D. H. Lawrence, seem recurrent in the history of poetry, and belong more to the study of consciousness than to the study of poetic tradition. The more rewarding problem for pondering is the young Tennyson's profounder distrust of his own creative powers. A god spoke in him, or a demon, and a revulsion accompanied the maturing of this voice. No really magical poem by Tennyson ever became quite the work he intended it to be, and this gap between his intention and his actual achievement saved him as a poet, though it could not save him altogether. Most considerable poems by Tennyson do not mean what they meant to mean, and while this is true of all poets whatsoever to some degree, Tennyson is the most extreme instance I know of the imagination going one way, and the will going quite another. Blake thought that the Milton of *Paradise Lost* had to be rescued from himself, an opinion that most recent

Miltonists find dubious, perhaps without fully understanding it. But Tennyson's best poems are a much more radical version of Blake's paradox; they address themselves simultaneously and overtly to both a conventional and a "diabolic" reading.

Partly this is due to the prevalence in Tennyson's poetic mind of the "damned vacillating state" of the early *Supposed Confessions*. No lyric by Tennyson is more central to his sensibility than *Mariana*, entirely a poem of the autonomous imagination running down into isolated and self-destructive expectation. Wordsworth, in his sublime Tale of Margaret, wrote the contrary to Tennyson's poem, for Margaret is destroyed by an imaginative hope that will not take account of the mundane. The hope is all too willing to be fed, and the prevalence of the imagination could hardly be more dangerous. Wordsworth does, here and in *Michael*, what Tennyson could only approximate in *Dora*; the poet creates a consciousness narrower and purer than his own, and measures his own malady of self-concern by its distance from that pure intensity. Mariana, unlike Margaret, is a poetess, and she sings a Dejection ode that Tennyson scarcely ventured to write in his own person. Her disease is Romantic self-consciousness, and no bridegroom can come to heal her. "She could not look on the sweet heaven," for much the same cause as the singer of Blake's *Mad Song* turns his back to the east and rejects the comforts of the sun. Wilful and unwilling, she is poised between two states of being, one in which the world has been taken up into the mind (the mind of a Picturesque rather than Descriptive poet) and the other in which the solipsistic mind rejects the world as an unreal intruder; hence the landscape of her poem, which as a poetic achievement could not be overpraised. The poplar, seen as a phallic symbol by some recent Tennyson critics, is rather an indication of the border realm between the two states in which Mariana lives. She can neither absorb its presence nor utterly reject it, and it serves therefore to show how precarious her mode of existence is. The poem's strongest impulse is to see the world as phantasmagoria, in which case Mariana's lament would be transvalued and appear as an ironic cry of triumph for the autonomy of her vision. But there are other impulses in the poem, and "He cometh not" remains a lament.

The Shelleyan origins of Tennyson's female solitary, in *Mariana* and other poems, has been demonstrated ably by Lionel Stevenson, who unfortunately reduces this emblematic figure in both Shelley and Tennyson to Jung's archetype of the *anima*. The reduction is unnecessary in any case, since *Epipsychidion* demonstrates how consciously and deliberately Shelley used his epipsyche figure. Tennyson's use of his cynosure-female is presumably not as conscious or as deliberate, though no theory of the two Tennysons, and no prosaic psychoanalytic reduction, need be ventured in consequence. Tennyson's poetry is too many-sided for anyone to suggest plausibly that it was written by uneasy collaboration between a Shelley-Keats and a Victorian Christian humanist, and I intend no such notion in this essay. There is a profound sense of the limitations of poetry in both Keats and Shelley, but each learned how to convert this sense into an overt poetic strength. Tennyson wrote in an age of reform, both voluntary and involuntary, while the younger Romantics faced a time of apparent stasis, an exhaustion following an apocalyptic fervor. The temper of poetic imagination is peculiarly and favorably responsive to the thwarting of political hope, and Shelley and Keats and Byron gained immensely by their good fortune of having the era of Metternich and Castelreagh to contend against, little as they would appreciate so cynical a judgment. Like Beddoes and Darley, a half-generation before him, Tennyson found himself with a fiercely autonomous imagination confronting a time that neither challenged nor repelled such an imagination, yet also gave it no proper arena in which to function. Keats was of course not a political poet, indeed was far less one than Tennyson, but there still existed provocations for Keats's humanism and his naturalism to become combative. Browning found provocation enough in the Evangelicism of his parents, particularly his mother, but *Pauline* records too clearly how his Shelleyan sensibility failed guiltily before such a stimulus. Tennyson had no combative use to which an assertion of the imagination could be put, and no antidote therefore against any aesthetic corrosion that his moral doubts of imagination might bring about. The pride of imagination, and the distrust of it, had nowhere to go but within.

Sexual virginity for any poet, even a Jesuit, as Hopkins shows, is a kind of sickness unto action, a time of fear before the potential disorder of the strange. That Tennyson's Muse was (and always remained) Hallam has given Robert Graves occasion for innocent merriment, but need disturb no one any longer. The death of a beautiful young man strikes our social sense as a less appropriate theme for poetry than Poe's pervasive theme, but is of course much more traditional than Poe's preference in corpses. The sexual longings of a poet *qua poet* appear to have little relation to mere experience anyway, as for instance in the contrast between the sexually highly active Shelley with his crucial antithetical theme of the inadequacy of nature to the imagination from *Alastor* on, and the probably virginal Keats of *Endymion*, with his profoundly primary sense of satisfaction in natural experience. Still, there is a line of poetry that goes from the complexly sensual aspirations of Spenser through the bitter sexual frustrations of Milton and Blake (particularly relevant to his Notebook poems and *Visions of the Daughter of Albion*), then to the curious argument between Shelley and Keats in *Alastor* and *Endymion*, and on to the astonishingly delayed entries into sexual experience of Tennyson and of Yeats. The analytical sophistication in aesthetic realms that would allow a responsible sexual history of English poetry to be written is not available to us, and yet such a history must and should come. The hidden fulfillment of Wordsworth is the aesthetic puzzle of *The Prelude*, since the 1805 version is marred by the inclusion of the Julia and Vaudracour episode, and the 1850 version suffers from its exclusion. The *malaise* of Tennyson's early poetry is very like that of *The Wanderings of Oisin*, and the existence of Shelley and Keats as ancestor-poets-in-common is insufficient to explain the likeness. The tragedy of sexual intercourse, according to the older Yeats, was the perpetual virginity of the soul. The comedy of sexual intercourse is presumably the initial virginity of the body, but in poetry poised before experience the comedy tends to be negated, or rather displaced into the phantasmagoria of a Mariana, whose poem would be destroyed by the slightest touch of a comic spirit.

I am not, I would hope, alone in my puzzlement as to why Tennyson has not had the prestige of the hieratic in our time, while the more limited but precisely similar Mallarmé has. Tennyson's poems of the *Mariana* kind, centered on a self-embowered consciousness, are not less artful or persuasive than Mallarmé's, and are rather more universal in their implications. The English Decadence has, as its true monument, not Swinburne, admirable poet as he certainly was, but the more masterful Tennyson, whose "metaphysics of night" go beyond Malarme's in their elaborately indeliberate subtleties. Hallam's is necessarily a theory of pure poetry (as H. M. McLuhan shows) and while Tennyson could not allow himself to share the theory overtly, he inspired it by his early practice, and fell back on it implicitly to save his poetry time and time again. In a way that *In Memoriam* does not apprehend, the dead Hallam remained Tennyson's guardian angel.

Mariana is too pure a poem to test any argument by, so that an overview of its neighbors in early Tennyson seems likely to be helpful. *Recollections of the Arabian Nights* is a clearly Shelleyan poem, more confident indeed in its Shelleyan faith of imagination than any-

thing else of Tennyson's. It echoes *Kubla Khan* also, but not the
third part of that poem in which Coleridge to some degree withdraws
from the full implications of his own vision. Like the Poet-hero
of *Alastor*, Tennyson voyages through nature in search of a center
transcending nature, and he finds it in a pleasure-dome like that of
Kubla Khan or *The Palace of Art* or *The Revolt of Islam:*

> The fourscore windows all alight
> As with the quintessence of flame,
> A million tapers flaring bright
> From twisted silvers look'd to shame
> The hollow-vaulted dark, and stream'd
> Upon the mooned domes aloof
> In inmost Bagdat, till there seem'd
> Hundreds of crescents on the roof
>   Of night new-risen . . .

This is the young Tennyson's *Byzantium*, and perhaps it lingered
in the mind of the old Yeats, though more likely both poets were
recalling, however involuntarily, visions seen by Coleridge and by
Shelley. Reasonable sophisticates will smile at my connecting Tennyson's playful *Recollections* to Yeats's supreme lyric, but there is a
great deal legitimately to claim (or reclaim) for *Recollections of the
Arabian Nights*. It was Hallam's favorite among the 1830 *Poems*,
and his choice was a justified one, for the lyric is a complete and perfected miniature of Tennyson's poetic mind, and is even an *In Memoriam* in little. A very great, a consummate poet is at work in the
full strength of his sensibility, and can be felt with especial power
from the fifth line of this stanza on:

> Far off, and where the lemon grove
> In closest coverture upsprung,
> The living airs of middle night
> Died round the bulbul as he sung;
> Not he: but something which possess'd
> The darkness of the world, delight,
> Life, anguish, death, immortal love,
> Ceasing not, mingled, unrepress'd,
>   Apart from place, withholding time,
>   But flattering the golden prime
>   Of good Haroun Alraschid.

This stanza is at the poem's center of vision, and properly recalls
the song of Keats's nightingale, also sung to a poet in darkness, and
like this chant an overcoming of the limitations of space and time.

The companion-poem to *Recollections* is the impressive *Ode to Memory*, and it is palpable that both lyrics are love poems addressed to Hallam. Palpable to us and not presumably to Tennyson and Hallam, I suppose I ought to add, but then the *Ode to Memory* ends:

> My friend, with you to live alone,
> Were how much better than to own
> A crown, a sceptre, and a throne!
>
> O strengthen me, enlighten me!
> I faint in this obscurity,
> Thou dewy dawn of memory.

The *Recollections* opens with an inspiriting breeze that takes the poet back to what Hart Crane in *Passage* beautifully called "an improved infancy." In that unitary joy, Tennyson emulates the Poet-hero of *Alastor* and sets forth on his quest for the good Haroun Alraschid, who is already the supernatural Hallam of *In Memoriam*, a poet-king dwelling at the center of vision, a type of god-man still to come. To reach this absolute being, the poet-voyager sails, with "a majesty of slow motion in every cadence," as Hallam observed, until he enters "another night in night," an "imbower'd" world of "imprisoning sweets." The voyage suggests not only the quest of *Alastor*, but also the journey to the Bower of Bliss in Book II of *The Faerie Queene*. Tennyson, as many critics by now have noted, is the most discreetly powerful erotic poet in the language, and this early lyric is a masterpiece of subdued erotic suggestiveness. The penultimate stanza, with its confectioner's delight of a Persian girl, is merely an erotic evasion, but the final stanza, directly celebrating Hallam, is sustained by a lyric rapture remarkable even in the younger Tennyson.

In section CIII of *In Memoriam*, Tennyson finds an after-morn of content because of another voyage-vision in which Hallam is again at the center, the Muse presiding over a realized quest. But the playfulness of *Recollections of the Arabian Nights* is now gone, that poem's greatest admirer being dead. Perhaps remembering how much Hallam had loved the poem, Tennyson returns to its design at one of the climaxes in his book of elegies, in which his grief is assuaged by the compensatory imagination, and Hallam is resurrected as a Titan capable of reviving Tennyson's lesser Muses. In itself, section CIII has rightly been judged to be one of Tennyson's great lyrics, but one can wonder how many of the poet's readers have seen how very little the poem has to do with the supposed faith of *In Memo-*

riam. Bradley, the definitive commentator on the elegies for Hallam, interpreted the dream of section CIII with his usual good sense, but declined to see its clearly Promethean pattern of consolation. In Numbers 13:32–33, the spies of Moses report on the Anakim, "which come of the giants," and the report appals the murmuring Israelites. Like the Titans, the Anakim testify to a time when there were giants in the earth, when men walked with gods as equals. In the titanic section CIII Tennyson dreams "a vision of the sea" during his last sleep in the house of his childhood, and in the vision he leaves behind him not only childhood, but all that precedes a rising Prometheanism as well. The poet's lesser Muses, his Daughters of Beulah as Blake patronizingly would have named them, sing "of what is wise and good / And graceful" to a veiled statue of Hallam, the unknown god who must lead them to a greater music. A dove summons Tennyson to an apocalyptic sea, an outward-flowing tide on which he will be reunited with "him I loved, and love / For ever." The weeping Muses sail with the poet:

> And still as vaster grew the shore
>   And rolled the floods in grander space,
>   The maidens gather'd strength and grace
> And presence, lordlier than before;
>
> And I myself, who set apart
>   And watch'd them, wax'd in every limb;
>   I felt the thews of Anakim,
> The pulses of a Titan's heart.

Watching the ministering spirits of his own creativity, Tennyson suddenly shares their participation in a daemonic possession, an influx of power as the poet rises in the body to be one again with the giants in the earth. With this transformation his Muses sing not of what is, but ought to be: the death of war, the great race that is to come, and a new cosmos—the shaping of a star. The New Man, the first of the crowning race, Tennyson's Albion "appearing ere the times were ripe," and so dying an early and unnatural death, is necessarily Hallam, whose epiphany "thrice as large as man" is the saving culmination of section CIII, and indeed of all the elegies. The ship of the reunited lovers, both now Titans and accompanied by the nervous Muses, fearful lest their function be gone, sails at last toward a land of crimson cloud, a realm where vapor, sea, and earth come together, a world out of space and time and free of all merely human moralities.

One never ceases to be puzzled that *In Memoriam,* an outrageously personal poem of Romantic apotheosis, a poem indeed of vastly eccentric mythmaking, should have been accepted as a work of consolation and moral resolution in the tradition of Christian humanism. *In Memoriam*, viewed as one poem, is rather a welter of confusions, but its main movement is clear enough, and establishes the work as having considerably less relation to a Christian elegy than even *Adonais* has. Whatever Tennyson thought he was doing, the daemon of imaginative autonomy got hold of the poem's continuity, and made the poem an argument for a personal love about as restrained and societal as Heathcliff's passion, or Blake's in *Visions of the Daughters of Albion* or Shelley's in *Epipsychidion*. The vision of Hallam in sections CXXVI to CXXX for instance is a more extreme version of the transfiguration of Keats in the final stanzas of *Adonais*, and is a victory for everything in Tennyson that could accept neither God nor nature as adequate to the imaginative demands of a permanently bereaved lover who was also a professional poet.

No poet in English seems to me as extreme and fortuitous as Tennyson in his sudden moments of recognition of his own powers, bursts of radiance against a commonplace conceptual background that cannot accommodate such radiance. The deeply imaginative reader learns instinctively to listen to the song and not the singer, for Lawrence's adage is perfectly relevant to Tennyson. More relevant still was the prophetic warning of Hallam, in one sentence of his review that one wishes Tennyson had brooded upon daily, and so perhaps saved for poetry more fully than he did one of the major Romantic sensibilities:

> That delicate sense of fitness which grows with the growth of artist feelings, and strengthens with their strength, until it acquires a celerity and weight of decision hardly inferior to the correspondent judgments of conscience, is weakened by every indulgence of heterogeneous aspirations, however pure they may be, however lofty, however suitable to human nature.

Had Tennyson heeded this, he might have ended like the sinful soul of his own *The Palace of Art*, howling aloud "I am on fire within." One cannot be sure it would not have been the fitting end his imagination required.

1966

11
Browning's *Childe Roland:*
All Things Deformed
and Broken

"What in the midst lay but the Tower itself?" The quester, "after a life spent training for the sight," sees nothing but everything he has estranged from himself. Browning's poem, to me his finest, is a crucial test for any reader, but peculiarly so for a reader rendered aware of Romantic tradition, and the anxieties fostered by its influence. What happens in the poem, difficult to determine, perhaps impossible to know with final assurance, depends upon the reader's judgment of Roland, the poem's speaker. How far can he be trusted in recounting his own catastrophe?

On New Year's Day, 1852, in Paris, Browning strenuously resolved to write a poem a day, a resolution kept for a fortnight, producing successively in its first three days *Women and Roses*, "*Childe Roland to the Dark Tower Came*," and *Love Among The Ruins*. *Women and Roses*, as William Clyde DeVane commented, is wholly uncharacteristic of its poet, and is far likelier to make current readers think of Yeats than of Browning. Its curious structure alternates tercets and nine-line stanzas, the tercets introducing the roses of a dream-vision, and the longer stanzas presenting the poet's almost frantic responses to the vision's sexual appeal. Past, present, and future women dance to one cadence, each circling their rose on the poet's rose tree, and each evading his attempts "to possess and be possessed." Even the prophetic vision, a kind of Yeatsian *antithetical* influx, refuses the maker's shapings:

> What is far conquers what is near.
> Roses will bloom nor want beholders,
> Spring from the dust where our flesh moulders,
> What shall arrive with the cycle's change?
> A novel grace and a beauty strange.

157

> I will make an Eve, be the artist that began her,
> Shaped her to his mind!—Alas! in like manner
> They circle the rose on my rose tree.

Browning's experience of what Blake called the Female Will had been confined largely to his mother and his wife, neither of whom he had shaped to his mind; rather he had yielded to both. If *Women and Roses* indeed was "the record of a vivid dream" (DeVane), then the dream was of reality, and not a wish-fulfillment. A greater, though nightmare, vision of reality came the next day.

> My first thought was, he lied in every word,
>   That hoary cripple, with malicious eye
>   Askance to watch the working of his lie
> On mine, and mouth scarce able to afford
> Suppression of the glee, that pursed and scored
>   Its edge, at one more victim gained thereby.
>
> What else should he be set for, with his staff?
>   What, save to waylay with his lies, ensnare
>   All travellers who might find him posted there,
> And ask the road? I guessed what skull-like laugh
> Would break, what crutch 'gin write my epitaph
>   For pastime in the dusty thoroughfare,
>
> If at his counsel I should turn aside
>   Into that ominous tract which, all agree,
>   Hides the Dark Tower.

The cripple's motives, the actual look of him, even whether his mouth worked with suppressed glee or with terror, or compassion, or whatever, we will never know, for we have only Childe Roland's monologue, and it takes less than the first fifteen lines he speaks for us to suspect all his impressions. Whether, if we rode by his side, we too would see all things deformed and broken, would depend upon the degree to which we shared in his desperation, his hopelessness not only of his quest but of himself and of all questings and questers. Why not throw up the irksome charge at once? If Roland tempts us to this question, asked of Paracelsus by Festus in the second of Browning's Shelleyan quest-romances, we can be assuaged by the great charlatan's reply:

> A task, a task!
>   But wherefore hide the whole
>   Extent of degradation once engaged

In the confessing vein? Despite of all
My fine talk of obedience and repugnance,
Docility and what not, 'tis yet to learn
If when the task shall really be performed,
My inclination free to choose once more,
I shall do aught but slightly modify
The nature of the hated task I quit.
In plain words, I am spoiled . . .
                              . . . God! how I essayed
To live like that mad poet, for a while,
To love alone; and how I felt too warped
And twisted and deformed! What should I do,
Even though released from drudgery, but return
Faint, as you see, and halting, blind and sore,
To my old life and die as I began?
I cannot feed on beauty for the sake
Of beauty only, nor can drink in balm
From lovely objects for their loveliness;
My nature cannot lose her first imprint;
I still must hoard and heap and class all truths
With one ulterior purpose: I must know!
. . . .
                              . . . alas,
I have addressed a frock of heavy mail
Yet may not join the troop of sacred knights;
And now the forest-creatures fly from me,
The grass-banks cool, the sunbeams warm no more,
Best follow, dreaming that ere night arrive,
I shall o'ertake the company and ride
Glittering as they!

This company, in *"Childe Roland To The Dark Tower Came,"* has become "The Band" of failures, who glitter only in the Yeatsian Condition of Fire that Roland enters also in his dying:

There they stood, ranged along the hillsides, met
    To view the last of me, a living frame
    For one more picture! in a sheet of flame
I saw them and I knew them all.

The company of Browning scholars, notably DeVane, F. A. Pottle, W. O. Raymond, and Betty Miller, have charted for us the complexities of Browning's Shelleyan heritage, and his equivocal denial of that heritage. Mrs. Miller in particular reads *Childe Roland* in the context of the denial, as a poem of retribution appropriate to Browning's own sin in murdering his earlier, Shelleyan self as a sacrifice to his Oedipal anxieties, to his love for his Evangelical mother. The poem, like Coleridge's three poems of natural magic, *Christabel, The Ancient Mariner, Kubla Khan,* becomes a ballad of the imagination's revenge against the poet's unpoetic nature, against his failure to rise out of the morass of family romance into the higher romance of the autonomous spirit questing for evidences of its own creative election. Mrs. Miller's view seems to me the indispensable entry into Browning's darkest and most powerful romance, and once within we will find the fullest phenomenology of a consciousness of creative failure available to us in our language, fuller even than in Coleridge, whose censorious and magnificent intellect fought back too effectively against romance, in the holy name of the Logos. Browning embraced that name also, but in *Childe Roland* happily the embrace is evaded, and a terrible opening to vision is made instead.

If we go a day past *Childe Roland's* composition, to 3 January 1852, we find the indefatigable Browning writing *Love Among The Ruins,* where fallen Babylon exposes only a ruined tower:

> Now,—the single little turret that remains
>   On the plains,
> By the caper overrooted, by the gourd
>   Overscored,
> While the patching houseleek's head of blossom winks
>   Through the chinks—
> Marks the basement whence a tower in ancient time
>   Sprang sublime,
> And a burning ring. . . .

It is "the Tower itself," but a day later, still "the round squat turret, blind as the fool's heart," but seen now in the mundane, nightmare fallen away into ruin, and Browning, blind to the night's lessons, falls back on: "Love is best." Doubtless it is, when the quester is free to find it, or be found by it. Shelley, who knew more about love than Browning, or most men (before or since), had the capacity of a stronger visionary, to confront the image of nightmare in the mundane:

> —so, o'er the lagune
> We glided; and from that funeral bark
> I leaned, and saw the city, and could mark
> How from their many isles, in evening's gleam,
> Its temples and its palaces did seem

Like fabrics of enchantment piled to Heaven.
I was about to speak, when—"We are even
Now at the point I meant," said Maddalo,
And bade the gondolieri cease to row.
"Look, Julian, on the west, and listen well
If you hear not a deep and heavy bell."
I looked, and saw between us and the sun
A building on an island; such a one
As age to age might add, for uses vile,
A windowless, deformed and dreary pile;
And on the top an open tower, where hung
A bell, which in the radiance swayed and swung
We could just hear its hoarse and iron tongue:
The broad sun sunk behind it, and it tolled
In strong and black relief.—

. . . .

"And such," he cried, "is our mortality,
And this must be the emblem and the sign
Of what should be eternal and divine!—
And like that black and dreary bell, the soul,
Hung in a heaven-illumined tower, must toll
Our thoughts and our desires to meet below
Round the rent heart and pray—as madmen do
For what? they know not—till the night of death
As sunset that strange vision, severeth
Our memory from itself, and us from all
We sought and yet were baffled."

Though it is not traditional to find in this passage one of the "sources" of *Childe Roland*, it seems to me the truest precursor to Browning's poem, on evidence both internal and external. It lay deep in his mind as he wrote his poem, and emerged in the emblem of the commonplace yet unique tower where the quester is met by his career's ambiguous truth, and triumphantly accepts destruction by that truth. Externals can be postponed until Roland's truth meets us in the poem, but the internal evidence of Romantic tradition finds us even as we enter Roland's realm of appearances, and are accosted by his "hoary cripple," an amalgam of Spenser's Archimago, Spenser's Despair, Shakespeare's Gloucester from *Lear*, and perhaps Ahasuerus, the Wandering Jew of Shelley's *Queen Mab* and *Hellas*. Gloucester as seen by Cornwall, I should amend, for the verbal origins of *Childe Roland* are in the snatch of verse sung by Edgar before his father suffers Cornwall's version of the Dark Tower:

161

"Child Rowland to the dark tower came.
His word was still 'Fie, foh, and fum,
I smell the blood of a British man.' "

But the Browning version of the ogre is a *daimon* of self-betrayal, and the reader needs to trace influence in the manner of Borges, rather than of Lowes, if source-study is to help in reading this poem. Kafka and Yeats, Gnostic visionaries, are closer to the poem than Spenser and Shakespeare, or even Shelley, who in a true sense is the poem's pervasive subject, the betrayed ideal whose spirit haunts Roland, whose love chastizes Roland's way of knowing until it becomes a knowing that deforms and breaks all things it lights upon, and finds "all dark and comfortless," the blinded Gloucester's answer to Cornwall's vile taunt: "Where is thy luster now?"

To recognize Childe Roland as a Gnostic quester is to begin reading his poem as if it were a Borges parable of self-entrapment, another labyrinth made by men that men must decipher. A Gnostic quester is necessarily a kind of Quietist, for whom every landscape is infernal, and every shrine a squalor. In Shelleyan quest the objects of desire tend to touch the vanishing point of the visual and auditory, but the field of quest remains attractive, though not benign. Childe Roland moves in the Gnostic nightmare, where all natural context even looks and sounds malevolent, and the only goal of desire is to fail.

The greatest power of Browning's romance inheres not in its landscape (in which we are too ready to believe) but in the extraordinary, negative intensity of Childe Roland's consciousness, which brings to defeat an energy of perception so exuberant as to mock defeat's limits. This energy is very close to the remorseless drive of Shelley's Poet in *Alastor,* or of Shelley himself in *Epipsychidion.* The landscape of *"Childe Roland To The Dark Tower Came,"* like that of *Alastor,* is charged by the quester's own furious, self-frustrated energy, and cannot at last contain that energy. When Childe Roland burns through the context he has invented, in his closing epiphany, he sees and hears all things he has made and marred, or rather made by breaking, himself and his vision, everything finally except the landscape of estrangement he has been seeing all through the poem. "Burningly it came on me all at once," he says, and "it" is place imagined into full meaning, an uncovering so complete as to be triumph whatever else comes to him. The Roland who sets the slughorn to his lips does not accept a Gnostic conclusion, but ranges himself with those who have sounded the trumpet of a prophecy to unawakened earth. A poem that commenced in the spirit of *The Castle* or *Meditations In A Time of Civil War* concludes itself deliberately in the Orphic spirit of the *Ode To The West Wind*'s last stanza.

Browning dates his *Introductory Essay* on Shelley as "Paris, December 4th, 1851," a month before the composition of *Childe Roland*. The *Essay* on Shelley is, with one exception, Browning's only prose work of consequence, the exception being the *Essay on Tasso and Chatterton* done a decade before *Childe Roland*. In *Julian And Maddalo* the "windowless, deformed and dreary pile" with its "open tower" and "hoarse and iron tongue" of a tolling bell is the madhouse of Tasso's confinement, and one can surmise that "the round squat turret, blind as the fool's heart" has some intimate relation to the madness of poets. Chatterton, coupled with Tasso by Browning as a victimized mad poet, enters *Childe Roland* at the close with the slug-horn, a nonexistent instrument that appears only in his works, by a corruption of "slogan." As a cry-to-battle by a crazed, self-defeated poet, its appropriateness is overwhelming at *Childe Roland*'s end. The *Essay on Tasso and Chatterton* is essentially a defense of Chatterton's assumption of the mask of Rowley, anticipating Browning's extraordinary essay on Shelley, with its implicit defense of Browning's assumption of the many masks of his mature poetry. Contrasting Shakespeare as the objective poet to Shelley as the subjective (and thus helping Yeats to his antinomies of *primary* and *antithetical* in *A Vision*), Browning asks an unanswerable question about the unknowable objective artist:

> Did the personality of such an one stand like an open watchtower in the midst of the territory it is erected to gaze on, and were the storms and calms, the stars and meteors, its watchman was wont to report of, the habitual variegation of his everyday life, as they glanced across its open door or lay reflected on its four-square parapet?

No such question need be asked concerning the subjective poet, who is a seer, not a fashioner, and so produces "less a work than an effluence." The open tower of Shelley radiates "its own self-sacrificing central light," making possible what Browning calls "his noblest and predominating characteristic":

> This I call his simultaneous perception of Power and Love in the absolute, and of Beauty and Good in the concrete, while

163

he throws, from his poet's station between both, swifter, subtler, and more numerous films for the connection of each with
each, than have been thrown by any modern artificer of whom
I have knowledge . . .

Browning was thirty-nine when he wrote his Shelley essay, and
then its sequel in *Childe Roland.* At thirty-nine the imagination has
learned that no spring can flower past meridian, and in one sense we
can regard *Childe Roland* as a classical poem of the fortieth year.
Shelley had died in his thirtieth year, but his imagination might have
declined the lesson in any case, for no imagination was ever so impatient of our staler realities, and Browning, who was a superb reader
of Shelley, would have known this. Reading Shakespeare for his
Shelley essay, Browning came upon Edgar's assumption of a mask,
and his ballad-lines of the Dark Tower, and yoked together in his
creative mind highly disparate towers. The *Essay on Shelley* twice
names *Julian and Maddalo* as a major example of the poet's art, once
citing it among "successful instances of objectivity" together with
"the unrivalled Cenci." Browning is critically acute, for the landscape of *Julian and Maddalo* is not only marvelously rendered, but
is one of the rare instances in nineteenth-century poetry of a landscape *not* estranged from the self, and so not seen merely as a portion
of the self expelled:

> I rode one evening with Count Maddalo
> Upon the bank of land which breaks the flow
> Of Adria towards Venice: a bare strand
> Of hillocks, heaped from ever-shifting sand,
> Matted with thistles and amphibious weeds,
> Such as from earth's embrace the salt ooze breeds,
> Is this; an uninhabited sea-side,
> Which the lone fisher, when his nets are dried,
> Abandons; and no other object breaks
> The waste, but one dwarf tree and some few stakes
> Broken and unrepaired, and the tide makes
> A narrow space of level sand thereon,
> Where 'twas our wont to ride when day went down,
> This ride was my delight. I love all waste
> And solitary places; where we taste
> The pleasure of believing what we see
> Is boundless, as we wish our souls to be.

This rider experiencing the Sublime is the polar contrary to Childe
Roland, and to the mad poet dwelling in the "windowless, deformed

and dreary pile;/And on the top an open tower," who in some sense is Roland's *daimon* or true self. In the debate between Shelley (as Julian) and Lord Byron (as Count Maddalo) it is Shelley who insists on the quester's will as being central and capable, and Byron who maintains a darker wisdom, to which Shelley, unlike Roland (or Browning), quietly declines surrender:

> "—it is our will
> That thus enchains us to permitted ill—
> We might be otherwise—we might be all
> We dream of happy, high majestical.
> Where is the love, beauty, and truth we seek
> But in our mind? and if we were not weak
> Should we be less in deed than in desire?"
> "Ay, if we were not weak—and we aspire
> How vainly to be strong!" said Maddalo:
> "You talk Utopia." "It remains to know,"
> I then rejoined, "and those who try may find
> How strong the chains are which our spirit bind;
> Brittle perchance as straw . . . we are assured
> Much may be conquered, much may be endured,
> Of what degrades and crushes us. We know
> That we have power over ourselves to do
> And suffer—what, we know not till we try;
> But something nobler than to live and die—"

The passage might well be epigraph to *Childe Roland*. Shelley, the sun-treading spirit of imaginative reproach or true Apollo of *Pauline*, the "mad poet" who sought love as opposed to Paracelsus's quest for knowledge, the spirit still not exorcised in *Sordello*, gives to *Childe Roland* and its nightmare landscape a sense of a hidden god, a presence felt by the void of its total absence. Roland rides across a world without imagination, seeing everywhere "such starved ignoble nature," his own, as he follows "my darkening path" to its conclusion.

DeVane found much of the "source" material for Roland's landscape in Gerard de Lairesse's *The Art of Painting in All its Branches*, a book Browning remembered as having read "more often and with greater delight, when I was a child, than any other." Lairesse, celebrated by Browning in the late *Parleyings*, gathered together the horrible in painting, as he saw it, in his Chapter 17, *Of Things Deformed and Broken, Falsely called Painter-like*, and DeVane demonstrated how many details Browning took from the one chapter, probably unknowingly. Childe Roland, like Browning, is painter as well

165

as poet, and dies as a living picture, framed by "all the lost adventurers my peers," who like him found all things deformed and broken.

All this is the living circumference of *"Childe Roland To The Dark Tower Came"*; we move to the central meaning when we ponder the sorrow of this quester, this *aware* solipsist whose self-recognition has ceased to be an avenue to freedom. When Roland ceased to imagine (before his poem opens) he made it inevitable that he should be *found by* his phantasmagoria. By marching into that land of his own terrible force of failed will, he compels himself to know the degradation of what it is to be illuminated while himself giving no light. For this is the anxiety of influence, in that variety of poetic melancholy that issues from the terrible strength of post-Enlightenment literary tradition. Where *Childe Roland* excels, and makes its greatness as a poem, is in its unique and appalling swerve, its twist or Lucretian *clinamen* away from its precursors, from the whole line of internalized romance, and from Shelley in particular. This swerve is the vision of the end, where *all* the poets of the Romantic tradition are seen as having failed, to the degree where they stand together, ranged in the living flame, the fire the Promethean quester could not steal but had to burn through.

Yet Childe Roland dies in the courage of knowing—he too sees, and he knows, and so dies with a full intelligence as what Keats called an atom of perception; at the close, he ceases to be a figure of romance, for he knows too much.

Thomas Greene, in a superb insight, speaks of "the mystery and melancholy of romance, which always accepts less than total knowledge," since total knowledge successfully resists enchantment. Romance in *Childe Roland* passes into what George Ridenour has called "the typical mode," which though allegoric is yet allegorically self-contained, as though Browning's poem were that odd conceit, an allegory of allegorizing. Ridenour, in the most illuminating critical remarks yet made about the poem, relates the knight's trial by landscape (his reduced *geste*) to Browning's obsessive investigations into the nature of purposeful human act, and finds the poem to be finally a celebration. All men are questers, and capable of rising into the Burkean Sublime, however purposeless or compulsive their acts as they blunder toward goals both commonplace and unique, like the Dark Tower. Whether this is entirely celebration, since Roland fails his trial by landscape, may be doubted, but the triumphant surge of the end gives Ridenour considerable sanction, making his reading of the poem closer to what must be presumed as Browning's also than my own or Mrs. Miller's is.

If we follow Mrs. Miller by returning to the passage from *Paracelsus* quoted earlier in this essay, we can say that Roland is being punished, by himself, for having quested after knowledge rather than love, the punishment being to see all things as deformed and broken. One of Wordsworth's central insights is that to see without love, to see by knowing, is to deform and break, and Roland would thus exemplify a terrible Romantic truth. But this is to read as reductively as Roland sees, and to miss the awful greatness of Roland's landscape. Browning took Roland from Edgar's song, but giving the name to a quester means to invoke also, in some way, the rich romance associations of the name. In the *Chanson de Roland* the knight's loyalty to his lord, Charlemagne, is exemplary, and the final blast of his trumpet is a supreme self-sacrifice. In Ariosto though, Orlando is insane and disloyal through love's madness, with the love being silly, wretched, and unrequited at that. In contrast to Browning's Roland, we can say of Tasso, Chatterton, and Shelley, his precursors in the band of questers, what Yeats said of certain Irish poets and rebels who had confounded his expectations, that excess of love may have bewildered them until they died. But if the romance quest is, as Angus Fletcher suggests in his powerful study of allegory, an obsessive pattern of desire that becomes a compulsive act, then Browning's Roland too is journeying to rebeget himself, despite his conscious desire only to make an end, any end. Though he finds, and is annihilated in finding, an extraordinary if only partly communicable knowledge, the meaning of his quest was still in his search for love. Love of whom? Of his precursors, the band of brothers who, one by one, "failed" triumphantly at the Dark Tower. A poet's love for another poet is no more disinterested than any other variation upon family romance, but a final knowledge that it was indeed love may be the revelation that makes for a kind of triumph, though not a salvation, at a dark end.

1969

12
Ruskin as Literary Critic

Ruskin was born in London, on 8 February 1819, in the same year that Queen Victoria was born. His father, John James Ruskin, the son of a bankrupt, self-slain Edinburgh wine merchant, had prospered in partnership with the Domecq sherry vineyards, and aspired to raise himself out of his lower middle class position, though he was forced to put aside artistic and literary interests while he made his fortune. Ruskin's mother, Margaret Cox, was John James Ruskin's cousin, and had waited nine years to marry him, while he made his way in London. Energetic and shrewd as John James Ruskin was, he appears to have been a weaker character than his fiercely Evangelical wife, whose rigid nature dominated the formative years of her only child's life, and who clearly was responsible for the psychic malforming that made John Ruskin's emotional life a succession of disasters. Margaret Ruskin, before her son's birth, dedicated him to the service of God, intending him for the ministry. Nature intended otherwise, and made even of the infant Ruskin an aesthetic visionary, fascinated by the world of form and color. The world of language was revealed to the child, between the ages of four and fourteen, by daily Bible readings with his mother. That ten-year march and countermarch through the Book made Ruskin as Bible-soaked a writer as Milton or Blake, and formed the ultimate basis for the characteristic Ruskinian prose style, with its ornate and opulent diction, prophetic rhythm, and extraordinary emotional range.

Ruskin had the misfortune to be a child prodigy, as forced a one as John Stuart Mill. A poet at seven, educated largely at home, scarcely allowed friends, brooded over by a sternly loving mother and a totally indulgent and admiring father, Ruskin was ruined before his thirteenth birthday. He was ruined, one qualifies, in terms of his fully human potential, but not at all in regard to the unique gift that was his, and that his peculiar upbringing did much to nourish.

On his thirteenth birthday, Ruskin received the present of a copy of Samuel Rogers' long poem *Italy*, richly illustrated with steel engravings, including twenty-five plates from drawings by J. M. W. Turner. Immediately captured by Turner, Ruskin was to become an artist under this influence, but his painting like his poetry finally proved marginal, and the lasting effect of Turner was to confirm a critical gift of genius. As a critic of all the arts and of society, Ruskin became, and still remains, a unique figure in the European cultural tradition. This uniqueness was finally a uniqueness of sensibility, and cannot be understood apart from the history of sensibility.

The natural world Ruskin saw was half-created by his Romantic vision, a vision for which his personal sensibility provided the beginnings, but in which his great and essential teachers were Wordsworth and Turner, the dominant figures in the poetry and painting of their generation. Like Shelley before him, Ruskin was haunted throughout his life by Wordsworth's great *Ode: Intimations of Immortality from Recollections of Earliest Childhood*. The fundamental experience of the Ode, and of *Tintern Abbey*, is at one with the central and decisive experiences of Ruskin's life. Attempting to describe the unifying element in Ruskin's complex religious development, Derrick Leon, perhaps unintentionally, paraphrased *Tintern Abbey:*

> Ruskin's real communion, throughout his life, was the communion of the artist and poet: his *panis supersubstantialis* those rare moments of fully awakened consciousness when the mind is detached and deliberately at rest; when the usual egotism of being is deliberately suppressed, and the emotional faculties, cleansed of all human desire and sorrow, respond in serenity and joy to the mystery and beauty of the external world.

In his old age, Ruskin looked back at his essential character as a child, and recognized again his affinity to Turner, Wordsworth, and Shelley, though he did not hesitate to give the preference to himself, the failed poet, over those who had succeeded:

> I was different, be it once more said, from other children even of my own type, not so much in the actual nature of the feeling, but in the mixture of it. I had, in my little clay pitcher, vialfuls, as it were, of Wordsworth's reverence, Shelley's sensitiveness, Turner's accuracy, all in one. A snowdrop was to

me, as to Wordsworth, part of the Sermon on the mount; but I never should have written sonnets to the celandine, because it is of a coarse, yellow and imperfect form. With Shelley, I loved blue sky and blue eyes, but never in the least confused the heavens with my own poor little Psychidion. And the reverence and passion were alike kept in their places by the constructive Turnerian element; and I did not weary myself in wishing that a daisy could see the beauty of its shadow, but in trying to draw the shadow rightly, myself.

This self-congratulatory paragraph tells us why Wordsworth and Shelley were poets, and Ruskin only a critic, albeit a great one. Reverence, sensitiveness, and accuracy, taken together, are the theological virtues for criticism, but the combination can thwart creation. Ruskin, at the age of nine, was a better poet than Ruskin at twenty, when he won the Newdigate Prize at Oxford. At nine, Ruskin wrote good Wordsworthian verse, better perhaps than Wordsworth was writing in 1828:

> Skiddaw, upon thy heights the sun shines bright,
> But only for a moment; then gives place
> Unto a playful cloud which on thy brow
> Sports wantonly,—then floats away in air,—
> Throwing its shadow on thy towering height;
> And, darkening for a moment thy green side,
> But adds unto its beauty, as it makes
> The sun more bright when it again appears.

But, by 1839, Ruskin's imagination had not the patience to wait upon the restraints of verse. He knew the truth, or many divisions of it, and he sought the prophet's style in which to deliver it. Fortunately, the truth always remained a poet's truth, and relied on the sources of visionary experience, known to Ruskin from his childhood on, and confirmed in him by his discovery of the visual equivalent in Turner's work.

Ruskin's life, from the revelation of Turner on to his disastrous marriage, was a continuous process of self-discovery, assured and "organic" in its development. Foreign tours, with his parents, encouraged his passion for close observation of nature, for the study of geology and botany, and for incessant sketching and versifying. Even his unreciprocated first love, for Adele Domecq, daughter of his father's business partner, created no more disturbance than could be quieted by an outpouring of much pseudo-Byronic verse. The closeness of the family-circle was not affected by his studies at Christ

Church, Oxford, from January 1837 on, as Mrs. Ruskin imperturbably settled in that city and required her son to appear for tea every evening, with Ruskin's father hastening to join them from London every weekend. Despite the family presence, Ruskin had a successful career at Oxford, composing his first book, *The Poetry of Architecture*, while still an undergraduate. But an attack of tuberculosis delayed his taking a degree, and sent him abroad instead, creating the circumstances that altered his career. His return to the Vale of Chamouni, his confronting again the sight of the sublimity of Mont Blanc, renewed the sense of exaltation he had first encountered at the same spot when he was fifteen. The visionary dialectic of Wordsworth's *Tintern Abbey* was renewed in Ruskin, and prepared him for a climactic return to Chamouni in August 1842. In *that* moment of renewal, as Wordsworthian a "spot of time" as any in *The Prelude*, Volume I of *Modern Painters* had its genesis. Ruskin returned to England, gave up all plans of taking orders, and devoted himself to vindicating the genius of Turner's Romantic landscape art, on principles grounded in the critic's own visionary experience.

By the time Ruskin had to seek healing consolation through another return to Chamouni, in 1854, his critical reputation was established, and his personal life was fairly well set toward destruction. He had published the second volume of *Modern Painters*, *The Seven Lamps of Architecture*, and *The Stones of Venice*, and he had married Euphemia Gray in 1848 with motives that have puzzled the best of his biographers. The marriage was not consummated, and was annulled in 1854, after the lady fled back to her parents. She married the Pre-Raphaelite painter Millais, whom Ruskin had befriended and patronized, and the entire affair soon passed out of the realm of scandal. Ruskin himself remained reticent on the matter (his marriage is not mentioned in his autobiography, *Praeterita*) and devoted himself more passionately to his work, which increasingly moved from art criticism to social prophecy. As the friend of Rossetti, Carlyle, and the Brownings, as the foremost expositor of the visual arts ever to appear in Great Britain, and as a prose poet of extraordinary power who took the whole concern of man as his subject, Ruskin appeared to have realized himself during the years from 1854 to 1860. Volumes three and four of *Modern Painters* came out in 1856, eliciting from George Eliot the definitive comment: "He is strongly akin to the sublimest part of Wordsworth." By 1860, Ruskin ought to have been at the supreme point of his development, and in a sense he was, but not in terms of continuity, for by 1860 he was at the turning, and entered into what was at once his great decade and his tragedy.

In 1860, Ruskin stood forth as a prophet fully armed in *Unto This Last*, his most eloquent and vital book. The central experiences of his life had led him beyond Wordsworth's quietism, and returned him to the biblical origins of his vision. The "theoretic faculty" of man, our ability to enter into the state of aesthetic contemplation depicted in *Tintern Abbey*, had now to issue in the Hebraic and Protestant impulse to free all men toward finding the way to individual vision, to an enjoyment of the sense of something more divinely interfused. Eloquent as he always was, Ruskin rose to the heights of his rhetorical power in *Unto This Last*. If there is a kernel passage in his work, it is the one that climaxes:

> *There is no wealth but Life*—Life, including all its powers of love, of joy, and of admiration. That country is the richest which nourishes the greatest number of noble and happy human beings.

This is the moral force behind the apocalyptic yearnings of the fifth and final volume of *Modern Painters*, also published in 1860. A fully perceptive reader in that year might have seen Ruskin as being poised on the threshold of a creative period akin to the great years granted to a whole tradition of English poetic visionaries before him. The expectation would not have been altogether disappointed by Ruskin's works in the sixties, particularly by the sequence of *Munera Pulveris* (1863), *Sesame and Lilies* (1865), and *The Queen of the Air* (1869), but the decade essentially was one of brilliant decline, and two decades of writing after it showed the decline more consistently, until there came the final, intermittent brilliance of *Praeterita*, after which Ruskin had to be silent.

Part of the cause of this downward movement is found clearly enough by an examination of Ruskin's life from 1860 on. In that year Ruskin, already forty, met Rose La Touche, not yet ten, and their extraordinary love began. By 1860 Ruskin had no religious belief in any orthodox sense, having become intellectually agnostic, though his temperament remained a deeply Evangelical one. Rose was, at ten, something of a religious fanatic, and she evidenced already the tortured sensibility that was to result in the illness (at least partly mental) that killed her when she was twenty-five. Despite all the obvious barriers—of differences in age and belief, of the strong opposition of Rose's mother (who, perhaps unconsciously, seems to have desired Ruskin for herself)—Ruskin proposed marriage to Rose on her seventeenth birthday. Ambiguously, Rose delayed her answer for over a year, until correspondence between Ruskin's former wife and Mrs. La Touche revealed the supposed fact of his impotence. There followed a complex cycle of estrangements and reconciliations, concluding with a final reconciliation in 1874, by which time Rose's mental illness had become extreme. With her death, in 1875, Ruskin's long decline commenced. He became involved in spiritualism, and began to identify the memory of Rose with Dante's Beatrice and with Saint Ursula. One sympathetic biographer called the Ruskin of the late 1870s a morbid prig, and he was not far wrong. By 1878, Ruskin believed himself to have failed, in love and work alike, and with this sour belief came the onset of his own mental illness. He had been Slade Professor of Fine Art at Oxford since 1868, but the controversy with Whistler and subsequent trial, in 1877, caused him to resign that influential forum. He resumed the chair in 1883, but resigned again when it became clear he could no longer lecture coherently. Thenceforward he lived under what he termed the Storm Cloud, and his whole existence took on the beauty and terror of nightmare, haunted by the Evil One, who had intercepted all his desires, and who plagued him now in the shapes of peacock and cat. From this terror Ruskin partly rescued himself by a Wordsworthian return to childhood, celebrated by the writing of *Praeterita*. He returned also to a kind of religious belief, though he continued to hate the notion of justification by faith, and seems in his last days to have been more Catholic than Protestant in his outlook. In a final twilight period of deep peace alternating with total alienation from reality, Ruskin lived out his last days, dying on 20 January 1900.

There are three major areas of Ruskin's achievement: art, social, and literary criticism, and this essay is wholly devoted to only one of the three. I have allowed myself a broad interpretation of "literary criticism," since Ruskin is very much an anticipatory critic in regard to some schools of literary criticism in our own time. Ruskin is one of the first, if not indeed the first, "myth" or "archetypal" critic, or more properly he is the linking and transitional figure between allegorical critics of the elder, Renaissance kind, and those of the newer variety, like Northrop Frye, or like W. B. Yeats in his criticism. Even if he did not have this unique historical position, Ruskin would stand as one of the handful of major literary critics in nineteenth-century England, though his importance has been obscured by misapprehensions about his work. Most histories of literary criticism tag Ruskin as a "moral" critic which is true only in Ruskin's own terms, but not at all in conventional ones. An Oxford lecture delivered by him in 1870 makes clear the special sense in which Ruskin insists upon the morality of art:

> You must first have the right moral state, or you cannot have art. But when the art is once obtained, its reflected action enhances and completes the moral state out of which it arose, and, above all, communicates the exultation to other minds which are already morally capable of the like. For instance take the art of singing, and the simplest perfect master of it—the skylark. From him you may learn what it is to sing for joy. You must get the moral state first, the pure gladness, then give it finished expression, and it is perfected in itself, and made communicable to others capable of such joy. Accuracy in proportion to the rightness of the cause, and purity of the emotion, is the possibility of fine art. You cannot paint or sing yourself into being good men; you must be good men before you can either paint or sing, and then the colour and sound will complete in you all that is best . . .

In this passage the "right moral state" and "being good men" are phrases that suggest conventional moral attitudes, yet the only moral state mentioned is that of the skylark, "the pure gladness." Behind Ruskin's passage are Wordsworth and Shelley, both in their skylark poems, and in their insistence upon the poet's joy and on poems as necessarily recording the best and happiest moments of the happiest and best minds. Ruskin's literary theory is primarily a Wordsworthian one, and as such it shows a family resemblance to all such theories down to Wallace Stevens, with his eloquent, Paterian insistence that "the morality of the poet's radiant and productive atmosphere is the morality of the right sensation." Ruskin's morality, as a critical theorist, is a morality of aesthetic contemplation, like the morality of *Tintern Abbey*. It is not, in content, an Evangelical morality, though its fervor stamps it as a displaced version of Evangelicism. Ruskin's literary criticism has an explicit moral purpose, as Wordsworth's poetry does also, yet the purpose no more disfigures the criticism than it does the poetry. To understand Ruskin's criticism we need to study not only the pattern of Ruskin's life and career, but also the radical version of Romanticism his entire sensibility incarnated. Literary criticism rarely communicates the critic's own *experience* of literature, but in Ruskin's hands it very nearly always does, and in doing so touches upon the incommunicable. Ruskin did not believe that the imagination could create truth, but he did believe that it was the crucial faculty for the communication and interpretation of truth. Though Ruskin's judgment as a critic was fairly unsteady (he once declared Mrs. Browning's *Aurora Leigh* to be the greatest poem in the language), his central aesthetic experience was so powerful as to make him an almost miraculous medium for the truth of imagination to work through in order to reach sensibilities less uniquely organized than his own. In this respect, as in so many others, he resembles Wordsworth. Thus, speaking of Gothic as being representative of our universal childhood, Ruskin observes that all men:

> look back to the days of childhood as of greatest happiness, because those were the days of greatest wonder, greatest simplicity, and most vigorous imagination. And the whole difference between a man of genius and other men . . . is that the first remains in great part a child, seeing with the large eyes of children, in perpetual wonder, not conscious of much knowledge,—conscious, rather, of infinite ignorance, and yet infinite power; a fountain of eternal admiration, delight, and creative force within him, meeting the ocean of visible and governable things around him.

If this is the source of creative imagination, it follows tragically but pragmatically that the workings of the mature imagination must be compensatory, for the story of art must be one in which gain can come only through loss, and the subsequent memory of the glorious time preceding loss. This pattern is familiar to every reader of Wordsworth, and is nowhere more eloquently expressed than it is by Ruskin. In a letter (28 September 1847) written to Walter Brown, once his tutor at Christ Church, Ruskin states the central experience of his life in phrases directly borrowed from the *Intimations* Ode:

> . . . there was a time when the sight of a steep hill covered with pines cutting against blue sky, would have touched me with an emotion inexpressible, which, in the endeavour to communicate in its truth and intensity, I must have sought for all kinds of far-off, wild, and dreamy images. Now I can look at such a slope with coolness, and observation of *fact*. I see that it slopes at twenty or twenty-five degrees; I know the pines are spruce fir—"Pinus nigra"—of such and such a formation; the soil, thus, and thus; the day fine and the sky blue. All this I can at once communicate in so many words, and this

is all which is necessarily seen. But it is not all the truth: there is something else to be seen there, which I cannot see but in a certain condition of mind, nor can I make anyone else see it, but by putting him into that condition, and my endeavour in description would be, not to detail the facts of the scene, but by any means whatsoever to put my hearer's mind into the same ferment as my mind . . .

Ruskin's activity as a critic of all the arts, of society, and of nature, is a quest to fulfill that "endeavour in description." What makes him a tragic critic (if so odd a phrase may be allowed) is his post-Words-worthian and post-Turnerian sense of reality. In reply to Walter Brown's Wordsworthian statement of recompense for a loss of primal delight in nature, Ruskin wrote a letter (27 November 1847) which is an epilogue to the *Intimations* Ode:

. . . You say, in losing the delight I once had in nature I am coming down more to fellowship with others. Yes, but I feel it a fellowship of blindness. I may be able to get hold of people's hands better in the dark, but of what use is that, when I have no where to lead them but into the ditch? Surely, devoid of these imaginations and impressions, the world becomes a mere board-and-lodging house. The sea by whose side I am writing was once to me a friend, companion, master, teacher; now it is *salt water*, and salt water only. Is this an increase or a withdrawal of *truth*? I did not before lose hold or sight of the fact of its being salt water; I could consider it so, if I chose; my perceiving and feeling it to be more than this was a possession of higher *truth*, which did not interfere with my hold of the physical one.

This sense of loss haunts Ruskin's criticism, until at last it becomes the apocalyptic desire of his later works, from *Modern Painters* V (1860) on to *Praeterita* (1885–89). Kenneth Clark has said, very accurately, that Ruskin was by nature an impressionist, to which one can add that an apocalyptic impressionist is a very strange being; it is difficult to conceive of Revelation as Proust would have written it, yet that is what the prophetic Ruskin gives us. Ruskin remained true to Wordsworth and Turner in being interested primarily in *appearances*, and in taking those appearances as final realities. Yet Wordsworth learned how to evade the apocalyptic element even in the sublime modes of poetry, and Turner, like Keats, thought the earth and the sun to be enough. If there is a central meaning to Ruskin's great change about 1860, it is that his movement from description to prophecy refused to abandon the external world or the arts that he had learned to scrutinize so accurately. Instead Ruskin demanded more from both nature and art than even he had asked earlier, and so made more terrible the process of loss his sensibility had made inevitable. The Ruskin of the Storm Cloud is what Wordsworth would have been, had he allowed his characteristic dialectic of love between man and nature to survive, unchanged, the crisis of 1805, out of which *Peele Castle* was written as palinode.

This is the terrible pathos of Ruskin's art as a critic, that no one else has had so intense an intimation of loss within the imaginative experience itself. Remembering the vision that was his as a child, Ruskin could say that "for me, the Alps and their people were alike beautiful in their snow, and their humanity; and I wanted, neither for them nor myself, sight of any thrones in heaven but the rocks, or of any spirits in heaven but the clouds." This primary humanism never left Ruskin, as it did finally leave the older Wordsworth. What preserved it in Ruskin was the greater purity of his own Wordsworthianism; like the poet John Clare, he excelled Wordsworth as a visionary, and *saw* constantly what the greater poet could see only by glimpses:

> . . . My entire delight was in observing without being myself noticed,—if I could have been invisible, all the better. I was absolutely interested in men and their ways, as I was interested in marmots and chamois, in tomtits and trout. If only they would stay still and let me look at them, and not get into their holes and up their heights! The living inhabitation of the world—the grazing and nesting in it,—the spiritual power of the air, the rocks, the waters, to be in the midst of it, and rejoice and wonder at it, and help it if I could,—happier if it needed no help of mine,—this was the essential love *of Nature* in me, this the root of all that I have usefully become, and the light of all that I have rightly learned.

If we call Ruskin's view of nature or of the self a mythical one, we need to qualify the classification, as Ruskin scarcely believed his view of either to be the product of his own creative powers. Wordsworth, and most of the Romantics after him, sought continuity between the earlier and the future self even at the expense of present time; Wordsworth indeed is mute in the face of nature at the living moment. Ruskin, like Blake, celebrated the pulsation of an artery, the flash of apprehension in which the poet's work is done. And, again like Blake, Ruskin placed his emphasis on *seeing* as the special mark of imagination. For Ruskin, unlike Wordsworth, the deepest imaginative effects are connected with the finite phenomena of nature, and the minute particulars of artistic detail. Wordsworth valued most highly in poetry "those passages where things are lost in each other, and limits vanish," but Ruskin, regarding art or nature, never ceased to see firm, determinate outlines, and every subtlety of detail. Ruskin, unlike Wordsworth, would not sacrifice either the landscape or the moment to the quest for continuity. Wordsworth's rewards for such sacrifices were immense, as Ruskin well knew, for no other writer has felt or made others feel so great a sense of the renewal of the past in the present, through the renovating influence of nature. Ruskin was an extraordinary psychologist, though a largely involuntary one, and did not believe that the therapy for an individual consciousness could come largely through a pursuit of after-images. Yet he wished to believe this, frequently wrote in the Wordsworthian mode, and achieved his final, autobiographical vision and last broken intervals of lucidity primarily through following Wordsworth's example, by tracing the growth of his own imagination. If Ruskin became one of the ruins of Romanticism, and even one of its victims, he became also one of its unique masters, who could justify asserting that "the greatest thing a human soul ever does in this world is to see something, and tell what it saw in a plain way. Hundreds of people can talk for one who can think, but thousands can think for one who can see. To see clearly is poetry, prophecy and religion all in one." Yet to see clearly was finally no salvation for Ruskin, but only gave him a maddening sense of loss, in the self and in nature alike.

Ruskin never gave up insisting that all art, literature included, was worship, but this insistence does not make him either a "religious" or a "moral" critic of literature. Though he moved in outward religion from Evangelical Protestantism to agnostic naturalism and on finally to a private version of primitive Catholicism, Ruskin's pragmatic religion always remained a Wordsworthian "natural piety," in which aesthetic and spiritual experience were not to be distinguished from one another. Ruskin's literary taste was formed by the King James Bible, more than any other reading, and therefore from the start he associated expressive and devotional values. In this also he stands with the great Romantics, whose theories of the Imagination are all displaced, radical Protestant accounts of the nakedness of the soul before God.

179

Ruskin's own theory of the Imagination is clearly derived from Coleridge's, and it has been argued that all Ruskin adds to his master's account is a multiplication of unnecessary entities. Yet Ruskin does add to Coleridge's theory a confidence in the autonomy of the imagination that Coleridge himself never possessed. Indeed it is Coleridge whose criticism is distorted by the claims of conventional morality and institutional religion, and not Ruskin. Ruskin could not have written "that it has pleased Providence, that the divine truths of religion should have been revealed to us *in the form of* poetry" (italics mine) or that "an undevout poet is mad: in the strict sense of the word, an undevout poet is an impossibility." Because he lacked Coleridge's doubts, Ruskin allowed himself to elaborate upon Coleridge's categories, there being no point at which he felt the imagination had to yield to a higher or more assured faculty. If these elaborations have failed to be influential, they yet remain interesting in themselves and indicate where a less inhibited Romantic theory of Imagination may still quarry for its materials.

Fundamentally Ruskin favored two groups of poets, those like Dante, Spenser, Milton, and Wordsworth who dealt in detail with the whole destiny of man, from creation to apocalypse, and those he had loved in his own youth, like Scott and Byron. It is in the first that Ruskin's great strength as a critic lies, since he is given to special pleading for his childhood favorites. But there is an honorable place for special pleading in criticism, if it is done with the eloquent passion and exquisite discrimination of a Ruskin.

It is in his examination of the larger outlines of the structure of literature that Ruskin appears today to have been a major critical innovator. Because of his intimate knowledge of biblical and classical iconology, and of Dante, Spenser, and Milton as the heirs of such iconology, Ruskin arrived at a comprehensive theory of literature, which he never made fully explicit but which is evident throughout his criticism. One major assumption of this theory is that all great poetry whatsoever is allegorical; and that what it allegorizes is a fundamental myth of universal man, his fall from Paradise and his quest for a revelation that would restore him to Paradise. This myth is clearest in the Ruskin of the 1860s, of *The Queen of the Air,* and of *Sesame and Lilies.*

Though it is an obsession in the later Ruskin, a consciousness of this myth was always present in his criticism, since he relied from the start on a Wordsworthian experience of paradisal intimations within a wholly natural context. The Wordsworthian principle of continuity and dialectic of love between man and nature were generalized by the older Ruskin into the universal figures he had encountered in his early journeys from Genesis to Revelation. The symbols of *Modern Painters* V, *Munera Pulveris*, *Sesame and Lilies*, and *The Queen of the Air* are primarily biblical ones, even when Ruskin investigates the many guises of Athena in the elaborate mythologizings of *The Queen of the Air*. The Garden of Eden, the Serpent or Dragon, the unfallen maiden who replaces Mother Eve and becomes the prime hope of salvation; these are for Ruskin the principal figures in a mythopoeic fantasia of his own, which is almost too available for psychoanalytical reduction, of the kind to which Ruskin is generally subjected in our time. When, in *The Queen of the Air*, this fantasia is mixed with extraordinary excursions into botany, political economy, and primordial folklore, the result demands a reader more exuberant than most Ruskin scholars have been.

The Queen of the Air, in one of its aspects, resembles some works of Elizabethan mythography like Henry Reynolds' *Mythomystes*, but an even closer parallel can be found in Blake's poetry and prose. Like Ruskin, Blake counterpoints both classical and biblical myth against an imaginative story of his own, which in itself is a deliberate modification of Milton's accounts of Fall and Redemption. Ruskin does not seem to invent "Giant Forms" or titanic personages, as Blake does, but he invents and explores states-of-being in a manner very similar to Blake's, though he does not give them Blake's kind of categorical names. Ruskin's Athena is finally a goddess of his own creation, and as such she is one of the major myth-makings of the Victorian age.

Ruskin's earlier, and more Wordsworthian literary criticism, is dominated by the problem of landscape, in the same way that his later criticism centers on typological figures of redemption. *Modern Painters* III (1856) contains Ruskin's principal achievement as a literary critic before he entered upon his own mythical phase, but it is an achievement that has been misunderstood, partly because Ruskin's famous formulation of the Pathetic Fallacy has been misinterpreted. The theory of the Pathetic Fallacy is a searching criticism of Romanticism from within, for the sake of saving the Romantic program of humanizing nature from extinction through excessive self-indulgence. Ruskin is the first writer within the Romantic tradition to have realized the high spiritual price that had to be paid for Wordsworthianism, the human loss that accompanied the "abundant recompense" celebrated in *Tintern Abbey*.

Ruskin was, more so even than most artists and critics, a kind of natural phenomenologist, to use a term now in fashion, or simply, a man to whom things spoke, and who spent his life describing "the ordinary, proper, and true appearances of things to us." Ruskin knew that, as man and artist, his debts and affinities were to what he called the second order of poets, the "Reflective or Perceptive" group (Wordsworth, Keats, Tennyson) and not to the first order, the "Creative" group (Shakespeare, Homer, Dante). Ruskin's purpose in expounding the Pathetic Fallacy, which characterizes the second order, is not to discredit the Wordsworthian kind of poetry, but to indicate its crucial limitation, which he knew himself to share.

Wordsworth and his followers present states of mind that "produce in us a falseness in all our impressions of external things." A. H. R. Ball, the most sympathetic student of Ruskin's literary criticism, was convinced that the theory of the Pathetic Fallacy contradicted Ruskin's own imaginative theory, which may be true, but the contradiction, if it exists, is only a seeming one. Ruskin understood that Romantic poetry, and its imaginative theory, were grounded upon the Pathetic Fallacy, the imputation of life to the object-world. To believe that there is the one life only, within us and abroad, was to heal the Enlightenment's split in consciousness between adverting mind and the universe of things, but at the price that the intuitive phenomenologist in Ruskin understood and resented. The myth of continuity, in Wordsworth and in his followers, Ruskin included, is the result of a homogeneity of sense-experience, which can result only from reduction. The psychiatrist J. H. Van den Berg, in his fascinating study, *Metabletica*, traces this reduction to Descartes, who saw objects as localized space, extensiveness. Wordsworth's quest was to find a way out of all dualisms, Cartesian included, but ironically Wordsworth and his school followed Descartes, unknowingly, in reducing the present to an elaborated past, and making the future also only a consequence of the past. Ruskin's formulation of the Pathetic Fallacy is a profound protest against nineteenth-century homogeneities, particularly landscape homogeneities. It is perhaps sour wit, but it seems true to remark that Wordsworth could see only landscapes that he had seen before, and that no landscape became visible to him that he had not first estranged from himself.

Ruskin's protest is against this estrangement of things, and against the Romantic delight in seeing a reduction, and then elevating that reduction to the ecstasy of enforced humanization. Van den Berg remarks somberly that the Romantic inner self became necessary when contacts between man and the external world became less valued. Ruskin's rejection of Romantic mythopoeia as the Pathetic Fallacy shows a similar distrust of Wordsworthian self-consciousness, but the later Ruskin put such distrust aside, and became the major Romantic myth-maker of the Victorian era. The aesthetic tragedy of Ruskin is that works like *Sesame and Lilies* and *The Queen of the Air* are giant Pathetic Fallacies, but the mingled grandeur and ruin of those books only make them still more representative of post-Romantic art, and its central dilemma. Ruskin may yet seem the major and most original critic that Romanticism has produced, as well as one of its most celebrated avatars.

1965

13
The Place of Pater:
Marius The Epicurean

The Aesthetic Movement in England (*circa* 1870–1900) is usually tracked to its sources in the literary Paris of the 1850s. The poets Théophile Gautier and Charles Baudelaire are thus viewed as being the inventors of the new sensibility exemplified in the life and work of Algernon Swinburne, James Whistler, Walter Pater, and their immediate followers—George Moore, Oscar Wilde, Aubrey Beardsley, Simeon Solomon, Ernest Dowson, Lionel Johnson, Arthur Symons, and the young William Butler Yeats. Whistler, an American and a painter, rightly felt that he owed everything to Paris and himself and nothing to English tradition. But behind Swinburne and Pater were three generations of English Romanticism, from the poetry of Blake and Wordsworth on through to the Victorian Romanticism of the Pre-Raphaelite poets and painters. In the midst of this tradition one finds a more direct source of English Aestheticism: the literary theories of Arthur Henry Hallam, as set forth in a review of his friend Alfred Tennyson's poetry some twenty years before Gautier and Baudelaire created their sensibility out of Delacroix, Poe, and their own complex natures.

Yeats remarked that he had found his literary aesthetics in Hallam before coming under Pater's influence. Hallam contrasted Shelley and Keats as "poets of sensation" with Wordsworth as a "poet of reflection":

> Susceptible of the slightest impulse from external nature, their fine organs trembled into emotion at colors, and sounds, and movements, unperceived or unregarded by duller temperaments . . . So vivid was the delight attending the simple exertions of eye and ear, that it became mingled more and

more with their trains of active thought, and tended to absorb their whole being into the energy of sense.

Marshall McLuhan observed that the theme of Hallam's essay is
usually the theme of Pater and of T. S. Eliot: the Copernican revolution in poetry that saw a change in the direction of poetic art, from
"the shaping of the poetic object . . . to the shaping of psychological
effects in the reader," as McLuhan phrases it. Eliot disliked Pater's
work, as he disliked most of the Romantic tradition, but critics tend
now to agree that he has a place in that tradition despite himself.

Walter Pater's place in Romantic tradition was a consciously
chosen one, and only recently have readers begun to see again what
that place was. In his lifetime Pater was a shadowy but famous figure, vaguely blamed by the public as being the half-sinister and
withdrawn theorist whom extravagant disciples—Wilde, Beardsley,
Moore—would cite as the authority for their more extreme stances
in art and in life. This Pater of popular tradition is so vivid a part of
literary folklore that any critic ought to be wary of clearing away
the myth. We would lose the "tremendous Ritualist" who had lost
all faith, and who burned his poems because they had been too pious,
but who felt frustrated nonetheless when he was prevented (by his
friends) from being ordained. A still greater loss would be the Pater
who is reputed to have walked the Oxford meadows in the cool of
the evening, murmuring that the odor of the meadow-sweet gave
him pain: "It is the fault of nature in England that she runs too much
to excess."

Aside from his assured place in the great line of English eccentrics,
Pater is one of the central figures in the continuity between Romanticism, Modernism, and the emergent sensibility still in the process of
replacing Modernism today. Pater's most ambitious and extensive
work, the historical novel *Marius The Epicurean*, is in itself one of
the more remarkable fictional experiments of the later nineteenth
century, but it has the added value now of teaching us something
about our own continuity with the past that otherwise we could not
wholly know.

Currently fashionable sensibility, two-thirds of the way through
the century, is perhaps another ironic disordering of Paterian sensibility. Pater is halfway between Wordsworth and ourselves. But he
is more than a link between, say, the sensibility of Keats and that
of the late Yeats or late Stevens; he is a kind of hinge upon which
turns the single gate, one side of which is Romantic and the other

modern poetry. Marius himself may be little more than an idealized version of Pater's own self-consciousness, and yet Marius, more than any fictional character of our age, is the representative modern poet as well as the representative man of literary culture who remains the only audience for that poet. If one holds in mind a handful of our age's lyrical poems at their most poignant, say Yeats's *Vacillation* and *The Man and the Echo*, with Stevens's *The Course of a Particular* and *Of Mere Being*, and imagines a possible poet who might make those poems into a story, one gets the sensibility and even the dimmed, half-willing, self-defeated fate of Pater's Roman quester.

"His Sensations and Ideas" is the subtitle of *Marius The Epicurean*. At the center of the novel is the flux of sensations; at its circumference whirl a succession of ideas of the good life, all of them inadequate beside the authenticity of the central flux. This inadequacy is highly deliberate:

> . . . with this sense of the splendour of our experience and of its awful brevity, gathering all we are into one desperate effort to see and touch, we shall hardly have time to make theories about the things we see and touch. What we have to do is to be for ever curiously testing new opinions and courting new impressions, never acquiescing in a facile orthodoxy. . . .

That is Pater at his most central, in the famous "Conclusion" to *The Renaissance*, written in 1868. Thinking of this "Conclusion," and of its effect on the "Tragic Generation" of Wilde, Aubrey Beardsley, Ernest Dowson, Lionel Johnson, and their companions, Yeats eloquently complained that Pater "taught us to walk upon a rope, tightly stretched through serene air, and we were left to keep our feet upon a swaying rope in a storm." Pater's reply is more eloquent still:

> While all melts under our feet, we may well catch at any exquisite passion, or any contribution to knowledge that seems by a lifted horizon to set the spirit free for a moment, or any stirring of the senses, strange dyes, strange colours, and curious odours, or work of the artist's hands, or the face of one's friend. Not to discriminate every moment some passionate attitude in those about us, and in the brilliancy of their gifts some tragic dividing of forces on their ways, is, on this short day of frost and sun, to sleep before evening.

Eliot complained that Pater was neither a critic nor a creator but a moralist, whether in *Marius, The Renaissance*, or elsewhere. Clearly

Pater, whenever he wrote, was all three, like Eliot himself. The confusion of purposes, in both men, was well served by a late version of Romantic art, the usual mode for each being a flash of radiance against an incongruous or bewildering background. In this "privileged" or "timeless" moment of illumination, the orthodox religious quest of the later writer found its equivocal conclusion, but the skeptical, more openly solipsistic Pater tended to remain within a narrower vision, confined to what he himself naturalistically could see.

Because of this restraint, *Marius* is a surprisingly unified narrative for all its surface diversity. At first reading one can feel that its motto might well be the tag from Nennius affixed by David Jones to his *Anathemata:* "I have made a heap of all that I could find," or perhaps Eliot's line in *The Waste Land:* "These fragments I have shored against my ruins." Pater gives us the tale of Cupid and Psyche from Apuleius, an impressionistic account of the *Pervigilium Veneris,* a supposed oration of Cornelius Fronto, a version of a dialogue of Lucian, and a paraphrase of selected meditations of Marcus Aurelius. Critics have suspected his motives: they argue that Pater resorted to imitation because he could not invent a story, create a character, dramatize a conflict, or even present a conversation. This is true enough. We hardly *hear* anything said in Pater's novel, and few events occur that are not historical. Critics less prejudiced than Eliot have also questioned the accuracy of Pater's summations of philosophical creeds, and others have indicated the absence of all theological content from the presentation of Christianity in the closing pages of the book. All true, and all irrelevant to the achievement of *Marius,* which remains a unified reverie or aesthetic meditation upon history, though a history as idealized and foreshortened as in Yeats's *A Vision,* a thoroughly Paterian work.

Pater and Yeats made magical associations between aspects of the Renaissance and their own times. Yeats extended the parallel to different phases of Byzantine culture, with an arbitrariness justified by his needs as a lyrical poet not content with the limitations of lyric. Pater's *Marius* is founded on a more convincing and troubling resemblance, between Victorian England in the 1880s and Rome in the Age of the Antonines, two summits of power and civilization sloping downward in decadence. The aesthetic humanism of Marius, poised just outside of a Christianity Pater felt to be purer than anything available to himself, is precisely the desperately noble and hopeless doctrine set forth in the "Conclusion" to *The Renaissance.* Like Pater, Marius is committed to the universe of death, loving it the better for every evidence of decay. "Death is the mother of beauty" in Pater as in his immediate ancestor, the poet of the *Ode to Psyche* and the *Ode on Melancholy*, and in his immediate descendant, the poet of *Sunday Morning* and *Esthétique du Mal*. There is a morbidity in Pater, not present in Keats or in Stevens, the spirit of sadomasochism and inversion, the infantile regressiveness of his *The Child in the House*, and the repressed destructiveness that emerges in some of his *Imaginary Portraits*. Something of this drifts into *Marius The Epicurean*, through the subtly evaded homosexuality of the love of Marius first for Flavian and then for Cornelius, and in the reveries on human and animal victims of pain and martyrdom. But what morbidity there is distracts only a little from the central theme of the book, which is Pater's own version of Romanticism, his individual addition of strangeness to beauty. For Wordsworth the privileged moments, "spots of time," gave precise knowledge of how and to what extent his power of mind reigned over outward sense. "I see by glimpses now," Wordsworth lamented, but the glimpses revealed the glory of human imagination, and recalled a time when the poet stood alone, in his conscious strength, unaided by religious orthodoxies. For Pater the spots of time belonged to the ascendancy of what Wordsworth called "outward sense," and the dying Marius is still an "unclouded and receptive soul," sustained by "the vision of men and things, actually revealed to him on his way through the world." The faith, to the end, is in the evidence of things seen, and in the substance of things experienced. Certainly the closest analogue is in the death poem of Stevens, *Of Mere Being*, where the palm that rises at the end of the mind, the tree of mere being, has on it the life-enhancing aureole of an actual bird:

> The bird sings. Its feathers shine . . .
> The bird's fire-fangled feathers dangle down.

The burden of *Marius The Epicurean* is the burden of modern lyric, from Wordsworth to Stevens, the near solipsism of the isolated sensibility, of the naked aesthetic consciousness deprived of everything save its wavering self and the flickering of an evanescent beauty in the world of natural objects, which is part of the universe of death. As a critic, Pater derived from Ruskin, and went further in alienation. This stance of experiential loss and aesthetic gain is familiar enough to contemporary analysts in several disciplines. It was while Pater labored at the composition of *Marius* that the unconscious was formally "discovered" (about 1882), and thus the

Romantic inner self received its definitive formulation. Societies (Victorian and Antonine) disintegrate, and individuals (Pater and Marius) lose all outward connections. Pater would have understood immediately the later description of the unconscious proposed by the phenomenologists: an index of the remoteness in the self's relationships with others. The famous description of the Mona Lisa in Pater's *Renaissance*, anthologized by Yeats as the first modern poem, is just such a vision of the unconscious: what J. H. Van den Berg, the phenomenological psychiatrist, defines as "the secret inner self, the innerworld in which everything the world has to offer is shut away." Van den Berg, as it happens, is referring to Rilke's account of Leonardo's lady and her landscape, but Rilke writes of the painting much in Pater's spirit. The landscape, Rilke observes, is as estranged as the lady, "far and completely unlike us." Both represent what Van den Berg calls "things-in-their-farewell," a beauty purchased by estrangement.

This, I think, is the most relevant context in which to read *Marius The Epicurean*. *Marius* is the masterpiece of things-in-their-farewell, the great document in English of the historical moment when the unconscious came painfully to its birth. Where Wordsworth and Keats, followed by Mill and Arnold, fought imaginatively against excessive self-consciousness, Pater welcomes it, and by this welcome inaugurates, for writers and readers in English, the decadent phase of Romanticism, in which, when honest, we still find ourselves. What Pater, and modernist masters following him, lack is not energy of apprehension, but rather the active force of a synthesizing imagination, so titanic in Blake and Wordsworth. Yet this loss—in Yeats, Joyce, Stevens—is only an honest recognition of necessity. Except for the phenomenon of a last desperate High Romantic, Hart Crane, the faith in the saving, creative power of the imagination subsides in our time. Here too Pater is the hinge, for the epiphanies of Marius only help him to live what life he has; they do not save him, nor in the context of his world, or Pater's, or ours, can anyone be saved.

As an artist, Pater was essentially a baroque essayist, in the line of Sir Thomas Browne and De Quincey, and the aesthetic achievement of Marius is of a kind with the confessions of those stylists. Yeats, at least, thought *Marius* to be written in the only great modern prose style in English. One can add Yeats, in his still undervalued prose, to the line of Browne, De Quincey, and Pater, and indeed the influence of Pater remains to be traced throughout all of Yeats's prose, early or late, particularly in the marvelous *Autobiographies*.

Criticism has said little to the purpose about this late tradition of highly mannered prose, whose elaborate and conscious harmonies have an affinity with the relatively more ascetic art of James, and reach their parodistic climax in Joyce. Our expectations of this prose are mistaken when we find it to be an intrusion, of any kind, between ourselves and its maker; it is as much of his vision as he can give to us, and its self-awareness is an overwhelming attempt to exorcize the demon of discursiveness. The marmoreal reverie, whether in *Marius* or in Yeats's *Per Amica Silentia Lunae* and *A Vision*, is allied to other modernist efforts to subvert the inexorable dualism of form and content.

Pater has the distinction of being one of the first major theorists in the modern phase of this effort. He rejected the organic analogue of Coleridge, by which any work of art is, as it were, naturalized, because he feared that it devalued the intense and solitary effort of the artist to overcome natural limitation. In his essay on *The School of Giorgione* he could speak of art as "always striving to be independent of the mere intelligence, to become a matter of pure perception, to get rid of its responsibilities to its subject or material." This ideal is impossible, and prompts the famous and misleading formula: "All art constantly aspires towards the condition of music." What stimulated Pater to this extravagance was his obsessive concern with what Stevens states so simply in one of his *Adagia*: "One has a sensibility range beyond which nothing really exists for one. And in each this is different." The peculiar structure of *Marius The Epicurean* emanates from the primacy Pater gives to sensibility, in his own special sense of that complex faculty.

Paterian "sensibility" is nothing less than the way one sees, and so apprehends, everything of value in human experience, or in the art that is the best of that experience. Poetry and *materia poetica,* Stevens says, are the same thing. *Marius* is a gathering of *materia poetica,* taken out of one moment of European history, on the chance of illuminating a later moment. The late Victorian skeptic and Epicurean, of whom Pater and Wilde are definitive, is emancipated from his immortality, and suffers the discontent of his own passion for ritual. Pater, as was notorious, studied the nostalgias of religion only in terms of form and ceremony. The passionate desire for ritual, in Pater and in his Marius, as in the Yeats of *A Prayer For My Daughter,* is not a trivial matter, because the quest involved is for the kind of innocence and beauty that can only come from custom and from ceremony. The social aspect of such innocence may be pernicious, but fortunately Pater, unlike Yeats, offered only visionary politics.

Marius The Epicurean is constructed as a series of rituals, each of which is absorbed into its successor without being destroyed, or even transcended. As art was ritual for Pater, so life is ritual for Marius, the ordering principle always being that no form or possibility of life (or of art) is to be renounced in favor of any other. This could be described, unkindly and unfairly, as a kind of polymorphous perversity of the spirit, a refusal to pay the cost of choosing a single aim for culture, or of meeting the necessity of dying by a gracious yielding to the reality principle. What can be urged against Pater, fairly, is that he evaded the novel's ultimate problem by killing off Marius before the young man grasps the theological and moral exclusiveness of Christianity. Marius could not remain Marius and renounce; forced to make the Yeatsian choice between perfection of the life and perfection of the work he would have suffered from a conflict that would have destroyed the fine balance of his nature. Whether Pater earns the structural irony of the novel's concluding pages, as a still-pagan Marius dies a sanctified Christian death, is quite legitimately questionable.

But, this aside, Pater's novel is unflawed in its odd but precise structure. The four parts are four stages on the life's way of Marius, but the continuities of ritual pattern between them are strong enough to set up a dialectic by which no apparent spiritual advancement becomes an aesthetic retreat. The consequence is that the spiritual quest is not from error to truth, but only from alienation to near-sympathy. Thus the first part opens with the most humanly appealing presentation of a belief in the book, as we are given the ancestral faith of Marius, "the Religion of Numa." Here there is no skepticism, but a vision of home and boyhood, the calm of a natural religion that need not strain beyond the outward observances. The world of sense is at home in the child and his inherited faith, which climaxes by his initiation into the world of literature, beautifully symbolized by the story of Cupid and Psyche. The tentative love of Marius for Flavian is precisely the awakening of the literary sense under the awareness of death that Pater traces in the "Conclusion" to *The Renaissance*, and the premature death of Flavian, his one masterpiece left imperfect, inaugurates the first crisis Marius must suffer.

Resolving this crisis is the "conversion," by himself, of Marius to Epicureanism, the doctrine of Aristippus. Though Epicureanism (and its Stoic rival, as represented by Aurelius and Fronto) is supposedly the dominant element of only the second part of the novel, its presence in the book's title is no accident, as in the broad sense Marius, like Pater, lives and dies an Epicurean. For the Epicureanism involved is simply the inevitable religion of the Paterian version of sensibility, or the "aesthetic philosophy" proper. "Not pleasure, but fullness of life, and 'insight' as conducing to that fullness—energy, variety, and choice of experience . . . ," is Pater's best summary of the doctrine, with his added warning that "its mistaken tendency would lie in the direction of a kind of idolatry of mere life, or natural gift. . . ."

The first crisis of this Epicureanism comes at the close of Part II, with Marius's recoil from the sadistic games of the arena, a recoil fascinating for everything that it suggests of the repressed masochism of both Marius and his creator. Like Flaubert, that other high priest of the religion of art, Pater has a way of wandering near the abyss, but *Marius* is no *Salammbô*, and finds no place in the litany of the Romantic agony. But the cruelty of the world, the pain and evil that border so near to Marius's exquisite realm of sensation and reverie, awaken in him a first movement of skepticism toward his own Epicureanism.

Part III develops this sense of limitation with regard to the fruits of sensibility, but by exploiting a more fundamental flaw in the Paterian vision. The self-criticism here is illuminating, not just for this book but for the whole of Pater, and explains indeed the justification for the elaborately hesitant style that Pater perfected. Isolation has expanded the self, but now threatens it with the repletion of solipsism. The Stoic position of Aurelius and Fronto is invoked to contrast its vision of human brotherhood with the more selfish and inward cultivation of Aristippus. But the limits of Stoicism are rapidly indicated also, even as exemplified in its noblest exponent, the philosophic emperor. The climax of Part III comes with marvelous appropriateness, in the quasi-Wordsworthian epiphany experienced by Marius, alone in the Sabine Hills. Moved by the unnamed Presence encountered in this privileged hour, Marius is prepared for the supernatural revelation that never quite appropriates him in the fourth and final part of the novel.

Here, in the closing portion, Pater's skill in construction is most evident. Part IV builds through a series of contrasts to its melancholy but inevitable conclusion. We pass from the literary neo-Platonism of Apuleius with its fanciful daemons aiding men to reach God, on to the aesthetically more powerful vision of the Eucharist, as Marius is drawn gradually into the Christian world of Cornelius and Cecilia. This approach to grace through moral sympathy is punctuated beautifully by a triad of interventions. The first is the dialogue in which the great satirist Lucian discomfits a young philosophic enthusiast, teaching the Paterian lesson that temperament alone determines our supposed choice of belief. Next comes a review of a diary of observed sufferings by Marius, coupled with an account of recent Christian martyrdoms. Finally there is the deeply moving last return home by Marius. Reverently, he rearranges the resting-places of his ancestors, in full consciousness that he is to be the last of his house. He goes out to his fate with the Christian knight, Cornelius, offering up his life in sacrifice for his friend, and dies anonymously among unknown Christians, his own quest still unfulfilled. "He must still hold by what his eyes really saw," and at the last Marius still longs to see, and suffers from a deep sense of wasted power. He is a poet who dies before his poems are written, and even the great poem that is his life is scarcely begun. The attentive reader, confronted by Marius's death, is saddened by the loss, not of a person, but of a major sensibility. And for such losses, such yieldings of a fine sensibility to the abyss, there are no recompenses.

We return always, in reading Pater, to the "Conclusion" of *The Renaissance*, where he spoke his word most freely. The lasting power of *Marius The Epicurean* stays with us not as an image, or series of images, but as a memory of receptivity, the vivid sense of a doomed consciousness universal enough to encompass all men who live and die by a faith in art:

> . . . we have an interval, and then our place knows us no more. Some spend this interval in listlessness, some in high passions, the wisest, at least among "the children of this world," in art and song. For our one chance lies in expanding that interval, in getting as many pulsations as possible into the given time. Great passions may give us this quickened sense of life, ecstasy and sorrow of love, the various forms of enthusiastic activity, disinterested or otherwise, which come naturally to many of us. Only be sure it is passion—that it does yield you this fruit of a quickened, multiplied consciousness. Of this wisdom, the poetic passion, the desire of beauty, the love of art for art's sake, has most; for art comes to you professing frankly to give nothing but the highest quality to your moments as they pass, and simply for those moments' sake.

1967

14
Lawrence, Eliot, Blackmur, and the Tortoise

Art was too long for Lawrence; life too close.
R. P. Blackmur

As a judicial critic, R. P. Blackmur approximates the Arnold of our day. He *ranks* poets. His essay "Lord Tennyson's Scissors: 1912–1950" creates a new scriptural canon out of modern poetry in English. Class I: Yeats, Pound, and Eliot. Plenty of other classes, but all their members standing below Pound and Eliot. In a rather sad class, the violent school, lumped in with Lindsay, Jeffers, Roy Campbell, Sandburg, etc., are D. H. Lawrence and Hart Crane. Lawrence and Crane "were outside the tradition they enriched. They stood at the edge of the precipice which yawns to those who lift too hard at their bootstraps."

Presumably, Blackmur bases this judgment upon two of his own more influential essays: "D. H. Lawrence and Expressive Form" and "New Thresholds New Anatomies: Notes on a Text of Hart Crane." Both essays will be sizable relics when most specimens of currently fashionable analysis are lost. But because they attempt so little *description* and so much value judgment they will be relics at best. By their documentation we will remember what illusions were prevalent at a particular moment in the history of taste.

Blackmur is a critic of the rhetorical school of I. A. Richards. The school is spiritually middle-aged to old; it is in the autumn of its emblematic body. Soon it will be dead. "Lord Tennyson's Scissors" is only an episode in the school's dying. But, as criticisms die so grudgingly, the essay is worth clinical attention.

Northrop Frye has recently said that all selective approaches to tradition invariably have some ultracritical joker concealed in them. A few sentences from Frye's *Anatomy of Criticism* are enough to place Blackmur's pseudodialectics as false rhetoric:

The dialectic axis of criticism, then, has as one pole the total acceptance of the data of literature, and as the other the total acceptance of the potential values of those data. This is the real level of culture and of liberal education, the fertilizing of life by learning, in which the systematic progress of scholarship flows into a systematic progress of taste and understanding. On this level there is no itch to make weighty judgments, and none of the ill effects which follow the debauchery of judiciousness, and have made the word critic a synonym for an educated shrew. Comparative estimates of value are really inferences, most valid when silent ones, from critical practice, not expressed principles guiding its practice.

What I propose to do here is to examine Blackmur's "debauchery of judiciousness" in his criticism of Lawrence, and to suggest where it is inadequate to the poetry.

Poetry is the embodiment of a more than rational energy. This truth, basic to Coleridge and Blake, and to Lawrence as their romantic heir, is inimical to Blackmur's "rationally constructed imagination," which he posits throughout his criticism. Eliot's, we are to gather, is a rational imagination, Lawrence's is not. Eliot is orderly; the lines beginning "Lady of silences" in *Ash-Wednesday* convey a sense of controlled hysteria. Lawrence is merely hysterical: the concluding lines of *Tortoise Shout* are a "ritual frenzy." The great mystics, and Eliot as their poetic follower, saw their ultimate vision "within the terms of an orderly insight." But Lawrence did not. Result: "In them, reason was stretched to include disorder and achieved mystery. In Lawrence, the reader is left to supply the reason and the form; for Lawrence only expresses the substance."

The underlying dialectic here is a social one; Blackmur respects a codified vision, an institutionalized insight, more than the imaginative Word of an individual Romantic poet, be he Blake or Lawrence or Crane. In fairness to Blackmur one remembers his insistence that critics are *not* the fathers of a new church, as well as his quiet rejoinder to Eliot's *After Strange Gods:* "The hysteria of institutions is more dreadful than that of individuals." But why should the order of institutions be more valid for poetry than the order of a gifted individual? And why must order in poetry be "rational," in Blackmur's minimal sense of the word? Lawrence's poetry, like Blake's, is animate with mental energy: it does not lack *mind.* For it is precisely in a quality of mind, in imaginative invention, that Lawrence's poetry excels. Compared to it, the religious poetry of Eliot suggests everywhere an absence of mind, a poverty of invention, a reliance upon the ritual frenzy of others.

Blackmur, who is so patient an exegete of verse he admires, will not even grant that Lawrence's poetry is *worth* descriptive criticism:

> You cannot talk about the art of his poetry because it exists only at the minimum level of self-expression, as in the later, more important poems, or because, as in the earlier accentual rhymed pieces written while he was getting under way, its art is mostly attested by its badness.

Neither half of this confident judgment is true, but Blackmur has a thesis about Lawrence's poetry that he wants very much to prove. The poetry does not matter if the essay can be turned well to its despite. For Lawrence, according to this critic who denies his fatherhood in a new faith, is guilty of the "fallacy of expressive form." Blackmur's proof-of-guilt is to quote Lawrence external to his poetry, analyze the quotation, and then to quote without comment some fragments of Lawrence's verse ripped from context. But the fact is that Lawrence was a bad critic of his own poetry. Lawrence may have believed in "expressive form"; his poetry largely does not.

Blackmur quotes the final lines of *Medlars and Sorb Apples:*

> Orphic farewell, and farewell, and farewell
> And the *ego sum* of Dionysos
> The *sono io* of perfect drunkenness.
> Intoxication of final loneliness.

Here, for Blackmur, "the hysteria is increased and the observation becomes vision, and leaves, perhaps, the confines of poetry." We can begin by restoring the context, so as to get at an accurate description of these "hysterical" lines. For the tone of *Medlars and Sorb Apples* is very quiet, and those final lines that Blackmur would incant as "ritual frenzy" are slow with irony, if that word is still available in the discussion of poetry. The Orphic farewell is a leave-taking of a bride left in the earth, and no frenzy accompanies it here.

Medlars and Sorb Apples might be called a natural emblem poem, as are most of the *Birds, Beasts and Flowers* sequence; one of the signatures of all things. In the "brown morbidity" of the medlar, as it falls through its stages of decay, Lawrence tastes the "delicious rottenness" of Orphism, the worship of the "Dionysos of the Underworld," god of isolation and of poetry. For the retorts of medlars and sorb apples distill the exquisite odor of the autumnal leave-taking of the year, essence of the parting in Hades of Orpheus and Eurydice.

The intoxication of this odor, mingled with Marsala, provides that gasp of further isolation that imaginatively completes the loneliness of the individual soul. The poem is an invocation of this ultimate loneliness as the best state of the soul. The four final lines are addressed directly to medlar and sorb apples as an Orphic farewell, but different in kind from the Eurydice-parting, because of Lawrence's identification of Orpheus with Dionysos. This Orphic farewell is a creative vivification, a declaration of Dionysiac being, a perfect lonely, intoxicated finality of the isolated self of the poet. What smells of death in the autumnal fruit is life to him. Spring will mean inevitable division, crucifixion into sex, a genuine Orphic farewell to solipsistic wholeness. The poem is resolved finally as two overlapping cycles, both ironically treated.

Tortoise Shout is Blackmur's prime example of "the hysteria of expression" in Lawrence, where "every notation and association, every symbolic suggestion" possible is brought to bear upon "the shrieking plasm of the self." In contrast, Eliot's Rose Garden with Virgin is our rational restorative to invocatory control.

Eliot's passage is a simple, quite mechanical catalogue of clean Catholic contradictions, very good for playing a bead-game but not much as imaginative meaning. The Virgin is calm and distressed, torn and most whole, exhausted and life-giving, etc. To Blackmur, these ritualistic paradoxes inform "nearly the same theme" as *Tortoise Shout*. Unless *Ash-Wednesday* takes all meaning as its province, I am at a loss to know what Blackmur thinks he means. He invites us to "examine the eighteen pages of the poems about tortoises" with him, but as he does not do any examining, we ought perhaps to read them for ourselves.

The Tortoise poems, a continuous sequence, communicate a homely and humorous, if despairing, love for the tortoise, in itself and as emblematic of man and all created nature involved in sexual division and strife. The Tortoise-Christ identifications have throughout them a grim unpretentious joy, which Blackmur, on defensive grounds, takes as hysteria.

Baby Tortoise, the first poem, celebrates the infant creature as Ulyssean atom, invincible and indomitable. The best parallel is Whitman, in his praise of animals who do not whine about their condition. "No one ever heard you complain." The baby tortoise is a life-bearer, a Titan against the inertia of the lifeless. But he is a Titan circumscribed by a demiurge like Blake's Urizen; this is the burden of the next poem, *Tortoise Shell*, which seems to me closer to Blake than

anything else by Lawrence or by Yeats. Blake's Urizen, the Old Man
of the Compasses, draws horizons (as his name and its derivation
indicate). The Nobodaddy who made the Tortoise in its fallen condition circumscribes with the cross:

> The Cross, the Cross
> Goes deeper in than we know,
> Deeper into life;
> Right into the marrow
> And through the bone.

On the back of the baby tortoise Lawrence reads the terrible
geometry of subjection to "the mystic mathematics of the city of
heaven." Under all the eternal dome of mathematical law the tortoise
is subjected to natural bondage; he exhibits the long cleavage of
division. An arbitrary division, a Urizenic patterning, has been made,
and the tortoise must bear it eternally. Lawrence's earlier tone of
celebration is necessarily modulated into a Blakean and humanistic
bitterness:

> The Lord wrote it all down on the little slate
> Of the baby tortoise.
> Outward and visible indication of the plan within,
> The complex, manifold involvedness of an individual creature
> Plotted out.

Against this natural binding the tortoise opposes his stoic individuality, his slow intensity. In *Tortoise Family Connections* his more-
than-human independence is established, both as against Christ:

> He does not even trouble to answer: "Woman, what have I to
>   do with thee?"
> He wearily looks the other way

and against Adam:

> To be a tortoise!
> Think of it, in a garden of inert clods
> A brisk, brindled little tortoise, all to himself—
> Adam!

The gentle homeliness that follows, in *Lui Et Elle* and *Tortoise Gal-
lantry*, is punctuated by a purely male bitterness, in preparation for
the great and climactic poem of the series, *Tortoise Shout*.

This last poem is central in romantic tradition, deriving ultimately
as much from Wordsworth as from Whitman. Parallel to it is Melville's enigmatic and powerful *After The Pleasure Party*:

For, Nature, in no shallow surge
Against thee either sex may urge,
Why hast thou made us but in halves—
Co-relatives? This makes us slaves.
If these co-relatives never meet
Self-hood itself seems incomplete.
And such the dicing of blind fate
Few matching halves here meet and mate.
What Cosmic jest or Anarch blunder
The human integral clove asunder
And shied the fractions through life's gate?

Lawrence also is not concerned with asking the question for the answer's sake:

Why were we crucified into sex?
Why were we not left rounded off, and finished in ourselves,
As we began,
As he certainly began, so perfectly alone?

The subject of *Tortoise Shout* is initially the waking of the tortoise into the agony of a fall into sexual division, a waking into life as the heretofore silent creature screams faintly in its arousal. The scream may be just audible, or it may sound "on the plasm direct." In the single scream Lawrence places all cries that are "half music, half horror," in an instructive ordering. The cry of the newborn, the sound of the veil being rent, the "screaming in Pentecost, receiving the ghost." The ultimate identity, achieved in an empathy dependent upon Wordsworthian recollection, is between the tortoise-cry in orgasm, and Christ's Passion on the Cross, the connecting reference being dependent upon the poem *Tortoise Shell*.

The violence of expression here, obscene blasphemy to the orthodox, has its parallels in Nietzsche and in Yeats when they treat the Passion. Lawrence structures this deliberate violence quite carefully. First, a close account of the tortoise in coition, emphasizing the aspects of the act beyond the tortoise's single control. Then a startling catalogue (the form from Whitman, the mode from Wordsworth) of memories of boyhood and youth, before the major incantation assigned by Blackmur to the realm of the hysterical.

The passage of reminiscence works by positing a series of similitudes that are finally seen as a composite identity. The cries of trapped animals, of animals in passion, of animals wounded, animals newborn, are all resolved on the human plane as the infant's birth-pang, the mother singing to herself, the young collier finding his mature voice. For all of these represent:

> The first elements of foreign speech
> On wild dark lips.

The voice of the solitary consciousness is in each case modified, usually by pain, into the speech of what is divided, of what is made to know its own separateness. Here, as in Wordsworth's great *Ode*, the awareness of separateness is equated to the first intimations of mortality.

The last protesting cry of the male tortoise "at extremity" is "more than all these" in that it is more desperate, "less than all these" in that it is faintest. It is a cry of final defeat:

> Tiny from under the very edge of the farthest far-off horizon of life.

One sees why Lawrence has chosen the tortoise; the horizon of separateness-in-sexual-division could not be extended further and still be manageable in a poem of this kind. From this extreme Lawrence carries us to the other pole of human similitude, Christ or Osiris being divided, undergoing ultimate dismemberment:

> The cross,
> The wheel on which our silence first is broken,
> Sex, which breaks up our integrity, our single inviolability, our
>   deep silence,
> Tearing a cry from us.
>
> Sex, which breaks us into voice, sets us calling across the deeps,
>   calling, calling for the complement,
> Singing, and calling, and singing again, being answered, having
>   found.
>
> Torn, to become whole again, after long seeking for what is lost,
> The same cry from the tortoise as from Christ, the Osiris-cry of
>   abandonment,
> That which is whole, torn asunder,
> That which is in part, finding its whole again throughout the
>   universe.

Much of the meaning in this is conveyed through rhythmical mastery; the scattering and reuniting of the self is incanted successively, now widening, now narrowing.

The cross here is the mechanical and mathematical body, the fallen residue of Blake's Human Form Divine. It is also the circumscribed tortoise body, as adumbrated in *Tortoise Shell*. As such, the cross is a demonic image, symbolizing enforced division (into male and female, or *in* the self, or self kept from another self) and torture (tearing on the wheel, crucifixion). The tortoise, torn asunder in coming together, and perpetually caught in that cyclic paradox, utters the same cry as the perpetually sacrificed Osiris in his vegetative cycle. Christ's cry of forsakenness, to Lawrence, is one with these, as the divine nature is torn apart in the Passion. The sexual reduction in this last similitude is imaginatively unfortunate, but as interpretation does not issue from Lawrence alone.

Blackmur, defending Eliot as a dogmatic critic and poet, has written that "conviction in the end is opinion and personality, which however greatly valuable cannot satisfy those who wrongly expect more." The remark is sound, but Blackmur has been inconsistent in its application.

Lawrence, as a Romantic poet, was compelled by the conventions of his mode to present the conceptual aspect of his imagery as self-generated. I have borrowed most of this sentence from Frye's *Anatomy of Criticism*, where it refers to Blake, Shelley, Goethe, and Victor Hugo. What Frye calls a mode of literature, mythopoeia, is to Blackmur "that great race of English writers whose work totters precisely where it towers, collapses exactly in its strength: work written out of a tortured Protestant sensibility." We are back in a social dialectic external to criticism being applied to criticism. Writers who are Protestant, romantic, radical, exemplify "the deracinated, unsupported imagination, the mind for which, since it lacked rational structure sufficient to its burdens, experience was too much." This dialectic is out of Hulme, Pound, and Eliot, and at last we are weary of it. Under its influence Blackmur has tried to salvage Wallace Stevens as a late Augustan, while Allen Tate has asserted that Yeats's romanticism will be invented by his critics. That the imagination needs support can perhaps be argued; that a structure properly conservative, classical, and Catholic enough is its necessary support is simply a social polemic, and irrelevant to the criticism of poetry.

Lawrence himself, if we allow ourselves to quote him out of context, can be left to answer his judicious critic:

> What thing better are you, what worse?
> What have you to do with the mysteries
> Of this ancient place, of my ancient curse?
> What place have you in my histories?

1958

15
Poetic Misprision:
Three Cases

> Attacking bad books is not only a waste
> of time but also bad for the character.
> Auden

> While an author is yet living we estimate his powers by his worst
> performance, and when he is dead we rate them by his best.
> Johnson

Secondary Worlds is a bad book, and Auden's worst performance. These four lectures in memory of T. S. Eliot deal in turn with *Thomas Cranmer*, a pious verse drama by Charles Williams; Icelandic sagas; the three opera libretti by Auden and Chester Kallman; the relation between Christian belief and the writing of poetry. Since the title, *Secondary Worlds*, refers to works of art as against "the primary world of our everyday social experience," the rationale for printing these four talks as a book must be their linked relevance to what has long been Auden's overt polemic against the Romantic view of poetry. Coleridge's ill-chosen terms, Primary and Secondary Imagination, are here subverted by Auden's wit, since by secondary Auden, unlike Coleridge, does mean "inferior."

Of all Auden's writings, *Secondary Worlds* comes most directly out of the neo-Christian matrix of modern Anglo-Catholic letters: Eliot, Williams, C. S. Lewis, Tolkien. I search in vain only for references to Dorothy Sayers. Auden compensates with a quotation from *The Future of Belief*, by Leslie Dewart, a book one might not otherwise know:

> The Christian God is not *both* transcendent and immanent.
> He is a reality other than being Who is present to being, by
> which presence He makes being to be.

"To believe this," Auden modestly says, "is to call into question the art of poetry and all the arts." In *The Dyer's Hand*, an admirable performance, Auden remarked that "the imagination is a natural human faculty and therefore retains the same character whatever a man believes." In his new book, the imagination of a humane man-of-letters and talented comic poet appears to be hardening, which would be a loss.

207

Johnson definitively stated the difficulties of devotional verse when he observed that the good and evil of Eternity were too ponderous for the wings of wit. The mind sinks under them, and must be content with calm belief and humble adoration, attitudes admirable in themselves but perhaps not conducive to the writing of poems. One of Auden's many virtues is that, unlike Eliot and other literary Christians, he has spared us, and mostly refrained from devotional verse. *For the Time Being,* a work dear to many churchwardenly critics, is a long and unhappy exception, but even it, unlike much Eliot, does not offer us the disciplined humility of the poet as our aesthetic experience.

It is of course one thing to deprecate the possibility of Christian poetry, or of poetry being Christian, and quite another to deprecate poetry itself, all poetry. In Auden's criticism, and particularly *Secondary Worlds,* the two are not always kept apart. When this happens, I find it is bad for my character. On a higher level the experience of reading Auden then becomes rather like reading Kilmer's *Trees.* "Poems are made by fools like me," yes, and by Dante, Milton, Blake, and Homer, but only God makes primary worlds. Or, as Auden says:

> . . . it is possible that artists may become both more modest and more self-assured, that they may develop both a sense of humour about their vocation and a respect for that most admirable of Roman deities, the god *Terminus.* No poet will then produce the kind of work which demands that a reader spend his whole life reading it and nothing else. The claim to be a "genius" will become as strange as it would have seemed to the Middle Ages.

It is possible that other artists may become more like Auden. It is likelier that other critics may become more like him for, with Arnold and Eliot, he is a poet-critic who appeals greatly to critics, little as the splendor of becoming a "poet of professors" appeals to him. Books about Auden all tend to be fairly good, just as books about, say Wallace Stevens, tend to be quite bad. This is probably not because admirers of Stevens love him less well than the lovers of Auden, but because more genuinely difficult poets do not reduce to structures of ideas and images so readily as Auden does.

Auden's poetry now maintains a general esteem among academic critics. If one's judgment of Auden's poetry is more eccentric, one needs to take up the sad burden of literary dissent. Auden has been

accepted as not only a great poet but also a Christian humanist sage
not because of any conspiracy among moralizing neo-Christian aca-
demicians, but because the age requires such a figure. Eliot is gone,
and Auden now occupies his place, though with a difference. The
difference is refreshing; Auden is wittier, gentler, much less dogmatic, and does not feel compelled to demonstrate the authenticity
of his Christian humanism by a judicious anti-Semitism. He has more
wisdom and more humor than Eliot, and his talent is nowhere near
so sparse, as the enormous range of his lyrics shows. I think it unfortunate that he should find himself in apostolic succession to Eliot,
but *Secondary Worlds* seems to indicate that the succession is not
unwelcome to him.

Much of *The Dyer's Hand*, despite its generosity as criticism, is
darkened by Auden's obsessive doubts about the value of art in the
context of Christianity. Similar doubts have maimed many writers,
Tolstoi and Hopkins in particular. Insofar as Auden's uneasiness has
prevented him from devotional poetry, he has gained by it, but unfortunately the effect upon him has been larger, and has resulted in
a trivialization of his art. As a songwriter he remains supreme, being
certainly the best in English in the century, but as a reflective poet
he suffers from the continual evanescence of his subject matter. As
a satirist, he may have been aided, yet the staple of his poetry is neither song nor satire but rumination on the good life, and his notion
of the relation between Christianity and art has troubled that rumination. Auden is one of the massive modern sufferers from the malady of Poetic Influence, a variety of melancholy or anxiety-principle
that our studies have evaded. Poetic Influence, in this sense, has little
to do with the transmission of ideas and images from an earlier poet
to a later one. Rather, it concerns the poet's sense of his precursors,
and of his own achievement in relation to theirs. Have they left him
room enough, or has their priority cost him his art? More crucially,
where did they go wrong, so as to make it possible for him to go
right? In this revisionary sense, in which the poet creates his own
precursors by necessarily misinterpreting them, Poetic Influence
forms and malforms new poets, and aids their art at the cost of in-
creasing, finally, their already acute sense of isolation. Auden, like
Byron, gives the continual impression of personal sincerity in his
poetry, but again like Byron this sincerity is the consequence of a
revisionary swerve away from the sincerity of the precursor. In
Byron's case of Poetic Influence the great precursor was Pope, with

his highly dialectical sincerity; with Auden the prime precursor is Hardy, and the poetic son's sincerity is considerably more dialectical than the father's.

Auden, in his very fine *New Year Letter* (1 January 1940, at the height of his poetic power), wrote an important poem about Poetic Influence. His precursors are invoked there as a summary tribunal sitting in perpetual session:

> Though
> Considerate and mild and low
> The voices of the questioners,
> Although they delegate to us
> Both prosecution and defence,
> Accept our rules of evidence
> And pass no sentence but our own,
> Yet, as he faces them alone,
> O who can show convincing proof
> That he is worthy of their love?

He names these fathers and judges: Dante, Blake, Rimbaud, Dryden, Catullus, Tennyson, Baudelaire, Hardy, and Rilke, connecting this somewhat miscellaneous ninefold (except for Dryden, there for his mastery of the middle style) by their common sense of isolation, fit companions "to one unsocial English boy." Of all these, Auden's most characteristic poetry is closest to Hardy's, not merely in its beginnings, and like Hardy Auden remains most convincing as a ruminator upon human incongruities, upon everything valuable that somehow will not fit together. Auden's best poems, such as the justly esteemed *In Praise of Limestone*, brood upon incongruities, swerving from Hardy's kind of poem into a more double-natured sense of ruinous circumstance and thwarted love, yet retaining their family resemblance to Hardy. But where Hardy's strenuous unbelief led him to no worse redundancies than an occasional sharp striving after too palpable an irony, Auden's self-conscious belief and attendant doubt of poetry mar even *In Praise of Limestone* with the redundancy of uneasy and misplaced wit:

> But if
> Sins can be forgiven, if bodies rise from the dead,
> These modifications of matter into
> Innocent athletes and gesticulating fountains,
> Made solely for pleasure, make a further point;
> The blessed will not care what angle they are regarded from,
> Having nothing to hide.

The blessed, as Auden says so often in prose, need neither to read nor to write poems, and poems do not describe their sanctity with much success, as Auden also sadly notes, contemplating the verse of Charles Williams. Close thy Auden, open thy Stevens, and read:

> If, then, when we speak of liberation, we mean an exodus; if when we speak of justification, we mean a kind of justice of which we had not known and on which we had not counted; if when we experience a sense of purification, we can think of the establishing of a self, it is certain that the experience of the poet is of no less a degree than the experience of the mystic and we may be certain that in the case of poets, the peers of saints, those experiences are of no less a degree than the experiences of the saints themselves. It is a question of the nature of the experience. It is not a question of identifying or relating dissimilar figures; that is to say, it is not a question of making saints out of poets or poets out of saints.

1969

Borges: A Compass for the Labyrinth

For the gnostic in Borges, as for the heresiarch in his mythic Uqbar, "mirrors and fatherhood are abominable because they multiply and disseminate that universe," the visible but illusory labyrinth of men. Gnostics rightly feel at ease with Jung, and very unhappy with Freud, as Borges does, and no one need be surprised when the ordinarily gentlemanly and subtle Argentine dismisses Freud "either as a charlatan or as a madman," for whom "it all boils down to a few rather unpleasant facts." Masters of the tale and the parable ought to avoid the tape-recorder, but as Borges succumbed, an admirer may be grateful for the gleaning of a few connections between images.

The gnostic gazes into the mirror of the fallen world and sees, not himself, but his dark double, the shadowy haunter of his phantasmagoria. Since the ambivalent God of the gnostics balances good and evil in himself, the writer dominated by a gnostic vision is morally ambivalent also. Borges is imaginatively a gnostic, but intellectually a skeptical and naturalistic humanist. This division, which has impeded his art, making of him a far lesser figure than gnostic writers like Yeats and Kafka, nevertheless has made him also an admirably firm moralist, as these taped conversations show.

Borges has written largely in the spirit of Emerson's remark that the hint of the dialectic is more valuable than the dialectic itself. My own favorite among his tales, the cabbalistic *Death and the Compass*, traces the destruction of the Dupin-like Erik Lönnrot, whose "reckless discernment" draws him into the labyrinthine trap set by Red Scharlach the Dandy, a gangster worthy to consort with Babel's Benya Krik. The greatness of Borges is in the aesthetic dignity both of Lönnrot, who at the point of death criticizes the labyrinth of his entrapment as having redundant lines, and of Scharlach, who just before firing promises the detective a better labyrinth, when he hunts him in some other incarnation.

The critics of the admirable Borges do him violence by hunting him as Lönnrot pursued Scharlach, with a compass, but he has obliged us to choose his own images for analysis. Freud tells us that: "In a psychoanalysis the physician always gives his patient (sometimes to a greater and sometimes to a lesser extent) the conscious anticipatory image by the help of which he is put in a position to recognise and to grasp the unconscious material." We are to remember that Freud speaks of therapy, and of the work of altering ourselves, so that the analogue we may find between the images of physician and romancer must be an imperfect one. The skillful analyst moreover, on Freud's example, gives us a single image, and Borges gives his reader a myriad; but only mirror, labyrinth, compass will be gazed at here.

Borges remarks of the first story he wrote, *Pierre Menard, author of the Quixote,* that it gives a sensation of tiredness and skepticism, of "coming at the end of a very long literary period." It is revelatory that this was his first tale, exposing his weariness of the living labyrinth of fiction even as he ventured into it. Borges is a great theorist of poetic influence; he has taught us to read Browning as a precursor of Kafka, and in the spirit of this teaching we may see Borges himself as another Childe Roland coming to the Dark Tower, while consciously not desiring to accomplish the Quest. Are we also condemned to see him finally more as a critic of romance than as a romancer? When we read Borges—whether his essays, poems, parables, or tales—do we not read glosses upon romance, and particularly on the skeptic's self-protection against the enchantments of romance?

Borges thinks he has invented one new subject for a poem—in his poem *Limits*—the subject being the sense of doing something for the last time, seeing something for the last time. It is extraordinary that so deeply read a man-of-letters should think this, since most strong poets who live to be quite old have written on just this subject, though often with displacement or concealment. But it is profoundly self-revelatory that a theorist of poetic influence should come to think of this subject as his own invention, for Borges has been always the celebrator of things-in-their-farewell, always a poet of loss. Though he has comforted himself, and his readers, with the wisdom that we can lose only what we never had, he has suffered the discomfort also of knowing that we come to recognize only what we have encountered before, and that all recognition is self-recognition. All loss is of ourselves, and even the loss of falling-out of love is, as Borges would say, the pain of returning to others, not to the self. Is this the wisdom of romance, or of another mode entirely?

What Borges lacks, despite the illusive cunning of his labyrinths, is precisely the extravagance of the romancer; he does not trust his own vagrant impulses. He sees himself as a modestly apt self-marshaller, but he is another Oedipal self-destroyer. His addiction to the self-protective economy and overt knowingness of his art is his own variety of the Oedipal anxiety, and the pattern of his tales betrays throughout an implicit dread of family-romance. The gnostic mirror of nature reflects for him only Lönnrot's labyrinth "of a single line which is invisible and unceasing," the line of all those enchanted mean streets that fade into the horizon of the Buenos Aires of his phantasmagoria. The reckless discerner who is held by the symmetries of his own mythic compass has never been reckless enough to lose himself in a story, to our loss, if not to his. His extravagance, if it still comes, will be a fictive movement away from the theme of recognition, even against that theme, and towards a larger art. His favorite story, he says, is Hawthorne's *Wakefield*, which he describes as being "about the man who stays away from home all those years."

1969

On Ginsberg's *Kaddish*

Allen Ginsberg speaks of himself as having turned aside "to follow my Romantic inspiration—Hebraic-Melvillian bardic breath." That he is a very literary poet is the most obvious of his qualities. He cites Blake and Shelley, Whitman and Hart Crane, as well as Pound and W. C. Williams, those more baleful influences on recent verse fashion. In his best poems, *America* in the *Howl* pamphlet, and *Death to Van Gogh's Ear!* in this volume, he does establish himself as a legitimate though querulous follower of the main Romantic tradition in poetry, the line that in English runs from Blake and Wordsworth to *The Broken Tower* of Crane. But his major efforts, *Howl* and *Kaddish*, are certainly failures, and *Kaddish* a pathetic one.

Ginsberg's genuine poetic flaws are not in structure or in the control of rhetoric. Granted his tradition, he has a surer grasp of the shape of his poem and a firmer diction than almost all of his academic contemporaries, so many of whom have condemned him as formless. A little sympathetic study will establish that most of his larger poems move with inevitable continuity, finding their unity by repetitive techniques akin to those of Christopher Smart's *Jubilate Agno*. Smart's model was ultimately the King James Bible, which is the dominant influence on the technique of Blake and perhaps of Whitman. Ginsberg is hardly a biblical poet, but clearly he is trying to write a kind of religious poetry, and just as clearly he has read the displaced religious poetry of Romanticism with some technical profit.

The sadness is that his content, and not his form, is largely and increasingly out of control. His dominant notion as to form derives from Blake's "Exuberance is Beauty," the belief that the energy embodied in poetry finds only its outward boundary in reason and order, and can make that boundary where it will, at the limit of the poet's informing desire. But Blake's exuberance is the result of powerful imaginative control over the content of his own experience and visualization. Ginsberg is ruined poetically by his wilful addiction to a voluntaristic chaos, by a childish social dialectic as pernicious as any he seeks to escape. The ruin is very evident in *Kaddish*, a poem that is a prayer for the death anniversary of Ginsberg's mother, and also (as the title implies) an attempt at a sanctification of the name of God.

The poem opens, movingly, with the son and poet walking the streets of the city, remembering the death of his mother three years before. It passes, through sustained and harrowing memories of childhood and youth, to an agonized summary of the helplessness of love confronted by the separating power of mental disease. Having faced these horrors, the poet seeks some consolation, some radiance that can impinge upon the mystery of mortality. Ginsberg's epigraph is from *Adonais*, and he arouses in the reader some expectation that all this pathos and sorrow have been evoked toward some imaginative end. But this is what he gives us as a climax to his poem:

Lord Lord great Eye that stares on All and moves in a black cloud
caw caw strange cry of Beings flung up into sky over the waving trees

> Lord Lord O Grinder of giant Beyonds my voice in a boundless field in
> Sheol

All that is human about these lines is in the circumstances of their incoherence. Their single grace is in the irony, however unintended, of their self-reference. We have suffered an experience akin to but not our own, only to discover that its subject has nothing to say. Why then has he written his poem? Ginsberg's voice, which seemed to have possibilities of relevance, will at this rate soon enough constitute a boundless field of Sheol.

1961

16
The Central Man: Emerson, Whitman, Wallace Stevens

I begin with three quotations. The first is from Emerson's *Journals*, written in 1846 when Emerson was forty-two:

> We shall one day talk with the central man, and see again in the varying play of his features all the features which have characterized our darlings, and stamped themselves in fire on the heart: then, as the discourse rises out of the domestic and personal, and his countenance waxes grave and great, we shall fancy that we talk with Socrates, and behold his countenance: then the discourse changes, and the man, and we see the face and hear the tones of Shakespeare,—the body and the soul of Shakespeare living and speaking with us, only that Shakespeare seems below us. A change again, and the countenance of our companion is youthful and beardless, he talks of form and color and the riches of design; it is the face of the painter Raffaele that confronts us with the visage of a girl, and the easy audacity of a creator. In a moment it was Michael Angelo; then Dante; afterwards it was the Saint Jesus, and the immensities of moral truth and power, embosomed us. and so it appears that these great secular personalities were only expressions of his face chasing each other like the rack of clouds. Then all will subside, and I find myself alone. I dreamed and did not know my dreams.

My second quotation is from Whitman's great poem, perhaps his most moving, *As I Ebb'd with the Ocean of Life,* written in 1859 when the poet was forty:

> As I wend to the shores I know not,
> As I list to the dirge, the voice of men and women wreck'd,
> As I inhale the impalpable breezes that set in upon me,
> As the ocean so mysterious rolls toward me closer and closer,

> I too but signify at the utmost a little wash'd-up drift,
> A few sands and dead leaves to gather,
> Gather, and merge myself as part of the sands and drift.

Finally, from a crucial poem by Wallace Stevens, *Asides on the Oboe*, written in 1940 when the poet was sixty-one:

> If you say on the hautboy man is not enough,
> Can never stand as God, is ever wrong
> In the end, however naked, tall, there is still
> The impossible possible philosophers' man,
> The man who has had the time to think enough,
> The central man, the human globe, responsive
> As a mirror with a voice, the man of glass,
> Who in a million diamonds sums us up.

Between two visions of the central man, we have an approximation of the central man himself, most authentic when he ebbs, and merges himself, wrecked, as part of the sands and drift, man absolute, but man on the dump, a savior who could not save himself.

Emerson, writing in his Journal on 27 June 1846, made another of his magnificent claims for the poet as the true man at the center of men:

> The Poet should instal himself and shove all usurpers from their chairs by electrifying mankind with the right tone, long wished for, never heard. The true centre thus appearing, all false centres are suddenly superseded, and grass grows in the Capitol.

Whitman, less than a decade later, found the true center momentarily appearing in himself, and wrote the exuberant song that proclaims all false centers as being suddenly superseded. Many superb and scholarly critics have charted for us the painful and fascinating processes by which Emerson evaded and Whitman abandoned their mutual sense of centrality. The heir of both these bards, as many of the same critics have noted, is Wallace Stevens, whom it is no longer eccentric to regard as the ironically yet passionately balanced fulfillment of the American Romantic tradition in poetry. Mr. Yvor Winters, with exquisite judgment, pioneered in condemning Emerson, Whitman, the later Stevens, and Hart Crane together. The condemnation, however little one credits it, has perhaps a value to the man who made it, but the critical insight that first saw these poets as a continuous tradition can scarcely be overpraised. Mr. Winters is perhaps too majestic a moralist to be accepted as a judicial critic. He has, after all, recently offered us *The Cricket* of Frederick Goddard Tuckerman as the best poem written in the English language during the whole of the nineteenth century. But the history of criticism will deal reverently with Mr. Winters; in an age during which a formidable array of minor poets-turned-critics convinced the academies that twentieth-century verse had somehow repudiated its immediate heritage, and mysteriously found its true parentage in the seventeenth century; in so odd and unnatural a time the voice of Winters was heard proclaiming, with perfect truth, that almost all poetry written in English since the age of sensibility, of the mid-eighteenth century, was inescapably Romantic, whatever its contrary desires. Descriptive accuracy is the true strength of Winters; no matter that all the Romantics, from Blake and Wordsworth to Emerson and Whitman, to Stevens and Yeats and Crane, have been withered by the Winters's vision. A man who can tell us, accurately and powerfully, what he dislikes, does us a greater service than our host of churchwardenly purveyors of historical myths of decline.

Though there is a powerful and direct influence of Emerson upon Whitman and a subtler, less direct effect of Whitman on Stevens this will not be a discussion of poetic influence, a process about which all too little is presently known anyway. Nor do I want to isolate a definite tradition in American poetry, though I would agree that the tradition certainly exists, as so many critics have demonstrated. My concern is with three struggles between the Romantic Imagination (as domesticated in America) and the hard "given" of natural experience, the inescapable necessity of confronting the Not-Me, in search through that confrontation of a mode of consciousness that partook of life and not, like the mere reflective faculty, of death. Like the major English Romantics, but with a twist quite their own, Emerson and Whitman implicitly came to realize that the imagination had to separate from nature if it was to go beyond nature—but, rather like Wordsworth, they resisted this implicit realization, and attempted to treat nature and imagination as reciprocal rather than antithetical terms. Geoffrey Hartman, in his remarkable study of Wordsworth, has given us a definitive analysis of how Wordsworth resisted his own imaginative emancipation. The results of such resistance were for a time glorious, and later, as all agree, deplorable. In Emerson and Whitman a similar process exists, but not as a continuity in time, and not with such drastic clarity. Emerson, as his greatest admirers have admitted, is too antithetical a thinker and poet to have been of a single mind at any time on the relation of his imagination to nature, and Whitman, admirably but disconcertingly, is at his best, I think, when he is trying to say not less than everything simultaneously about the self and its world. Stevens, for all his endless ironies, is considerably clearer than either of these, and can be studied in this matter as directly as we study Wordsworth or Shelley. But, with Emerson and with Whitman, we do well to emulate these founders of our imaginative literature and proceed by indirection, tracking a part of a matter, because by tracking we cannot hope to come upon the whole of it.

In June 1827, not long after his twenty-fourth birthday, Emerson at Concord composed one of the finest of his earliest poems, *The River*. It is perhaps the most Wordsworthian of his poems; indeed it echoes, consciously or not, *Tintern Abbey* in its opening lines, and I would guess that it derives fairly directly from a realization of an experience parallel to that recorded in *Tintern Abbey*. Emerson begins:

> Awed I behold once more.
> My old familiar haunts; here the blue river,
> The same blue wonder that my infant eye
> Admired, sage doubting whence the traveller came,—
> Whence brought his sunny bubbles ere he washed
> The fragrant flag-roots in my father's fields,
> And where thereafter in the world he went.
> Look, here he is, unaltered, save that now
> He hath broke his banks and flooded all the vales
> With his redundant waves.

Decades later, in *Walden*, Thoreau used a similar conceptual image with more power:

> The life in us is like the water in the river. It may rise this year higher than man has ever known it, and flood the parched uplands. . . .

Clearly, in his meditation on the Concord River, Emerson is both celebrating the flooding of his own parched uplands, and lamenting also the sundering from his own earlier self that such flooding has brought about. The rock the poet gazes upon is also the ground of his father's faith to which he will not return. For the poem continues:

> Here is the rock where, yet a simple child,
> I caught with bended pin my earliest fish,
> Much triumphing,—and these the fields
> Over whose flowers I chased the butterfly,
> A blooming hunter of a fairy fine.

> And hark! where overhead the ancient crows
> Hold their sour conversation in the sky:—
> These are the same, but I am not the same,
> But wiser than I was, and wise enough
> Not to regret the changes, tho' they cost
> Me many a sigh.

The note to this poem by Edward Waldo Emerson details "the changes":

> In the same month in which these lines were written, their author told his brother, in a letter, that he meditated abdicating the profession, for "the lungs in their spiteful lobes sing sexton and sorrow whenever I only ask them to shout a sermon for me."

The poem, to this point, is a moving but weak version of *Tintern Abbey*, and its next movement is an even more simplistic version of an admonishing Wordsworthian Nature:

> Oh, call not Nature dumb;
> These trees and stones are audible to me,
> These idle flowers, that tremble in the wind,
> I understand their faery syllables,
> And all their sad significance. The wind,
> That rustles down the well-known forest road—
> It hath a sound more eloquent than speech.
> The stream, the trees, the grass, the sighing wind,
> All of them utter sounds of 'monishment
> And grave parental love.

The speeches that cannot be uttered, the sermons, expounding the God of grave parental love, that cannot now be delivered, are surpassed by the admonishing wind. Emerson raises himself to a more intensely imaginative apprehension of his state in his poem's conclusion. Speaking of the sounds of nature, he acknowledges his separation from them:

> They are not of our race, they seem to say,
> And yet have knowledge of our moral race,
> And somewhat of majestic sympathy,
> Something of pity for the puny clay,
> That holds and boasts the immeasurable mind.
> I feel as I were welcome to these trees
> After long months of weary wandering,
> Acknowledged by their hospitable boughs;

221

They know me as their son, for side by side,
They were coeval with my ancestors,
Adorned with them my country's primitive times,
And soon may give my dust their funeral shade.

There are echoes here again of *Tintern Abbey*, appropriately
enough of its conclusion, and the echoes strengthen the full emergence of the heretofore concealed major theme of the poem, which is
the sense of imminent mortality that stems from the self's awareness
of a break in continuity, of its separation from its own earlier existence. Nature is wholly other from us, and yet extends to us, through
the Wordsworthian myth of reciprocity, a majestic sympathy, the
agape of a monistic entity for a dualistic absurdity, for the ghost in
the machine, the immeasurable mind held in the puny clay of mortal, of Adamic flesh. After five years of weary wandering, Wordsworth returned with Dorothy to the banks of the Wye, there to cast
up his gain and his loss, and to insist that nature would not allow
her worshipper to fall into the death-in-life of alienation from her.
The young Emerson, after long months of weary wandering, returns
to the banks of the Concord, to insist also that nature has a care for
him, but he very movingly claims less than Wordsworth. His nature
awaits the sad gift of his mortality, and offers only the comfort of
ancestral rest, and not a Wordsworthian renovation of the self. Emerson's *The River* is *Tintern Abbey* stripped of the saving aspects of
personal myth, and though it certainly lacks the sublimity of Wordsworth's great meditation, it is also a confrontation of reality that is
free of fictions; remarkably unlike the mature Emerson, it is a poem
of guilt, and of measured and sincere defeat, a defeat accepted without remorse. Most important, at least for my purposes, it is as uncharacteristic a nature poem as Emerson ever wrote. By a paradox
Emersonian enough, had he continued writing in this mode, I believe
that Emerson would have become a better poet than he finally became, but he would not have become the immediate begetter of Whitman, and the ultimate forebear of Stevens and of Crane. The mature
Emerson wanted a humanized nature so badly that he made his poems, or the bulk of them anyway, egregious short-cuts to that end.
The great artist in Wordsworth knew better, and was content to wait
upon nature, developing the remarkable ambushing techniques that
resulted in the visions of the Simplon Pass and of Snowdon, and in
the visionary dreariness of the "spots of time." The poetic humanism
of Emerson, finding itself upon a stonier ground, had not the patience
to wait upon nature's revelation of herself. Wordsworth is a gradual-

ist of the imagination; his awesome strength is manifested by slowly but massively mounting effects, wonderfully balanced in image and idea. Impatience with revelation is almost a definition of mysticism, and mysticism is in fact antithetical to poetry. If we can understand how and why Emerson declined the Wordsworthian *aesthetic* lesson, then we can better understand, I hope, how and why the Romantic imagination domesticated itself in American poetry in so extreme and ironic a form, a form that made Stevens and Crane the inevitable heirs of the Whitmanian strain, a strain of visionary irony that is not yet worked out, and may indeed be the future as it has been the past of what is most central in our poetry.

It is not too much to say (nor very original to say) that the starting-point of Romantic poetry in America is Emerson's marvelous (and marvelously confused) little book, *Nature*, the last three chapters of it in particular. In chapter VI, "Idealism," Emerson affirms that "Nature is made to conspire with spirit to emancipate us." Emerson does not immediately tell us what we are to be emancipated from, but it finally becomes clear that we are to be made free from nature itself. The Imagination Emerson defines as the use that the Coleridgean or higher Reason makes of the material world, and Shakespeare, the most central of poets, is celebrated for having tossed the creation like a bauble from hand to hand. Chapter VII, "Spirit," ends with a consideration of "what discord is between man and nature," thus preparing the way for the eighth and final chapter, "Prospects," which gives us Emerson at his most apocalyptic. The prose-poem sung by the Orphic poet states magnificently a highly visionary account of Man's Fall, one that verges on the Blakean heresy of identifying the Creation and the Fall. Yet here too, at his most rapturous, Emerson is not unconfused. Blake's version of the Fall is properly a protest against all dualisms—Pauline, Cartesian, Lockean. A unitary Man fell, and his fall created dualistic man and dualistic nature. Emerson's Orphic poet is himself both dualist and monist, monist in his vision of what should be, but oddly dualist in what is. Yet if we set aside, arbitrarily, the statement that "the foundations of man are not in matter, but in spirit," we are left with the closest American equivalent to Blakean myth ever hazarded:

> Man is the dwarf of himself. Once he was permeated and dissolved by spirit. He filled nature with his overflowing currents. Out from him sprang the sun and moon; from man the sun, from woman the moon. The laws of his mind, the periods of his actions externized themselves into day and night, into

223

the year and the seasons. But, having made for himself this huge shell, his waters retired; he no longer fills the veins and veinlets; he is shrunk to a drop. He sees that the structure still fits him, but fits him colossally. Say, rather, once it fitted him, now it corresponds to him from far and on high. He adores timidly his own work. Now is man the follower of the sun, and woman the follower of the moon. Yet sometimes he starts in his slumber, and wonders at himself and his house, and muses strangely at the resemblances betwixt him and it.

This rhapsody can bear much analysis, yet is best summed up later in the conclusion to *Nature* by Emerson himself: "The ruin or the blank that we see when we look at nature, is in our own eye." At the very end of *Nature*, the Orphic poet is allowed to sing again, magnificent in his prophetic assurance of a restoration to come: "The kingdom of man over nature, which cometh not with observation—a dominion such as now is beyond his dream of god,—he shall enter without more wonder than the blind man feels who is gradually restored to perfect sight."

The late Stephen Whicher acutely remarked on this extraordinary if momentary assertion of the autonomy of the imagination on Emerson's part. "The lesson he would drive home," Whicher wrote, "is man's entire independence. The aim of this strain in his thought is not virtue, but freedom and mastery." Whicher, among others, showed how this strain in Emerson degenerated into anarchic egoism, but I would myself want to call that another strain. I think this aspect of Emerson simply did not develop, and that except for a literal handful of poems it simply disappeared. Why this happened I do not know; only that to find it again one must go to Emerson's legacy in Whitman, and in our time to Stevens and to Crane. And yet there is at least one lyric by Emerson where we can find it as powerfully present as it has been among us again, the marvelous poem called *Bacchus*, in which Emerson dares to identify himself with that central man who is yet to come, and who was prophesied by the Orphic Poet of *Nature*. I am myself a little startled to note that *Bacchus* was written in 1846, the same year that Emerson mused on the central man in his Journals. Why the apocalyptic impulse suddenly returned to Emerson after a decade in which it had been in abeyance, I do not know, but there are elements of it also in the Lectures on *Representative Men*, delivered in January 1846, and it provides all the more vital elements in the volume of *Poems*, published by Emerson on Christmas Day, 1846. That year saw what Emerson darkly and rightly took to be a slaveholders' war of oppression against Mexico, and perhaps such a year oddly fired the apocalyptic impulse in Emerson, making him feel again the troubled exultation of being a prophet against his own time. Whatever the cause, Emerson in the summer of 1846 wrote what I take to be his greatest and most ecstatic poem, a furiously energetic rhapsody worthy of its title and subject, and one of the most audacious chants of poetic incarnation and self-recognition in the language, a poem worthy of the Coleridge of *Kubla Khan*, or of Emerson's own Orphic poet, though the mysteries celebrated in this lyric are properly more Dionysian than Orphic.

Emerson's Platonic motto to *Bacchus*, as scribbled in his own copy of the *Poems* of 1846, is: "The man who is his own master knocks in vain at the doors of poetry," but the mastery here is clearly not that of nature, no matter how idealistically viewed, but of possession, and the possessing force is that of the central man, or man at the center of men, the human globe. The wine called for in the poem is not a natural beverage, but comes from an archetypal vine underlying all lands, rooted in Styx and Erebus, and turning demonic woe to angelic delight. The contraries of heaven and hell are married together, to give a bread and wine for apocalypic communion as opposed to the ashes and dilution we buy every day. As Emerson's chant mounts to its first climax, the communion is seen as being wholly and passionately humanistic. Where Stevens, in *The Auroras of Autumn*, speculates upon:

> The vital, the never-failing genius,
> Fulfilling his meditations, great and small.
>
> In these unhappy he meditates a whole,
> The full of fortune and the full of fate,
> As if he lived all lives, that he might know . . .

so, here, Emerson "may float at pleasure through all natures," and drink a "wine which is already man." In the intoxication of major man, a Blakean vision is granted Emerson, a vision in which:

> . . . the poor grass shall plot and plan
> What it will do when it is man.

Here at least, Emerson, entirely his own man, nevertheless joined himself to what is most vital in Romantic tradition, the double program of the naturalization of the human heart and the humanization of the natural world.

When Walt Whitman, in a late lyric, addressed the ceaseless swell of the tides, he could still ask the highly Emersonian and highly rhetorical question:

> What central heart—and you the pulse—vivifies all? what
> boundless aggregate of all?
> What subtle indirection and significance in you? what clue to
> all in you? what fluid, vast identity,
> Holding the universe with all its parts as one—as sailing in a
> ship?

The answers are all one answer, and the central heart belongs to the central man, to Whitman, who had had the time to see enough anyway, whether or not rumination had gone on long enough. Like Emerson, Whitman evidently passed through a phase of self-recognition in which the world and the self were made new, and the world seemed humanized in the powerful afterglow of the radiantly found self. Yet the historical dialectic of American Romantic poetry, which finds its thesis in Emerson's *Bacchus*, finds its authentic antithesis in Whitman, in any of a number of major efforts, but particularly in what seems to me (as it has seemed to R. W. B. Lewis) to be Whitman's absolute poem, *As I Ebb'd with the Ocean of Life*. Whether or not one would want to select precisely the poems by Emerson and Whitman that I have chosen as being the central poems is of course an individual and arbitrary matter, but there is a universal and inevitable tendency among us these days to turn most readily to Emerson at his most apocalyptic and to Whitman at his most despairing. The Orphic, primary Emerson and the tragic, antithetical Whitman are what we want and need. The Emerson who confuses himself and us by reservations that are not reservations, and the Whitman who will not cease affrming until we wish never to hear anything affirmed again—these poets we are done with, and in good time. If we are to understand Wallace Stevens, if we are indeed to follow Stevens in the difficult task of rescuing him and ourselves from his and our own ironies, then we need to have these two ancestral poets at their strongest, rather than at their most prevalent. For Stevens, and Hart Crane after him, are the synthesis of the two violent strains that have made American so extreme a Romanticism.

One could wish that Whitman had kept his apparently ironic original title for *As I Ebb'd*, which was *Bardic Symbols*. A later title, *Elemental Drifts*, is purely descriptive in its suggestiveness, but also conveys something of Whitman's own sense of the breakdown of self in this poem. Just as *Bacchus* is a poem of the summer vision, so this poem written thirteen years later is profoundly autumnal, in a way reminiscent of major odes by Shelley and by Keats. Like the *Ode to the West Wind*, Whitman's poem starts out of the poet's realization that he is an unheard prophet, that he is a failed poet. And like the ode *To Autumn*, Whitman's is a poem of naturalistic acceptance, of a tragic sense of completion. More like Shelley's ode, *As I Ebb'd* is a lament for an apocalyptic failure, that is, for a last judgment that an individual has failed to pass upon himself, and so resigns to nature. It is a crucial paradox that Shelley and Whitman should have written their most searching and fully organized shorter poems out of the realization that their imaginations had failed, or rather, that they had failed their imaginations.

One way of grasping Whitman's *As I Ebb'd* is to begin with the notion that it is a poem of the circumference rather than of the center, a poem whose speaker is minor man, man wandering "the rim, the sediment that stands for all the water and all the land of the globe." The antithetical statement to Emerson's Orphic Poet could hardly be more complete than this, a poet crying out his victimization by everything that lies outside the self:

> Nature here in sight of the sea taking advantage of me to dart
> upon me and sting me,
> Because I have dared to open my mouth to sing at all.

Shelley's *Ode to the West Wind* moves from natural invocation, to an abandonment of a human self, to a final choice by the human of a human self, in the minimal conviction that nature without a human seer and transformer is doomed to mere repetitiveness, to the same dull round of creations and destroyings. Whitman's *As I Ebb'd* is characteristically a more imaginatively extreme version of the same dialectic. Whitman moves from an invocation both of nature and of the self naturalized, to an entire, self-mocking abandonment of his central ambitions, and finally to a realization that all is not entirely lost for the self even in its ironic naturalization.

Whitman's poem records a seizure of the self "by the spirit that trails in the lines underfoot," a Jobean spirit that finds itself in the sea-drift, "these little shreds indeed standing for you and me and all." Yet, in conscious defeat, Whitman's imaginative impulse remains that of the central man in reverse, the poet as representative of all, not as hero but as the child of earth throwing himself upon the breast of his father, a wrestling Jacob holding the angel "so firm till you answer me something." "Breathe to me," Whitman whispers to the paternal beach, "While I hold you close the secret of the murmuring I envy," the murmuring being the maternal song of the moaning sea. And, having learned the secret, which appears to be that man, that "loose windrow," is still somehow at the center, that it is "just as much for us that sobbing dirge of nature," Whitman is able to bring his great elegy of the self to its agnostic but trusting conclusion: "Whoever you are, we too lie in drifts at your feet." There, at the rim of being, the forces of sea and land converge upon their loving if wrecked child, the human self, and everything is at home in us again, for we are the destined receiver, though not the maker, of all sounds and songs.

The synthesis of this dialectic I seek to present is Stevens, neither an Orphic celebrator nor a despairer at the circumference, but an asserter or re-asserter, however self-qualified, of the imaginative fable of the Central Man. The dialectical recoil to *As I Ebb'd with the Ocean of Life* is in that magnificent ode, *The Idea of Order at Key West:*

> For she was the maker of the song she sang.
> The ever-hooded, tragic-gestured sea
> Was merely a place by which she walked to sing.

The denunciations of *Bacchus:* "We buy ashes for bread;/We buy diluted wine," are echoed by this major quester for *The American Sublime:* "What wine does one drink?/What bread does one eat?" The brilliant ironists and philosophical critics, most notably Helen H. Vendler and J. Hillis Miller, would insist that Stevens offers no answers but ironic evasions to these questions, that he abides in a reality of "The empty spirit/In vacant space," a metaphysical reduction beyond metaphysics, a sense of nothingness returning upon itself. No one reads Stevens daily for a decade, as I have, without remarking upon the constant irony of diction and syntax as well as the more obvious irony of Stevens's personae and of his imagery. But a qualified assertion remains an assertion; it is *not* an asserted qualification, and one might well write an essay entitled *The Qualified Assertions of Percy Bysshe Shelley,* for the most passionate of all Romantics was also the most deeply involved in his own consciousness of prophetic irony, just as Blake was. Stevens, as a poet, had a "wintry temperament," as Helen Vendler justly remarks. It is also true, as Hillis Miller notes, that in Stevens's poetry: "Speed also makes possible a vision of being—in the moment of its disappearance." That sentence, applied to Shelley, is the total formula of his lyric practice, of his favorite imagery of dwindling and vanishing, of the fading morning and evening star, of the lark's song in its evanescence, and of that outrageous and exuberant speed that utterly characterizes the greatest of all qualified asserters. There are passages in *An Ordinary Evening in New Haven* that are the purest Shelley, and Stevens is at his most Romantic when he appears to be most wintry, when he qualifies and hastens the most, so "That all the extreme postures of the spirit are present in a single moment," to quote Miller again. We need to thrust aside utterly, once and for all, the critical absurdities of the Age of Eliot, before we can see again how complex the Romantics were in their passionate ironies, and see fully how overwhelmingly Stevens and Crane are their inheritors and continuators, as they are of Emerson and Whitman as well.

The Central Man Stevens celebrates, in a sense of celebration that transcends all ironies, was of course not himself, but a "prodigious shadow." Still, of this shadow Stevens could say "He was not man yet he was nothing else," and when this shadow spoke he could insist: "My solitaria / Are the meditations of a central mind." So prevalent is this figure in Stevens that one approaches him best where he appears to be absent, as I will attempt to do now, by an overview of *The Auroras of Autumn,* a poem of the circumference, like *As I Ebb'd* or Emerson's early *The River,* rather than a poem of the center, like *Bacchus* or *Asides on the Oboe,* or Stevens's major poem of the center, *Notes Toward a Supreme Fiction.*

Fundamentally, *The Auroras of Autumn* is a Wordsworthian poem, in that its central theme is gain and loss as associated with the workings of the creative or secondary imagination, the shaping spirit of Coleridge. Wordsworth claimed that for the loss of an earlier glory of primary imagination, of plain but exalted sight, he had received "abundant recompense," but *The Auroras* is primarily a poem of loss, since the gain in the poem appears in the ambiguous figuration of the Northern lights. Yet Stevens attempts to resolve the ambiguity in a positive way, and only a forcing ironist, determined to confront an unqualified hopelessness, would contest the fresh innocence that Stevens allows himself to attain.

I do not know if *The Auroras of Autumn* has a specific literary source, but we may bring both Emerson and Emily Dickinson to our consideration of the poem, if only as starting points. In his fine essay on *The Poet* (1843), more a hymn of praise than an essay, Emerson allows himself to say of the Poet: "He is a sovereign, and stands on the center." There follows a playfully rhapsodic little fable that might be termed the primary thesis of a little Auroras dialectic, as it were, with Emily Dickinson providing the antithetical term and Stevens's marvelous poem the troubled synthesis. Here is Emerson:

> . . . the experience of each new age requires a new confession, and the world seems always waiting for its poet. I remember when I was young how much I was moved one morning by tidings that genius had appeared in a youth who sat near me at table. He had left his work and gone rambling none knew whither, and had written hundreds of lines, but could not tell whether that which was in him was therein told; he could tell nothing but that all was changed,—man, beast, heaven, earth and sea. How gladly we listened! how credulous! Society seemed to be compromised. We sat in the aurora of a sunrise which was to put out all the stars. Boston seemed to be at twice the distance it had the night before, or was much farther than that. Rome,—what was Rome? Plutarch and Shakespeare were in the yellow leaf, and Homer no more should be heard of. It is much to know that poetry has been written this very day, under this very roof, by your side. What! that wonderful spirit has not expired! These stony moments are still sparkling and animated! I had fancied that the oracles were all silent, and nature had spent her fires; and behold! all night, from every pore, these fine auroras have been streaming.

Here the auroras humorously signify nature renovated through the imagination. Emily Dickinson, confronting the auroras, found a very different signification:

> Of Bronze—and Blaze—
> The North—Tonight—
> So adequate—it forms—
> So preconcerted with itself—
> So distant—to alarms—
> An unconcern so sovereign
> To Universe, or me—

This poem ends in a premonition of the destruction of the self:

> When I, am long ago,
> An Island in dishonored Grass—
> Whom none but Beetles, know.

Charles R. Anderson, commenting upon this poem, emphasizes its grim lesson that "the mortal poet corrupts his true nature if he attempts to be divine," for "the poet must remain earth-bound." Here at least Dickinson is far from the Emersonian vision of the central man. Subtle as Stevens's vision is in *The Auroras of Autumn*, I think it accurate to say that it is further from Dickinson than from Emerson, in that the Northern Lights are seen finally as signifiying the desperate necessity for an assertion of the autonomy of the human imagination, and even for its freedom from every worn conception of existence. The aurora terrifies, because imaginative freedom terrifies, but the poet's courage is to insist that the aurora *is* benevolent and innocent.

The Northern Lights are first seen in Stevens's poem as a quest after the center of night, an aspiration to find the serpent of necessity, of time and mutability, in a nest distinct from the autumnal landscape, for the earthly nest now yields us no peace. When the lights appear next, in the second part of the sequence, they confront the poet with an inhuman imagination, a sublime that appalls:

> The season changes. A cold wind chills the beach.
> The long lines of it grow longer, emptier,
> A darkness gathers though it does not fall
>
> And the whiteness grows less vivid on the wall.
> The man who is walking turns blankly on the sands.
> He observes how the north is always enlarging the change,
>
> With its frigid brilliances, its blue-red sweeps
> And gusts of great enkindlings, its polar green,
> The color of ice and fire and solitude.

The gathering darkness is the impending shadow of mortality, a shadow that slays imaginative vision. As yet the Northern Lights promise no compensatory balm for such loss, and hint only at the nightmare alienation of a world like the Antarctic of Coleridge's *Ancient Mariner*. When the lights next appear in the poem, in the magnificent section VI, their splendor confronts the poet with the challenge and fear of a total questioning of the capability of human imagination to match the power of reality:

> This is nothing until in a single man contained,
> Nothing until this named thing nameless is
> And is destroyed. He opens the door of his house

231

> On flames. The scholar of one candle sees
> An Arctic effulgence flaring on the frame
> Of everything he is. And he feels afraid.

This is of course one of the greatest passages in Stevens, and one of the most sublime in modern verse. The scholar of one candle is the poet, and the crisis he reaches in *The Auroras of Autumn* will be repeated, in bleaker form, in Stevens's *The Rock*. Here, at the circumference of vision, the adequacy of the imagination must be tested, until the poet can affirm, however qualifiedly, that:

> ... these lights are not a spell of light,
> A saying out of a cloud, but innocence.
> An innocence of the earth and no false sign
>
> Or symbol of malice.

No matter that this is followed by one of Stevens's characteristic "as ifs"; for out of this innocence of the earth emerges finally, however tenuously, the figure of the rabbi, the humanist teaching his congregation the doctrine of the hallowing of the commonplace, and from that teaching there comes again a vision of the possible impossible, the central man:

> The vital, the never-failing genius,
> Fulfilling his meditations, great and small.

The last word in this tradition belongs not to Stevens but to a poet who should have died after him but died decades before, the tragic Hart Crane. The poet who said he entered the broken world to trace the visionary company of love spoke of himself also as the "derelict and blinded guest" of his own vision, not as its rightful inhabitant, yet he inherited from Whitman, with full authenticity, the burden of aspiring to be the central man of the Emersonian dream.

Yvor Winters has summed up Crane's career by invoking the Winters's reduction of Emerson. "The Emersonian doctrine," he writes, "which is merely the romantic doctrine with a New England emotional coloration, should naturally result in madness if one really lived it; it should result in literary confusion if one really wrote it. Crane accepted it; he lived it; he wrote it; and we have seen what he was and wrote."

Against this one must mildly observe that we have not yet seen all that Crane was, nor have we as yet seen all that there is to be seen in what he wrote. Winters warns us against demonic possession;

232

Emerson warns us against death-in-life, the life without imagination that is not worth living. Whatever the dangers of the Emersonian vision of the center, we have no choice but to seek the light of that vision, for it is the major example yet given us in America of what Stevens might have called the human making choice of a human self.

1965

17
Notes Toward a Supreme Fiction:
A Commentary

>   ... to me I feel
> That an internal brightness is vouchsafed
> That must not die, that must not pass away.
>   Why does this inward lustre fondly seek
> And gladly blend with outward fellowship?
> Why do *they* shine around me whom I love?
> Why do they teach me, whom I thus revere?
>   Wordsworth, *The Recluse*

Stevens had the radiant fortune that attends only the great poets:
his most ambitious poem is his best. The six hundred and fifty-
nine lines of *Notes Toward a Supreme Fiction* constitute his central
attempt to relieve the imaginative poverty of his time, and they
establish him as I think the central poet of that time, bringing to us
the consolations of a healing poetic humanism as Wordsworth
brought them to his contemporaries. Nothing else in twentieth-
century poetry written in English matches the magnificence of
Stevens's *Notes*, for Stevens has all that Yeats sorely lacked, the
wisdom and love whose absence renders the powers of poetry
inadequate to the firm dignity of merely natural man. One reads
and studies Yeats with growing wonder at the talents that could
transform so much that was prose nonsense into genuine poetry,
and yet with growing distaste for the vision of man that informs
a play like *Purgatory* or a poem like *The Gyres*. One turns with
relief to Stevens, whose gifts as a poet were as immense as those
of Yeats, but who remained always a man speaking to men,
and never sought to become an oracle with mummy truths to tell.

    The tentativeness of Stevens's title is neither humility nor
irony, for the poem is an attempt at a final belief in a fiction known
to be a fiction, in the predicate that there is nothing else. The
fiction is broadly poetry itself, and poetry is necessarily the
subject of Stevens's poem. The *Notes* move toward the creation of a
fictive hero who quite simply will become the real, and thus
bring to a climax the whole movement of poetry in the Romantic
tradition. In the closing sections of the third part of *Notes*, Stevens
is able to gather together, in an astonishing splendor of
integration, all the major themes of Romantic poetry, and so
brings to a present perfection everything that is most vital in the
imaginative legacy of Blake and of Wordsworth.

Notes opens with eight lines of dedication, appropriately celebrating the relationship of loving friendship, for in the mutuality of such confrontation there appear all the characteristics of the Supreme Fiction. The love of friends, as a marriage of reality and the imagination, depends upon an abstraction in Stevens's sense of that word, and clearly is subject to the necessities of change and of pleasure that serve further to define Stevens's version of the Romantic Imagination. The moment of communion caught in the dedication is one of the enlargements of life, bringing a central man into being through two men sitting at rest together, peaceful in a world still undergoing the living change of natural process, yet made vividly transparent by the light of common day.

It Must Be Abstract

Stevens gives the first part of *Notes* the admonitory title *It Must Be Abstract*. Elsewhere in his work the idea of abstraction is what more usually would be called "fabrication." The possible poet has the power to abstract or withdraw himself from outworn conceptualizations of reality, and to live in the world, yet outside the existing conceptions of it, and he can do this only by fabricating his fictions. When these fictions become supreme, in the work of a central poet, a Wordsworth or a Stevens, it is because the abstracted reality has been married to the possible sublimities of the imagination. To follow the poet by so halting a paraphrase leads to another kind of abstracting tendency, from which only the experience of reading his poem can save us. It is because *Notes* creates an extraordinary actuality that the attentive reader is able to capture a state of so being in the poem's presence as to feel that consciousness has taken the place of imagination.

Yet the poem's gift of such consciousness is properly deferred, in the exuberant premise that the reader is a "prodigious scholar" of the imaginative quest, an ephebe entering upon poetic maturity. Even as *The Comedian as the Letter C* mixed the modes of allegorical romance and spiritual autobiography (a thoroughly Romantic mixture) so the *Notes* mixes quest romance with the poetry of vision, again according to Romantic precedent. Stevens presents us with a long poem whose continuity is utterly dependent upon the impatient obsessions of an imagination determined to possess reality without altering it. He therefore declines the normal chronology of quest; the ephebe seeks, does not find, and finds, but all in a simultaneity. Stevens has no truth to make us free except the truths that together define the Supreme Fiction: the truth of separation or withdrawal of the imagination from its worn coverings and reality from its stale disguises; the truth of mutability and natural renewal; and the great truth of *Harmonium*, a humanism of love liberated through pleasure.

It Must Be Abstract begins by adjuring the ephebe to see the sun as it is, without evasion by a single metaphor. Yet the sun, in one of Stevens's most compelling and pervasive metaphors, is identified with man, or rather that brave man, our idea of the sun, is at one with the major abstraction or first idea, our idea of the human. The poet's first abstraction or saving withdrawal of the real from the unreal must be to divest the sun of its mythologies. As a modern humanist the poet begins by a rejection of invisibles: God, "a voluminous master folded in his fire," is dead, and since "the death of one god is the death of all," then "Phoebus is dead, ephebe." What remains is the project that was and is the joint venture of man and the sun, to "be in the difficulty of what it is to be."

The verbal play of the first poem of *It Must Be Abstract* warns the ephebe against taking himself too seriously. This warning is made explicit in the second poem, which deals with the ennui that lurks in our awareness of the first idea. The ravishments of truth are fatal to the truth itself, and a poem seeking to widen consciousness must warn us against self-consciousness. Not to have the first idea is best, for to desire is the only way to know again that we are of the veritable sun, that we possess within us the sublime potential of the central man. The ephebe must begin then with a sense of loss, of poverty, and so throw away the unrealities of unimaginative existence "as morning throws off stale moonlight and shabby sleep."

This much is prologue; with the third poem of *It Must Be Abstract* Stevens touches on greatness as he considers how the poem refreshes life:

> We move between these points:
> From that ever-early candor to its late plural
>
> And the candor of them is the strong exhilaration
> Of what we feel from what we think, of thought
> Beating in the heart, as if blood newly came,
>
> An elixir, an excitation, a pure power.
> The poem, through candor, brings back a power again
> That gives a candid kind to everything.

The belief here is also that of Coleridge and Wordsworth; the rapture, authentic and heartening, is Stevens's own. The gift of candor is evidenced at the start of this poem, with the fine admission that poetry's refreshment of life allows us to "share, for a moment, the first idea." To share, not to appropriate for ourselves, and to confront the redeeming idea of the human only as a brief relational event: Stevens has grasped, with imaginative sureness, the honest despair of Romantic humanism. The ever-early candor is in the nakedness out of which poems or vividly transparent encounters come; the late plural ensues from the imagination's generosity in giving back to us a world of such mixed motion and such imagery that our essential nakedness is clothed by a fictive covering. In a primal chant of exuberant response, Stevens illustrates the candid kind that is the poem's gift:

> We say: At night an Arabian in my room,
> With his damned hoobla-hoobla-hoobla-how,
> Inscribes a primitive astronomy
>
> Across the unscrawled fores the future casts
> And throws his stars around the floor. By day
> The wood-dove used to chant his hoobla-hoo
>
> And still the grossest iridescence of ocean
> Howls hoo and rises and howls hoo and falls.
> Life's nonsense pierces us with strange relation.

One knows, from elsewhere in Stevens, that the wood-dove is the bird who represents "the interior paramour," the Blakean emanation or Shelleyan epipsyche, the Muse the poet creates and loves. Even without such knowledge, this spirited chant declares itself as a manifesto of the imagination, part of the late plural the poem bestows. The Arabian, as much as Wordsworth's Arab in *The Prelude*, is a figure of capable imagination, and his incantation helps save the visionary faculty for the poet, inscribing an order across the uncertainties of futurity, and munificently throwing the excess of his gift at random around the floor. If the wood-dove's chant is no longer present as external reminder of visionary potency to the poet, the ocean remains; and its very inadvertence constitutes another song of fixed accord between reality and imagination. The rise and fall, grossly nonsensical, pierces us to recognition of relationship, teaches us again to separate what we need from what seems to be beyond our need.

A Commentary

Stevens is more adept than most poets at creating a dialectic of distinctions, and proceeds in the next two poems to distinguish such
visionary naturalism from any form of pantheism. Sections IV and V
of *It Must Be Abstract* are as rigorous as Blake in disengaging the
origins of imagination from unredeemed nature. The poem springs
from our realization

> that we live in a place
> That is not our own and, much more, not ourselves
> And hard it is in spite of blazoned days.

Even the first idea, of ourselves as man, was not our own, for
"there was a muddy centre before we breathed." The myth of earth
precedes the myth of major man, and the painfully thought "I am"
of Adam is the muddy precedent to the sophistications of consciousness. Something of progressive alienation between man and earth,
already expressed in the absence of the wood-dove's song, is emphasized in the movement from Eve, who "made air the mirror of herself," to ourselves, for whom "the air is not a mirror but bare board."

In Section V the elegant pathos of this alienation is transformed
by an extravagance of color into a pitying mockery of minor man,
the ephebe as he has become. The lion's roar, elephant's blare, and
bear's snarl meet their antithesis in the ephebe's utterance:

> But you, ephebe, look from your attic window,
> Your mansard with a rented piano. You lie
>
> In silence upon your bed. You clutch the corner
> Of the pillow in your hand. You writhe and press
> A bitter utterance from your writhing, dumb,
>
> Yet voluble dumb violence.

With something beyond mere irony Stevens insists on this ephebe
as one of "the heroic children whom time breeds against the first
idea." It takes a kind of heroism to lash the lion, but to be bred
against the idea of man is clearly to exhibit the lesser fortitude. Halfway through *It Must Be Abstract* Stevens has brought the ephebe's
quest to a nadir.

We are made to start again where we must, "in the difficulty of
what it is to be." Section VI subtly alters the entire tone of the work,
as a gentler insistence on the continued possibility of relationship
begins to draw the object-world and the poet together again. Stevens
is very much a poet of the human seasons, like Keats, and Section VI

of *It Must Be Abstract* is his hymn to the weather and the giant man the weather almost evokes. A quietly modulated chant salutes what the poet has "imagined well," and then touches near to a revelation, more moving for its candid confession that this presence of the human in weather is "not to be realized," is not wholly capable of a saving abstraction from falseness:

> My house has changed a little in the sun.
> The fragrance of the magnolias comes close,
> False flick, false form, but falseness close to kin.
>
> It must be visible or invisible,
> Invisible or visible or both:
> A seeing and unseeing in the eye.
>
> The weather and the giant of the weather,
> Say the weather, the mere weather, the mere air:
> An abstraction blooded, as a man by thought.

"We cannot write the order of the variable winds," Emerson remarked, and went on to question how the law of our shifting moods and susceptibility was to be penetrated, though the two orders differed "as all and nothing." If the giant of the weather could be confronted, then the first idea could be thought again, and wholly within the context of natural experience. But the giant has not yet been encountered on this imaginative quest; the weather, like the sun, must be met without evasion. The mere weather, the mere air, must be abstracted from the outworn idealizations that pass for reality. In such nakedness of withdrawal, of a separation that fabricates again, the abstraction is realized, as a man is blooded, when he has had time to think enough.

From here to the end of *It Must Be Abstract* the poet feels free to approach again, though very gently, his fiction of major man, the giant of imagination concealed within each ephebe. Section VII celebrates those "times of inherent excellence" which are Stevens's modest equivalents of the state celebrated by Wordsworth in *Tintern Abbey*. There is an instructive sadness in contemplating the exhaustions that attend the increases of self-awareness in Romantic tradition. Wordsworth, in the sublimity of his natural strength, could speak of his eye as being made quiet by the power of harmony and the deep power of joy. Stevens too speaks of a gift akin to that of seeing into the life of things, but the gift has become "extreme, fortuitous, personal," though it can still be described as "moments of

awakening . . . in which we more than awaken." The movement between Wordsworth and his eloquent heir is that between "balances
that we achieve" and "balances that happen," and the elevation
achieved by Stevens is serenely precarious. From that height we "behold the academies like structures in a mist."

It is to one of these mistily perceived structures that the next section refers, the "castle-fortress-home" in which an expedient hypothesis of the major man might be housed. Section VIII is Stevens
in the vitality of his ironic extravagance, which habitually precedes
the direct presentation of what is hottest and purest in his heart, a
vision of major man. So we proceed from the "crystal hypothesis" of
the MacCullough, who remains merely MacCullough, to the major
man who evades our tautologies. That imagined thing, the first idea,
moves in on the MacCullough through a process of incarnation that
is a contemporary equivalent to the Romantics' visions of the cyclic
rebirth of the Poetical Character. Even the MacCullough may be
transformed into a figure of the youth as virile poet, the "beau linguist" conceived as a young god:

> If MacCullough himself lay lounging by the sea,
>
> Drowned in its washes, reading in the sound,
> About the thinker of the first idea,
> He might take habit, whether from wave or phrase,
>
> Or power of the wave, or deepened speech,
> Or a leaner being, moving in on him,
> Of greater aptitude and apprehension,
>
> As if the waves at last were never broken,
> As if the language suddenly, with ease,
> Said things it had laboriously spoken.

Under such conditions the MacCullough too would sing beyond
the genius of the sea. From this chant of a possible incarnation,
Stevens descends to deliberate the advent of a more probable version
of the major man. We must put aside the idiom of apotheosis, "the
romantic intoning, the declaimed clairvoyance" and be content
plainly to propound a coming of the major man more subtly modest
in its manner. So at least Stevens claims, though his poem partly re-
futes him. Stevens was at once curiously shy and passionately defensive in regard to the Romantic, and clearly apotheosis can be the
origin of the major man, as the third part of *Notes* will show. But

It Must Be Abstract, in its two final sections, seeks another tone, at once toughly reasonable and displaying a proud poverty, as befits a bad time for the imagination. It is the Stevens who wrote *The Man On The Dump* whose voice is heard as an undersong in Sections IX and X, yet the overt declaration is for the major man as an immediacy of vision:

> He is and may be but oh! he is, he is,
> This foundling of the infected past, so bright,
> So moving in the manner of his hand.
>
> Yet look not at his colored eyes. Give him
> No names. Dismiss him from your images,
> The hot of him is purest in the heart.

The gestures of the major man are visible in the here and now, free of the illnesses of history, but so dangerous is it to categorize vision that again the ephebe is urged to become an ignorant man, and to avoid the despotism of the eye. All these elaborations of a central theme are brought together in the last section of *It Must Be Abstract,* where major man makes his appearance, not the poet as a young god but the poet as an old tramp, the comedian:

> in his old coat,
> His slouching pantaloons, beyond the town,
>
> Looking for what was, where it used to be.
> Cloudless the morning. It is he. The man
> In that old coat, those sagging pantaloons,
>
> It is of him, ephebe, to make, to confect
> The final elegance, not to console
> Nor sanctify, but plainly to propound.

On that clear morning, abstracted into reality, the major man comes, seeking the difficulty of what was, and presenting in himself the difficulty of what it is to be. The ultimate elegance is the imagined land, to be fabricated by the ephebe out of this battered hero who is beyond loss. The whole burden of *Notes* rests upon those closing lines and their admonition; where Wordsworth could offer to console and sanctify, the maker of the Supreme Fiction for us has a more elemental task. He must render us able to conceive of the fresh possibility of life, yet he can show us nothing that is more fecund as particle than as principle. The natural man of Wordsworth and Keats,

242

the visionary man of Blake and Shelley—these could be manifested in the singular, in the struggle of a poet to realize himself, whether by growth or rebirth. Our idea of man is a final belief in a last-ditch sense of finality; major man is "abler in the abstract than in his singular," a figure of capable imagination only when withdrawn from his not very fecund world. Confronted by this "inanimate, difficult visage," we know as ephebes that our hard obligation is "plainly to propound" what we have abstracted, to present without ornament the naked poem, the vulnerable confrontation.

It Must Change

There is much in *It Must Be Abstract* that grows into the reader's consciousness with the inevitability of greatness, yet one's experience of *Notes* is that the poem becomes better as it develops, *It Must Change* being superior to the first part, and *It Must Give Pleasure* finer still. *Notes* could therefore be judged an uneven poem, but the ascending intensity of the work is certainly a matter of design, a movement from the essential prose of our condition in *It Must Be Abstract* to the ecstatic celebration of the marriage between flesh and air in *It Must Give Pleasure*.

The principal Romantic vision of mutability stems from Spenser, who lamented natural change and yet found in the cycle of the months an augury of salvation, an eternal principle surviving amid the particles of decay. In Blake this hopeful view of natural cycle survives in the vision of the world of Los at the close of the first book of *Milton*, but the larger emphasis falls on mutability as ironic repetition, "the Orc cycle" of meaningless eternal recurrence from which man must learn to fight free. Shelley's later poems, particularly *Adonais* and *The Triumph of Life*, tend to share this dark vision, and a mocking analogue seems to lurk in Byron's treatment of nature in *Don Juan*. This negative judgment upon natural cycle, to be found again in the later Yeats, has no relevance to Stevens, who shares the more positive Spenserianism of Wordsworth and Keats, an attitude that recognizes the tragedy of mutable existence, but insists also on the necessity of celebrating the values of organic repetition. The heroic faith in the merely natural of Keats in particular, who praised as true humanists those who "seek no wonder but the human face," is carried on in Stevens, who could say that "the adventurer/In humanity has not conceived of a race/Completely physical in a physical world." One feels behind the exquisite fables of *It Must Change* the faithless faith of Keats's tragic naturalism, though the overt presence of Keats is not felt, as it certainly is in Stevens's rapturous *Credences of Summer*, or as Wordsworth is felt in *Sunday Morning* or Coleridge in the *Final Soliloquy of the Interior Paramour*.

The first two sections of *It Must Change* are devoted to a celebration of the advent of spring that is worthy to be compared with any similar celebration in English poetry. Even as the absence of imagination had itself to be imagined, so deadest winter is a tribute to the saving power of change:

> It means the distaste we feel for this withered scene
>
> Is that it has not changed enough. It remains,
> It is a repetition.

The booming of the returning bees, "as if they had never gone," defies our sense of things past, and comically defies also the pronunciamentos by which we would invest nature with our shabby notions of immortality. Against our unimaginative denial of the reality of change, the booming of the bees asserts a beginning, not a resuming:

> Why, then, when in golden fury
>
> Spring vanishes the scraps of winter, why
> Should there be a question of returning or
> Of death in memory's dream? Is spring a sleep?
>
> This warmth is for lovers at last accomplishing
> Their love, this beginning, not resuming, this
> Booming and booming of the new-come bee.

Without this bee that never settles, without its generations that follow in their universe, the land we inhabit "would be a geography of the dead," to cite *Somnambulisma*, one of Stevens's most crucial shorter poems. Such a geography of the dead is exemplified in Section III of *It Must Change* by the great statue of the General Du Puy. This noble rider was "an inhuman bronze," a monument to the past so rigid as to divest the past of all reality, and so the General belonged:

> Among our more vestigial states of mind.
> Nothing had happened because nothing had changed.
> Yet the General was rubbish in the end.

From this ironic apprehension Stevens suddenly modulates to passionate directness in Section IV, in itself a complete and profoundly

244

moving poem. The origin of change is proclaimed as a marriage of
contraries, without which is no progression. But Stevens is offering
us rapture, not dialectics:

> Winter and spring, cold copulars, embrace
> And forth the particulars of rapture come.
>
> Music falls on the silence like a sense,
> A passion that we feel, not understand.
> Morning and afternoon are clasped together
>
> And North and South are an intrinsic couple
> And sun and rain a plural, like two lovers
> That walk away as one in the greenest body.

Change, in this vision, is a sharing, the living antithesis to the
death-in-life that is merely a remaining with oneslf. Radiant by virtue
of this truth, the poem raises itself to the pure and productive atmosphere in which the interior paramour is invoked:

> Follow after, O my companion, my fellow, my self,
> Sister and solace, brother and delight.

After this, the poem's midpoint, there are no flats or resting places
in *Notes*, no section that is not poetry of the highest order. Section
V of *It Must Change* is Stevens at his most characteristic, recalling
Sunday Morning and other poems in *Harmonium*. The island solitude
in a wide water without sound reappears, blue with the color of
imagination, and "a green baked greener in the greenest sun" of summer's reality. The "possible red" of the autumnal vision is suggested
also, preparing us for its full development later, in *It Must Give
Pleasure*, Section III. The planter of *It Must Change*, Section V, is
an imaginative brother to the woman who meditates on death and
change in *Sunday Morning*, and like her he understands that death
and change are the mothers of beauty. He is the man positively affected by change in a positive light, and he dies in the dignity of major man:

> An unaffected man in a negative light
> Could not have borne his labor nor have died
> Sighing that he should leave the banjo's twang.

This meditation on dying well is followed by an ecstasy of bird
song, in a Shelleyan poem that traces the natural destiny of the relational event, from the dialogue of sparrow and crackled blade to the

necessity of the dialogue's petrification. The vatic cry of Shelley to the west wind is heard again in this fresh confrontation of life by life:

> Bethou me, said sparrow, to the crackled blade,
> And you, and you, bethou me as you blow,
> When in my coppice you behold me be.
>
> Ah, ké! the bloody wren, the felon jay,
> Ké-ké, the jug-throated robin pouring out,
> Bethou, bethou, bethou me in my glade.

Together, "these bethous compose a heavenly gong," but the fate of these natural confrontations is such that they cannot be transformed into the living dialogue of change that exists between humans, as in the Dedication of *Notes*. Because their song cannot change it becomes:

> A single text, granite monotony,
>
> One sole face, like a photograph of fate,
> Glass-blower's destiny, bloodless episcopus,
> Eye without lid, mind without any dream—

This is the anatomy of monotony, that where man is not, nature is barren, as one of Blake's aphorisms phrases it. But Stevens ends more in Shelley's spirit than in Blake's, with the hint that all dialogue must fail at last:

> Bethou him, you
> And you, bethou him and bethou. It is
> A sound like any other. It will end.

Though it must change, though its personal exchange of words will end, the supreme relationship of love becomes the fiction of the following section, a defense of "the easy passion, the ever-ready love / Of the lover that lies within us." The easiness of this passion, condemned by moralists for the very mutability that marks it as genuine, is paralleled to the scholar's heat "for another accessible bliss." The lover too experiences:

> The fluctuations of certainty, the change
> Of degrees of perception in the scholar's dark.

This theme of lovers' confrontation is raised to its apotheosis in Section VIII, a passage at once comically grotesque and seriously moving. Ozymandias, Shelley's king-of-kings, whose shattered relics presided over a desert in ironic pride, is confronted by his interior paramour, the bride of his imagination, who bears the splendidly Stevenesque name of Nanzia Nunzio. Stripped more nakedly than nakedness, she demands of him that she be clothed "in the final fila- ment," the fictive covering bestowed by the inflexible order of reality upon the imaginative vision it contemplates embracing. The works of Ozymandias, like all the pride of a reality seeking to deny change, are sunk in the sand, but:

> A fictive covering
> Weaves always glistening from the heart and mind.

The monument of Ozymandias, like his empire, could not bear change; the fictive covering of living relationship, woven by heart and head together, weaves always in the present, and glistens with the motion of its making. Since the poem is itself a fictive covering, it too must change, which is the central point of Section IX, following. Not only must the poem resist the intelligence almost successfully, but it must take on a different form with each fresh reading. That miracle Stevens does not accomplish, but he approaches it as nearly as any poet of our time. Haunting him in Section IX of *It Must Change* is the fearful question every poet in the Romantic tradition is compelled to ask: "Does the poet evade us, as in a senseless ele- ment?" The true Romantic Agony is the fear of solipsism, the horror of becoming a monster like Blake's Urizen, self-absorbed in the deathly perfection of silence. To avoid this fate the poet performs his difficult quest:

> He tries by a peculiar speech to speak
>
> The peculiar potency of the general,
> To compound the imagination's Latin with
> The lingua franca et jocundissima.

That Stevens achieves this will I think become increasingly more evident, though it seems clear that he has a larger proportion of the imagination's Latin in his compound than he might have hoped. That he has spoken something of the peculiar potency of the general is proved in the concluding section of *It Must Change*, where the joy of imagination is released in splendor:

> The casual is not
> Enough. The freshness of transformation is

247

> The freshness of a world. It is our own,
> It is ourselves, the freshness of ourselves,
> And that necessity and that presentation
>
> Are rubbings of a glass in which we peer.
> Of these beginnings, gay and green, propose
> The suitable amours. Time will write them down.

That necessity is the will to change, expressed by the west wind, still a potent Romantic image; that presentation is the way of change. The west wind transforms our world and ourselves, and we peer into a freshness, gay and green with the color of reality. If we cannot quite choose the suitable amours such freshness deserves, we can at least propose them. The proposers will not record the results, but the time that will write them down is a redemptive agent, and for the refreshment of transformation we can afford that certain toll.

It Must Give Pleasure

The third part of *Notes* gives us a continual though difficult greatness. Four of the sections, the Canon Aspirin group, V to VIII, are I think the height of Stevens's achievement, and can scarcely be matched in English poetry since the Romantics. They are to Stevens what the Byzantium poems are to Yeats; the central works of a clarified vision, but their difficulties are more subtly integrated with their themes than the complexities of Yeats's poems, and much more relevant to a reality centered in common experience. Like the Byzantium poems and Keats's odes, they concern the poet's stance in relation to his own poetry, and they render the teleology of the imaginative life with an appropriate intensity.

The Supreme Fiction, now seen as the poem of reality, or nature conceived as a general being and human universe, must begin and end in delight, in the poet's creative joy and the reader's exuberant response. Pleasure is the power that liberates vision, that shows us the new earth given to us by the great marriage between reality and imagination, specifically celebrated by Stevens in *It Must Give Pleasure*, Section IV, the prelude to the Canon Aspirin poems. The necessity of joy for the poet is of course the explicit theme of much of Coleridge and Wordsworth, but Stevens is again deliberately their poverty-stricken heir. The joy of the Romantics elevates its possessor to the experience of a theophany, and becomes an intimation of immortality. The pleasure Stevens exalts is another rich confirmation of mortality, as indeed it was for Keats, and leads to a manifestation of major man, the real man slumbering within us.

The first section of *It Must Give Pleasure* is founded on a contrast between mediated and unmediated vision and their resultant songs, a contrast set forth to perfection in Keats's ode *To Psyche*. Stevens presents first the "facile exercise" of religious celebration: "To sing jubilas at exact, accustomed times." Opposed to this is "the difficultest rigor" of the humanist poet who sees the unmediated vision:

> On the image of what we see, to catch from that
>
> Irrational moment its unreasoning,
> As when the sun comes rising, when the sea
> Clears deeply, when the moon hangs on the wall
>
> Of heaven-haven. These are not things transformed.
> Yet we are shaken by them as if they were.
> We reason about them with a later reason.

The "doctrine," for want of a better word, of *Notes* is expressed in this passage with finality, persuasiveness, and an astonishing economy of verbal gesture. The "unreasoning" here is that nakedness of confrontation that yields only to "a later reason," the poet's imaginative broodings. In such directness of life meeting life, of two realities brought face to face, we are moved as if the everyday had been transformed, though no transformation exists. "Think of the earth," Moneta exclaims to Keats in *The Fall of Hyperion*, and that thinking is also part of Stevens's "later reason," which becomes the subject of Section IV of *It Must Give Pleasure* (where the first line is nearly identical with the final line of Section I). Between this first statement of a reality now beyond the necessity for abstraction, and the chant celebrating a marriage of reality and imagination, come two poems presenting the waiting bride and the heroic bridegroom. The bride is "the blue woman," or poetic imagination, of Section II; the groom is the "lasting visage" of Section III, red with the color of autumn reality. In the fourth poem they appear, respectively, as "the maiden Bawda" and "a great captain." Together the three sections serve to introduce the Canon Aspirin poems, at once the climax of *Notes* and the fulfillment of Stevens's poetic promise, his "theory of poetry" so fleshed as to rival Rilke's visions of the poet's adequacy.

The blue woman, interior paramour of the poet's creative desire, does not wish for more than sensuous reality; enough for her that she remembers the full sequence of the seasons. She too sees what is in the difficulty of what it is to be:

> The blue woman looked and from her window named
>
> The corals of the dogwood, cold and clear,
> Cold, coldly delineating, being real,
> Clear and, except for the eye, without intrusion.

She sees in "the harmonious heat of August," when the world is largest, and our attendant credences are most intense. The powerful chant of Section III brings into counterpoise with this summer of our content the red countenance of autumn, where the human visage falls back into the rock that is the gray particular of man's self:

> A lasting visage in a lasting bush,
> A face of stone in an unending red,
> Red-emerald, red-slitted-blue, a face of slate. . . .

In this landscape the human is seen from afar, and is weathered down, like "the spent feeling leaving nothing of itself." Yet, amid these "red-in-red repetitions never going away," where we would expect to find only "an effulgence faded," we find instead the possibility of an Orphic salvation:

> A dead shepherd brought tremendous chords from hell
>
> And bade the sheep carouse. Or so they said.
> Children in love with them brought early flowers
> And scattered them about, no two alike.

As the expression of a faith that sees repetition becoming revival, the soldier of reality growing deathless in his ruddy ancientness, this passage has many parallels elsewhere in Stevens's poetry. Here it leads us back to reasoning "of these things with a later reason," but now "these things" are not only the real seen plainly but also our sense of a perfection grasped and come again, the blue woman and her revived lover. Of what we have thus seen we make "a place dependent on ourselves," a marriage place between the blue air and the red flesh:

> There was a mystic marriage in Catawba,
> At noon it was on the mid-day of the year
> Between a great captain and the maiden Bawda.

They take one another as a sign "to stop the whirlwind, balk the elements," for this is a marriage between sun and moon, a natural meeting that shatters the context of nature. But it remains a confrontation in this world, the human making choice of a human self:

> They married well because the marriage place
> Was what they loved. It was neither heaven nor hell.
> They were love's characters come face to face.

From this marriage proceeds the Supreme Fiction, whose exponent, major man, now enters the poem in the exhilarating person of the Canon Aspirin, Stevens's finest invention. The Canon is the cure for our current headache of unreality, even as Saint John prophesies the cure of the backache of our fallen history in a later poem by Stevens. In his activity the Canon first becomes the angel of reality, then is tempted too far in his benevolent impositions, and finally is surpassed by the poet himself, who discovers an order that his created angel could only impose. The Canon therefore has his limitations, but that is only to say that one instance of the Supreme Fiction is finally inferior to its maker's desires.

We begin with an introduction very much in the luxurious *Harmonium* manner, which rapidly modulates into a rhetoric of sensible ecstasy, to appropriate one of Stevens's happiest phrases:

> We drank Meursault, ate lobster Bombay with mango
> Chutney. Then the Canon Aspirin declaimed
> Of his sister, in what a sensible ecstasy
>
> She lived in her house. She had two daughters, one
> Of four, and one of seven, whom she dressed
> The way a painter of pauvred color paints.

No sequence of greatly ambitious poetry, one might have believed, could afford to open with such deliberate banality. It is because Stevens is daring so fiercely Romantic a vision that he begins in such deceptive inconsequence. The Canon, one soon understands, is not far from being "that brave man," our abstraction of the sun. His sister is an abstraction of the moon, mother of the months, and her two daughters make up the lunar cycle, as one is the four weeks and the other the seven days. Because we are exploring the real, "without intrusion," the daughters are seen in their essential poverty, our poverty:

> But still she painted them, appropriate to
> Their poverty, a gray-blue yellowed out
> With ribbon, a rigid statement of them, white,

With Sunday pearls, her window's gayety.
She hid them under simple names. She held
Them closelier to her by rejecting dreams.

The words they spoke were voices that she heard.
She looked at them and saw them as they were
And what she felt fought off the barest phrase.

This is the most moving of Stevens's insistences on seeing the very thing itself and nothing else. The Canon's sister, coloring the existence of her children, sees that nothing must stand between them and the shapes they take. In tribute the Canon hums a fugue of praise, but in the sleeping nights his sister transcends all praise, demanding of sleep that it bestow on her children "only the unmuddled self of sleep, for them." With this last rejection of the illusions of moonlight, we are prepared for the angelic greatness of the Canon.

The Canon's apotheosis is the subject of Section VI, the first of three sections forming a miniature dialectic among themselves. In this triad, Section VI states the thesis of the Canon's quest toward an integration of all reality, fact and thought together. Section VII is the antithesis, presenting the Canon's surrender of his quest to the angelic impatience that imposes rather than discovers order. The synthesis is in Section VIII, which one does not hesitate to call Stevens's finest poem, where the poet's discovery of reality is both given and celebrated. Sections IX and X, following, are commentaries on this discovery, after which *Notes* concludes with an invocation of the soldier, who is man embattled in the real world even as the poet is man embattled in the fictive or verbal universe.

Section VI is at once the most Miltonic and the most strenuously heroic of Stevens's poems. At long midnight, when "normal things had yawned themselves away," the Canon sleeps himself into an awareness of naked reality, and reaches a point "beyond which fact could not progress as fact," and where thought must begin. The Canon therefore reconceives night, and in this conceptual effort becomes the angel of reality, joining fact and thought together at that point of nakedness where they meet:

So that he was the ascending wings he saw
And moved on them in orbits' outer stars
Descending to the children's bed, on which

They lay. Forth then with huge pathetic force
Straight to the utmost crown of night he flew.
The nothingness was a nakedness, a point

> Beyond which thought could not progress as thought.

The Canon's Miltonic flight brings him to that metaphysical point where fact and thought alike have reached their limits, where reality and the imagination join in desperation. The Canon's heroism is in the intensity of his integrating choice, his refusal to reject either order:

> He had to choose. But it was not a choice
> Between excluding things. It was not a choice
>
> Between, but of. He chose to include the things
> That in each other are included, the whole,
> The complicate, the amassing harmony.

This choice is Wordsworthian rather than Blakean, for it insists that the context of fact or nature can be harmonized with the more exuberant context of the poet's apocalyptic desires. The problem in such a harmonization is to cultivate the highly anti-apocalyptic virtue of patience. Like Wordsworth, the Canon needs to wait upon the initiative of nature, but instead "he imposes orders as he thinks of them," in Section VII. Though this "is a brave affair," the exhausted Canon has forgotten that "to impose is not to discover." The passion of Stevens slowly mounts in an extraordinary emotional progression as he states his own version of a Romantic faithless faith:

> To discover an order as of
> A season, to discover summer and know it,
>
> To discover winter and know it well, to find,
> Not to impose, not to have reasoned at all,
> Out of nothing to have come on major weather,
>
> It is possible, possible, possible. It must
> Be possible.

No desperation could be more dignified, for Stevens speaks out of the barrenness of the fertile thing that can become no more, the giant of the weather in his nobility and his essential poverty. Utterly vulnerable, except for the Supreme Fiction, the poet prepares to confront the real, and calls upon the angel he has created to be silent and listen to the ultimate poem:

> It must be that in time
> The real will from its crude compoundings come,

> Seeming, at first, a beast disgorged, unlike,
> Warmed by a desperate milk. To find the real,
> To be stripped of every fiction except one,
>
> The fiction of an absolute—Angel,
> Be silent in your luminous cloud and hear
> The luminous melody of proper sound.

After this it is only a question of a final belief, for all possible pro-
logues are ended. Stevens rises to his own challenge and gives us his
ultimate poem, the supreme achievement of post-Romanticism and
the culmination of Coleridgean and Blakean poetic theory. As much
as with Rilke's best poetry, we are convinced that this is "the luminous melody of proper sound":

> What am I to believe? if the angel in his cloud,
> Serenely gazing at the violent abyss,
> Plucks on his strings to pluck abysmal glory,
>
> Leaps downward through evening's revelations, and
> On his spredden wings, needs nothing but deep space,
> Forgets the gold centre, the golden destiny,
>
> Grows warm in the motionless motion of his flight,
> Am I that imagine this angel less satisfied?
> Are the wings his, the lapis-haunted air?
>
> Is it he or is it I that experience this?
> Is it I then that keep saying there is an hour
> Filled with expressible bliss, in which I have
>
> No need, am happy, forget need's golden hand,
> Am satisfied without solacing majesty,
> And if there is an hour there is a day,
>
> There is a month, a year, there is a time
> In which majesty is a mirror of the self:
> I have not but I am and as I am, I am.

If Blake had taken this final step, he would have celebrated his
own Spectre of Urthona, the crippled temporal will of every man, as
the earthly maker of that heavenly maker, Los the Poetic Genius.
Had Wordsworth crossed into this desperately triumphant poetic
humanism, *The Prelude* would have been followed by a poem of the
kind of *Notes,* and there are hints of such a poem in the early *Recluse*

fragment. A less tragic Keats might have lived into so prodigious an exaltation of the poetic self, but the pressures of ill-fortune created instead the purgatorial *Fall of Hyperion*. What the poet comes to believe, in Stevens's late plural of Romantic tradition, is that his disinterested joy in his own creation is more than a final good. In that profoundest of satisfactions, the stance of the creator before his own isolated and splendid artifact, the poet ceases to possess but is, at last in the full difficulty of what it is to be. Most central is that he ceases to have the sense of possessing himself, but is one with that self. In that heroic integration, what is outside the self can be dismissed without fear of solipsistic self-absorption, for the self has joined major man:

> These external regions, what do we fill them with
> Except reflections, the escapades of death,
> Cinderella fulfilling herself beneath the roof?

The rest of *Notes* is epilogue. The song of the birds rises again in Section IX, renewing the vast repetitions that both constitute and exalt our lives, "until merely going round is a final good." In the last section of *It Must Give Pleasure* the poet invokes the universe he has created, "my green, my fluent mundo," with a homely affection appropriate to his achieved peace.

Notes ends with an address to the soldier of reality, the brother to the poet as the soldier of imagination. An exact balance between the humility and the pride of poetry is attained in the poem's conclusion:

> The soldier is poor without the poet's lines,
>
> His pretty syllabi, the sounds that stick,
> Inevitably modulating, in the blood.
> And war for war, each has its gallant kind.
>
> How simply the fictive hero becomes the real;
> How gladly with proper words the soldier dies,
> If he must, or lives on the bread of faithful speech.

Stevens was to create a tone of even greater simplicity and dignity than this in the best poem of his final period, *The Rock*, but at the expense of some of the human warmth of this conclusion. Here, the poet and the soldier make their dwelling in that place formed by the imagination, in which being there together is enough.

1965

18
A. R. Ammons:
"When You Consider
The Radiance"

Nature centres into balls,
And her proud ephemerals,
Fast to surface and outside,
Scan the profile of the sphere;
Knew they what that signified,
A new genesis were here.
Emerson, *Circles*

In 1955, A. R. Ammons, in his thirtieth year, published his first
book of poems, *Ommateum, with Doxology*. *Ommateum* consists
of thirty Whitmanian chants, strongly influenced by the metric of
Ezra Pound (though by nothing else in Pound). *Doxology* is an
intricate religious hymn, in three parts, more ironic in tone than in
direction. In the lengthening perspective of American poetry,
the year 1955 will be remembered as the end of Wallace Stevens's
career, and the beginning of Ammons's, himself not Stevens's
heir but like Stevens a descendant of the great originals of
American Romantic tradition, Emerson and Whitman. Beyond its
experimentation with Poundian cadences, *Ommateum* shows no
trace of the verse fashions of the fifties; I cannot detect in it the
voice of William Carlos Williams, which indeed I do not hear
anywhere in Ammons's work, despite the judgments of several
reviewers. The line of descent from Emerson and Whitman to the
early poetry of Ammons is direct, and even the Poundian
elements in *Ommateum* derive from that part of Pound that is
itself Whitmanian.

   Ommateum's subject is poetic incarnation, in the mode of
Whitman's *Sea-Drift* pieces, Emerson's *Seashore*, and Pound's
Canto II. The Whitman of *As I Ebb'd with the Ocean of Life* is
closest, suggesting that poetic disincarnation is Ammons's true
subject, his vitalizing fear. In the "Foreword" to *Ommateum*
he begins his list of themes with "the fear of the loss of identity."
The first poem of the volume, the chosen beginning of this poet's
outrageously and wonderfully prolific canon, is an assumption of
another's identity. This other, "Ezra," is neither Pound nor the
biblical scribe of the Return, but a suddenly remembered
hunchback playmate from childhood, brought back to the poet's

consciousness by a report of his death in war. The whole of Ammons
is in this first poem, but half a lifetime's imaginings will be necessary
to transfigure this shore-burst into the radiance already implicit here:

So I said I am Ezra
and the wind whipped my throat
gaming for the sounds of my voice
   I listened to the wind
go over my head and up into the night
Turning to the sea I said
   I am Ezra
but there were no echoes from the waves
The words were swallowed up
   in the voice of the surf
or leaping over swells
lost themselves oceanward
   Over the bleached and broken fields
I moved my feet and turning from the wind
   that ripped sheets of sand
   from the beach and threw them
   like seamists across the dunes
swayed as if the wind were taking me away
and said
   I am Ezra
As a word too much repeated
falls out of being
so I Ezra went out into the night
like a drift of sand
and splashed among the windy oats
that clutch the dunes
of unremembered seas

As in the *Ode to the West Wind* and *As I Ebb'd with the Ocean
of Life*, so here the poet's consciousness is assaulted by the elements
he seeks to address, reproved by what he hopes to meet in a relationship that will make him or keep him a poet. The motto of Ammons's first poem might be Whitman's:

Nature here in sight of the sea taking advantage
   of me to dart upon me and sting me,
Because I have dared to open my mouth to
   sing at all.

Later in *Ommateum*, Ammons echoes *As I Ebb'd* more directly,
recalling its terrifying contraction of the self:

> Me and mine, loose windrows, little corpses,
> Froth, snowy white, and bubbles,
> (See, from my dead lips the ooze exuding at last,
> See, the prismatic colors glistening and rolling,)
> Tufts of straw, sands, fragments . . .

This becomes, in his ninth chant, Ammons's emblem of the last stage of "peeling off my being":

> but went on deeper
> till darkness snuffed the shafts of light
>   against the well's side
>   night kissing
>   the last bubbles from my lips

The Emersonian ambition to be possessed fully by the Transcendental Self is Ammons's early theme as it was Whitman's, and is still pervasive in Ammons's latest lyrics, but turned now in a direction avoided by his precursors:

> When you consider the radiance, that it does not withhold
> itself but pours its abundance without selection into every
> nook and cranny not overhung or hidden; when you consider
>
> that birds' bones make no awful noise against the light but
> lie low in the light as in a high testimony; when you consider
> the radiance, that it will look into the guiltiest
>
> swervings of the weaving heart and bear itself upon them,
> not flinching into disguise or darkening; when you consider
> the abundance of such resource as illuminates the glow-blue
>
> bodies and gold-skeined wings of flies swarming the dumped
> guts of a natural slaughter or the coil of shit and in no
> way winces from its storms of generosity; when you consider
>
> that air or vacuum, snow or shale, squid or wolf, rose or lichen,
> each is accepted into as much light as it will take, then
> the heart moves roomier, the man stands and looks about, the
>
> leaf does not increase itself above the grass, and the dark
> work of the deepest cells is of a tune with May bushes
> and fear lit by the breadth of such calmly turns to praise.

This extraordinary poem, *The City Limits*, marks one of the limits of Ammons's art, and almost releases him from the burden of his main tradition. "The guiltiest swervings of the weaving heart," for a poet as poet, are those that swerve him away from his poetic fathers into an angle of fall that is also his angle of vision. For an Emersonian poet, an American Romantic, the angle of vision becomes the whole of life, and measures him as man. Sherman Paul, acutely measuring Emerson's own angle, provides the necessary gloss for this Emersonian poem, *The City Limits*:

> The eye brought him two perceptions of nature—nature ensphered and nature atomized—which corresponded to the distant and proximate visual powers of the eye. These powers, in turn, he could have called the reasoning and understanding modes of the eye. And to each he could have assigned its appropriate field of performance: the country and the city.

We can surmise that the sorrow of all Emersonian poets, from Whitman to Ammons and beyond, comes from the great central declaration: "I become a transparent eyeball; I am nothing; I see all; the currents of the Universal Being circulate through me; I am part or particle of God." But if "Thought is nothing but the circulations made luminous," then what happens when the circulations are darkening? The currents of the Universal Being do not cease to circulate, ever, and the "mathematic ebb and flow" of Emerson's *Seashore* is no consolation to temperaments less rocky than Emerson's own (one thinks not only of Whitman, but of middle Stevens, and late Roethke). To a grim consciousness like Frost's in *Directive*, the wisdom of the Emerson of *The Conduct of Life* is acceptable, admirable, even inevitable, and this late Emersonian strain may never be so worked out in our poetry as to vanish. But Ammons has none of it, and the toughness of his own consolations and celebrations comes out of another tradition, one that I do not understand, for everything that is Southern in American culture is necessarily a darkness to me. Ammons is a poet of the Carolina as well as the Jersey shore, and his relation to Whitman is severely modified by rival spirits of place. The Ezra-poet is as obsessed with sandstorms as any Near Easterner; for him the wind makes sheets of sand into sea mists. In *The City Limits* the radiance, despite its generosity, cannot reach what is overhung or hidden, and what is wholly hidden cannot be accepted into the light it will not take. There is for Ammons a recalcitrance or unwilling dross in everything given, and this "loneliness" (to use one of his words for it) marks his verse from *Ommateum* on as more than a little distinct from its great precursors.

I am writing of Ammons as though he had rounded his first circle in the eye of his readers, and there is no other way to write about him, even if my essay actually introduces him to some of its readers. The fundamental postulates for reading Ammons have been set down well before me, by Richard Howard and Marius Bewley in particular, but every critic of a still emergent poet has his own obsessions to work through, and makes his own confession of the radiance. Ammons's poetry does for me what Stevens's did earlier, and the High Romantics before that: it helps me to live my life. If Ammons is, as I think, the central poet of my generation, because he alone has made a heterocosm, a second nature in his poetry, I deprecate no other poet by this naming. It is, surprisingly, a rich generation, with ten or a dozen poets who seem at least capable of making a major canon, granting fortune and persistence. Ammons, much more than the others, has made such a canon already. A solitary artist, nurtured by the strength available for him only in extreme isolation, carrying on the Emersonian tradition with a quietness directly contrary to nearly all its other current avatars, he has emerged in his most recent poems as an extraordinary master, comparable to the Stevens of *Ideas of Order* and *The Man With the Blue Guitar*. To track him persistently, from his origins in *Ommateum* through his maturing in *Corsons Inlet* and its companion volumes on to his new phase in *Uplands* and *Briefings* is to be found by not only a complete possibility of imaginative experience, but by a renewed sense of the whole line of Emerson, the vitalizing and much maligned tradition that has accounted for most that matters in American poetry.

Emerson, like Stevens and Ammons after him, had a fondness for talking mountains. One thinks of Wordsworth's old men, perhaps of the Virgilian Mount Atlas, of Blake's Los at the opening of Night V, *The Four Zoas*, of Shelley's Mont Blanc, which obstinately refuses however to take on human form, and affronts the humane revolutionary with its hard, its menacing otherness. Emerson's Monadnoc is genial and gnomic:

> "Monadnoc is a mountain strong,
> Tall and good my kind among;
> But well I know, no mountain can,
> Zion or Meru, measure with man.
> For it is on zodiacs writ,
> Adamant is soft to wit:
> And when the greater comes again

> With my secret in his brain,
> I shall pass, as glides my shadow
> Daily over hill and meadow.
> . . . .
> Anchored fast for many an age,
> I await the bard and sage,
> Who, in large thoughts, like fair pearl-seed,
> Shall string Monadnoc like a bead."

Emerson is not providing the golden string to be wound into a ball, but one of a series of golden entities to be beaded on a string. Monadnoc awaits the Central Man, the redemptive poet of *Bacchus*. Thoreau, in his fine poem on the mountains, characteristically avoids Emerson's humanizing of an otherness, and more forcefully mountainizes himself:

> But special I remember thee,
> Wachusett, who like me
> Standest alone without society.
> Thy far blue eye,
> A remnant of the sky,
> Seen through the clearing or the gorge,
> Or from the windows of the forge,
> Doth leaven all it passes by.
> . . . .
> Upholding heaven, holding down earth,
> Thy pastime from thy birth;
> Not steadied by the one, nor leaning on the other,
> May I approve myself thy worthy brother!

Wachusett is not to be strung like a bead, however strong the bard and sage. Thoreau is a more Wordsworthian poet than Emerson, and so meets a nature ruggedly recalcitrant to visionary transformations. Ammons, who has a relation to both, meets Emerson's kind of mountains, meets a nature that awaits its bard, even if sometimes in ambush. In *Ommateum*, there is not much transformation, and some ambuscade, and so the neglect encountered by the volume can be understood. Yet these chants, setting aside advantages in retrospect, are remarkable poems, alive at every point in movement and in vision. They live in their oddly negative exuberance, as the new poet goes out into his bleak lands as though he marched only into another man's phantasmagoria. One chant, beginning "In the wind my rescue is," to be found but mutilated in the *Selected Poems* (1968), states the poet's task as a gathering of the stones of earth into one place. The wind, by sowing a phantasmagoria in the poet's eyes,

262

draws him "out beyond the land's end," thus saving him "from all those ungathered stones." The shore, Whitman's emblem for the state in which poets are made and unmade, becomes the theater for the first phase of Ammons's poetic maturity, the lyrics written in the decade after *Ommateum*. These are gathered in three volumes: *Expressions of Sea Level* (1964), *Corsons Inlet* (1965), and *Northfield Poems* (1966), which need to be read as a unit, since the inclusion of a poem in one or another volume seems to be a matter of whim. A reader of Ammons is likeliest to be able to read this phase of him in the *Selected Poems*, whose arrangement in chronological order of composition shows how chronologically scrambled the three volumes are.

Ammons's second start as a poet, after the transcendental waste places of *Ommateum*, is in this *Hymn:*

> I know if I find you I will have to leave the earth
> and go on out
>   over the sea marshes and the brant in bays
> and over the hills of tall hickory
> and over the crater lakes and canyons
> and on up through the spheres of diminishing air
> past the blackset noctilucent clouds
>   where one wants to stop and look
> way past all the light diffusions and bombardments
> up farther than the loss of sight
>   into the unseasonal undifferentiated empty stark
>
> And I know if I find you I will have to stay with the earth
> inspecting with thin tools and ground eyes
> trusting the microvilli sporangia and simplest
>   coelenterates
> and praying for a nerve cell
> with all the soul of my chemical reactions
> and going right on down where the eye sees only traces
>
> You are everywhere partial and entire
> You are on the inside of everything and on the outside
>
> I walk down the path down the hill where the sweetgum
> has begun to ooze spring sap at the cut
> and I see how the bark cracks and winds like no other bark
> chasmal to my ant-soul running up and down
> and if I find you I must go out deep into your
>   far resolutions
> and if I find you I must stay here with the separate leaves

The chants of *Ommateum* were composed mostly in a single year, from the Spring of 1951 to the Spring of 1952. In 1956, Ammons fully claims his Transcendental heritage in his *Hymn,* a work of poetic annunciation in which the "you" is Emerson's "Nature," all that is separate from "the Soul." The *Hymn's* difficult strength depends on a reader's recognition that the found "you" is: "the NOT ME, that is, both nature and art, all other men and my own body." Juxtapose a crucial passage of Emerson, and the *clinamen* that governs the course of Ammons's maturity is determined:

> The world proceeds from the same spirit as the body of
> man. It is a remoter and inferior incarnation of God, a projec-
> tion of God in the unconscious. But it differs from the body in
> one important respect. It is not, like that, now subjected to the
> human will. Its serene order is inviolable by us. It is, there-
> fore, to us, the present expositor of the divine mind. It is a
> fixed point whereby we may measure our departure.

Emerson's fixed point oscillates dialectically in Ammons's *Hymn.* Where Emerson's mode hovers always around metonymy, parts of a world taken as the whole, Ammons's sense of the universe takes it for a symptom. No American poet, not Whitman or Stevens, shows us so fully something otherwise unknown in the structures of the national consciousness as Ammons does. It cannot be said so far that Ammons has developed as fluent and individual a version of the language of the self as they did, but he has time and persistence enough before he borrows his last authority from death. His first authority is the height touched in this *Hymn,* where everything depends upon a precision of consequences "if I find you." "The unassimilable fact leads us on," a later poem begins, the leading on being Ammons's notion of quest. If all that is separate from him, the "you," is found, the finding will be assimilated at the final cost of going on out "into the unseasonal undifferentiated empty stark," a resolution so far as to annihilate selfhood. One part of the self will be yielded to an apprehension beyond sight, while the other will stay here with the earth, to be yielded to sight's reductiveness, separated with each leaf.

This is the enterprise of a consciousness extreme enough to begin another central poem, *Gravelly Run,* with a quietly terrifying sense of what will suffice:

> I don't know somehow it seems sufficient
> to see and hear whatever coming and going is,
> losing the self to the victory
>   of stones and trees,

of bending sandpit lakes, crescent
round groves of dwarf pine:

for it is not so much to know the self
as to know it as it is known
by galaxy and cedar cone . . .

But as it is known, it is only a "surrendered self among / unwel-
coming forms." The true analogue to this surrender is in the curious
implicit threat of Emerson's Orphic poet:

We distrust and deny inwardly our sympathy with nature.
We own and disown our relation to it, by turns. We are like
Nebuchadnezzer, dethroned, bereft of reason, and eating grass
like an ox. But who can set limits to the remedial force of
spirit?

The remedial force of spirit, in this sense, is closest to being that
terriblest force in the world, of which Stevens's Back-ache complains.
Ammons, who knows he cannot set limits to such force, warns himself perpetually "to turn back," before he comes to a unity apparently equal to his whole desire. For his desire is only a metonymy,
and unity (if found) compels another self-defeating question:

You cannot come to unity and remain material:
in that perception is no perceiver:
    when you arrive
you have gone too far:
    at the Source you are in the mouth of Death:

you cannot
    turn around in
the Absolute: there are no entrances or exits
    no precipitations of forms
to use like tongs against the formless:
    no freedom to choose:

to be

    you have to stop not-being and break
off from *is* to *flowing* and
    this is the sin you weep and praise:
origin is your original sin:
    the return you long for will ease your guilt
and you will have your longing:

    the wind that is my guide said this: it
should know having

given up everything to eternal being but
direction:

how I said can I be glad and sad: but a man goes
   from one foot to the other:
wisdom wisdom:
   to be glad and sad at once is also unity
and death:
   wisdom wisdom: a peachblossom blooms on a particular
tree on a particular day:
   unity cannot do anything in particular:

are these the thoughts you want me to think I said but
   the wind was gone and there was no more knowledge then.

The wind's origin is its original sin also; were it to give up even direction, it would cease to be *Guide*, as this poem is entitled. If the wind is Ammons's Virgil, an Interior Paramour or Whitmanian Fancy remains his Beatrice, guiding him whenever wind ceases to lead. The poetic strength of *Guide* is in its dialectical renunciation of even this daimonic paramour. For the wind speaks against what is deepest and most self-destructive in Ammons. "Break off from *is* to *flowing*" is a classic phrasing of the terrible dream that incessantly afflicts most of our central poetic imaginations in America. "Unity cannot do anything in particular"; least of all can it write a poem.

The wind, Ammons's way to knowledge, is certainly the most active wind in American poetry. In *Ommateum*, the wind is a desperate whip, doubting its own efficacy in a dry land. It moves "like wisdom," but its poet is not so sure of the likeness. In the mature volumes, it is more a blade than a whip, and its desperation has rendered it apologetic:

Having split up the chaparral
blasting my sight
the wind said
   You know I'm
     the result of
forces beyond my control
I don't hold it against you
I said
It's all right I understand

For the wind "dies and never dies," but the poet goes on:

consigned to
form that will not

let me loose
except to death
till some
syllable's rain
anoints my tongue
and makes it sing
to strangers:

To be released from form into unity one dies or writes a poem;
this appalling motive for metaphor is as desperate as any wind.
Wind, which is "not air or motion/but the motion of air," speaks to
a consciousness that is not spirit or making, but the spirit of making,
the Ezra-incarnation in this poet:

I coughed
  and the wind said
Ezra will live
to see your last
  sun come up again

I turned (as I will) to weeds and
the wind went off
  carving
monuments through a field of stone
  monuments whose shape
wind cannot arrest but
taking hold on
changes

While Ezra
  listens from terraces of mind
wind cannot reach or
weedroots of my low-feeding shiver

When the poet falls (as he must) from this Ezra-eminence, the
terraces of mind dissolve:

The mind whirls, short of the unifying
reach, short of the heat
  to carry that forging:
after the visions of these losses, the spent
seer, delivered to wastage, risen
  into ribs, consigns knowledge to
  approximation, order to the vehicle
of change . . .

He is never so spent a seer as he says, even if the price of his ascensions keeps rising. If from moment to moment the mode of motion is loss, there is always the privileged *Moment* itself:

> He turned and
> stood
>
> in the moment's
> height,
>
> exhilaration
> sucking him up,
>
> shuddering and
> lifting
>
> him
> jaw and bone
>
> and he said
> what
>
> destruction am I
> blessed by?

The burden of Ammons's poetry is to answer, to name that enlargement of life that is also a destruction. When the naming came most complete, in the late summer of 1962, it gave Ammons his two most ambitious single poems, *Corsons Inlet* and *Saliences*. Though both poems depend upon the context of Ammons's canon, they show the field of his enterprise more fully and freely than could have been expected of any single works. *Corsons Inlet* is likely to be Ammons's most famous poem, his *Sunday Morning*, a successfully universalizing expression of a personal thematic conflict and its apparent (or provisional) resolution. But *Saliences*, a harder, less open, more abstract fury of averted destructions, is the better poem. *Corsons Inlet* comforts itself (and us) with the perpetually renewed hope of a fresh walk over the dunes to the sea. *Saliences* rises past hope to what in the mind is "beyond loss or gain/beyond concern for the separate reach." Both the hope and the ascension beyond hope return us to origins, and can be apprehended with keener aptitude after an excursus taking us deeper into Ammons's tradition. Ammons compels that backward vision of our poetry that only major achievement exacts, and illuminates Emerson and all his progeny as much as he needs them for illumination. Reading Ammons, I brood on all

American poetry in the Romantic tradition, which means I yield to Emerson, who is to our modern poetry what Wordsworth has been to all British poetry after him; the starting-point, the defining element, the vexatious father, the shadow and the despair, liberating angel and blocking-agent, perpetual irritant and solacing glory.

John Jay Chapman, in what is still the best introductory essay on Emerson, condensed his estimate of the seer into a great and famous sentence: "If a soul be taken and crushed by democracy till it utter a cry, that cry will be Emerson." In the year 1846, when he beheld "the famous States/Harrying Mexico/With rifle and with knife!", Emerson raised the cry of himself most intensely and permanently:

> Though loath to grieve
> The evil time's sole patriot,
> I cannot leave
> My honied thought
> For the priest's cant,
> or statesman's rant.
>
> If I refuse
> My study for their politique,
> which at the best is trick,
> The angry Muse
> Puts confusion in my brain.

The astonished Muse found Emerson at her side all through 1846, the year not only of the Channing *Ode*, but of *Bacchus* and *Merlin*, his finest and most representative poems, that between them establish a dialectic central to subsequent American poetry. In *Bacchus*, the poet is not his own master, but yields to daimonic possession. In *Merlin*, the daimonic itself is mastered, as the poet becomes first the Bard, and then Nemesis:

> Who with even matches odd,
> Who athwart space redresses
> The partial wrong,
> Fills the just period,
> And finishes the song.

The poet of *Bacchus* is genuinely possessed, and yet falls (savingly) victim to Ananke—he is still *human*. The poet of *Merlin* is himself absorbed into Ananke and ceases to be human, leaving *Bacchus* much the better poem. To venture a desolate formula about American poetry: our greater poets attain the splendor of Bacchus, and then attempt to become Merlin, and so cease to be wholly human and begin to fail as poets. Emerson and his descendants dwindle, not when they build altars to the Beautiful Necessity, but when they richly confuse themselves with that Necessity. Poetry, Emerson splendidly observed, must be as new as foam and as old as the rock; he might also have observed that it had better not itself try to be foam or rock.

A strain in Ammons, ecological and almost geological, impels him towards identification with the American version of Ananke, and is his largest flaw as a poet. Robert Bly brilliantly parodied this strain by printing a passage from *The Mushroom Hunter's Field Guide* under the title, *A. R. Ammons Discusses The Lacaria Trullisata*:

> The somewhat distant,
> broad, purplish
> to violaceous gills,
> white spore
>
> Deposit, and
> habitat
> on sand distingu-
> ish it. No
> part of the fruit-
>
> Ing body is ever
> glutinous.
> *Edibility.* The question
> is academic: It is
>
> Impossible to get
> rid of
> all the sand.

And so on. The Ammonsian literalness, allied to a similar destructive impulse in Wordsworth and Thoreau, attempts to summon outward continuities to shield the poet from his mind's own force. *A Poem Is A Walk* is the title of a dark, short prose piece by Ammons that tries "to establish a reasonably secure identity between a poem and a walk and to ask how a walk occurs, what it is, and what it is for," but establishes only that a walk by Ammons is a sublime kind of Pythagorean enterprise or Behmenite picnic. Emerson, who spoke as much wisdom as any American, alas spoke darkly also, and Ammons is infuriatingly Emersonian when he tells us a poem "is a motion to no-motion, to the still point of contemplation and deep realization. Its knowledges are all negative and, therefore, more positive than any knowledge." *Corsons Inlet, Saliences,* and nearly a hundred other poems by Ammons are nothing of the kind, his imagination be thanked, rather than this spooky, pure-product-of-America mysticism. Unlike Emerson, who crossed triumphantly into prose, Ammons belongs to that company of poets that *thinks* most powerfully and naturally in verse, and sometimes descends to obscure quietudes when verse subsides.

Corsons Inlet first verges on, and then veers magnificently away from worshipping the Beautiful Necessity, from celebrating the way things are. "Life will be imaged, but cannot be divided nor doubled," might be the poem's motto; so might: "Ask the fact for the form," both maxims being Emerson's. Ammons's long poem, *Tape for the Turn of the Year,* contains the self-admonishment: "get out of boxes, hard/forms of mind:/go deep:/penetrate/to the true spring," which is the initial impulse of *Corsons Inlet.* The poet, having walked in the morning over the dunes to the sea, recollects later in the day the release granted him by the walk, from thought to sight, from conceptual forms to the flowings and blendings of the Coleridgean Secondary Imagination. Released into the composition of *Corsons Inlet,* he addresses his reader directly (consciously in Whitman's mode) to state both the nature of his whole body of poetry, and his sense of its largest limitation:

> I allow myself eddies of meaning:
> yield to a direction of significance
> running
> like a stream through the geography of my work:
>   you can find
> in my sayings
>
>   swerves of action
>   like the inlet's cutting edge:
>
>   there are dunes of motion,
> organizations of grass, white sandy paths of remembrance
> in the overall wandering of mirroring mind:
>
> but Overall is beyond me: is the sum of these events
> I cannot draw, the ledger I cannot keep, the accounting
> beyond the account:

Within this spaced restraint, there is immense anguish, and the anguish is not just metaphysical. Though this anguish be an acquired wisdom, such wisdom proffers no consolation for the loss of quest.

The anguish that goes through *Corsons Inlet*, subdued but ever salient, is more akin to a quality of mind in Thoreau than to anything in Emerson or Whitman. What Transcendentalists wanted of natural history is generally a darkness to me, and I resort to the late Perry Miller for some light on "the Transcendental methodology for coping with the multifarious concreteness of nature. That method is to see the particular as a particular, and yet at the same time so to perceive it as to make it, of itself, yield up the general and the universal." But that is too broad, being a Romantic procedure in general, with neither the American impatience nor the American obsession of particularity clearly distinguished from Wordsworthianism. Wordsworth was wonderfully patient with preparations for vision, and was more than content to see the particulars flow together and fade out in the great moments of vision. Emerson scanted preparations, and held on to the particulars even in ecstasy. In Thoreau, whatever his final differences with his master, the Emersonian precipitateness and clarity of the privileged moment are sharpened. When I read in his *Journals*, I drown in particulars and cannot find the moments of release, but *The Natural History of Massachusetts*, his first true work, seems all release, and very close to the terrible nostalgias *Corsons Inlet* reluctantly abandons. William Ellery Channing, memorializing Thoreau clumsily though with love, deluges us with evidences of those walks and talks in which Overall was never beyond Thoreau, but came confidently with each natural observation. But Ammons, who would want to emulate Thoreau, cannot keep the account; his natural observations bring him wholly other evidences:

> in nature there are few sharp lines: there are areas of
> primrose
>   more or less dispersed;
> disorderly orders of bayberry; between the rows
> of dunes,
> irregular swamps of reeds,
> though not reeds alone, but grass, bayberry, yarrow, all . . .
> predominantly reeds:

All through the poem beats its hidden refrain: "I was released from . . . straight lines," "few sharp lines," "I have drawn no lines," "but there are no lines," "a wider range/than mental lines can keep," "the waterline, waterline inexact," "but in the large view, no/lines or changeless shapes." A wild earlier poem, called *Lines*, startlingly

exposes Ammons's obsession, for there nature bombards him, all but
destroys him with lines, nothing but lines:

> Lines flying in, out: logarithmic
>   curves coiling
> toward an infinitely inward center: lines
>   weaving in, threads lost in clustral scrawl,
>   weaving out into loose ends,
> wandering beyond the border of gray background,
>   going out of vision,
>   not returning;
> or, returning, breaking across the boundary
>   as new lines, discontinuous,
>   come into sight:
> fiddleheads of ferns, croziers of violins,
>   convoluted spherical masses, breaking through
>   ditchbanks where briar
> stem-dull will
>   leave and bloom:
>   haunch line, sickle-like, turning down, bulging, nuzzling
> under, closing into
>   the hidden, sweet, dark meeting of lips:
>   the spiraling out
> or in
>   of galaxies:
>   the free-running wavy line, swirling
> configuration, halting into a knot
> of curve and density: the broken,
>   irreparable filament: tree-winding vines, branching
> falling off or back, free,
>   the adventitious preparation for possibility, from
>   branch to branch, ash to gum:
> the breaker
>   hurling into reach for shape, crashing
>   out of order, the inner hollow sizzling flat:
> the longnecked, uteral gourd, bass line
>   continuous in curve,
>   melodic line filling and thinning:
> concentrations,
>   whirling masses,
>   thin leaders, disordered ends and risks:
> explosions of clusters, expansions from the
>   full radial sphere, return's longest chance:
>   lines exploring, intersecting, paralleling, twisting,
> noding: deranging, clustering.

This is Ammons's Mad Song, his equivalent of Stevens's *A Rabbit As King of the Ghosts*, another poem of the mind's mercilessness, its refusal to defend itself against itself. "Deranging, clustering" is the fear and the horror, from which *Corsons Inlet* battles for release, mostly through embracing "a congregation/rich with entropy," a constancy of change. The poet who insists he has drawn no lines draws instead his poem out of the "dunes of motion," loving them desperately as his only (but inadequate) salvation, all that is left when his true heaven of Overall is clearly beyond him. Yet this remains merely a being "willing to go along" in the recognition not of the Beautiful but the Terrible Necessity:

> the moon was full last night: today, low tide was low:
> black shoals of mussels exposed to the risk
> of air
> and, earlier, of sun,
> waved in and out with the waterline, waterline inexact,
> caught always in the event of change:
>   a young mottled gull stood free on the shoals
>   and ate
> to vomiting: another gull, squawking possession, cracked a crab,
> picked out the entrails, swallowed the soft-shelled legs, a ruddy
> turnstone running in to snatch leftover bits:
>
> risk is full: every living thing in
> siege: the demand is life, to keep life: the small
> white blacklegged egret, how beautiful, quietly stalks and spears
>   the shallows, darts to shore
>   to stab—what? I couldn't
>   see against the black mudflats—a frightened
>   fiddler crab?

This great and very American passage, kin to a darker tradition than Ammons's own, and to certain poems of Melville and Hart Crane, is *Corsons Inlet*'s center, the consequence of the spent seer's consignment of order to the vehicle of change. I remember, each time I read it, that Ammons is a Southerner, heir to a darker Protestantism than was the immediate heritage of the New England visionaries or of Whitman. But our best Southern poets from Poe and Timrod through Ransom, Tate, Warren, have not affected his art, and a comparison to a Southern contemporary like James Dickey indicates sharply how much Ammons is the conscious heir of nineteenth-century Northern poetry, including a surprising affinity to

Dickinson in his later phase of *Uplands* and *Briefings*. But, to a North Carolinian one hundred years after, Transcendentalism comes hard and emerges bitterly, with the Oversoul reduced from Overall to "the overall wandering of mirroring mind," confronting the dunes and swamps as a last resource, the final form of Nature or the Not-me.

From the nadir of "every living thing in/siege," *Corsons Inlet* slowly rises to a sense of the ongoing, "not chaos: preparations for/ flight." In a difficult transitional passage, the poet associates the phrasal fields of his metric with the "field" of action on every side of him, open to his perception "with moving incalculable center." Looking close, he can see "order tight with shape"; standing back, he confronts a formlessness that suddenly, in an extraordinary epiphany, is revealed as his consolation:

> orders as summaries, as outcomes of actions override
> or in some way result, not predictably (seeing me gain
> the top of a dune,
> the swallows
> could take flight—some other fields of bayberry
>   could enter fall
>   berryless) and there is serenity:
>
>   no arranged terror: no forcing of image, plan,
> or thought:
> no propaganda, no humbling of reality to precept:
>
> terror pervades but is not arranged, all possibilities
> of escape open: no route shut, except in
>   the sudden loss of all routes:

"No arranged terror" is the crucial insight, and if we wish to inquire who would arrange terror except a masochist, the wish will not sustain itself. The poem's final passage, this poet's defense, abandons the really necessary "pulsations of order," the reliable particulars, for what cannot suffice, the continued bafflement of perceiving nothing completely. For Ammons, the seer of *Ommateum* and the still-confident quester of the *Hymn*, this bafflement is defeat, and enjoying the freedom that results from scope eluding his grasp is hardly an enjoying in any ordinary sense. The poem ends bravely, but not wholly persuasively:

> I see narrow orders, limited tightness, but will
> not run to the easy victory:

> still around the looser, wider forces work:
>   I will try
>   to fasten into order enlarging grasps of disorder, widening
>   scope, but enjoying the freedom that
>   Scope eludes my grasp, that there is no finality of vision,
>   that I have perceived nothing completely,
>   that tomorrow a new walk is a new walk.

Origin is still his original sin; what his deepest nature longs for, to come to unity and yet remain material, is no part of *Corsons Inlet*, which grants him freedom to choose, but no access to that unity that alone satisfies choice. The major poem written immediately after *Corsons Inlet* emerges from stoic acceptance of bafflement into an imaginative reassurance that prompts Ammons's major phase, the lyrics of *Uplands, Briefings,* and the work-in-progress:

> Consistencies rise
> and ride
> the mind down
> hard routes
>   walled
> with no outlet and so
> to open a variable geography,
>   proliferate
> possibility, here
> is this dune fest
>   releasing,
> mind feeding out,
> gathering clusters,
> fields of order in disorder,
> where choice
> can make beginnings,
>   turns,
>   reversals,
> where straight line
> and air-hard thought
> can meet
> unarranged disorder,
>   dissolve
> before the one event that
> creates present time
> in the multi-variable
>   scope:

Saliences thus returns to *Corsons Inlet*'s field of action, driven by that poet's need not to abide in a necessity, however beautiful. Saliences etymologically are out-leapings, "mind feeding out," not taking in perceptions but turning its violent energies out into the field of action. If *Corsons Inlet* is Ammons's version of *The Idea of Order at Key West* (not that he had Stevens's poem in mind, but that the attentive reader learns to compare the two), then *Saliences* is his *The Man With the Blue Guitar*, a discovery of how to begin again after a large and noble acknowledgement of dark limitations. *Saliences* is a difficult, abstract poem, but it punches itself along with an overwhelming vigor, showing its exuberance by ramming through every blocking particular, until it can insist that "where not a single single thing endures,/the overall reassures." Overall remains beyond Ammons, but is replaced by "a round/quiet turning,/beyond loss or gain,/beyond concern for the separate reach." *Saliences* emphasizes the transformation of Ammons's obsessive theme, from the longing for unity to the assertion of the mind's power over the particulars of being, the universe of death. The Emersonianism of Ammons is constant; as did Whitman, so his final judgment of his relation to that great precursor will be: "loyal at last." But *Saliences* marks the *clinamen;* the swerve away from Emerson is now clarified, and Ammons will write no poem more crucial to his own unfolding. Before *Saliences*, the common reader must struggle with the temptation of naming Ammons a nature poet; after this, the struggle would be otiose. The quest that was surrendered in *Guide*, and whose loss was accepted in *Corsons Inlet*, is internalized in *Saliences* and afterward.

Saliences approximates (indeliberately) the subtle procedure of a subtradition within Romantic poetry that goes from Shelley's *Mont Blanc* to Stevens's *The Auroras of Autumn*. The poet begins in an austere, even a terrifying scene of natural confrontation, but he does not describe the scene or name the terror until he has presented fully the mind's initial defense against scene and terror, its implicit assertion of its own force. So *Saliences* begins with a vision of the mind in action "in the multi-variable/scope." A second movement starts with the wind's entrance ("a variable of wind/among the dunes,/making variables/of position and direction and sound") and climaxes at the poem's halfway point, which returns to the image of the opening ("come out of the hard/routes and ruts,/pour over the walls/of previous assessments: turn to/the open,/the unexpected, to new saliences of feature." After this come seventy magical lines of Ammons upon his heights (starting with: "The reassurance is/that through change/continuities sinuously work"), lines that constitute one of a convincing handful of contemporary assurances that the imagination is capable always of a renovative fresh start.

The dune fest, which in the poem's opening movement is termed a provocation for the mind's release from "consistencies" (in the sense of Blake's Devourer), is seen in the second movement as *Corsons Inlet*'s baffled field of action:

> wind, a variable, soft wind, hard
> steady wind, wind
> shaped and kept in the
> bent of trees,
> the prevailing dipping seaward
> of reeds,
> the kept and erased sandcrab trails:
> wind, the variable to the gull's flight,
> how and where he drops the clam
> and the way he heads in, running to loft:
> wind, from the sea, high surf
> and cool weather;
> from the land, a lessened breakage
> and the land's heat:
> wind alone as a variable,
> as a factor in millions of events,
> leaves no two moments
> on the dunes the same:
>   keep
> free to these events,
> bend to these
> changing weathers:

This wind has gone beyond the wind of *Guide,* for it has given up everything to eternal being, even direction, even velocity, and contents itself to be shaped and kept by each particular it encounters. Knowing he cannot be one with or even like this wind, knowing too he must be more than a transparency, an Eye among the blind particulars, the poet moves to a kind of upper level of Purgatory, where the wind ceases to be his guide, and he sees as he has not seen before:

> when I went back to the dunes today,
>   saliences,
> congruent to memory,
> spread firmingly across my sight:
> the narrow white path
> rose and dropped over
> grassy rises toward the sea:
> sheets of reeds,
> tasseling now near fall,

> filled the hollows
> with shapes of ponds or lakes:
> bayberry, darker, made wandering
> chains of clumps, sometimes pouring
> into heads, like stopped water:
>   much seemed
> constant, to be looked
> forward to, expected:

It is the saliences, the outleapings, that "spread *firmingly* across my sight," and give him assurances, "summations of permanence." The whole passage, down through the poem's close, has a firm beauty unlike anything previous in Ammons. Holding himself as he must, firmly apart from still-longed-for unity, he finds himself now in an astonishing equilibrium with the particulars, containing them in his own mind by reimagining them there:

>   . . . in
>   the hollow,
>   where a runlet
>   makes in
>   at full tide and fills a bowl,
>   extravagance of pink periwinkle
>   along the grassy edge,
>   and a blue, bunchy weed, deep blue,
>   deep into the mind the dark blue
>   constant:

The change here, as subtle as it is precarious, only just bears description, though the poet of *Uplands* and *Briefing* relies upon it as though it were palpable, something he could touch every way. The weed and the mind's imaginative constancy are in the relation given by the little poem, *Reflective*, written just afterward:

>   I found a
>   weed
>   that had a
>
>   mirror in it
>   and that
>   mirror
>
>   looked in at
>   a mirror
>   in

279

me that
had a
weed in it

In itself this is slight; in the context provided by *Saliences* it is exact and finely wrought. The whole meaning of it is in "I *found*," for *Saliences* records a finding, and a being found. Because of this mutual finding, the magnificent close of the poem is possible, is even necessary:

where not a single single thing endures,
the overall reassures,
deaths and flights,
shifts and sudden assaults claiming
limited orders,
the separate particles:
earth brings to grief
much in an hour that sang, leaped, swirled,
yet keeps a round
    quiet turning,
beyond loss or gain,
beyond concern for the separate reach.

I think, when I read this passage, of the final lines of Wordsworth's great Ode, of the end of Browning's *Love Among the Ruins*, of the deep peace Whitman gives as he concludes *Crossing Brooklyn Ferry*, and of Stevens closing *As You Leave the Room:*

An appreciation of a reality

And thus an elevation, as if I left
With something I could touch, touch every way.

And yet nothing has been changed except what is
Unreal, as if nothing had been changed at all.

This is not to play at touchstones, in the manner of Arnold or of Blackmur, but only to record my experience as a reader, which is that *Saliences* suggests and is worthy of such company. Firm and radiant as the poem is, its importance for Ammons (if I surmise rightly) transcends its intrinsic worth, for it made possible his finest poems. I pass to them with some regret for the splendors in *Selected Poems* I have not discussed: *Silver, Terrain, Bridge, Jungle Knot, Nelly Myers, Expressions of Sea Level*, and for the long poem, *Tape for the Turn of the Year*, a heroic failure that is Ammons's most original and surprising invention.

Uplands, published in the autumn of 1970, begins with a difficult, almost ineluctable lyric, *Snow Log*, which searches for intentions where they evidently cannot be found, in the particulars of fallen tree, snow, shrubs, the special light of winter landscape; "I take it on myself," the poet ends by saying, and repeats the opening triad:

> especially the fallen tree
> the snow picks
> out in the woods to show.

Stevens, in the final finding of the ear, returned to the snow he had forgotten, to behold again "nothing that is not there and the nothing that is." *Snow Log* seems to find something that is not there, but the reader is left uncertain whether there is a consciousness in the scene that belongs neither to him nor to the poet. With the next poem, *Upland*, which gives the volume both its tonality and title, the uncertainty vanishes:

> Certain presuppositions are altered
> by height: the inversion to
> sky-well a peak
> in a desert makes: the welling
>
> from clouds down the boulder fountains:
> it is always a
> surprise out west there—
> the blue ranges loose and aglide
>
> with heat and then come close
> on slopes leaning up into green:
> a number of other phenomena might
> be summoned—
>
> take the Alleghenies for example,
> some quality in the air
> of summit stones lying free and loose
> out among the shrub trees: every
>
> exigency seems prepared for that might
> roll, bound, or give flight
> to stone: that is, the stones are
> prepared: they are round and ready.

A poem like this is henceforth Ammons's characteristic work: shorter and more totally self-enclosed than earlier ventures, and less reliant on larger contexts. He has become an absolute master of his

art, and a maker of individual tones as only the greater poets can
accomplish:

> ... the stones are
> prepared: they are round and ready.

Upland does not attempt to define "some quality in the air" that
alters presuppositions and makes its stones prepared for anything at
any time. The poem disturbs because it compels us to accept the
conflicting notions (for us) of surprise and preparation as being no
conflict for the intentionality held by those summit stones. It satisfies
as much as disturbs because something in us is not wholly apart from
the summit stone's state-of-being; a natural apocalypticism is in the
air, and pervades our rare ascensions to the mind's heights. Ammons, who is increasingly wary of finalities, praises hesitation in the
next lyric, *Periphery:*

> One day I complained about the periphery
> that it was thickets hard to get around in
> or get around for
> an older man: it's like keeping charts
>
> of symptoms, every reality a symptom
> where the ailment's not nailed down:
> much knowledge, precise enough,
> but so multiple it says this man is alive
>
> or isn't: it's like all of a body answering
> all of pharmacopoeia, a too
> adequate relationship:
> so I complained and said maybe I'd brush
>
> deeper and see what was pushing all this
> periphery, so difficult to make any sense
> out of, out:
> with me, decision brings its own
>
> hesitation: a symptom, no doubt, but open
> and meaningless enough without paradigm:
> but hesitation
> can be all right, too: I came on a spruce
>
> thicket full of elk, gushy snow-weed,
> nine species of lichen, four pure white
> rocks and
> several swatches of verbena near bloom.

All the poems in *Uplands* have this new ease, but the conscious mastery of instrument may obscure for us the prevalence of the old concerns, lightened by the poet's revelation that a search for saliences is a more possible quest than the more primordial romancing after unity. The concerns locate themselves still in Emerson's mental universe; Ammons's *Periphery*, like Dickinson's *Circumference*, goes back to the astonishing *Circles* of 1840 with its insistence that "the only sin is limitation" and its repeated image of concentricity. The appropriate gloss for Ammons's *Periphery* (and for much else in *Uplands*) is: "The natural world may be conceived of as a system of concentric circles, and we now and then detect in nature slight dislocations which apprise us that this surface on which we now stand is not fixed, but sliding." Ammons calls so being apprised "hesitation," and his slight dislocation is the radiant burst of elk, snow-weed, lichen, white rocks, and verbena that ends *Periphery* so beautifully.

In *Uplands* and the extraordinary conceptions of the recent volume, *Briefings*, the motions of water have replaced the earlier guiding movements of wind. *If Anything Will Level With You Water Will*, the title of one fine poem, is the credo of many. "I/mean the telling is unmediated," Ammons says of a rocky stream, and his ambition here, enormous as always, is an unmediated telling, a purely visionary poetry. It is not a poetry that discourses of itself or of the outward particulars, or of the processes of the poet's mind so much as it deals in a purer representation than even Wordsworth could have wanted. The bodily eye is not a despotic sense for Ammons (as it became for Thoreau) who has not passed through a crisis in perception, but rather has trained himself to sense those out-leapings later available to the seer (like Emerson) who had wisdom enough to turn back from Unity. For pure representation in the later Ammons, I give *Laser* (from *Uplands*) as a supreme example:

> An image comes
> and the mind's light, confused
> as that on surf
> or ocean shelves,
> gathers up,
> parallelizes, focuses
> and in a rigid beam illuminates the image:
>
> the head seeks in itself
> fragments of left-over light

to cast a new
direction,
any direction,
to strike and fix
a random, contradicting image:

but any found image falls
back to darkness or
the lesser beams splinter and
go out:
the mind tries to
dream of diversity, of mountain
rapids shattered with sound and light,

of wind fracturing brush or
bursting out of order against a mountain
range: but the focused beam
folds all energy in:
the image glares filling all space:
the head falls and
hangs and cannot wake itself.

I risk sounding mystical by insisting that "an image" here is neither the poetic trope nor a natural particular, but what Ammons in-
veterately calls a "salience"; "the image glares filling all space." Not
that in this perception there is no perceiver; rather the perceiving is
detached, disinterested, attentive without anxiety or nostalgia. Perhaps this is only Ammons's equivalent of the difficult "half create"
of *Tintern Abbey* or Emerson's "I am nothing; I see all," but it seems
to ensue from the darker strain in him, that goes back to the twenty-
sixth poem in *Ommateum*, "In the wind my rescue is," which stated
a hopeless poetic quest: "I set it my task/to gather the stones of
earth/into one place." In *Uplands*, a profound poem, *Apologia pro
Vita Sua*, makes a definitive revision of the earlier ambition:

I started picking up the stones
throwing them into one place
and by sunrise I was going far away
for the large ones
always turning to see never lost
the cairn's height
lengthening my radial reach:

the sun watched with deep concentration
and the heap through the hours grew

> and became by nightfall
> distinguishable from all the miles around
> of slate and sand:
>
> during the night the wind falling
> turned earthward its lofty freedom and speed
> and the sharp blistering sound muffled
> toward dawn and the blanket was
> drawn up over a breathless face:
>
> even so you can see in full dawn
> the ground there lifts
> a foreign thing desertless in origin.

"Distinguishable" is the desperate and revelatory word. To ask, after death, the one thing, to have left behind "a foreign thing desertless in origin," the cairn of a lifetime's poems, is to have reduced rescue into a primordial pathos. Yet the poem, by its virtue, renders more than pathos, as the lyric following, on the same theme, renders more also:

> Losing information he
> rose gaining
> view
> till at total
> loss gain was
> extreme:
> extreme & invisible:
> the eye
> seeing nothing
> lost its
> separation:
> self-song
> (that is a mere motion)
> fanned out
> into failing swirls
> slowed &
> became continuum.

Offset is the appropriate title; this is power purchased by the loss of knowledge, and unity at the expense of being material. *Uplands*, as a volume, culminates in its last lyric, *Cascadilla Falls*, placed just before the playful and brilliant long poem, *Summer Session 1968*, in which Ammons finds at last some rest from these intensities. Despite its extraordinary formal control and its continuous sense of a

285

vision attained, *Uplands* is a majestically sad book, for Ammons does not let himself forget that his vision, while uncompromised, is a compromise necessarily, a constant knowing why and how "unity cannot do anything in particular." The poet, going down by Cascadilla Falls in the evening, picks up a stone and "thought all its motions into it," and then drops the stone from galactic wanderings to dead rest:

> the stream from other motions
> broke
> rushing over it:
> shelterless,
> I turned
>
> to the sky and stood still:
>
> I do
> not know where I am going
> that I can live my life
> by this single creek.

From this self-imposed pathos Ammons wins as yet no release. Release comes in the ninety delightful lyrics gathered together in *Briefings* (first entitled, gracefully but misleadingly, *Poems Small and Easy*), this poet's finest book. Though the themes of *Briefings* are familiarly Ammonsian, the mode is not. Laconic though transfigured speech has been transformed into "wasteful song." The first poem, *Center*, places us in a freer world than Ammons would give us before:

> A bird fills up the
> streamside bush
> with wasteful song,
> capsizes waterfall,
> mill run, and
> superhighway
> to
> song's improvident
> center
> lost in the green
> bush green
> answering bush:
> wind varies:
> the noon sun casts
> mesh refractions

on the stream's amber
bottom
and nothing at all gets,
nothing gets
caught at all.

The given is mesh that cannot catch because the particulars have been capsized, and so are unavailable for capture. The center is improvident because it stands at the midmost point of mind, not of nature. *Briefings* marks an end to the oldest conflict in Ammons; the imagination has learned to avoid apocalyptic pitch, but it has learned also its own painful autonomy in regard to the universe it cannot join in unity. With the confidence of this autonomy attained, the mind yet remains wary of what lurks without, as in *Attention:*

Down by the bay I
kept in mind
at once
the tips of all the rushleaves
and so
came to know
balance's cost and true:
somewhere though in the whole field
is the one
tip
I will someday lose out of mind
and fall through.

The one particular of dying remains; every unmastered particular is a little death, giving tension to the most triumphant even among these short poems. *Hymn IV*, returning to the great *Hymn* and two related poems of the same title, seals up the quest forever:

You have enriched us with
fear and contrariety
providing the searcher
confusion for his search

teaching by your snickering
wisdom an autonomy
for man
Bear it all
and keep me from my enemies'
wafered concision and zeal
I give you back to yourself
whole and undivided

I do not hear bitterness in this, or even defiance, but any late Emersonian worship of the Beautiful Necessity is gone. With the going there comes a deep uncertainty in regard to poetic subject, as *Looking Over the Acreage* and several other poems show so poignantly. The ironically moving penultimate poem of *Briefings* still locates the poet's field of contemplation "where the ideas of permanence/and transience fuse in a single body, ice for example,/or a leaf," but does not suggest that the fusion yields any information. The whole of *Briefings* manifests a surrender of the will-to-knowledge, not only relational knowledge between poetic consciousness and natural objects, but of all knowledge that is too easy, that is not also loss. Amid astonishing abundance in this richest of his volumes, I must pick out one lyric as representative of all the others, for in it Ammons gives full measure of a unique gift:

He held radical light
as music in his skull: music
turned, as
over ridges immanences of evening light
rise, turned
back over the furrows of his brain
into the dark, shuddered,
shot out again
in long swaying swirls of sound:

reality had little weight in his transcendence
so he
had trouble keeping
his feet on the ground, was
terrified by that
and liked himself, and others, mostly
under roofs:
nevertheless, when the
light churned and changed

his head to music, nothing could keep him
off the mountains, his
head back, mouth working,
wrestling to say, to cut loose
from the high, unimaginable hook:
released, hidden from stars, he ate,
burped, said he was like any one
of us: demanded he
was like any one of us.

It is the seer's horror of radical light, his obduracy to transcendence, that moves the seer himself, moves him so that he cannot know what he should know, which is that he cannot be like ourselves. The poem's power is that we are moved also, not by the horror, which cannot be our own, but by the transcendence, the sublime sense we long to share. Transcendent experience, but with Emerson's kind of Higher Utilitarianism ascetically cut off by a mind made too scrupulous for a new hope, remains the *materia poetica* of Ammons's enterprise. A majestic recent poem like *The City Limits* suggests how much celebration is still possible even when the transcendent moment is cruelly isolated, too harshly purified, totally compelled to be its own value. Somewhere upon the higher ridges of his Purgatory, Ammons remains stalled, unable for now to break through to the Condition of Fire promised by *Ommateum*, where instead of invoking Emerson's Uriel or Poe's Israfel he found near identity with "a crippled angel bent in a scythe of grief" yet witnessed a fiery ascent of the angel, fought against it, and only later gained the knowledge that "The eternal will not lie/down on any temporal hill."

1970

19
Bacchus and Merlin: The Dialectic of Romantic Poetry in America

That far-reaching idea of time, which seems to expand our thoughts
with limitless existence, gives to our mental struggles a greatness they
could not have before had. We each of us feel within our own bosoms a
great, an immortal foe, which if we have subdued, we may meet with
calmness every other, knowing that earth contains no greater; but
which if we have not, it will continually appear in those petty
contests with others by which we do but show our own cowardice.
Jones Very (1838)

In what follows I propose to examine four "first volumes" of
American poetry as part of a personal critical quest after the
governing dialectic I sense in our poetry's central tradition, our
version of Romanticism. Though I will glance as I progress at
poems by Bryant and Poe, Whitman and Dickinson, Frost
and Stevens, my intent here is to use as texts-for-study only the
following books: Emerson's *Poems* (1846); E. A. Robinson's
The Torrent and the Night Before (1896); Hart Crane's *White
Buildings* (1926); Alvin Feinman's *Preambles* (1964). These
choices, though arbitrary, are not idiosyncratic, as my discussion
should evidence. This essay is meant as prolegomenon to a
projected large study of American Romantic poetry, to be
conducted on the principles of a revisionist theory of poetic
influence, and its consequences for practical criticism. Poetic
misprision, rather than influence, might be a better name (however
ironical) for the process I am studying, which appears to be a
normal mode of continuity in most post-Enlightenment poetry, but
is particularly evident in American poetry of the nineteenth and
twentieth centuries.

Emerson. Much more enlightened, more roving, more manifold,
subtler than Carlyle; above all, happier. One who instinctively
nourishes himself only on ambrosia, leaving behind what is
indigestible in things . . . he simply does not know how old he
is already and how young he is still going to be . . .
Nietzsche

On Christmas Day, 1846, Emerson's *Poems* appeared. The poet was forty-three, and had published much of his most characteristic prose; *Nature* in 1836, and the two series of *Essays* in 1841 and 1844. Like so many American poets, Emerson was a late starter; few of his important poems precede his thirtieth year, and most were written after he turned forty. The few early exceptions would include *The River* (1827) and some extraordinary chants of self-recognition in the 1831 *Journals*, which resemble certain sermons of Meister Eckhart in their dangerously intense realization that the soul's substance is uncreated, and their conclusion that the soul alone is the Law. By 1832, the *Journals* show a dialectical recoil: "It is awful to look into the mind of man and see how free we are. . . . inside, the terrible freedom!" Throughout Emerson's great period (1832–41, with a sudden but brief resurgence in 1846) there is a dialectic or interplay between the assertion of imagination's autonomy, and a shrewd skepticism of any phenomenon reaching too far into the unconditioned. This rhythm appears again in the Emersonian Whitman in his great years (1855–60), in Dickinson throughout her life, and in every Emersonian poet we have enjoyed since (Cummings, Hart Crane, Roethke) except for poets who stem from the later, resigned Emerson (*The Conduct of Life*, particularly the essay *Fate*), including Robinson and Frost. The relation of Stevens to Emerson, early and late, is too complex for summary, being hidden, perhaps partly an unconscious one, and will receive some consideration further on in this essay.

The notable poems in Emerson's first volume are *The Sphinx* (probably 1840), *Uriel* (1845), *Hamatreya* (1845–46), *The Humblebee* (1837), *Woodnotes* (1840–41), *Monadnoc* (1845), *Ode: Inscribed To William H. Channing* (1846), *The Forerunners* (date unknown), *Merlin* (1846), *Bacchus* (1846), *Saadi* (1842), and *Threnody* (1842–43). From late in 1845 and almost all through 1846, Emerson seems to have revived in himself something of his earlier Transcendental fury. Stephen Whicher dated 1841 as the end of Emerson's "Period of challenge" and the start of his long "Period of acquiescence," a useful enough categorizing if we grant the year 1846 as an exception. The year's prelude is in *Uriel*, a late response to the furor following the Divinity School Address, and Frost's candidate for the best American poem. The poem turns on Uriel's "sentiment divine":

> "Line in nature is not found;
> Unit and universe are round;
> In vain produced, all rays return;
> Evil will bless, and ice will burn."

The poem is deliberately and successfully comic in a unique mode, indeed, the positive magic of poetic influence (as exalted by Borges) appears to be at work, and at moments Frost is' writing the poem, even as Yeats writes certain passages in *The Witch of Atlas* or Stevens in *The Recluse*, or Dickinson in Emerson's *The Humble-Bee*. But *Uriel* (again like some Frost) is very dark in its comedy, and records the inner cost of angelic defiance:

> A sad self-knowledge, withering, fell
> On the beauty of Uriel;
> In heaven once eminent, the god
> Withdrew, that hour, into his cloud;
> Whether doomed to long gyration
> In the sea of generation,
> Or by knowledge grown too bright
> To hit the nerve of feebler sight.

Line in human nature is not to be found either, least of all in Emerson's spiral of a spirit. The Eternal Return is perpetual in the single soul, and Emerson anticipates the doctrines of Yeats as well as Nietzsche. Self-knowledge withers because it teaches the terrible truths of the grand essay, *Circles*; Uriel too is only a proud ephemeral whose revelation must be superseded. Emerson's wisdom, by limiting the self's discourse, gives the poem firm outline; Uriel sings out when possessed but then gyres into a cloudy silence.

Monadnoc, a powerful ramble of a poem, now absurdly undervalued, shows the same discretion, allowing much everyday lumber to ballast the ascents to vision. Its direct modern descendant, Stevens's *Chocorua To Its Neighbor*, suffers from refusing similar ballast; it is a purer but not a better poem. Monadnoc expects to disappear in the mightier chant of the Major Man it awaits, a god no longer in ruins. Chocorua celebrates only the shadow of the Major Man, but already begins to disappear in that celebration:

> Upon my top he breathed the pointed dark.
> He was not man yet he was nothing else.
> If in the mind, he vanished, taking there
> The mind's own limits, like a tragic thing
> Without existence, existing everywhere.

This is painfully said, but since the mind is the mountain's, Chocorua himself is being skeptically raised to sublimity, where limits vanish. Monadnoc is a sturdier Titan, and sees a form, not a shadow of centrality. In Emerson's poem, we find the shadow, in the mountain:

Thou seest, O watchman tall,
Our towns and races grow and fall,
And imagest the stable good
For which we all our lifetime grope,
In shifting form the formless mind,
And though the substance us elude,
We in thee the shadow find.

Probably Emerson was not aware he echoed the *Intimations* Ode here, as in so many other places:

... thou Eye among the blind,
That, deaf and silent, read'st the eternal deep,
Haunted for ever by the eternal mind,—
Mighty Prophet! Seer blest!
On whom those truths do rest,
Which we are toiling all our lives to find,
In darkness lost, the darkness of the grave;

Wordsworth addresses the Child, Emerson Monadnoc, but the Other is the same; Monadnoc is a "Mute orator," sending "conviction without phrase," to "succor and remede/The shortness of our days," promising "long morrow" to those of "mortal youth." The Child, though silent, prophesies the same good news. The movement from *Intimations* to *Monadnoc* to *Chocorua* is not one of successive *clinamens*, of swerves away from a downward course, but of what students pursuing Poetic Influence might term the *tessera* or link, a different and subtler kind of revisionary ratio. In the *tessera*, the later poet provides what his imagination tells him would complete the otherwise "truncated" precursor poem and poet, a "completion" that is as much misprision as a revisionary swerve is. I take the term *tessera* from the psychoanalyst Jacques Lacan, whose own revisionary relationship to Freud might be given as an instance of *tessera*. In his *Discours de Rome* (1953), Lacan cites a remark of Mallarmé's, which "compares the common use of Language to the exchange of a coin whose obverse and reverse no longer bear any but worn effigies, and which people pass from hand to hand 'in silence.' " Applying this to the discourse, however reduced, of the analytic subject, Lacan says: "This metaphor is sufficient to remind us that the Word, even when almost completely worn out, retains its value as a *tessera*." Lacan's translator, Anthony Wilden, comments that this "allusion is to the function of the *tessera* as a token of recognition, or 'password.' The *tessera* was employed in the early mystery religions where fitting together again the two halves of a broken piece of pottery was used as a means of recognition by the initiates." In this sense of a completing link, the *tessera* represents any later poet's attempt to persuade himself (and us) that the precursor's Word would be worn out if not redeemed as a newly fulfilled and enlarged Word of the ephebe.

By concluding *Monadnoc* with a *tessera* related to Wordsworth's Great Ode, Emerson overcomes not only the dominant (if hidden) major influence upon his mature poetry, but frees his greater poems of the following year from the excessive authority of the single poem that haunts all of the Transcendentalists. Here is part of a memorable disaster of influence, Christopher Pearse Cranch's *The Ocean*, where the *Intimations* Ode and *Asia's Song* from *Prometheus Unbound* oddly combine:

> Now we've wandered from the shore,
> Dwellers by the sea no more;
> Yet at times there comes a tone
> Telling of the visions flown,
> Sounding from the distant sea
> Where we left our purity:
> Distant glimpses of the surge
> Lure us down to ocean's verge;
> There we stand with vague distress,
> Yearning for the measureless,
> By half-wakened instincts driven,
> Half loving earth, half loving heaven,
> Fearing to put off and swim,
> Yet impelled to turn to Him,
> In whose life we live and move,
> And whose very name is Love.

Thoreau, a stronger poet, handles the Great Ode (in pieces like *Music* and *Manhood*) by swerving from it, a *clinamen* already remarked by his editor Carl Bode when he speaks of the "striking bias" the Wordsworthian theme takes on in such poems. But Emerson was as close as Cranch to the *Ode;* it was not to him a point of departure, but a finality, and he handles it accordingly. Thoreau, throughout his use of the *Ode* in his *Journal*, emphasizes a music within, remembering that: "There was a time when the beauty and the music were all within . . . When you were an organ of which the world was but one poor broken pipe." Wordsworth turns to a music in the later time, but emphasizes the lost glory as a light, something seen. What for Wordsworth is a movement from the despotic eye to

295

the liberating ear becomes in Thoreau a double loss, involving both senses. Emerson, from 1831 on a more consistent Wordsworthian than the more drastic (and even more American) Thoreau, wavers more cunningly from the *Ode*. Monadnoc takes the Child's place, for the stone Titan is free of the tragic rhythm by which the Child is father of the Man. In this *tessera*, Wordsworthian Nature is perhaps over-humanized, and Monadnoc becomes a Transcendentalist rather too benign, less a flaw in the poem than it might be, since the whole work demands so generous a suspension of our skepticism.

Skepticism, the powerful undersong in Emerson's dialectic, returns in *Hamatreya*, as awesome a rebuff to a naturalistic humanism as Yeats's great sonnet *Meru* in the *Supernatural Songs*, and proceeding from much the same sources as *Meru*. *Hamatreya* is the necessary prelude to what is most difficult yet inviting in Emerson's two supreme poems, *Merlin* and *Bacchus*. Because of the dominance of certain pseudo-critical shibboleths for several decades, there is a certain fashion still to deprecate all of Emerson's poetry, with the single exception of *Days*. Mathiessen pioneered in grudgingly accepting *Days* as the one Emerson poem that seemed readable by Eliotic standards. I suspect the poem passed because Emerson condemns himself in it, though only for not being Emersonian enough. *Days*, in Emerson's canon, is a miniature of his later retreat into the acceptance of Necessity. Necessity speaks as the Earth-Song in *Hamatreya*, is defied by the Dionysiac spirit of the poet in *Bacchus*, but then subsumes that spirit in *Merlin*. The three poems together evidence Emerson's major venture into his own cosmos in the *Poems* of 1846, and are the furthest reach of his imagination beyond his Wordsworthian heritage, since the *May-Day* volume and later work largely return to the Wordsworthianism of *Monadnoc* and *Woodnotes*.

The passage copied from the *Vishnu Purana* into his 1845 *Journal* by Emerson has one crucial sentence: "Earth laughs, as if smiling with autumnal flowers to behold her kings unable to effect the subjugation of themselves." In Emerson's poem, this laughter is darkened, for this is a Mortality Ode:

> Earth laughs in flowers, to see her boastful boys
> Earth-proud, proud of the earth which is not theirs;
> Who steer the plough, but cannot steer their feet
> Clear of the grave.

The Earth-Song ends in the spirit of Stevens's *Madame La Fleurie*, provoking an extraordinary quatrain that presents Emerson's savage *tessera* to the conclusion of Wordsworth's *Ode*:

> When I heard the Earth-song
> I was no longer brave;
> My avarice cooled
> Like lust in the chill of the grave.

The forsaken courage here is Wordsworth's Stoic comfort at the *Ode*'s close. "Thoughts that do often lie too deep for tears," prompted by a flower that *blows*, that still lives, become only "avarice," unsuited to our deep poverty, when we hear the earth's true song in its laughing flowers. Since Emerson is to American Romanticism what Wordsworth is to the British or parent version, a defining and separating element in later American poetry begins to show itself here. Emerson had more cause, always, to fear an imminent mortality than Wordsworth did (though in fact both poets lived to be quite old), but he shared with Wordsworth a healthy realism toward natural dangers. I cannot think of another major American writer who is so little credulous in regard to preternatural phenomena as Emerson, who had no patience for superstition, even when manifested as folklore. As an admirer of Sir Thomas Browne, Emerson might have been expected to be at least a touch Yeatsian in this region, but every journal reference to the occult is strongly disparaging. Wordsworth too is reluctant, even when he approaches the form of romance. The largest aspect of the supernatural, the life-after-death, so pervasive in romance traditions as well as folk superstitions, makes no thematic appeal to Emerson or Wordsworth, neither of whom could imagine a life apart from the natural. Wordsworth's "immortality," as many critics have noted, is less Platonic or Christian than it is primordial, personal, almost literal, resembling most closely the child's undivided consciousness, not yet sundered to the self-realization of mortality. But Emerson, though he longed for this, and loved the *Ode* as much as any poem, could not as a poet accept this "immortality" either. Robert C. Pollock, in his fine study of Emerson's "Single Vision," shows how much that vision emphasizes man's "continual self-recovery." Wordsworth's vision declined to offer so much, for his temperament was harsher and his experience less exuberant. But Pollock is writing of the earlier Emerson, whose last major expression is in *Bacchus*, not the Emerson who is partly inaugurated by *Merlin*, the essay *Experience*, and the essay on Montaigne in *Representative Men*. *Hamatreya* is another prelude to this Emerson, who speaks his whole mind in the great essay *Fate*:

But Fate against Fate is only parrying and defence: there are also the noble creative forces. The revelation of Thought takes man out of servitude into freedom. We rightly say of ourselves, we were born and afterward we were born again, and many times. We have successive experiences so important that the new forgets the old, and hence the mythology of the seven or the nine heavens. The day of days, the great day of the feast of life, is that in which the inward eye opens to the Unity in things, to the omnipresence of law:—see that what is must be and ought to be, or is the best. This beatitude dips from on high down on us and we see. It is not in us so much as we are in it. If the air come to our lungs, we breathe and live; if not, we die. If the light come to our eyes, we see; else not. And if truth come to our mind we suddenly expand to its dimensions, as if we grew to worlds. We are as lawgivers; we speak for Nature; we prophesy and divine.

This insight throws us on the party and interest of the Universe, against all and sundry; against ourselves as much as others. A man speaking from insight affirms of himself what is true of the mind: seeing its immortality, he says, I am immortal; seeing its invincibility, he says, I am strong. It is not in us, but we are in it. It is of the maker, not of what is made. All things are touched and changed by it. This uses and is not used. It distances those who share it from those who share it not.

Wordsworth, with his extraordinary precision in measuring the spirit's weather, said of his "spots of time" that they gave knowledge of to what extent and how the mind held mastery over outward sense. In the passage above the spirit's weather is perpetual cyclone, and the mind's mastery is beyond extent or means. This is more than very American; for glory and loss, it is as central a passage as American literature gives, more so even than the splendid and much-maligned "transparent eyeball" passage in *Nature*, which is to the earlier Emerson what being thrown "on the party and interest of the Universe . . . against ourselves" is to the later. Though the Stevens of *Ideas of Order* mocks the first Emerson (see *Sailing After Lunch*: "To expunge all people and be a pupil/Of the gorgeous wheel and so to give/That slight transcendence to the dirty sail,/By light . . .") the greater Stevens of *The Auroras of Autumn* reaches the resolution of *Fate*, precisely attaining the late Emersonian balance (or rather oscillation) between Fate and Necessity. The anxiety of influence abided in Stevens, who continued to satirize his American ancestor (as in the Mr. Homburg of *Looking Across the Fields and Watching the Birds Fly*, whose enterprise is "To think away the grass, the trees, the clouds,/Not to transform them into other things"). Burrowing away somewhere in Stevens's imagination were memories of reading *The Conduct of Life* (where the essay *Illusions* contains *The Rock* in embryo) and *Letters and Social Aims* (where the long, meandering *Poetry and Imagination* holds more of Stevens's poetics than Valéry or Santayana do). I instance Stevens in relation to *Fate*, but the essay touches, directly or dialectically, a company of American poets that includes also Whitman, Dickinson, Melville, Tuckerman, Robinson, Frost, Jeffers, Aiken, Crane, Roethke, and Ammons, none of whom would have completed the self's circle without it, or at least without modifying into a somewhat different self. That this influence was neither as benevolent as a confirmed Emersonian would have it (see H. H. Waggoner's *American Poets*) nor as destructive as Yvor Winters insisted (*In Defense of Reason*), need not surprise anyone who has reflected upon the long course of Wordsworth's influence upon British poets (or Milton's, before that).

The central passage of *Fate* exhilarates and dismays, as it should; Emerson's "Fate" is Indian enough to be at last unassimilable by him or by us. A *Journal* entry contrasts the Greek "Fate" as "private theatricals" in contrast to India, where "it is the dread reality, it is the cropping-out in our planted gardens of the core of the world: it is the abysmal Force, untameable and immense." This Force inspires a shaman rather than a humanizing poet, an augurer not a prophet, the poet of *Merlin* but not of the misnamed and sublime *Bacchus*. Force is irrational, but the inspiration of Bacchus, though more than rational, is the "later reason" of Stevens's *Notes*, or more historically the Idealist Reason that Coleridge and Wordsworth took (though only in part) from assorted Germans. With the contrast between *Bacchus* and *Merlin*, we can attempt to clarify two allied strains in Emerson (they cannot be regarded only as early and late, *Nature* and *Self-Reliance* against *The Conduct of Life*, because traces of each can be found from youth through age). Clarification must begin with the 1846 *Journal*, where something of the complexity of Emerson's last great year can be recovered.

In his disgust with the politics of Polk and Webster, in the year of our aggression against Mexico, Emerson consciously turned to the Muse, but with a skeptical reserve: "The life which we seek is expansion; the actual life even of the genius or the saint is obstructive." But, in some mysterious passages, as in the one on the Central Man

299

that I examined in an earlier essay, the reserve vanishes. Here is another, premonitory of Nietzsche's Overman, of Whitman's Self, and (much diminished) of Stevens's Major Man (particularly in the second and third paragraphs, with which compare *Notes Toward a Supreme Fiction*, Part I, Sections IX–X):

> He lurks, *he* hides,—he who is success, reality, joy, power, that which constitutes Heaven, which reconciles impossibilities, atones for shortcomings, expiates sins, or makes them virtues, buries in oblivion the crowded historical Past, sinks religions, philosophies, nations, persons to legends; reverses the scale of opinion, of fame; reduces sciences to opinion, and makes the thought of the moment the key to the universe and the egg of history to come. . . .
>
> This is he that shall come, or if he come not, nothing comes; he that disappears on the instant that we go to celebrate him. If we go to burn those that blame our celebration, he appears in them.
>
> Hoe and spade; sword and pen; cities, pictures, gardens, laws, bibles, are prized only because they were means he sometimes used: so with astronomy, arithmetic, caste, feudalism. We kiss with devotion these hems of his garment. They crumble to ashes on our lips.

This is not Christ, but rather an Orphic god-poet, such a divinity as Emerson assumed Hafiz to have celebrated. This is also not the Force or Necessity apotheosized by shamans and bards. Is Emerson constant in distinguishing the three: Christ, Central Man, *Ananke?* As a poet, yes; in prose, not always, for there (despite the fallacious assumptions of Winters) he refuses to "label and ticket, one thing, or two," as he rightly charges the mystic with doing. The 1846 *Journal* frequently approximates Blake, not least when it attacks the mystic, like Swedenborg, as being a Devil turned Angel: "The mystic, who beholds the flux, yet becomes pragmatist on some one particular of faith, and, what is the mischief, seeks to accredit this new jail because it was builded by him who has demolished so many jails." Fearing even an antinomian or visionary dogmatism, the mature Emerson refuses distinctions where we, as his ephebes, badly want and need them. Uriel, like Nature, hates lines, knowing that all new generation comes when matter rolls itself into balls. In the midst of the 1846 *Journal*, there is a great antithetical prayer: "O Bacchus, make them drunk, drive them mad, this multitude of vagabonds, hungry for eloquence, hungry for poetry." The great poem *Bacchus*, to me Emerson's finest, comes in answer to this prayer. As I have commented on it in an earlier essay, I wish here only to look again at its marvelous close:

> Let wine repair what this undid;
> And where the infection slid,
> A dazzling memory revive;
> Refresh the faded tints,
> Recut the aged prints,
> And write my old adventures with the pen
> Which on the first day drew,
> Upon the tablets blue,
> The dancing Pleiads and eternal men.

Stevens's *Large Red Man Reading* aloud "the great blue tabulae" gives to earth-returning ghosts "the outlines of being and its expressings, the syllables of its law," a characteristic reduction of the greater Emersonian dream. Emerson's poem goes as far as apocalyptic poetry can go, but the impulse for refreshing and recutting was stronger even than *Bacchus*, and gave Emerson *Merlin*, scarcely a lesser poem, but a dangerous and divided work. *Bacchus* asks for more than Wordsworth did, for a renovation as absolute as Blake's vision sought. The poetic faculty is to free man from his own ruins, and restore him as the being Blake called Tharmas, instinctual innocence triumphantly at home in his own place. Stevens, at his most hopeful, asserted that the poem refreshes life so that we share, but only for a moment, the First Idea, which belonged to Tharmas. Like Wordsworth, Stevens yields to a version of the Reality Principle. Blake and Emerson do not, but Emerson departs from Blakean affinities when, in his extraordinary impatience, most fatedly American of qualities, he seeks terms with his Reality Principle only by subsuming it, as he does in *Merlin*. Not *Bacchus*, but *Merlin*, seems to me the archetypal American poem that our best poets keep writing, once they have passed through their crises of individuation, have found their true limit, and then fail to accept any limit as their own. The American Muse is a *daimon* of disorder, whose whispered counsel in the dark is: "Evade and multiply." Young and old at once, bewilderingly from their start, the great among our poets seek to become each a process rather than a person, Nemesis rather than accident, as though it could be open to any imagination to be enthroned where only a handful have ever come.

If a single American has incarnated our *daimon*, it is Emerson, not our greatest writer but merely our only inescapable one, to be found

301

always where Whitman asked to be sought, under our boot-soles, effused and drifted all through our lives and our literature, just as he is to be found on every page, almost in every line, of Whitman. Denied or scorned, he turns up again in every opponent, however orthodox, classical, conservative or even just Southern. Why he stands so much at the center may always be a mystery, but who else can stand in his place? Nineteenth-century American culture is the Age of Emerson, and what we undergo now seems more than ever his. A good part of what has been urged against him, even by very negative critics like James Truslow Adams and Winters, is true, but this appears to mean mostly that Emerson did subsume something inevitable in the national process, that he joined himself forever to the American version of what Stevens called "fatal Ananke . . . the final god."

Merlin, a text in which to read both the American Sublime and the American poetic disaster, was finished in the summer of 1846, but had its origins in the *Journal* of 1845, in a strong doggerel:

> I go discontented thro' the world
> Because I cannot strike
> The harp to please my tyrannous ear:
> Gentle touches are not wanted,
> These the yielding gods had granted.
> It shall not tinkle a guitar,
> But strokes of fate
> Chiming with the ample winds,
> With the pulse of human blood,
> With the voice of mighty men,
> With the din of city arts,
> With the cannonade of war,
> With the footsteps of the brave
> And the sayings of the wise,
> Chiming with the forest's tone
> When they buffet boughs in the windy wood,
> Chiming with the gasp and moan
> Of the ice-imprisoned flood.
> I will not read a pretty tale
> To pretty people in a nice saloon
> Borrowed from their expectation,
> But I will sing aloud and free
> From the heart of the world.

It is almost the universal motto of the American poet, from Whitman down to the recent transformation of W. S. Merwin into the nearly impersonal bard of *The Lice* and *The Carrier of Ladders*.

From the "gentle touches" of *Green With Beasts* ("the gaiety of three winds is a game of green/Shining, of grey-and-gold play in the holly-bush") Merwin has gone to Emersonian "strokes of fate" ("We are the echo of the future/On the door it says what to do to survive /But we were not born to survive/Only to live") and Merwin is probably the representative poet of my own generation. Learned accomplishment will not suffice where the Muse herself masks as Necessity; if Emerson was aware that this was a masking, he failed to show it, an imaginative failure, fine as the finished *Merlin* is:

> Thy trivial harp will never please
> Or fill my craving ear;
> Its chords should ring as blows the breeze,
> Free, peremptory, clear ...
> . . . .
> The kingly bard
> Must smite the chords rudely and hard,
> As with hammer or with mace;
> That they may render back
> Artful thunder, which conveys
> Secrets of the solar track,
> Sparks of the supersolar blaze.
> Merlin's blows are strokes of fate ...

"Artful thunder" is cousin to "fearful symmetry," reversing the parodistic awe of an argument from apparent design but still mockingly urging us to yield to an other-than-human splendor and terror. Power is *Merlin's* subject, "strokes of fate" as the essay *Fate* defines them: "why should we fear to be crushed by savage elements, we who are made up of the same elements?" We are ourselves strokes of fate, on this view, and most ourselves in Merlin the Bard, whose "mighty line/Extremes of nature reconciled." The dangers, social and solipsistic, of so amazingly unconditioned a bardic vision crowd upon us in the poem's second part, with great eloquence:

> Perfect-paired as eagle's wings,
> Justice is the rhyme of things;
> Trade and counting use
> The self-same tuneful muse;
> And Nemesis,
> Who with even matches odd,
> Who athwart space redresses
> The partial wrong,
> Fills the just period,
> And finishes the song.

No reader of Emerson ought to brood on these lines without juxtaposing them to the magnificent and famous *Journal* entry of April 1842, in which Emerson gave his fullest dialectic of Nemesis, which *Merlin* seems to slight:

> In short, there ought to be no such thing as Fate. As long as we use this word, it is a sign of our impotence and that we are not yet ourselves. There is now a sublime revelation in each of us which makes us so strangely aware and certain of our riches that although I have never since I was born for so much as one moment expressed the truth, and although I have never heard the expression of it from any other, I know that the whole is here,—the wealth of the Universe is for me, everything is explicable and practicable for me. And yet whilst I adore this ineffable life which is at my heart, it will not condescend to gossip with me, it will not announce to me any particulars of science, it will not enter into the details of my biography, and say to me why I have a son and daughters born to me, or why my son dies in his sixth year of joy. Herein, then, I have this latent omniscience coexistent with omni-ignorance. Moreover, whilst this Deity glows at the heart, and by his unlimited presentiments gives me all Power, I know that tomorrow will be as this day, I am a dwarf, and I remain a dwarf. That is to say, I believe in Fate. As long as I am weak, I shall talk of Fate; whenever the God fills me with his fulness, I shall see the disappearance of Fate.
>
> I am *Defeated* all the time; yet to Victory I am born.

But Merlin, who can no more be defeated than Nemesis can be thwarted, becomes one with the spirit that "finishes the song." There is nothing like this unity with the serpent Ananke before Emerson in American poetry (or in English) but all too much after. Before Emerson, we can take Bryant and Poe as representative of the possibilities for Romantic poetry in America, and see in both of them a capable reservation that Emerson abolished in himself. Bryant's *The Poet* is very late (1863) but presents a stance firmly established by more than fifty years of composing good poetry. "Make thyself a part/Of the great tumult," Bryant tells the poet, but the same poem severely contrasts the organized violence within the mind and the unorganized violence of nature:

> A blast that whirls the dust
>   Along the howling street and dies away;
> But feelings of calm power and mighty sweep,
> Like currents journeying through the windless deep.

Poe, despite his celebrated and angelic ambitions for the poet, follows Shelley and Byron in emphasizing the pragmatic sorrows of Prometheanism, even as Bryant follows Cowper and Wordsworth in a Stoic awareness of the mind's separation from its desired natural context. *Israfel* remains a poem of real excellence because in it the mind is overwhelmed by auguries of division, betwen the angelic bard and his wistfully defiant imitator below, who is reduced to doubting his divine precursor's powers where they are to be brought down into nature: "He might not sing so wildly well/A mortal melody." Bryant and Poe are both of them closer to English Romantic consciousness than the Emerson of *Merlin* and *Fate*, who thus again prophesied what Wright Morris calls "the territory ahead," the drastic American Romanticism of heroic imaginative failure, or perhaps a kind of success we have not yet learned to apprehend. For the doctrine of *Merlin* is dangerous in that it tempts our poets to a shamanism they neither altogether want nor properly can sustain.

The best Emersonian poets are, by rationally universal agreement, Whitman and Dickinson, who found their own versions of a dialectic between Bacchus and Merlin. I pass though to smaller but still powerful figures, to trace the vagaries of Nemesis in three later "first volumes" of our poetry. For the oscillation between poetic incarnation (Bacchus) and the merging with Necessity (Merlin) is most evident and crucial in each new poet's emergence and individuation. Emerson our father, more than Whitman the American Moses, has become the presiding genius of the American version of poetic influence, the anxiety of originality that he hoped to dispel, but ironically fostered in a more virulent form than it has taken elsewhere.

Emerson himself was a product of New England and a man of strong
moral habits. . . . He gave to American romanticism, in spite of its
irresponsible doctrine, a religious tone which it has not yet lost and
which has often proved disastrous. . . . there is a good deal of this
intellectual laziness in Robinson; and as a result of the laziness, there
is a certain admixture of Emersonian doctrine, which runs counter
to the principles governing most of his work and the best of it.
Yvor Winters

The Torrent and the Night Before (published late in 1896 by Robinson himself) remains one of the best first volumes in our poetry. Three of its shorter poems—*George Crabbe, Luke Havergal, The*

305

Clerks—Robinson hardly surpassed, and three more—*Credo, Walt Whitman* (which Robinson unfortunately abandoned), and *The Children of the Night* (reprinted as title-poem in his next volume)—are memorable work, all in the earlier Emersonian mode that culminates in *Bacchus.* The stronger *Luke Havergal* stems from the darker Emersonianism of *Experience* and *Fate*, and has a relation to the singular principles of *Merlin.* It prophesies Robinson's finest later lyrics, such as *Eros Turannos* and *For A Dead Lady*, and suggests the affinity between Robinson and Frost that is due to their common Emersonian tradition.

In *Captain Craig* (1902) Robinson published *The Sage*, a direct hymn of homage to Emerson, whose *The Conduct of Life* had moved him profoundly at a first reading in August 1899. Robinson had read the earlier Emerson well before, but it is fascinating that he came to essays like *Fate* and *Power* only after writing *Luke Havergal* and some similar poems, for his deeper nature then discovered itself anew. He called *Luke Havergal* "a piece of deliberate degeneration," which I take to mean what an early letter calls "sympathy for failure where fate has been abused and self demoralized." Browning, the other great influence upon Robinson, is obsessed with "deliberate degeneration" in this sense; Childe Roland's and Andrea del Sarto's failures are wilful abuses of fate and demoralizations of self. *The Sage* praises Emerson's "fierce wisdom," emphasizes Asia's influence upon him, and hardly touches his dialectical optimism. This Emerson is "previsioned of the madness and the mean," fit seer for "the fiery night" of *Luke Havergal:*

> But there, where western glooms are gathering,
> The dark will end the dark, if anything:
> God slays Himself with every leaf that flies,
> And hell is more than half of paradise.

These are the laws of Compensation, "or that nothing is got for nothing," as Emerson says in *Power.* At the depth of Robinson is this Emersonian fatalism, as it is in Frost, and even in Henry James. "The world is mathematical," Emerson says, "and has no casualty in all its vast and flowing curve." Robinson, brooding on the end of *Power*, confessed: "He really gets after one," and spoke of Emerson as walloping one "with a big New England shingle," the cudgel of Fate. But Robinson was walloped too well, by which I do not mean what Winters means, since I cannot locate any "intellectual laziness" in Emerson. Unlike Browning and Hardy, Robinson yielded too much to Necessity, and too rapidly assimilated himself to the tendency I have named Merlin. Circumstances and temperament share in Robinson's obsession with Nemesis, but poetic misprision is part of the story also, for Robinson's *tessera* in regard to Emerson relies on completing the sage's fatalism. From Emerson's categories of power and circumstance, Robinson fashions a more complete single category, in a personal idealism that is a "philosophy of desperation," as he feared it might be called. The persuasive desperation of *Luke Havergal* and *Eros Turannos* is his best expression of this nameless idealism that is also a fatalism, but *The Children of the Night*, for all its obtrusive echoes of Tennyson and even Longfellow, shows more clearly what Robinson found to be a possible stance:

> It is the crimson, not the gray,
>   That charms the twilight of all time;
> It is the promise of the day
>   That makes the starry sky sublime;
>
> It is the faith within the fear
>   That holds us to the life we curse;—
> So let us in ourselves revere
>   The Self which is the Universe!

The bitter charm of this is that it qualifies so severely its too-hopeful and borrowed music. Even so early, Robinson has "completed" Emersonian Self-Reliance and made it his own by emphasizing its Stoic as against its Transcendental or Bacchic aspect. When, in *Credo*, Robinson feels "the coming glory of the Light!", the light nevertheless emanates from unaware angels who wove "dead leaves to garlands where no roses are." It is not that Robinson believed, with Melville, that the invisible spheres were formed in fright, but he shrewdly suspected that the ultimate world, though existent, was nearly as destitute as this one. He is an Emersonian incapable of transport, an ascetic of the Transcendental spirit, contrary to an inspired saint like Jones Very or to the Emerson of *The Poet*, but a contrary, not a negation, to use Blake's distinction. Not less gifted than Frost, he achieves so much less because he gave himself away to Necessity so soon in his poetic life. Frost's Job quotes *Uriel* to suggest that confusion is "the form of forms," the way all things return upon themselves, like rays:

> Though I hold rays deteriorate to nothing,
> First white, then red, then ultra red, then out.

This is cunning and deep in Frost, the conviction that "all things come round," even the mental confusions of God as He morally blunders. What we miss in Robinson is this quality of savagery, the strength that can end *Directive* by saying:

> Here are your waters and your watering place.
> Drink and be whole again beyond confusion.

To be beyond confusion is to be beyond the form of forms that is Fate's, and to be whole beyond Fate suggests an end to circlings, a resolution to all the Emersonian turnings that see unity, and yet behold divisions. Frost will play at being Merlin, many times, but his wariness saved him from Robinson's self-exhaustions.

There is a fine passage in *Captain Craig* where the talkative captain asks: "Is it better to be blinded by the lights,/Or by the shadows?" This supposes grandly that we are to be blinded in any case, but Robinson was not blinded by his shadows. Yet he was ill-served by American Romanticism, though not for the reasons Winters offers. It demands the exuberance of a Whitman in his fury of poetic incarnation, lest the temptation to join Ananke come too soon and too urgently to be resisted. Robinson was nearly a great poet, and would have prospered more if he had been chosen by a less drastic tradition.

> What was the soil whence your anger sprang, who are deaf
> as the stones to the whispering flight of the Mississippi's rivers?
> What did you see as you fell? What did you hear as
> you sank? Did it make you drunken with hearing?
> John Wheelwright, *Fish Food:*
> *An Obituary to Hart Crane*

Hart Crane's *White Buildings* (1926) is *Harmonium's* only rival among first books of American poetry in our century. Almost every poem in it is valuable, but I will confine myself here only to *Emblems of Conduct, Voyages,* and two neglected and closely related lyrics, *Passage* and *Repose of Rivers. Emblems of Conduct* is centrally in the tradition of the Emerson of *Bacchus* (as is Samuel Greenberg, from whom most of the poem is quarried). *Passage* and *Repose of Rivers,* poems of autobiographical anguish, show an unwilling hesitation at confronting the tradition that chose Crane, while *Voyages* suggests the surrender to Nemesis that completes a now familiar dialectic. For Crane comes late in a powerful continuity of poets, and

critical scholarship only recently has begun to show us how conscious
his poetry necessarily is of its precursors.

Whitman and Dickinson are among these, as are also Poe, Emerson, Melville, Stevens, Eliot, even Pound and Cummings. But Whitman is the prime precursor, and his vision of the sea as Nemesis-crone
(what Blake called Tirzah, or mother of our mortal part) becomes
Crane's version of Ananke. I begin though with Dickinson, before
commenting on *Emblems of Conduct*, for her difficult relation to
Emersonianism is very close to Crane's less direct but equally equivocal stationing in regard to American Romanticism.

Bryant's lovely lyric, *To the Fringed Gentian*, appears to have
found its parodies in two of Dickinson's early lyrics, *The Gentian
weaves her fringes* and *Distrustful of the Gentian*, even as Emerson's
Bacchus seems parodied by *I taste a liquor never brewed—*. Crane
(after 1925, when he first read her) was strongly influenced by Dickinson, and used the opening lines of *The Gentian weaves her fringes*
as one of the epigraphs to the *Quaker Hill* section of *The Bridge*. I
cite the poem here not because Crane admired it, but to help define
Crane's visionary stance. Bryant takes the gentian as the *natural*
hope of heaven, which he is eager to share:

> I would that thus, when I shall see
> The hour of death draw near to me,
> Hope, blossoming within my heart,
> May look to heaven as I depart.

Dickinson parodies natural hope by giving her "departing blos-
soms" a proper Christian burial:

> It was a short procession,
> The Bobolink was there—
> An aged Bee addressed us—
> And then we knelt in prayer—
> We trust that she was willing—
> We ask that we may be.
> Summer—Sister—Seraph!
> Let us go with thee!
>
> In the name of the Bee—
> And the Butterfly—
> And of the Breeze—Amen!

The Bee, like Emerson's Humble-Bee, is Divinity, and—very
lightly—we may take Butterfly as Savior and Breeze as Holy Ghost.

Parody of a natural or analogical hope could hardly be taken farther, even by Dickinson's mastery. She is distrustful of finding sermons in gentians, even as she is of Bacchic possession. Crane temperamentally was more addicted to the latter than any American poet whatsoever, and he would have been delighted to find auguries of spiritual hope in natural particulars. To his sorrow, his condition compelled him to be a poet of Blakean Experience, and he learned, partly from Dickinson, to forgo the delights of natural analogy. A soul naturally Emersonian, he lacks from the start Emerson's (and Whitman's) power to rise from natural particulars to vision, and attains his visionary heights more in Dickinson's slant manner than in Blake's dialectical progression. Like Dickinson's, Crane's God is an Inquisitor, and the seer's vocation demands an extraordinary degree of self-consciousness. In his poem *To Emily Dickinson*, Crane praises her for having: "Achieved that stillness ultimately best, / Being, of all, least sought for." This praise is precise; Dickinson did not complete her quest, and yet attained a final harvest, which "needs more than wit to gather, love to bind. / Some reconcilement of remotest mind —." That reconcilement Crane knew always he could not reach.

Emblems of Conduct uses the purer Emersonianism of Samuel Greenberg to study the nostalgias of reconcilement. Greenberg's lyric *Conduct* takes its title and "chosen hero" from Emerson, and obscurely suggests a certain irony in the hero's apotheosis:

> . . . they bore the
> Chosen hero upon their shoulders,
> Whom they strangely admired, as
> The beach-tide summer of people desired.

R. W. B. Lewis summarizes *Emblems of Conduct* as showing "the reduction to mere historic memory of the once-living reality of the spiritual world." In Crane's poem, spiritual adorations become the property of "historians," which is to say, of all contemporary takers of communion: "Dull lips commemorating spiritual gates." A chosen hero is still borne on his adorers' shoulders but:

> By that time summer and smoke were past.
> Dolphins still played, arching the horizons,
> But only to build memories of spiritual gates.

The bard's Bacchic assumption still takes place, but as an autumnal ritual, to do memory's work. In two greater lyrics, entirely his own, *Passage* and *Repose of Rivers*, Crane brought this theme to a Dickinsonian perfection. The theme might be called "Bacchus frustrate," for it deviates from Emerson only in withdrawing from self-celebration. *Passage* moves from the more-than-Wordsworthian promise of "an improved infancy" to the Melvillean recognition of the "chimney-sooted heart of man." Such recognition turns the poet "about and back" until he finds, beneath an opening laurel, a thief, Time, with "my stolen book in hand." Memory, last spiritual refuge in *Emblems of Conduct*, breaks when "committed to the page." Ananke the serpent triumphs, as it will in Stevens's *The Auroras of Autumn*. On the beaches no longer paced by Whitman, the supreme Emersonian Bard, Necessity "leaned its tongue and drummed." Wheelwright's elegiac queries of the drowned Crane echo Crane's own greater questions: "What fountains did I hear? what icy speeches?" But broken memory permitted no replies.

Repose of Rivers, perhaps Crane's finest lyric, makes a partial answer, of which I wish to examine only a small aspect here, as preparation for a brief consideration of *Voyages*, where *White Buildings* enters wholly into the mode of *Merlin*, and Nemesis is celebrated as the Sea. The motto of *White Buildings*, from Rimbaud, is bitterly apocalyptic, and *Repose of Rivers*, in the manner of Blake, shows the seer passing a Last Judgment upon himself, according to the situation that he holds. Crane's situation is that of the seer who "entered once and quickly fled," and who stands now at the gates of vision, remembering not so much the glory of that single entrance as the terror of it. The memory of terror is a terror, and the stance is still that of Bacchus frustrate, self-condemned as unworthy of vision, and yet still subject to the sudden, involuntary opening of the gates. This kind of self-portrayal has a power almost unique even in Romantic tradition, and we have valued it too little in our encounters with Crane.

Voyages can best be approached through Whitman rather than Emerson, though its conclusions are very close to the late Emerson's. Whitman's *Sea-Drift* pieces are Crane's precursors, and Crane does not match them, beautiful as his achievement is. His saving link or *tessera* to *Sea-Drift* is a radical completion of Whitman, in which the Sea becomes not only the turner of Necessity's spindle but a gateway to fresh vision, to what might be beyond Nemesis. But this *tessera* is not sustained, and Crane's Word fails to promise him more than "some splintered garland for the seer." We can contrast one of the minor but still wonderful *Sea-Drift* poems, *The World below the Brine*:

The world below the brine,
Forests at the bottom of the sea, the branches and leaves,
Sea-lettuce, vast lichens, strange flowers and seeds, the
    thick tangle, openings, and pink turf,
Different colors, pale gray and green, purple, white,
    and gold, the play of light through the water,
Dumb swimmers there among the rocks, coral,
    gluten, grass, rushes, and the aliment of the swimmers,
Sluggish existences grazing there suspended, or slowly
    crawling close to the bottom,
The sperm-whale at the surface blowing air and spray, or
    disporting with his flukes,
The leaden-eyed shark, the walrus, the turtle, the
    hairy sea-leopard, and the sting-ray,
Passions there, wars, pursuits, tribes, sight in those
    ocean-depths, breathing that thick-breathing air, as so many do,
The change thence to the sight here, and to the subtle air
    breathed by beings like us who walk this sphere,
The change onward from ours to that of beings who
    walk other spheres.

For Whitman the two changes, "thence" and "onward," are necessarily slight, and he subtly stresses the final oneness of the three
spheres by giving us only suggestions of the higher worlds after the
heavy particularity of the deep. The world of the mother is not ours,
and yet we are one with it. Whitman knows it as an otherness that is
still *his* otherness, the discourse of the other in him, as Lacan would
say. Unconscious need, the Sea's desire for him, becomes a conscious
demand, his desire for return to her. Crane's situation was more
desperate, the discourse of his other more urgent, the movement
from need to demand much swifter. But Crane's conscious intellect
was stronger than Whitman's, little help finally as that is to man or
poet, barring unusual good fortune or timely aid from others. *Voyages* hymns a Nemesis of "sleep, death, desire" and yields more than
song to transmemberment, but fights back in full consciousness that
even song must find more loss than gain when it joins so total a
Necessity.

I instance only one passage, in the third stanza of *Voyages IV*.
The seer "must first be lost in fatal tides to tell" his word; yet this
"signature of the incarnate word / The harbor shoulders to resign in
mingling / Mutual blood," so that loss is transformed not into gain,
but only into further loss. Crane's love for Emil Opffer engulfs

his poetic word even as the love provokes the word, for the Sea of otherness is antithetical to the Muse that found Crane. But Crane knows all this, and *Voyages* struggles not to be canceled by such knowledge. *Voyages* does not struggle against its own largest impulse, which is to escape all limitation by finding an identity with the Sea. Whitman's major *Sea-Drift* poems, *Out of the Cradle* . . . and *As I Ebb'd* . . . , are stronger, and less limited poetry, because they struggle superbly to continue in a knowledge of limitation. Winters blamed Emerson for killing Crane, and for ruining his poetry. The accusation was audacious, and movingly extravagant, but Winters shrewdly recognized the legitimate destructiveness of an inescapable tradition, however little value he himself would grant to it.

> Thought thinks its ruin here without widening speculation. It finds what will not suffice . . . Yet Feinman's poetry performs so total an *epoché* on "discursions fated and inept" that only the stumble toward a preamble is left. For so rigorous a sensibility, writing verse must be like crossing a threshold guarded by demons . . .
> Geoffrey Hartman

Preambles and Other Poems, Alvin Feinman's first and still his only volume, was published in 1964, when the poet was thirty-five. The poet and critic, John Hollander, in a note written for his anthology of contemporary poetry, characterized his selections from Feinman as "perhaps the most difficult of those in this collection. Their difficulty is not that of allusion, nor of ellipsis, nor of problematical form, however, but the phenomenological difficulty of confronting the boundary of the visual and the truly visionary." To instance the three other really difficult but excellent poets of my generation, as examples of Hollander's kinds of difficulty, I would cite Geoffrey Hill for sustained indirection of allusiveness, John Ashbery for ellipsis, and A. R. Ammons for problematical form. Feinman presents the greatest difficulties of these four profoundly rewarding poets, difficulties not only for the reader, however energetic and generous, but clearly for the poet himself as well. Feinman's prime precursor is Crane, as Ashbery's is Stevens, and Ammons's (happily for him) the more remote Emerson, or a kind of merged Emerson-Whitman figure. Like Crane, Feinman begins with a volume of difficult yet frequently radiant lyrics, but unlike Crane he has not been able to go on to the larger form of internalized quest or visionary romance, and his inability (thus far) to continue appears to have doomed his remarkable volume to neglect.

The great poems in *Preambles and Other Poems* are the title-poem (this poet's longest, at eighty-four lines), *November Sunday Morning*, *Pilgrim Heights*, and the brief *Circumferences* that ends the volume. Only these will be considered here; all are in the line of descent from Emerson, and all mingle the two modes I have called Bacchus and Merlin. Here is *November Sunday Morning*:

> And the light, a wakened heyday of air
> Tuned low and clear and wide,
> A radiance now that would emblaze
> And veil the most golden horn
> Or any entering of a sudden clearing
> To a standing, astonished, revealed . . .
>
> That the actual streets I loitered in
> Lay lit like fields, or narrow channels
> About to open to a burning river;
> All brick and window vivid and calm
> As though composed in a rigid water
> No random traffic would dispel . . .
>
> As now through the park, and across
> The chill nailed colors of the roofs,
> And on near trees stripped bare,
> Corrected in the scant remaining leaf
> To their severe essential elegance,
> Light is the all-exacting good,
>
> That dry, forever virile stream
> That wipes each thing to what it is,
> The whole, collage and stone, cleansed
> To its proper pastoral . . .
>   I sit
> And smoke, and linger out desire.

"Cleansed/To its proper pastoral," for here there is no boundary between the visual and the visionary, and the poet is naturalized again as shepherd of the Invisible. In the torments of his quest for an enabling act of the mind, Feinman arrives at only a handful (or fewer) of such privileged moments. *November Sunday Morning* is his only poem of a celebratory kind and all it celebrates is a certain cleansing light, but actually seen. And, vision seen, the poet rests quietly on heights, and lingers out desire. When he considers the radiance, he declares it as correction, that which cleanses each thing to what it is. Emerson might have marveled at so ascetic a privilege, but would have recognized this as Bacchic in his own sense, though reduced.

Stevens could begin only by reduction, to each variation upon the First Idea, each nothing that yet *was*. Feinman, as all his perceptive readers painfully realize, scarcely can bear to begin at all. This restricts his readers necessarily to those few who are prepared to tolerate his reluctance, for who can wish, even now, to be invited into so stark a theater of mind? Feinman's American ancestors, culminating in Crane, move toward the reader, in the large, vitalistic gestures of natural abundance, but Feinman's difficult art is the closest equivalent we have to Valéry and the even more painfully achieved middle phases of Rilke. I dwell on difficulty because there is no evading it in discussing *Preambles and Other Poems*. Their difficulty is their necessity, and in a subtle sense defines their dialectical stance as Bacchus or poetic possession and Merlin or Necessity itself. The central vision in the volume is of the mind, ceaselessly an *activity*, engaged in the suffering process of working apart all things that are joined by it:

> And so
> The mind in everything it joins
> And suffers to redeem apart
> Plays victim to its own intent...
> *(Preambles)*

> ... history

> At the close will cripple to these things:
> A body without eyes, a hand, the vacant
> Presence of unjoined, necessary things.
> *(Landscape, Sicily)*

> And always the tips of the fingers of both her hands
> will pull or twist at a handkerchief
> like lovely deadly birds at a living thing
> trying to work apart something exquisitely,
> unreasonably joined.
> *(Relic)*

> Only this presence destined
> As a weather from its source

Toward broad or violent unleashings
Fables of the suffered and the joined
(*Three Elementary Prophecies*)

...I
Who have called you upright, destiny, or wall,
—How we exchange circumferences within
The one footfall that bruises us asunder.
(*Circumferences*)

This is the power of the mind over the universe of sense, not a power of renovation upon a universe of death (as in Wordsworth) but a tragedy of mind, victim to its own intent, which is to make by separations. Every joining of particulars in this poet's universe enforces a vacancy, every linkage indeed *vacates*, yet his sensibility finds exquisiteness only where we are bruised asunder. In Stevens, to "abstract" tends to dissociate, and probably Stevens should have used the latter word for his reductions to the First Idea. His immediate stimulus was Valéry, who had insisted "there are no names for those things amongst which one is completely alone," and who defined the characteristic of consciousness as "a process of perpetual exhaustion, of detachment without rest or exclusion from everything that comes before it, whatever that thing may be—an inexhaustible activity." No visionary poet could work within the limits of consciousness thus construed, and the visionary strain in Stevens became progressively more attenuated. Stevens had a mixed temperament, neither as wintry nor as Floridian as it sometimes appeared, and the poetics of Valéry were thus not wholly inimical to him. But Feinman's poetic temperament is Emersonian; like Crane, he is wholly a visionary, but afflicted (unlike Crane) with a critical consciousness in the mode of Valéry. He cannot create by dissociation, but only by joinings, like Whitman and Crane, joinings to which nevertheless he cannot give credence. His horror of the visual becomes, in the poems, a defense against madness, and still another hindrance to the fabling his gift requires.

Wordsworth, who in his wisdom feared the bodily eye as the most despotic of the senses, the one most likely to usurp the mind's mastery, has affected American poets (after the time of Bryant, when the influence was more direct) largely through the misprision of Transcendentalism. Thoreau is the major American instance of this misprision, since his *clinamen* from Wordsworth is the actual reversal of *The Prelude*'s warning, and apotheosizes the eye. Emerson, always more dialectical, vacillates in *Nature,* where the eye that sees the radiance is the same eye that radiance employs to behold us. Crane's furious synesthesia betrays an Emersonian uneasiness with pure vision, yet Crane is tormented by particulars of light, and testifies frequently to the eye's tyranny. Feinman, following Crane, is obsessed by light and by sharp outline, self-consciously knowing the eye's threat to his poetry, but unable to evade a terrible, continuous effort to merge with the God Ananke in the form of "Light . . . the all-exacting good." *November Sunday Morning,* a chilled epiphany, approximates the skeptical rapture of Shelley at nearly his most intense, yet lacks the mellowness of Shelley's urbanity (or of the Crane of the lovely *Sunday Morning Apples,* a possible source of Feinman's poem). It remains unique among this poet's work as the one venture where the joined is accepted, and "each thing" is redeemed without being pulled apart by the mind. "Wounded by apprehensions out of speech,/I hold it up against a disk of light—," Crane says of the "stone of lust" in *Possessions,* a poem in *White Buildings* whose presence is felt in nearly every poem in Feinman's book, in every hope of "all violences stayed and sudden light." Strongest of these hopes is *Pilgrim Heights:*

> Something, something, the heart here
> Misses, something it knows it needs
> Unable to bless—the wind passes;
> A swifter shadow sweeps the reeds,
> The heart a colder contrast brushes.
>
> So this fool, face-forward, belly
> Pressed among the rushes, plays out
> His pulse to the dune's long slant
> Down from blue to bluer element,
> The bold encompassing drink of air
>
> And namelessness, a length compound
> Of want and oneness the shore's mumbling
> Distantly tells—something a wing's
> Dry pivot stresses, carved
> Through barrens of stillness and glare:
>
> The naked close of light in light,
> Light's spare embrace of blade and tremor
> Stealing the generous eye's plunder
> Like a breathing banished from the lung's
> Fever, lost in parenthetic air.

Raiding these nude recesses, the hawk
Resumes his yielding balance, his shadow
Swims the field, the sands beyond,
The narrow edges fed out to light,
To the sea's eternal licking monochrome.

The foolish hip, the elbow bruise
Upright from the dampening mat,
The twisted grasses turn, unthatch,
Light-headed blood renews its stammer—
Apart, below, the dazed eye catches

A darkened figure abruptly measured
Where folding breakers lay their whites;
The heart from its height starts downward,
Swum in that perfect pleasure
It knows it needs, unable to bless.

With only a few companions—Ashbery's *Soonest Mended*, Ammons's *Saliences*, Geoffrey Hill's *Annunciations* among them—this stands for me as one of the fully achieved and central poems by a poet of my generation. The miraculously subtle movement of the first stanza is a reduction or *epoché* on the "somewhat more loudly sweep the string" theme, here treated not as the advent of a greater subject but as the promise, altogether precarious, of a momentary end to an oxymoronic agony of near-solipsism. Agony, yet this is upon the heights, from which the heart at least must start downward, for life and poetry to go on. The poet's eye, dazed by its Bacchic intoxication with all the shore's particulars, yields its plunder first to a visionary light that might as well be a darkness to it, and then more fortunately to a sudden sense of otherness ("Apart, below. . . . A darkened figure abruptly measured"). With this startling end to a perfect pleasure of solipsistic, Bacchic repletion, the poet's consciousness abandons a height "unable to bless" and descends "Where folding breakers lay their whites," to a scene where the ocean offers itself, obliquely indicating a new context where blessing is possible.

This ought to be the constant mode of *Preambles and Other Poems*, suggesting a way out of the impasse of blocked vision, of the world encountered in the Greenberg-Crane *Emblems of Conduct*. But Feinman, wherever his second and subsequent volumes may reach as vision, yields in most of his first volume to the Emersonian Necessity. Apart from *November Sunday Morning* and *Pilgrim*

Heights, he enters the realms of Merlin, most strikingly in his title-poem. *Preambles* is too long to give complete here, and is most inadequately represented by excerpts. Its title marks it as this poet's bracketing of his quest, and necessarily it is a driving, dissociative composition, with the unenviable distinction of being the most genuinely difficult poem of real coherence and value by an American poet of this century. Though thoroughly justifiable, the difficulty is preamble to Feinman's failure to make a canon of poems, to the slow waste of his genius. Though there are parallel problems in consciousness in Valéry and Rilke, those poets fortunately were free of the peculiarly American malady of seeking to be Ananke, which in Feinman's case becomes the deplorable quest to write the last possible poem, a work that takes the post-Romantic consciousness so far as to make further advances in self-consciousness intolerable. More than any poet, Feinman is the victim of what Wyndham Lewis called the Demon of Progress in the Arts, which makes Feinman one of the most American of poets.

Preambles is in three parts, each of seven quatrains. The first rejects "All/Discursion fated and inept," everything in the poet's past scrutinies that ended in irrelevance, which comes to not less than everything except for a handful of particulars out of *the given:*

> I would cite
> Wind-twisted spaces, absence
> Listing to a broken wall . . .

> . . . such things
> As thwart beginnings, limit . . .

> . . . *Archai*

> Bruited through crumbling masteries
> To hang like swollen apples
> In the river, witnesses
> Stilled to their clotted truth . . .

The problem with poetry of this rare kind, a poetry of "whole meaning" as Conrad Aiken termed *Preambles,* is eloquently presented by Priscilla Washburn Shaw in her commentary on Valéry's *Le Sylphe:*

> For those readers who demand that metaphor be firmly anchored so that the links of comparison are readily visible and uni-directional, an image like "ma tendre corbeille," and still

more "la ceinture," is somewhat unsatisfactory, and even obscure. No explanation, or series of explanations, can totally satisfy if what is really desired is a tighter connection between image and referent, because it is just this which has deliberately been avoided. This desire is present in even quite sophisticated readers, and it is probably a fundamental aspect of our attempt to understand the world intellectually and emotionally.

Preambles goes beyond Valéry by not only postponing or transposing such attempts to understand, but abrogating them, thus moving to the limits of the intelligible. Where Valéry beautifully restores our pleasure in particulars ("Les images sont nombreuses/a l'égal de mes regards"), the second part of *Preambles,* with strange serenity, surrenders to a process that ends the private mind:

> . . . To each defeat a signature
>
> The just reconnaissance
> That even fruit, each excellence
> Confirms its course   A leisure
> As of sap or blood arrested
>
> Only once and to the prime
> Its issue vivifies . . .

What is left "of every severed thing" completes the poem's third part:

> The *ecce* only, only hands
> Or hardnesses, the gleam a water
> Or a light, a paused thing
> Clothes in vacua killed
>
> To a limbless beauty   Take
> These torn possessives there
> Where you plead the radiant
> Of your truth's gloom   Own
>
> To your sleep, your waking
> The tread that is walked
> From the inner of its pace
> The play of a leaf to an earth.

I feel the immense distinction of this each time I read it, and am as chilled by it as I am by the closing measures of Emerson's *Merlin* or the splendid closing paragraphs of *Fate* where we are exhorted to build altars to the Beautiful Necessity. Criticism has yet to do justice to Feinman's poetry, particularly *Preambles*, but that is because it comes at us asking more than poetry can (or should) ask. The closing poem in Feinman's volume, *Circumferences*, movingly presents the dilemma and the triumph (which are one) of his vision:

> Dawn under day, or dawning, lake, late edge,
> Assumptive pure periphery where one thrust prominence
> Now give me back my eyes, my stride almost
> A next abode, and source   O gathering, your smile
> Is softer and more slow than the guileless surf
> Drying forever at a farthest shore   I
> Who have called you upright, destiny, or wall,
> —How we exchange circumferences within
> The one footfall that bruises us asunder.

This knowing return to what Lacan terms the *Stade du miroir*, on the part of so rigorous a sensibility, so remorselessly advanced a consciousness, is more than yet another instance of the indestructibility of unconscious desire, more than a gently smiling acknowledgement of the equivocal role of primal narcissism in the forming of poetic vision, even at its purest. The poet, just at the point of dawn, studies his reflection in a lake, perhaps relents a little at his own stern questing, and ends his poetry's first phase by the one footfall that bruises him and his image asunder. The obliteration of the other is an exchange of circumferences, a realization of Emerson's wisdom in *Circles:* ". . . we seek with insatiable desire . . . to lose our sempiternal memory . . . in short to draw a new circle." But the history of Emerson's progeny—of Robinson, Crane, Feinman as representative poets, and of so many more—suggests that no new circles can be drawn in this great but darkening tradition.

1970

20
"To Reason with a Later Reason": Romanticism and the Rational

The classical definition of Romantic poetry is by August Wilhelm Schlegel, who saw it as "the expression of a secret longing for the chaos which is perpetually striving for new and marvellous births, which lies hidden in the very womb of orderly creation." This definition has always seemed to me quite wrong, if applied to the tradition in Romanticism that interests me the most, the invention of two new kinds of poetry by Blake and Wordsworth, respectively, and the development of these two kinds by British and American poets down to the present day. *Contra* Schlegel, it may be affirmed that Romantic poetry from Blake down to Yeats and Wallace Stevens has no quarrel with "orderly creation," and makes no case against reason. The polemic of Romantic, which is to say, of the most vital modern poetry, is directed against inadequate accounts of reason, but not against reason itself. Though the greatest of Romantic theorists, Coleridge, rightly saw poetry as being the product of a more than rational energy, he tended also to emphasize the imaginative reinforcement of reason as being the proper goal of that energy. And Blake, the most extreme partisan of the Imagination ever to appear among men, spoke nevertheless of the necessity for reason as a dialectical counterpoise to energy lest, as he put it, the Prolific choke in an excess of its own delights. The great enemy of poetry in the Romantic tradition has never been reason, but rather those premature modes of conceptualization that masquerade as final accounts of reason in every age. It is not reason that menaces the shaping spirit, but the high priests of rationalization, the great men with the compasses who have marked out circumferences, from Descartes, Bacon, Newton, and Locke down to subtler limiters of the imaginative horizon in Hegel, Marx, Freud, and their various

323

revisionist disciples. Romanticism, in what seems its central tradition, at least in our language, is a revolt not against orderly creation, but against compulsion, against conditioning, against all unnecessary limitation that presents itself as being necessary. As such, Romanticism is a doomed tradition, yet a perpetually self-renewing one. All Romantics are the last Romantics, and no artistic tradition of such eminence has ever so consistently proclaimed its own self-immolation.

The vitality of Romantic tradition appears to inhere in its universality—we are, all of us, largely involuntary Romantics, however intensely we proclaim our overt beliefs to be anti-Romantic. Our characteristic therapy, the Freudian one, which is necessarily in the true sense our religion, since it is the myth in which we believe without conscious effort—that therapy is Romantic in its practice, though not in its theory. The pragmatic goal of Freudian therapy, whether in its pure or revisionist forms, is to free the patient for the ordeal of Romantic love. The rhetorical disguise of the revisionists that masks this quest as a search for "full satisfaction of psychic needs," is a poor one, but profoundly interesting as part of a pattern of disguise that runs throughout the history of rationalizations that seek to conceal inverted Romantic centers. Blake called this pattern "Druidism," by which he meant an archetypal natural religion, and he insisted that all rationalisms were concealed natural religions, mysteries celebrating one limiting context or another as being necessary to curb the full creative freedom of human energy.

I am not, therefore, in this essay, going to conduct a vendetta against inadequate dialectics in the name of various poets. I propose to take a series of major Romantic texts, chosen not for pattern but simply for their eminence and centrality as poems, and to trace through them their uncovering of "Druidism," their apocalyptic demonstrations that the garments of ideology or of supposed thought that we wear must be thrown aside if we are to explore our human imaginative heights and depths. I will begin with the climactic passage of Blake's brief epic, *Milton*, and with Wordsworth's *Resolution and Independence*, a lyric that invents the most characteristic modern genre of poetry, the crisis poem. I will then glance at two descendants of Wordsworth's genre in the next generation, Keats's *Ode to Psyche* and Shelley's *Ode to the West Wind*, and will pass on to four modern summits of poetry in the Romantic tradition— Yeats's *Dialogue of Self and Soul* and one of his *Supernatural Songs* —two crucial poems of D. H. Lawrence, the early *Under the Oak*

and the death-poem *Shadows;* two similar lyrics by Hart Crane—
the early *Passage* and the death-poem, *The Broken Tower*, until I
come to rest at the extreme limits of Romantic tradition, in the concluding sections of Wallace Stevens's *Notes Toward A Supreme
Fiction*, which will appear, increasingly, to have been the central or
representative poem of our time and place, even as Stevens, I think,
will seem to be as much the crucial poet of his time as Wordsworth
and Tennyson were of theirs.

Blake's Milton confronts his emanation, the supreme embodiment,
in female form, of his created world, the totality of his desire. And,
as even lesser men do, in the confrontation of Romantic love, he
identifies himself, he chooses to be all that he can be:

> To bathe in the Waters of Life; to wash off the
>   Not Human
> I come in Self-annihilation & the grandeur of
>   Inspiration
> To cast off Rational Demonstration by Faith in
>   the Saviour
> To cast off the rotten rags of Memory by
>   Inspiration
> To cast off Bacon, Locke & Newton from
>   Albions covering
> To take off his filthy garments, & clothe
>   him with Imagination
> To cast aside from Poetry, all that is
>   not Inspiration . . .

This great declaration attains its zenith a few lines further on:

> To cast off the idiot Questioner who is
>   always questioning,
> But never capable of answering; who sits
>   with a sly grin
> Silent plotting when to question, like a
>   thief in a cave . . .

Blake's "idiot Questioner" is a complex entity, but essentially he
is identifiable with the reasoning Spectre or fallen Urizen in every
man. Perhaps, most simply, he is the mind of the age, any age, as it
gets into the mind of the individual, and so becomes the individual
mind's debased, minimal notion of right reason. And, in another aspect, he is the anxiety and mode of self-doubt current in any age,
the kind of melancholia that allies all versions of right reason and
any age's notion of true madness. Blake is able to cast him off be-

cause he too is recognized by the poet as a mere garment, an outer covering and not a necessity. Blake is writing personal myth, like Shelley after him, and like Joyce and Yeats and Lawrence and Hart Crane in our own time. Though this has been a major Romanticism, it has been less prevalent than the other tradition in Romantic poetry, the tradition of nakedness or decreation, of a poetry of confrontation that hesitates at the threshold of myth, but declines altogether to cross over into it. Here Wordsworth is the fountainhead, with Keats following him in his own day, and Stevens in ours.

The characteristic modern lyric of real ambition is generally a variant of the Wordsworthian crisis poem, the ultimate models being *Tintern Abbey, Resolution and Independence,* and the *Intimations* Ode. This does not mean, of course, that the reliance of later poets upon Wordsworth is always overt or conscious; it means only, and yet all-importantly, that Wordsworth perfected the genre that Coleridge in fact had invented. In the crisis lyric, the poet seeks to save himself for poetry. The price of failure is madness, or death-in-life; the reward of success is only to have written the poem, and to be free for the struggle with the next poem. *Resolution and Independence* is a poem about not being able to do what Blake's Milton does, to cast off the coverings of anxiety and of self-torturing analysis. The case of the poem against reason is the case made by Wallace Stevens in a late poem, where the Backache that is fallen human history says to Saint John, the poet of the Apocalypse:

> The mind is the terriblest force in the world, father,
> Because, in chief, it, only, can defend
> Against itself. At its mercy, we depend
> Upon it.

The thought that protects us from thought is not reason but a later reason, as Stevens calls it in *Notes Toward A Supreme Fiction,* making a distinction at odds with the more philosophical antinomy of the reason and understanding. Stevens declares:

> But the difficultest rigor is forthwith,
> On the image of what we see, to catch from that
>
> Irrational moment its unreasoning,
> As when the sun comes rising, when the sea
> Clears deeply, when the moon hangs on the wall
>
> Of heaven-haven. These are not things transformed.
> Yet we are shaken by them as if they were.
> We reason about them with a later reason.

That is what *Resolution and Independence* is about, Wordsworth's saving attempt to catch from an irrational moment its unreasoning, its special power of clarification. Stevens's "irrational moment," Wordsworth's "spot of time," Pater's "privileged moment," Joyce's "epiphany," Yeats's moments when he is blessed and can bless, Browning's "good moment," Blake's "moment in each day that Satan's Watch Fiends cannot find," Lawrence's moments of breakthrough, Hart Crane's sudden revelations—clearly these all belong to one Romantic family, significant as their differences are. Pater's "privileged moment" is perhaps the most comprehensive of these epiphanies, and it is a series of privileged moments that I want to examine in this exploration. There are, I think, two major modes in Romantic reasonings with a later reason, both of which manifest themselves in the poetry of Yeats, Stevens, Crane, Lawrence, and many lesser figures in our time. Both modes are present in Blake and Wordsworth alike, but a different one is predominant in each. One, and it is primarily Blakean, is the mode of passionate assertion of a vision so overwhelming that it cuts through the cloven fiction or discursive antithesis of transcendence and immanence. The other, primarily Wordsworthian, is the affirmation of the privileged moment, not an attack on an antithesis, but a laying hold on both sides of the antithesis simultaneously.

Resolution and Independence is a poem dealing with the passage from crisis to what will suffice, that place of spirit from which one can again start to live and to write. The poet stands almost at the midpoint of his existence—he is thirty-two, soon to be married, and fearful that his vision has fled. He contemplates the acedia and ruin of his brother poet, Coleridge, and sees in him the entire line of the doomed poets of Sensibility, from Chatterton to Burns, the bards who in their youth began in gladness, but who fell one by one into the despondency that preceded total alienation. From this terrible anxiety, this grief without a name, Wordsworth is rescued by a privileged moment that scarcely yields itself even to the later reason of the imagination. Nothing the Leech-gatherer *says* makes a difference —it is the uncanny shape, the *kind* of speech, above all, the preternatural *stationing* of such a figure in the lonely place, that finds Wordsworth, that brings him home to consolation and to the secure stay of a possible fresh start for a life of poetry.

Keats, in the *Ode to Psyche*, the most original and I think most important poem he ever wrote, follows Wordsworth by internalizing a privileged moment, yet also approaches Blake (whom he had probably never read) by making his central poem an overt declaration of imaginative autonomy. Though this independence is urged against the religious and mythological past as well as against the mind's notions of limitation, there is a deeper sense in which the *Ode to Psyche*, like *Resolution and Independence*, conducts its polemic against the rags that masquerade as the rational coverings of imagination. The enemy within, for both poems, is what Blake called the Spectre, the isolated selfhood, rationalizing its fears of death and deprivation into a morality of natural confinement. What blocks the saving vision, Keats cries out in the *Nightingale* Ode, is the dull brain that perplexes and retards, even as Wordsworth's fearful thoughts, his anxieties about an indefinite future, perplex and retard psychic recovery in *Resolution and Independence*. Part of the answer given by the imagination as later reason comes from sight, but the sight is largely one of the inner eye. In the climactic moment of the *Ode to Psyche*, Keats sees and knows his own vision, and is raised to poetic priesthood by it. Confronting a revived Psyche, reunited with her Eros, he celebrates this vision of the human-soul-in-love; "I see, and sing, by my own eyes inspired." He concludes his poem with one of the greatest stanzas in the language, where an earthly paradise is re-created "in some untrodden region of the mind," with the work done by a new kind of thought, accompanied by pleasant pain, as the mind moves further out into its unused potential.

Stevens, as I will try to indicate at the close of this essay, is very much in the tradition of Wordsworth and Keats. He believes that even the naturalizing mind can save us from itself. Yeats, Lawrence, and Crane are more in Blake's and Shelley's tradition, more involved in a thoroughgoing apocalypticism in which both the forms of thought and the coverings of nature are put aside.

A backward glance at Shelley's most famous lyric, the revolutionary *Ode to the West Wind*, can serve to re-introduce this strain in the Romantic Later Reason. Shelley is an Orphic phenomenon, so great and startling a throwback that criticism is still largely bewildered when it attempts to meet him on his own ground, which is well up in the atmosphere anyway. And, more than Blake, Wordsworth, and Keats, more than Yeats or Lawrence or Crane, more probably than Stevens, Shelley was what we now call an intellectual, a skeptic fiercely questioning even of his own, quite literal inspiration. And that of course is what the *Ode to the West Wind* is "about," inspiration, or rather blocked inspiration. I have read and loved the poem for twenty years, and published several interpretations of it, without noticing until now that the subject central to it is that the poet has more inspiration than a human frame can handle; that, beautifully and quite formally, the poem stations itself out on that perilous ridge at the extreme verge of being, where the Orphic power *must* shatter it, where the poet must be rent apart. Against this *sparagmos*, the poem fights grandly, and wins a broken and noble victory. For it is not a natural force that threatens to rip the poet apart, but the power of his own mind, and if the energy that pours through him is more than rational, and it is, yet it is the strength of the rational component in that energy that menaces him the most. Out of the abyss of self the great Voice roars forth, but it is a voice of mind, of the most terrible force in the world, of consciousness turned against itself. If only the mind can defend us against itself, then Shelley's plangent yet defiant plea must be addressed to the mind, and it is. I will do two things for you that you cannot do for yourself, he declares to the wind. I will *modulate* you, give you tone, bring you into the realm of the aesthetic, and I will make you, through *my* lips, to unawakened earth, the trumpet of a prophecy. This is prophecy as choice, as the mind making a decision, as the self purged of excessive self-concern through the very power of self to heal its own torments. The poem hesitates, finally, at the brink of revelation, at the edge of an apocalyptic uncovering that will strip the year of its seasons, and show man again what Blake's Milton tried to show him, the instruction that Yeats takes up again in his *Supernatural Songs* when he declares, following Blake, that:

> Thought is a garment, and the soul's a bride
> That cannot in that trash and tinsel hide.

That couplet sums up the theme of the Later Reason. Yeats, just short of seventy, writes the *Supernatural Songs* in the *persona* of Ribh, an imaginary hermit whose Christianity, like Blake's, does not admit of any dualism. In the major poem of the series, *Ribh considers Christian Love insufficient*, a Blakean attack is made, not upon *agapè*, but upon conceptualizations of the divine, and of divine love. In four stanzas of extraordinarily mounting passion, Ribh moves from a hatred "that can clear the soul / Of everything that is not mind or sense" to a greater and more cleansing hatred, to "turn / From every thought of God mankind has had." When the inspired hermit declares that "Hatred of God may bring the soul to God," he is not stating paradox, and he compels us to contemplate deeply what he means by "hatred." "At stroke of midnight," in the apocalyptic presence of the last things, "soul cannot endure/A bodily *or* mental furniture." Soul here is imagination, the higher faculty of the Later Reason, weary of all discursive or analytic entities, seeking not a mystical unknowing, but a visionary identity between creator and creation, the state of being that Blake called Eden, and that Yeats, in *A Vision*, locates at the Fifteenth Phase, at the fullness of the moon. "Man's life is thought," the last of the *Supernatural Songs* will affirm, but man's thought leads only to "the desolation of reality." Life and thought are a garment; the soul, in its marriage with a final reality, must go naked. With less than the power of Blake's Milton, but in an accent more our own, Yeats has found again one of the two major Romantic modes of the Later Reason.

He had found the more characteristic one, of the saving moment, many times before, from *The Wild Swans at Coole* on, but never more powerfully than in *A Dialogue of Self and Soul*, a fierce dramatization of the Romantic case against the rational coverings that mockingly assume the face of reason. Soul, in this poem, speaks for the Western rational tradition, and for its related world of moral virtue, of life viewed as the development of character. Self speaks for personality as against character, for impulse against moral virtue, and primarily for imagination or the later reason against an exhausted reason that seeks now only to know its own deathly limits. Of the two parts of the poem, the first or dialogue proper centers on a crucial moment in which the awareness of death is so heightened that the moment becomes privileged, an epiphany demanding a last integration before man dissolves into the night. The second part is the Self's passionate declaration, in the manner of Blake, that it has cast off the covering of death-in-life, the self-denials of remorse.

If there *is* a division between the major Romantics and their most remarkable modern followers, a division greater than the passage of years by itself could make in a unified vision, then that division falls against the Romantic moderns. The power of mind in Blake and Wordsworth is awesome, but in Yeats and Stevens it is intermittent. The triumphs of rhetoric in Yeats and Stevens, at their finest, are as compelling as similar intensities in Blake and Wordsworth, but the strength and range of imagination is nowhere near so great. The Spectre or work-a-day reason argues back powerfully in Blake's *Jerusalem*, and is right on its own terms, while the Idiot Questioner within Wordsworth, in *Resolution and Independence*, nearly wins the victory over the desperately sincere poet. Yeats is a deliberate glorifier of the Self, and his self-dramatization does not give the Soul a chance to state its case with full persuasiveness. There is almost always a touch of the obscurantist in Yeats, as one would expect from an occultist, and it is not absent here. The soul or character is conceived too piously, and the Self's stance is taken too easily. Yet it is taken with majestic power, and the joy of the remarkable last stanza merits its Blakean tone:

> I am content to follow to its source
> Every event in action or in thought;
> Measure the lot; forgive myself the lot!
> When such as I cast out remorse
> So great a sweetness flows into the breast
> We must laugh and we must sing,
> We are blest by everything,
> Everything we look upon is blest.

This is the epiphany, the privileged moment in which mind and body, subject and object, are brought together by the energizing strength of the Romantic imagination. Yeats, as anyone reading his very last poems can see, did not abide in this moment. His last poems return to a violent emotionalism, to the self-sanctified fury of "the foul rag-and-bone shop of the heart." At his final point, thought did not yield to a later reason, but to mere irrationalism, and a dangerous antihumanism. The latest Yeats celebrates flux, and praises violence almost for its own sake. The later reason of Romanticism was as difficult to sustain as any reason is, and we are wrong, I think, to praise even one of the greatest of poets when he turns from our condition and its deepest needs.

D. H. Lawrence, whom the older Yeats so deeply and understandably admired, is in much of his poetry and many of his novels and polemical writings another prophet of irrationalism, but his central poems and novels are well within the most relevant aspects of the Romantic tradition, and make their own highly individual contribution to the Romantic vision of a later reason. The insights of his finest novels, *The Rainbow* and *Women in Love,* are condensed in the relatively early and very Blakean *Under the Oak,* while the blind vitalism and consequent irrationalism of the later novels like *Lady Chatterly's Lover* and *The Plumed Serpent* are compensated for by the sane and majestic death-poems, like *Bavarian Gentians* and *Ship of Death,* and particularly by the poem called *Shadows,* which moves me as much as any verse of our century.

The speaker of *Under the Oak* is experiencing a moment of vision, a moment so intense and privileged that the whole natural context in which he stands becomes a confinement set against him, a covering that must be ripped asunder though his life run out with it. He speaks to the reader, the "you" of the poem, his rational, his too-rational companion underneath the sacrificial Tree of Mystery, and his impatience chastises our rationalizations and hesitations, our troubled refusal to yield ourselves to a moment of vision. Like Balder slain by the mistletoe, the poet is sacrificed to the chthonic forces, and struggles against a Druidic adversary, as in Blake's tradition. We are excluded, unless we too can break the barrier of natural and rational confinement:

> Above me springs the blood-born mistletoe
> In the shady smoke.
> But who are you, twittering to and fro
> Beneath the oak?
>
> What thing better are you, what worse?
> What have you to do with the mysteries
> Of this ancient place, of my ancient curse?
> What place have you in my histories?

At the end, Lawrence felt the full strength of that ancient curse. The marvel of his death poems is that they raise the ancient blessing of the Romantic Later Reason against the curse, and triumph over it. So, in the sublime opening of *Shadows*:

> And if tonight my soul may find her peace
> in sleep, and sink in good oblivion,
> and in the morning wake like a new-opened flower
> then I have been dipped again in God, and new created.

The poem turns on an imagistic contrast between the new-opened flowers of a still-unfolding consciousness, and the lengthening and darkening shadows of mortality. The imagination's antagonist in the poem is not to be found in the actual shadows, but in a reasonable conception of mortality, a conception that would make what Lawrence calls "good oblivion" impossible. In a related death poem, *The End, The Beginning*, Lawrence writes:

> If there were not an utter and absolute dark
> of silence and sheer oblivion
> at the core of everything,
> how terrible the sun would be,
> how ghastly it would be to strike a match, and
>   make a light.

> But the very sun himself is pivoted
> upon a core of pure oblivion,
> so is a candle, even as a match.
>
> And if there were not an absolute, utter forgetting
> and a ceasing to know, a perfect ceasing to know
> and a silent, sheer cessation of all awareness
> how terrible life would be!
> how terrible it would be to think and know, to
>   have consciousness!
>
> But dipped, once dipped in dark oblivion
> the soul has peace, inward and lovely peace.

Renewal depends upon the expunging of self-consciousness, as much as it did in *Resolution and Independence*. Lawrence's death-poem, *Shadows*, is finally a hymn of renovation, of the privileged moments becoming "a new morning." This promise made to Lawrence is akin to what Hart Crane, in his beautiful, early, and very Wordsworthian lyric, *Passage*, calls "an improved infancy." Here, the ravening consciousness, associated with memory and time, is the thief hiding beneath the opening laurel of poetic accomplishment, the thief who steals the book the poet should compose. The poet bravely affirms that he has come to argue with the laurel, for the poet has foreknowledge of the lesson of transience, the burden of realizing that all the privileged moments of vision must pass. *Passage* ends with the young poet's momentary defeat, but Crane's finest poem, his elegy for his own poetic self, *The Broken Tower*, ends in the poet's victory over his own Idiot Questioner, his shattered, remorseful, spectral intellect. The rational self-questioner is allowed the full force of his case against the poet's imagination:

> And so it was I entered the broken world
> To trace the visionary company of love, its voice
> An instant in the wind (I know not whither hurled)
> But not for long to hold each desperate choice.
>
> My word I poured. But was it cognate, scored
> Of that tribunal monarch of the air
> Whose thigh embronzes earth, strikes crystal Word
> In wounds pledged once to hope—cleft to despair?

Satan or the Accuser within the self is the tribunal monarch of the air, and on his own terms he is right to claim the poet. What saves

Crane, though "saves" is both too hopeful and too orthodox a term in this context, is the power of his own imagination, which builds another tower of spirit, "healed, original now, and pure," to replace the broken tower of his earlier self. The imagination is redemptive because it can operate like a later reason, because it can take a momentary apprehension of release and build that apprehension into a faith, because again it can follow the Romantic path of moving from the privileged moment to a declaration of the mind's autonomy, to a casting-out of remorse and a freedom from outworn conceptions of the self.

The tradition I have been sketching is the tradition that culminates in Wallace Stevens, who was, I think, the representative poet of our time, and who may have been not only the best and most relevant poet writing in English in this century, but possibly also the finest poet our country has brought forth, the supreme example of the American imagination, the final perfection of the legacy of Emerson and Whitman. One makes these enormous claims not just for their shock value, but because it is time we see clearly just what we had in Stevens. Stevens's subject, as he kept saying, is the endlessly subtle relationship between reality and the imagination, and his central resource is the dialectic between the privileged moment and the endless continuum of things as they are. And Stevens, as was inevitable for a great poet coming so late in Romantic tradition, is a subtle qualifier. The great moments of affirmation, the declarations of faith in the imagination, are everywhere in his late, major phase, but they tend to sound more muted than they are. And his attack on what he calls the gaunt world of reason, as compared to the fat, green, fluent *mundo* of the imaginative man, is an ironic attack, and at heart an uneasy one. The mind, for him, is the great poem of winter, which constantly seeks to reduce illusion in the search for what will suffice. But reduction, for him, is worse than illusion, and it is no better than the excessive errors of a decadent sub-Romanticism that has substituted mental expansionism, the self-aggrandisement of the ego, for the true act of Romantic invention. Stevens's quest is for invention, or to use his word, discovery, which can remind us of the Blakean image of uncovering, of seeking a revelatory awareness. The poem, for Stevens, is found, not imposed, in an order already implicit in the *materia poetica* that makes up our lives.

Stevens's deliberate masterpiece, perhaps too deliberate, is his attempt to write the central poem, *Notes Toward a Supreme Fiction*. It is a poem about what Stevens calls poverty, imaginative need, and about the re-imagining of the first idea, which is primal human perception stripped of all fictions. The reduction of the wintry mind is fleshed by a series of fables, of which the last is the finest, the fable of the Canon Aspirin, which I shall rapidly rehearse. The Canon is a hedonist, a humane and humanistic one, who dreams an Angel, creates a fiction, even as he himself is a fiction made by a poet, Stevens. In his angelic dream he achieves Miltonic dimensions, and reaches the limits both of reduction, "a point,/Beyond which fact could not progress as fact.", and of expansion, "a point/Beyond which thought could not progress as thought." In his dream, the Canon chooses "the whole,/The complicate, the amassing harmony," an imaginative reconciliation of mind and fact. But the Canon is not a poet, and does not abide in his choice; he cannot sustain his own exercise of a later reason. He falls down into the imposition of mock order on reality, and his own creator, Stevens, disengages from him. If the poet has made an Angel, cannot he surpass his own creation in imaginative persistence, cannot he make his own humanity majestic by a recognition of his own powers? The satisfactions of belief, in the older sense made obsolescent by the advance of reason, can be found now by conscious belief in a fiction of one's own creation, provided one remembers what the Canon Aspirin forgot, that a fiction is after all, alas, not true. The ancient Romantic burden of extreme self-consciousness, with its attendant fears of a collapse into the death-in-life of solipsism, is relieved in a rhapsodic declaration of imaginative autonomy that is also an epiphany, a realization of the privileged moment, as the traditions of Blake and Wordsworth are brought together with radiant splendor:

> What am I to believe? If the angel in his cloud,
> Serenely gazing at the violent abyss,
> Plucks on his strings to pluck abysmal glory,
>
> Leaps downward through evening's revelations, and
> On his spredden wings, needs nothing but deep space,
> Forgets the gold centre, the golden destiny,
>
> Grows warm in the motionless motion of his flight,
> Am I that imagine this angel less satisfied?

In that superbly rhetorical question, a great tradition culminates. For the whole enterprise of Romanticism, as I understand it, was to show the power of the mind over a universe of death, to use Coleridge's reformulation of Milton. All dualisms, of mind and body, of subject and object, may be only the poor fictions of a tradition of reason, but they are the fictions that afflict us now, and will go on afflicting us where we are most afflicted, when we come face to face with one another. The great Romantic insight is that we die of loneliness because of our spectral dualities, we die daily because the self cannot bear the self. Our disease is of consciousness itself, and our doctor must be the constructive power of the mind, our ability to imagine as possible a being more healed, original, and pure than what we have become. Stevens allows his mind to pass a saving fiction on itself; he then goes further, and sees that fiction fail. But he does not allow himself to conclude in that failure; he stands back from his own creation, looks upon it, and smiles his work to see. The Canon Aspirin, in a Blakean sense, is both Lamb and Tyger, and Stevens rejoices in the satisfaction of having himself constructed something upon which to rejoice. He did not end there. He wrote poetry for twelve more years, including two great crisis poems in *The Auroras of Autumn* and *The Rock*, austerely beautiful poems purged of all illusion, including the last illusion or temptation of premature despair. The Northern Lights flash over the aging poet, intimating to him the impending totality of his own death, and the lights terrify at first, with their demonstration of a mindless or natural illumination greater than anything the power of mind can summon forth. Yet, of these lights, the poet finally affirms:

> So, then, these lights are not a spell of light,
> A saying out of a cloud, but innocence
> An innocence of the earth and no false sign
>
> Or symbol of malice.

And of the rock, reductive gray particular of man's life, he can say:

> It is the rock where tranquil must adduce
> Its tranquil self, the main of things, the mind
>
> The starting point of the human and the end.

This is to reason with a later reason, to arrive at "the more than rational distortion," in which the domain of the rational is pushed outward, into Keats's "untrodden region of the mind" or Blake's "Prolific."

Stevens's reasoning with a later reason can give us a final vision of the case of Romanticism against the disguises presented to us as reason by our analytical intellectual traditions. Stevens asks for the fiction that results from feeling, is pleased that the irrational is rational, and never forgets that the mind is the most terrible force in the world, since it alone can defend us against itself. The secret of Romanticism, from Blake and Wordsworth down to the age of Yeats and Stevens, increasingly looks like a therapy in which consciousness heals itself by a complex act of invention. The way between the mental errors of reductiveness and expansiveness is the path of invention, the finding of what will suffice through an act of discovery that is also a making. What is therapeutic about Stevens in particular, at the extreme verge of his tradition, is that he is always willing to construct something upon which to rejoice. It is fitting that in a bad time we discover ourselves to have had a great Romantic humanist of a poet among us. The man standing in the center, as Emerson prophesied, is still a poet. If we listen to him he will lead us beyond the quarrels of reason and imagination, and help us to live our lives in this bare land of things as they are, alone with the wind and the weather.

1966

21
Epilogue:
A New Romanticism?
Another Decadence?

There was a time when sensibility shifted only once or twice in a half-century. Communications are now all but instantaneous, and sensibility seems to shift once or twice each decade. What is around us, currently, presents itself as a radical newness, a kind of consciousness in which ways of apprehension and of feeling seem utterly different from what preceded them. The young have been alienated before, and the significance of their stance is lessened by the habit of an age that makes alienation a minimal mark of authenticity. But the aura of a younger generation's difference from its parents has not been this garish for several generations, and what looks like a really worsening world suggests to many that a time of troubles, heralding the breakup of an age, is at hand. A cheap apocalyptic intensity is in the air, and its electronic magnification appears to have overwhelmed taste, and not in music alone.

Whether, in such a time, detachment is valuable, or even possible, no one can know with certainty, but perhaps it can be found, if desired, through the study of analogous shifts in sensibility. Increasingly, observers of the contemporary scene tend to liken it to certain cultural movements of the past, and two in particular of these analogues seem to me valid. One is Romanticism, on the Continent and in England, from roughly 1770 to 1830 or so; the other is the Decadence, or Aestheticism, that once seemed the last wave of Romanticism, during the period, again roughly, of 1870 to 1900. Perhaps what we are enjoying or enduring now is the third wave of a cultural movement that becomes submerged in periods of societal consolidation, but always rises again in times of turbulence. The more spectacularly alienated of our youth, however mindlessly they exhibit their differences from the norm they deride, may in some sense be the heirs of Lord Byron and of Oscar Wilde.

Definitions of Romanticism are abundant, and generally unilluminating, it having been a political and social phenomenon as well as an artistic one. Besides, the term refers to timeless phenomena, as well as the recurrent appearances of a movement that began in the Europe of the late eighteenth century. Walter Pater, high priest of the English Decadence, defined it, as a strictly artistic phenomenon, as well as anyone has: "It is the addition of strangeness to beauty, that constitutes the romantic character in art; and the desire of beauty being a fixed element in every artistic organization, it is the addition of curiosity to this desire of beauty, that constitutes the romantic temper."

Strangeness, or curiosity, has a peculiar meaning in this context, a meaning highly relevant at our moment. Current sensibility ranges from Andy Warhol's heartfelt wish to be a machine all the way to creatures who wish only to be flowers. Both desires are late Romantic or Decadent, and if Mr. Warhol or any of the flower-flappers were enough of an artist, we might see a little strangeness added to beauty, as we sit together, pretending to reject the trash, here on our Western dump. But the dump is now more full than usual of images, and the images are primarily those of pop culture. I don't know whether High Culture is currently in a Romantic phase or not, since what passes for contemporary High Culture, in the subsidized reviews and the universities, is largely an affair of recently stuffed birds, with the various stuffers employing the plethora of foam rubber made available first by Modernism, or the Tradition of the New, or yet more recently by the Camp Sensibility or McLuhanism. But mass culture increasingly *is* in a Romantic or Decadent phase, and its images begin to acquire the strangeness or curiosity in which Pater pioneered. The phenomena of the Beardsley revival, of what the young look like, on the streets of London and New York, even of the apparent emergence of the hermaphrodite as a youthful sexual ideal, all testify to a Decadence analogous to that of *circa* 1870 to 1900. Pater, in his historical novel, *Marius The Epicurean*, implicitly compared the condition of late Victorian England to that of Rome in the age of the Antonines, the last high moment of a great civilization directly poised on the verge of Decline and Fall. So late-eighteenth-century Europe had seemed to various brooders in the days of the Romantic Revolution, and so it seems in our global empire today. As sensibility speeds up, what used to be the backgrounds, political and economic, of cultural ferments seem to shift into foregrounds, and no deep search need be made these days for the roots of genuine alienation, or of mere voluntary mindlessness.

The Romantic poet and New Left agitator Shelley wrote a sonnet, *England In 1819*, which some students recently tend to render as *America In 1968*, with our President taking the place occupied in the poem by the unhappy King George III. The rest of the *dramatis personae* can be left to any reader:

> An old, mad, blind, despised, and dying king,—
> Princes, the dregs of their dull race, who flow
> Through public scorn,—mud from a muddy spring,—
> Rulers who neither see, nor feel, nor know,
> But leech-like to their fainting country cling,
> Till they drop, blind in blood, without a blow,—
> A people starved and stabbed in the untilled field,—
> An army, which liberticide and prey
> Makes as a two-edged sword to all who wield,—
> Golden and sanguine laws which tempt and slay;
> Religion Christless, Godless—a book sealed;
> A Senate,—Time's worst statute unrepealed,—

Contemplating the election ahead (1968), with its likely but astonishing choice of major candidates, readers may amuse themselves with stanzas from the same poet's *Similes For Two Political Characters Of 1819*:

> As a shark and dog-fish wait
>   Under an Atlantic isle,
> For the negro-ship, whose freight
> Is the theme of their debate,
>   Wrinkling their red gills the while—
>
> Are ye, two vultures sick for battle,
>   Two scorpions under one wet stone,
> Two bloodless wolves whose dry throats rattle,
> Two crows perched on the murrained cattle,
>   Two vipers tangled into one.

Behind both poems, in the England of 1819, lay a country and a situation frighteningly like the here and now, a situation of domestic and foreign revolution and of middle- and upper-class reaction against both revolutions. Substitute the black people of the United States for the working people of England, and the Southeast Asian revolution for the French, and the situations tend to lose themselves in an identity that may account for the still-emerging cultural parallels. The English government under which the Romantic poets lived was engaged either in continental warfare or internal repression, or both together, for most of their lives. Their London is the city shown in William Blake's poem of that title in *Songs of Experience*, a city in which the traditional English liberties of free press, free speech, and the rights of petition and assembly were frequently denied. A country already shaken by war and anarchic economic cycles was beginning to experience the social unrest that had overthrown the French social order, and the British ruling class responded to this challenge by a vicious and largely effective repression. The wars against France, against which all of Blake's prophetic poetry protests with biblical passion, were typical of all modern wars fought by capitalistic countries. Enormous profits for the manufacturing classes were accompanied by inflation and by food shortages for the mass of poor people, and victory over Napoleon brought on all the woes endemic to a capitalist society when peace breaks out—an enormous economic depression, unemployment, hunger, and more class unrest.

This unrest, with no possibility of being channeled into organization or a protest vote, led to giant public meetings, riots, and what was called frame-breaking, a direct attempt to end technological unemployment by the destruction of machines. The government reacted by decreeing that frame-breaking was punishable by death, the "time's worst statute" that Byron denounced when he made his first speech in the House of Lords. The climax of popular agitation and government brutality came in August 1819 in the Peterloo Massacre at Manchester, where mounted troops charged a large, orderly, meeting that demanded parliamentary reform, the charge killing and maiming many of the unarmed protestors. For a moment, England stood on the verge of revolution, but no popular leaders of sufficient force and initiative came forward to organize the indignation of the mass of people, and the moment passed.

What our Peterloo was (Watts?) or more likely will be, it is a touch too early to know. Social rebellion, as time speeds up, cannot seem to accommodate itself to nonviolent resistance. That doctrine of Thoreau, Gandhi, and Martin Luther King was never presented with more eloquence than in Shelley's *The Masque of Anarchy*, written both to protest Peterloo and to warn British workers against premature armed rebellion against their oppressors. The Age of Violence had come to Europe freshly with Romanticism, as the dual

342

phenomenon comes to us again now. And with it, for the emancipated, came the night world of what later came to be called the Romantic Agony. Frustrated by the societal balking of the new birth of mixed creative and organic energy that had seemed the spirit of the age, many Romantics (and more mock-Romantics) found solace through various modes of internalization. The age of the doctrine of the creative imagination became also the age of literary drugtaking, and even of opium addiction. The age of the ethics of sexual release became also the age of the Marquis de Sade. Even on the more frivolous level of outward style and fashion, the age of egalitarian revolution became the age of the regency, of the English revival of dandyism and ornamental ostentation of every kind.

The parallels do not much favor us here, as the genius of that earlier age of excess still shines in their aberrations, where it yields again to mindlessness in ours. This scorn comes, alas, from more than a study of the nostalgias. Pursuing the gospel according to Leary, Allen Ginsberg gives us this as the mind-expanding and expanded product of poetic pharmacopoeia:

> Every possible combination of Being—all
> the old ones! all the old Hindu
> Sabahadabadie—pluralic universes
> ringing in Grandiloquent
> Bearded Juxtaposition,
> with all their minarets and moonlit
> towers enlaced with iron
> or porcelain embroidery . . .

One can compare:

> a dusky light—a purple *flash*
> crystalline splendor—light blue—
> *Green* lightnings—
> in that eternal and delirious misery
> wrath fires—
> inward desolations
> an horror of great darkness
> great things—on the ocean
> counterfeit infinity—

That is Coleridge, not in the majestic opium dream of *Kubla Khan*, but in an opium-induced manuscript jotting. Setting mere differences in talent aside, the second verse passage has the advantage of less self-consciousness and of more capacity for self-judgment. The same juxtapositions between the Burroughs of *Naked Lunch* and the fantasies of DeQuincey's *Confessions of an English Opium-Eater* would yield much the same results. "I was kissed, with cancerous kisses, by crocodiles; and laid, confounded with all unutterable slimy things, amongst reeds and Nilotic mud." It is authentic nightmare in DeQuincey, yet it adds strangeness to beauty.

The drug mystique of the present moment sometimes seeks the self-justification of religious longings, a quest set forth with great clarity by Norman Mailer, who can be an embarrassingly religious writer. It is difficult to estimate the full extent to which Romanticism resulted from a displacement of Protestant modes of feeling into purely secular contexts. These days, the same phenomenon appears to be at work, as the surviving elements of all the dead faiths are displaced, not into societal contexts, but into the amorphousness of an apparent social order that appears increasingly to be founded upon fraud and violence.

Romanticism insisted upon the autonomy of the individual, upon his freedom from traditions and conventions that had ceased to liberate form from chaos, and that instead had become mere stifling or blocking agents. In some clear sense, our current New Left is itself part of Romantic tradition, its rebelliousness ironically repeating a past creative outburst in a manner that could be judged a bit unoriginal. I think that the center of the dilemma for older observers of the New Left and of its less political contemporaries lies here; not unsympathetic as some of us over thirty are to such movements, we tend to wonder if we are not seeing mere organic repetition rather than a new birth of creative energy. Romanticism, except perhaps on the amatory level, where it did influence actual middle-class Victorian conduct as opposed to pretensions, remained always a relatively highbrow movement, as its late second wave in Aestheticism did also. But what we have now is a mass phenomenon, and even the vast increase in populations involved hardly accounts for the social diffusion of current sensibility. Though both Byron and Wilde, each in his own day, became highly marketable commodities, the business aspects of popular culture have changed in kind as well as degree in our own age.

If a Romantic artist, even one as extreme in feeling as Berlioz or Musset or Shelley, were to come upon us now, through some belated miracle of a Time Machine, I suppose he would not be much surprised, but he might be chagrined at our panoply. Anti-intellectualism of a carefully qualified variety, a preference for sensations over thought in some matters—these would be unifying commonplaces. But the dream of totally involving a spectator or reader or auditor might now seem an emotional nightmare, and the plunge into subjectivity might appear now to be a drowning in self-consciousness or in the desperate attempts to subdue a self-consciousness that is wholly consuming. To the Romantics it had seemed that everything was possible, but everything had meant a kind of regeneration, whether through art or through life. A purely physical or sensual art and life had never seemed possible, though a handful of extremists had dreamed toward it.

Romantic politics, whether now or then, relies on demonstrations or expressionism rather than inherited forms. The frame-breakers among the English working-class were perhaps the truest Romantics, and one can wonder why we have no contemporary parallel, no large group of computer-breakers rising among laborers, organized or not. The answer may be in the pervasiveness of our New Romanticism; our theorists of the computer revolution are themselves Romantic, in a tradition stemming directly from the Promethean Victor Frankenstein of Mary Shelley's novel. Frankenstein hated his own creation, once it had come to life, and he fled his responsibilities toward it. In consequence, it slew everyone close to him, and finally its creator himself.

The price paid for Romantic individualism, in life as in art, has always been high; the popular myth of the alienated artist or intellectual is largely based on the late, Decadent phase of Romanticism, but it is soundly based there. Erotic mysticism has early Romantic roots, but it flowered among the Decadents, and seems to be more prevalent just now than ever before. Allied to it is the diminishment, in the three stages of this tradition, of the idealization of the female, a dwindling process that could be traced through any number of representative figures. Byron frequently scoffed at the female and rarely pursued her (he generally was pursued), but he as frequently chanted her apotheosis. William Butler Yeats, who came out of the era of Pater and Wilde, was perhaps the last major poet in our culture who adhered to a high vision of heterosexual love. Nothing we have now seems linked in any way to the ancient hope that desire for a woman can be one of the enlargements of life, or a spiritual effort of any kind whatsoever. Here Romanticism seems to have gone into reverse; the movement is from a quest, however harrowing, for something beyond the self, to the contemporary Eros in which only a mirror is embraced.

345

With the fading of the Romantic dream of love, there fades now also the Romantic hero. Our representative novel is likely to be the *Herzog* of Saul Bellow, who is as central a writer as we have. Moses Herzog is a professional Romanticist, and very much a Romantic, but in the last ditch: narcissistic, masochistic, anachronistic, depressive, self-defeated, yet altogether charming, altogether a man of feeling, a sublime egotist. He is Man on the Dump, but speaks for all of us; an absurd case, but undeniably our version of the hero.

In one of his reveries, or imaginary letter-writings, Herzog, as a scholar of the subject, broods negatively upon Romanticism:

> . . . as the form taken by plebeian envy and ambition in modern Europe. Emergent plebeian classes fought for food, power, sexual privileges, of course. But they fought also to inherit the aristocratic dignity of the old regimes, which in the modern age might have claimed the right to speak of decline. In the sphere of culture the newly risen educated classes caused confusion between aesthetic and moral judgments. . . .

It is difficult to dispute this, and simple enough to see it as coming again today. In defense of Romanticism, Herzog answers his own dark analysis by defending the idea of Man against contemporary historicisms that urge a narrow repressiveness in place of the dream of a more perfect human being. Yet the sensibility of our moment is already post-Herzog, and Bellow speaks for a generation on the other side of the gap, for a late Romantic humanism that does not permeate what is emerging.

A country with the certain prospect of continuous external warfare, and imminent internal rebellion, is unlikely to reverse the direction in which its sensibility is moving. Cultural prophecy is a mug's game, but it is always fun and, like the imagination, it wishes to be indulged. We are a very long way from any kind of a realistic or classical reaction against the scene that escalates daily around us. Probably we will move directly from the High Romantic into the Decadent this time round, if indeed we have not largely started there. Gore Vidal's parody novel, *Myra Breckinridge*, may be as far as neopornography can go, or it may spark a kind of *art nouveau* of our time, in which a terrible elegance is born. What Bellow says of Herzog's students will be true of all of us: "It became apparent . . . that they would never learn much about the Roots of Romanticism but that they would see and hear odd things."

1968

Index

Index